T5-ASN-009

Complete Handyman do-it-yourself Annual

A COMPILATION OF SPECIAL INTEREST PROJECTS
FOR THE MODERNIZING AND CARE OF HOMES AND
FURNISHINGS, INDOORS AND OUTDOORS
Prepared by the Editors of MEREDITH BOOKS
Also published under the title,
HOMEOWNER'S DO-IT-YOURSELF YEARBOOK

1994

H. S. STUTTMAN CO., INC. *publishers* Westport, CT. 06889

Meredith® Press
is an imprint
of Meredith® Books

President, Book Group: Joseph J. Ward
Vice President, Editorial Director: Elizabeth P. Rice
Executive Editor: Maryanne Bannon
Project Manager: Kay Sanders
Production Manager: Bill Rose

Produced by North Coast Productions,
650 Mount Curve Blvd., St. Paul, MN 55116
Gene Schnaser, Editor
Jeanne Fredensborg, Managing Editor

Illustrations by Brian Jensen
Book design by Barbara Bowen

The editors of Meredith® Books are dedicated to giving you the information and ideas you need to enjoy do-it-yourself activities to their fullest. We guarantee your satisfaction with this book for as long as you own it. We welcome your comments and suggestions. Please address your correspondence to: Meredith Books, 1716 Locust Street, RW-240, Des Moines, IA 50309-3023.

Printing in the United States of America. First Edition.
Printing Number and Year: 5 4 3 2 1 98 97 96 95 94
ISBN: 696-20001-5

Special thanks to the many people, companies, and organizations who helped directly or indirectly to make this book possible. A special thank-you to all who contributed their time and talents to this edition, including John Shaughnessy, Rich Sharp, and Jeremy Powers of Mona, Meyer, McGrath & Gaven; Kathy Ziprik and Karen Suiter of Georgia-Pacific Corp.; Ramon Riba of the Truss Plate Institute; Jim Fassel of CJV Associates; Mike Mangan of MKM Communications, Donna Alexander of Stanley Tools; Roberta Hair of Symrah Licensing, Inc.; Timm Locke of the Western Wood Products Association; Maryann Olson of the American Plywood Association; Pamela Allsebrook of the California Redwood Association; the Minnesota Historical Society; Jay Holtzman of Donnelly & Duncan; Roger Heegaard of HomeStyles Plan Service; Stephen Jones of Pave Tech, Inc.; Nadine Olson of Borgert Products, Inc.; Mike Ferrara and Chad Stoianoff of Axiom Business Development Group; Patty Berg of Cold Spring Granite Company; plus Connie Schrader, Russ Barnard, Nancy Roberts, Patrick Spielman, Brian Ringham, Vince Koebensky, Jacob Schulzinger, Robert Scharff, Gary Green, and the dedicated crew of Jeanne, Kay, Brian, and Barb. For feature-by-feature credits and association and company addresses, see page 192.

Note to the Reader: The information, plans, and instructions in this book have come from a variety of sources. Every effort has been made to ensure the accuracy of data presented. However, due to differing conditions, tools, and individual skills, Meredith Books and the staff assume no responsibility for any injuries suffered, damages, or losses incurred during or as a result of following this information. Before beginning any project, review the plans and procedures carefully and, if any doubts or questions remain, consult local experts or authorities. Read and observe all of the safety precautions provided by any tool or equipment manufacturer, and follow all accepted safety procedures.

Preface

Good Projects, Good Neighbors

Welcome to the 1994 edition of the Homeowners' Do-It-Yourself Yearbook!

On the pages which follow you will find an exciting line-up of helpful information for the do-it-yourself homeowner, ranging from how to build your own workbenches to how to put a new roof on your home. Packed in between is an amazing variety of other ideas that show you how to use your hands, your skills, and your tools to improve your life and lifestyle.

As you'll see, the bulk of this year's annual is dedicated to helping you expand your do-it-yourself skills in and around the home. For most of us, our home is both the hub of our lives and the anchor of our personal fortunes. Projects that improve, refine, and enhance the place where we live can pay back in several ways. Just some of the rewards include the pleasure of working with our hands, seeing our investments in tools and labor pay off, and watching our projects add to the value of our personal estate.

We wish you success in all of your do-it-yourself endeavors. Above all, we hope that the project ideas in this book will ultimately enhance your life and the lives of those around you. Besides all the other challenges facing a do-it-yourself homeowner, one is the challenge of remaining a good neighbor as we tackle various projects. We often must use noisy tools and equipment, we sometimes need to mess up the yard, and on occasion we have to leave projects half done longer than we would like.

Occasionally do-it-yourselfers in general get a black eye because of the actions of a few: The one who keeps stacks of materials in the yard for months on end; the one who always starts hammering or sawing at sunrise; the one who cranks up a screeching leaf blower next to your backyard graduation party; the one who installs spotlights on the garage inadvertently aimed into your living room; the one who is always banging on the door to ask to borrow a tool.

Most of these *faux pas* are not intentional, but can work to tarnish the collective reputation of all do-it-yourselfers. Borrowing tools can be particularly tempting for beginners. The best advice is to avoid it if at all possible, and to either buy or rent the tools that you need. It might be fair to borrow a tool once, but if you need it a second time, then it is probably time to check the phone book for the closest rental store.

Likewise, being a good neighbor doesn't mean you have to open up your tool box for everyone down the block who has a project underway. Lending out tools can be risky business even among experienced do-it-yourselfers. First, if the borrower gets hurt while using your power tool, you may be the one in hot water. Second, you may find that tool missing when you need it for your own projects. Third, you can run the risk of the tool being misused, requiring expensive repairs or even replacement.

Some repair shops find that most homeowners bringing tools in for work had either borrowed them or had loaned them out to others. In most cases it is the tool owner who brings it in to get fixed. Even if a returned tool is still running, its useful life can be shortened drastically if it was misused. If a 3/8" drill, for example, was used to sand a porch deck for four hours instead of making occasional holes, half of its service life could have been used up.

How to get around it? The best approach, advises power tool expert Howard Silken, is to be up front and explain that your policy is not to lend your tools. Most do-it-yourselfers will understand. A second approach, if you can't say no, might be to lend only older tools that you have replaced with newer versions. That way you will be sure the tools you need are on hand for your own projects.

Being a good do-it-yourself neighbor mostly boils down to putting yourself in the other person's shoes. Problems sometimes can occur because we don't take time to think of how our projects will affect others, or we over-estimate tolerance levels. Evaluating the good-neighbor factor is a worthwhile consideration on any project, and it can add an extra element of success.

Gene Schnaser, Editor

Contents

DIY Enhancements

DIY Improvements

DIY Investments

DIY Achievements

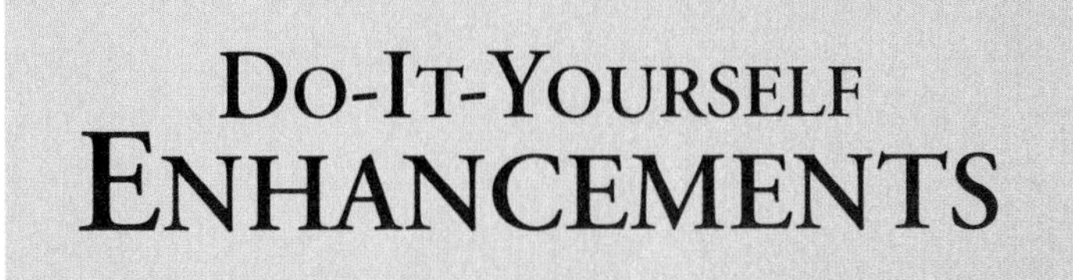

Do-It-Yourself Enhancements

Bungalow Update

How To Engineer A New Look For An Older Home In A Crowded Neighborhood

If you're like most people, your house and lot have some things you like and some things you wish were different. Perhaps you love the way the morning sun strikes the garden area off your bedroom, but you wish you could step outside with your morning coffee and sit in that sunlight yourself. Or maybe you have a lovely view from your deck—which would be perfect if only the deck were large enough to hold a few friends as well.

Every house has its own rewards and do-it-yourself outdoor projects can enhance your home's good features. They can help you expand your living space, give it variety, and add value to your property. By choosing projects carefully, you can create outdoor space as a retreat, a place for entertaining, or a shelter from the wind, rain, or too much sun. A simple structure can enhance the pleasures of outdoor living for a longer season each year.

Take, for example, the houses built during the 1930s and 40s, found in neighborhoods throughout the country, often situated on long, narrow lots in densely populated areas. With detached garages, their main floors are generally three or more feet above grade.

These homes offer unique potential for capturing outdoor living space, as shown by this make-over designed by the Western Wood Products Association. The distinctive window detailing of this home is repeated in several variations on the railings and fences. An old porch is hidden under a new entry deck (1) with built-in benches (1A). The craftsman-style squares of the deck railing can be built with overlapping slats or constructed with carefully fitted pieces. The drawing on page 10 shows both options.

The new planters (2) and front retaining wall (3) serve as an attractive entrance to the property and soften the change in grade from the lawn to the sidewalk. The new fence (4) is a simpler version of the deck railing. Positioning the gate (5) at the front corner of the house expands usable backyard space.

The improvements beyond the gate include a hose rack (11), a garbage can enclosure (20), a potting bench (9), and a storage fence (6)—all served by the driveway's pavement. The storage fence is a flat-roofed shed integrated with the lot-line fence.

On the site plans, the color coding suggests how a phased building program might be organized. The before and after plans identify which structures have been altered, added to, or newly created. Conceptual plans are available for the numbered projects (see end of article).

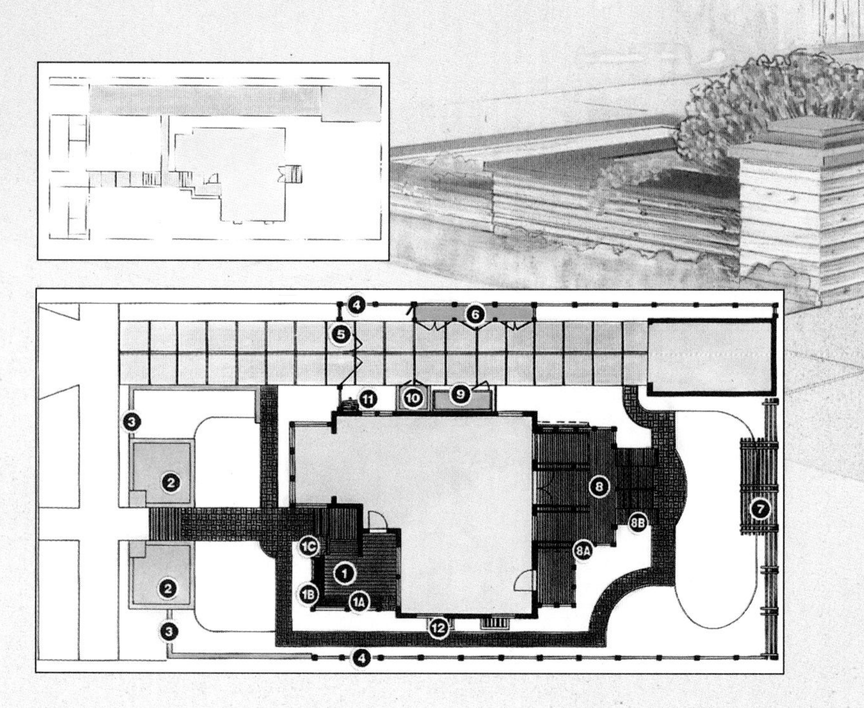

"Every house has its own rewards"

In the backyard, a traditionally styled deck (8) is finished with another variation of the craftsman style railing. The ledges on either side of the board steps (8B) are ideal for large pots with flowers and herbs. The trellis (8A) shelters the eating area from the sun and prevents a bird's eye view of the deck from the upper floors in nearby houses.

The posts of the back lot-line fence extend above the fence to support an arbor (7); it's an easy way to create a shady space in even the tiniest of backyards. If your house doesn't have a back door opening onto a potential deck area, consider converting a window to a door. It's inexpensive and can make a big difference in how you use your house and garden.

To begin your own make-over, draw a plan of your house on your lot. Keep it to scale. Consider your interior floor plan and determine the best locations for your outdoor spaces.

These elevation and plan views show the garage, back lot-line fence with arbor, and a portion of bricked area off the rear deck.

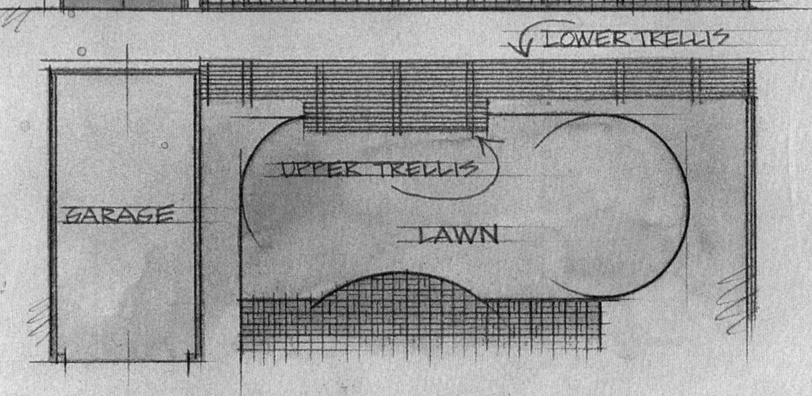

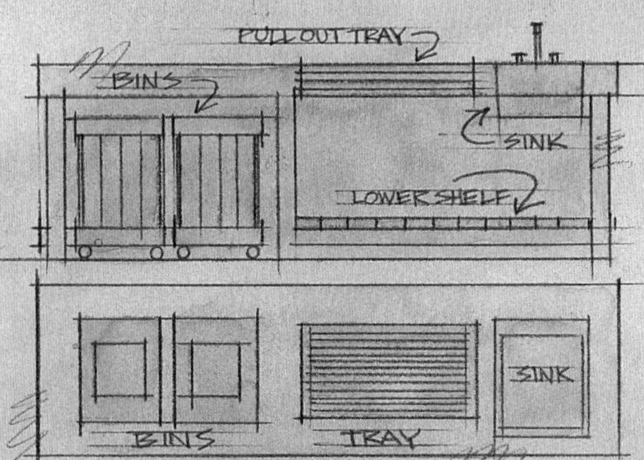

This simple potting bench (9) includes a faucet and sink (it hooks up to your garden hose and empties into a container), open slats on the top which allow spilled dirt to fall into a removable tray, two roll-out bins, and a shelf for extra supplies. It's easy to build, simple to use, and provides water at the bench in summer when it is needed.

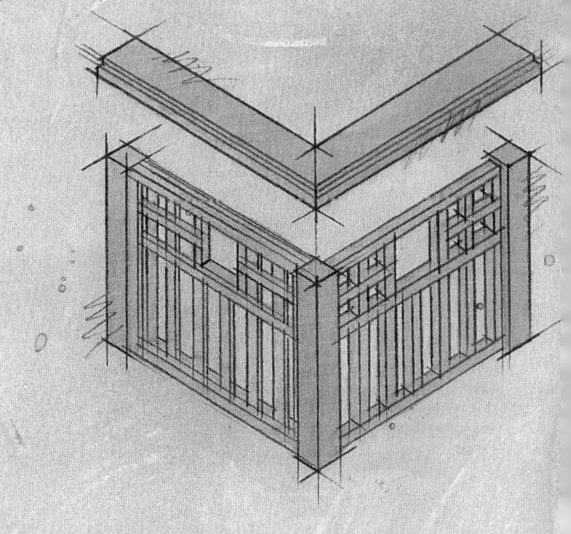

Craftsman-style detailing, borrowed from the home's windows and repeated in outdoor projects, can be achieved in two ways: simply run the horizontal members in front of the verticals for the railings and fences, or attach the horizontals first, and cut the verticals to fit.

Consider the position of the sun and where it will be at different times of the year. What direction do prevailing winds come from? How much privacy do you want? Give a priority rating to the projects you'd like to have.

Phased development is a good way to proceed. Build a project or two each year. By alternating large and small projects, you'll build on the work you've already done. Check with local code officials to review the ordinances which apply, and locate all underground utilities before starting.

Western woods work well for outdoor projects. They are handsome, dimensionally stable, hold paint and stains well, and machine easily. To order a packet of conceptual plans for the numbered projects ($10 postpaid), write Western Wood Products Association, Yeon Building, 522 SW Fifth Ave., Portland, OR 97204-2122. Ask for Set C.

Convert a window into a door and gain access to a raised deck (8) that is detailed to complement the house. The post of the back lot-line arbor/fence (7) is in the foreground; notice how simply the standard-sized pieces are joined together to create the trellis.

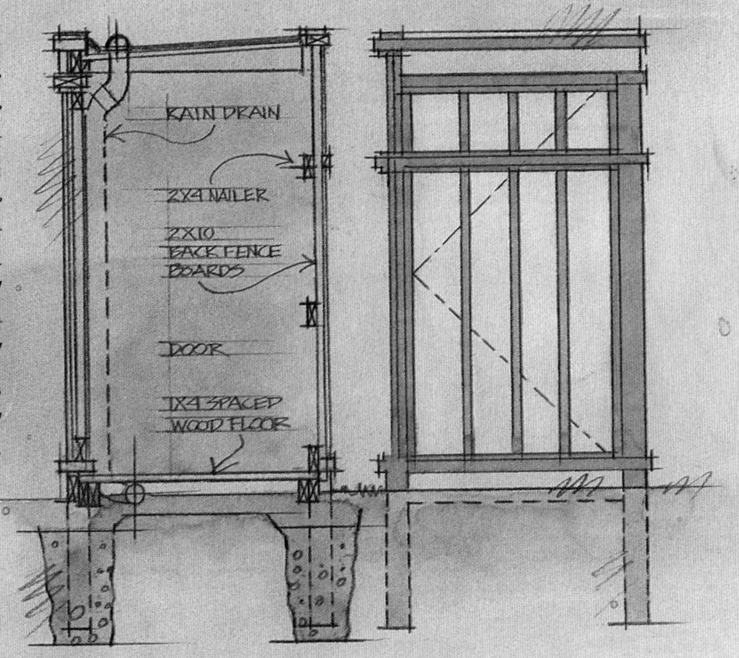

If you don't have room for a shed, but need outdoor storage, try this storage fence (6). The drawings at right show a section view and an end elevation. It can also be seen beyond the corner post of the deck in the illustration above. It's built and detailed like the fence, but has a roof and a decked floor. With 3′-deep storage, it can be built to any length.

Whitfield
THE NEW YORKER
ARCHITECTURE

WOOD HEAT

New Pellet Stoves Take The Drudgery Out Of Heating With Wood

Wood heating has undergone a big change since the first energy crisis in the Seventies when homeowners found wood heat fraught with problems and hard work. New high-tech stoves that burn pellets instead of logs are revolutionizing the home wood heating picture.

Already more than 200,000 of these new appliances are in use. Easy, direct-vent (no chimney) installation and clean, convenient feeding are just two main attractions.

If you love wood stoves but hate the work and the mess involved, pellet stoves are definitely worth investigating. They burn pellets made of highly flammable, organic waste material, which are automatically fed into the stove, much like the old coal stoker furnaces. Organic materials like sunflower or peanut shells and paper or wood waste products, such as softwood-cardboard or particleboard, are processed and formed into pellets which are easily poured into the stove's hopper.

Hardwood pellets are also available for the stoves; and special units also burn shelled corn.

One reason the new pellet stoves are generating excitement is because they are environmentally friendly. The fuels used and the burning process produce low pollution, measured as particulates per hour, and resulting emissions do not cause acid rain. Their exceptional performance has exempted them from EPA air quality regulations. Pellet stove emissions, at .3 to 1.5 grams per hour, are far below the 1988 EPA standards of 7.5 grams of particulate per hour that conventional noncatalytic wood-burning stoves can produce, along with acid rain and hazy skies. This makes pellet heat a viable option in areas where air pollution has resulted in restrictions or out-right bans on conventional wood heating.

Another reason pellet stoves are gaining a foothold is that installation is exceptionally easy. No chimney vent is required. Most models install with a simple flue and can be directly vented through a wall. Only a couple of inches of wall clearance is needed inside the home.

The new pellet fuel technology is found in freestanding units and fireplace inserts, in styles ranging from traditional to contemporary. Another basic buying decision is whether to choose a top-feeding unit or a bottom-feeding unit—the type of pellet fuel you want to burn can help you decide.

Pellet fuels are generally classified as either high-grade or low-grade, as determined by the ash content of the burnt fuel. Low-grade pellets, made from nut shells, cardboard, and shelled corn, have a high ash content; high-grade pellets, made from both hardwood and softwood wastes, have a low ash content. Top-feeding units can burn the high-grade fuels only, while the bottom-feeding unit can burn both grades of fuel.

Pellet stoves combine the heat of woodstoves with high-tech combustion systems that meter air and fuel. Pellets can be of sawdust, wood scrap, or agricultural waste.

Pellet stoves, such as the one from Pyro Industries shown at left, take the work out of wood heating. Some cast-iron units sell for about $2,000.

How a Pellet Stove Works

Pellet fuel appliances (PFAs) use advanced combustion technology to produce clean, efficient heat. Precise air/fuel controls and a combustion blower ensure complete burning of pellets. An adjustable fuel feeding system automatically meters the right amount of fuel to the burnpot; there is no need to stoke the fire in the middle of the night or re-light it when you return home from work. The components are: 1) the fuel hopper; 2) electronic auger system; 3) fuel chute; 4) fuel-metering cup; 5) airtight firebox; 6) fan to supply combustion air to the firebox; 7) second fan to distribute stove heat into the room, and 8) flue vent.

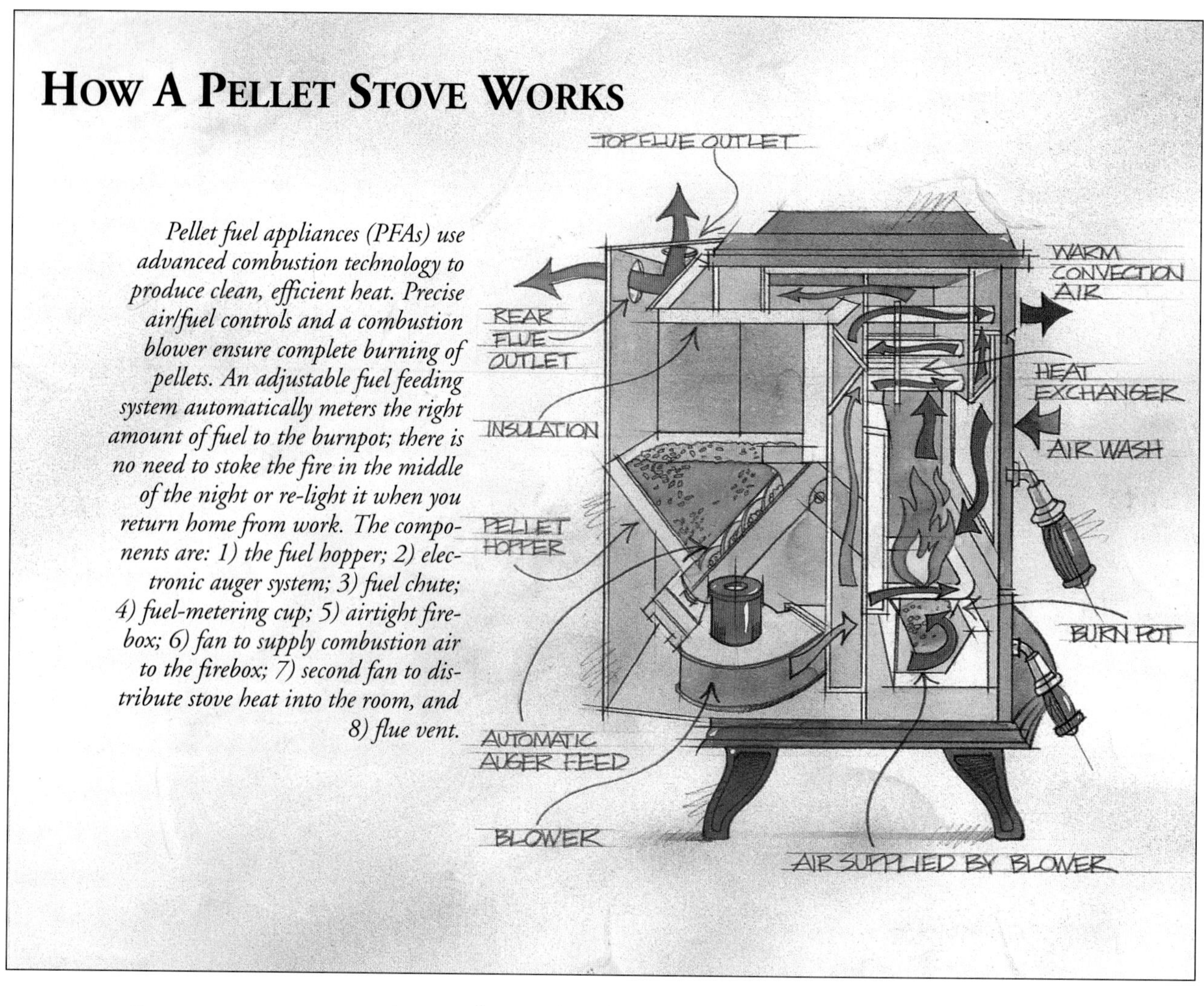

Stove Parts

A hopper in each unit, whether free-standing or a fireplace insert, holds the pellets used for fuel. The pellets are fed by an electronic, time-controlled auger system into an airtight firebox or burnpot, as some refer to it. One of the two fans used in these units helps to create a very hot fire, while a second fan distributes the heat into the room. Because the fans require electricity, a pellet stove may not be the best choice as a sole source of heating in case of a power failure. However, a battery backup system is available in some models.

Outside of the stove, floor protection is required, either standard ceramic or granite tile, or brick. No wall protection is needed, but the unit must be a couple of inches away from sidewalls. A simple, inexpensive flue expels vent exhaust gases outside—allowing installation on any exterior wall—or into an existing chimney system.

Should you buy a bottom-feeder or a top-feeder? In a bottom-fed stove, pellets are delivered to the firebox by a time-controlled screw auger from the underside of the burn box. Fresh pellets are pushed forward as previously introduced fuel is consumed. Because of an early problem with back burn (see Features To Check, page 16), safer designs now have the auger pushing pellets upward, forcing the noncombustibles to the side of the burn box. The result is continual exposure of fresh pellets to flame and combustion air.

With a top-fed stove, fuel is augered upward in a 45° angle to the side of and above the burn box. It has no continuous, unsafe, stream of pellets between the burn box and the feed hopper, so a stalled auger would not cause burn back.

Pellet Benefits

There are several advantages with the new pellet fuels. Converting waste products into pellets—more than 5 million cubic yards (800,000 tons) in 1992/93—eliminates that much waste in land fills. The Fiber Fuels Institute in Duluth, Minnesota estimates that this amount of waste would fill 45,000 70-foot-long semi trucks, forming a convoy stretching 600 miles. These fuels also burn for longer periods of time than wood logs, so you spend less time stoking the fire.

Pellet fuel is more convenient than cutting and storing your own wood; a ton of pellet fuel can be stored in a 4x4x5′ space, about half what is required for a cord of wood. Problems with bugs, dust, and smoke are also eliminated.

Perhaps the most important advantage is that the home remains free of contaminated air since the high internal operating temperatures of a pellet stove transform polluting gases into additional heat. And pellet fuel doesn't give off sulfur emissions, which cause acid rain, or produce creosote. The only tangible remains from this fuel are a small amount of ash.

Heat Costs

Since the use of pellet stoves is growing each year, manufacturers of pellets can now be found throughout the country. A single fueling of about 40 lbs. of pellets can provide heat for over 24 hours and, on a low setting, for up to two days. The price of pellets now ranges from $185 to $200 per ton. Pellets can be cost competitive, depending on the price of a cord of wood. The pellet stove typically uses 3/4 to 5 lbs. of fuel per hour with a heat output from 5,000 to 60,000 Btu per hour, depending on the type of fuel and the heat setting used. Homeowners using pellets as a primary heat source in cold climates can use up to 5 tons over a winter, but 2 to 3 tons is more typical.

The cost of a pellet stove can range from $1,700 to $3,000. This compares to a range of $1,200 to $2,000 for a wood-burning fireplace insert, or from $800 to $1,500 for a natural gas or propane stove.

Pellet stove models, such as the Erin, shown at top, and the Whitfield from Pyro Industries, shown at right, blend into a variety of decors.

Stoves which use pellets, photo left, require minimal sidewall clearance. A simple venting system allows installation on any exterior wall.

A typical pellet fuel stove will produce up to 50,000 Btu of heat, enough to warm a 2,400 sq. ft. home, and costs about 8 to 45 cents per hour to operate. The cost per hour also depends on the type of fuel and the heat setting used.

On a cost per million Btu basis, pellet stoves will cost about the same as oil to operate, about $11. This roughly compares to about $6 for a catalytic wood stove, $8 for natural gas, $15 for propane, and $26 for electricity.

Features to Check

Early bottom-fed pellet stoves had occasional problems with burn back. A stalled auger could stop the flow of pellets to the burn box resulting in the fire burning back through the auger tube and igniting pellets in the feed bin—a potentially dangerous situation. But by designing a break in the auger-fed system, stove manufacturers have solved this problem.

Among other improvements, newer models have two streams of fuel, one feeding into the other, with a gap separating the pellet flow between the hopper and the burn box. (Some units have a two-auger system where an intermediate hopper feeds a second auger.) Air space of 3½″ is provided between the two pellet streams. And some models allow the lower auger to continue to run for a minute when the unit is turned off, which clears fuel that could support burn back.

Some stoves have three safety devices for preventing burn back: 1) the hopper is isolated from the feed auger with no direct contact between them; 2) a motor-driven, fuel-metering cup provides fuel to the auger (the pellets drop down to the auger from 6″ above it), and 3) an electrical burner-limit switch shuts off power to the auger and the fuel metering cup if the temperature reaches 200° F.

Pellet Stove Contacts

A good contact for questions about these new fuels is the **Fiber Fuels Institute**, 5013 Miller Trunk Hwy., Duluth, MN 55811 (218/720-4319). Following are a dozen companies that make pellet fuel stoves and fireplace inserts.

Breckwell and Cadet, National Steelcrafters of Oregon Inc., 1875 W. 6th, Eugene, OR 97402 (503/683-3210).

Englander, England Stove Works, Inc., P.O. Box 206, Monroe, VA 24574 (804/929-0120).

Envirofire, Sherwood Industries, 6820 Kirkpatrick Crescent, Victoria, BC V8X 3X1 (604/652-6080).

Erin, Waterford Irish Stoves Inc., 16 Air Park Rd., West Lebanon, NH 03766 (603/298-5030).

Natural Fire, The Earth Stove, Inc., 1525 S. Western Ave., Marion, IN 46953 (317/662-0085).

Pellet Master, Enerpel, Inc., 533 Thain Rd., Lewiston, ID 83501 (208/743-5540).

Pellet Pro, Harman Stove Systems, 352 Mountain House Rd., Hallifax, PA 17032 (717/362-9080).

Quadra Fire, Alladin Steel Products, Inc., 401 N. Wynne St., Colville, WA 99114 (509/684-3745).

Reliance, Vermont Castings, Inc., Rte. 107, Box 501, Bethel, VT 05032 (802/234-2300).

Trager, Even-Temp Co., Inc., P.O. Box 127, Waco, NE 68460 (402/728-5255).

Venturi, Martin Industries Inc., P.O. Box 128, Florence, AL 35631 (205/767-0330).

Whitfield, Pyro Industries, Inc., 695 Pease Rd., Burlington, WA 98233 (206/757-9728).

Deck Supports

A Look At Ways To Give Your Deck A Solid Footing

One piece of folk wisdom that applies to do-it-yourself deck projects is this: If it's worthwhile doing, it's worthwhile doing right.

Because decks are a permanent structure, use all the care you would use in building a home. When planning your deck project be sure to check span tables to correctly size the lumber you will use. Plans and lumber in hand, the steps include pouring footings, then either pouring piers (or installing purchased piers or posts), then bolting a ledger to your home, installing a girder or stringers, and finally nailing down the decking.

Of all steps involved, one of the more important is making sure your deck will have adequate underpinnings. Whether you use a prepackaged deck plan or come up with your own, you will need to decide specifically how your deck will be supported. The type of structural support you build for your deck can determine how it will look and how long it will last.

Deck piers can be purchased ready-made, such as those shown above, or they can be made on-site in various styles using metal connectors.

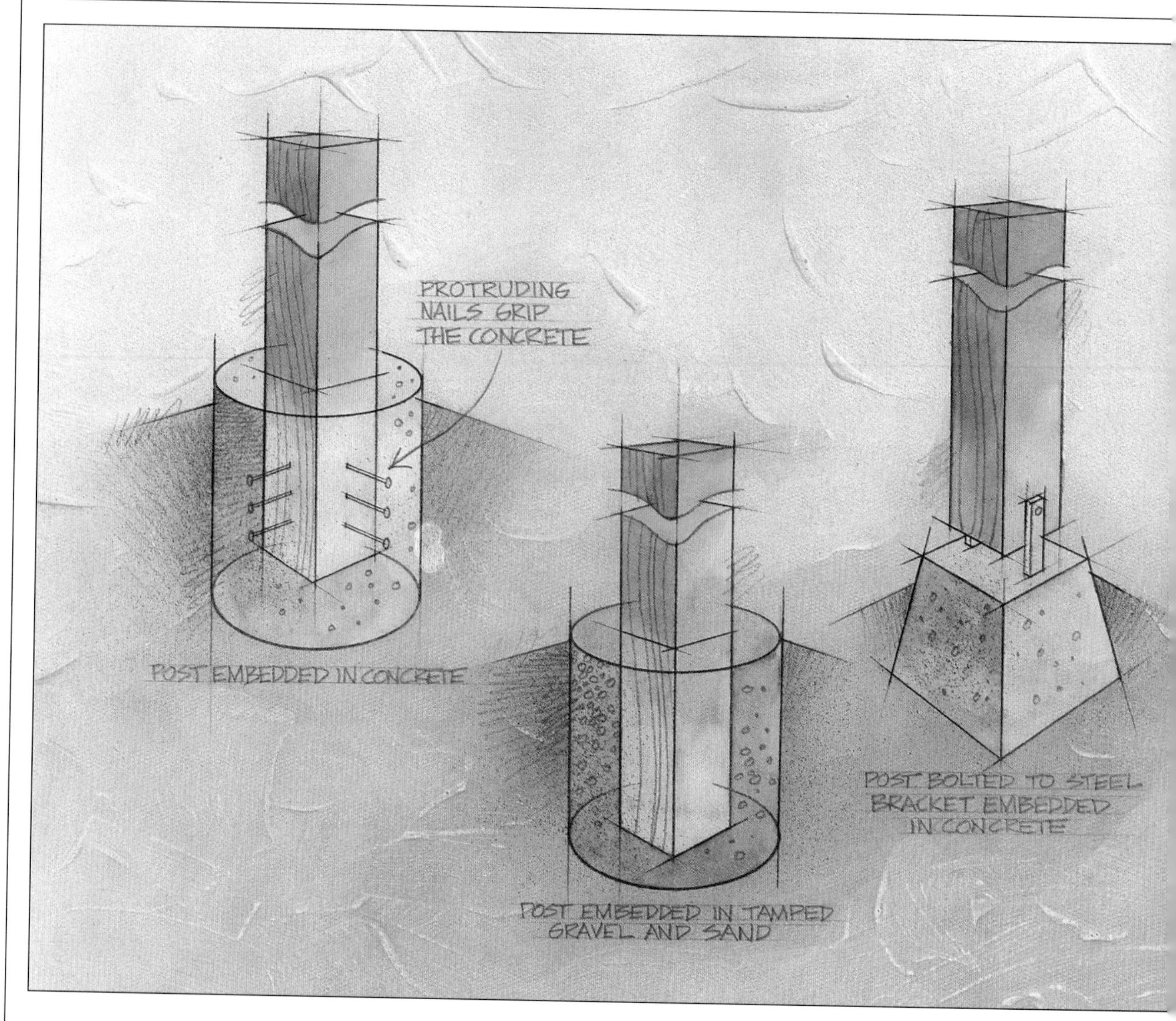

A deck can be supported directly by concrete footing or piers, or by upright support posts, which are often made of 4x4s or 4x6s. The two basic ways of installing posts are to set them in post holes and backfill around them, or to fasten the posts to the tops of footings or piers. Support posts kept from direct contact with earth or concrete will last longer.

After you finalize your deck plans, but before you buy your materials, check with local building code officials. Local codes may have specific requirements for footing depths, maximum spans, heights, and so forth. You may also be required to take out a permit to build your deck.

Here are more facts to help you choose which support system to use:

- If you embed your support posts in concrete or compacted earth, use pressure-treated lumber. If you are building with other lumber, including cedar or redwood, the posts should be set on top of concrete footings or piers. You can attach the posts to the concrete, using a variety of methods. In case of rot, embedded posts will be more difficult to replace than posts installed on piers.
- You can extend the tops of posts either to support the deck, or higher, to also help support deck railings. If you use posts as rail supports, you will probably have to extend them 32″ or more above the level of the deck.
- A minimum depth of 2′ for footings is generally recommended. But in freezing climates, you may need to sink the footings down to 6″ below the frostline—as deep as 4′ or more.
- You can use holes dug in stable soil as "forms" to pour concrete for footings. You can buy waxed cardboard forms for pouring footings in unstable soil or for pouring footings that will extend above ground level. You can cast your own piers to rest on the footings or you can buy them precast. (It is also possible to use

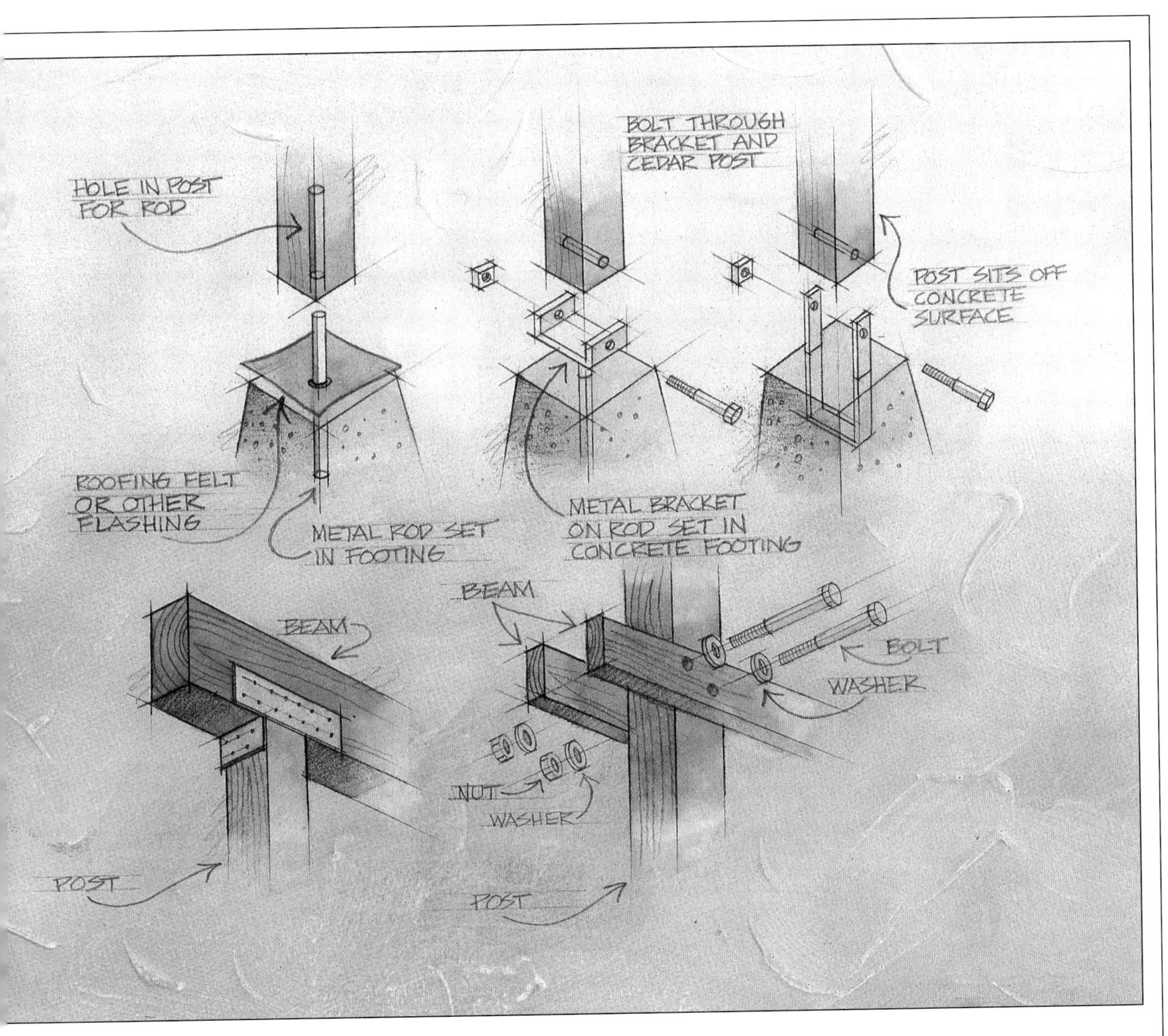

concrete blocks filled with concrete as piers.)

• The tops of concrete footings can end below, even with, or above ground level. If concrete around an embedded post extends above the ground, taper the top to help drain away moisture. Some deck builders, when using treated posts, like to keep footings about 18″ below ground level. Backfilling the top 18″ with compacted earth gives the post more stability during construction.

• Of the various ways of anchoring posts to concrete, metal connectors that keep posts up off the concrete may be the best. You can toenail posts into wooden blocks embedded in the concrete or set on pins embedded in concrete, but the blocks are likely to rot. These methods also don't resist upward lift from the wind as well as posts attached with metal connectors do. You anchor the connectors in concrete and then either nail or bolt the posts through holes in the connectors.

• Deck height can affect your choice of a support system. In some areas, low-level decks are built right on pressure-treated 4x4s set into the ground. High decks, 8′ or more, may require posts larger than those ordinarily used.

• Where you live, the type of deck you are planning, and your terrain will narrow your deck foundation options. If you need more help, check with building code officials, local lumber suppliers, or neighbors who have recently put up a deck, to find out commonly accepted practices in your area.

As posts are installed, make sure they are plumb and perpendicular. You can use a carpenter's level to check that each post is perfectly vertical during construction. Use braces or stakes as needed to keep posts in position. Once the posts are in, you will be ready to install beams, joists, and finally the decking itself.

NORTHERN EXPOSURE

Do-It-Yourself Sauna Kits Come Out Of The Basement

At last count, Finns were taking 200 million saunas a year to refresh both mind and body. What began as water thrown on hot rocks in an underground dugout later became a log cabin consisting of a hot-room, wash room, and dressing area. Today, saunas are no longer only built outdoors beside a lake and are no longer the exclusive domain of the Finns.

In homes across America, the sauna is moving out of the basement to the upper levels. As part of a master bath, for example, the modern sauna provides an economical route to rejuvenation. The cost of three saunas per week is only about $4 per month.

Although some enthusiasts prefer building the sauna structure straight from plans, do-it-yourselfers can capitalize on this Finnish legacy using kits specially packaged for easy assembly. Since no plumbing and almost no carpentry work are involved, it is possible to assemble a sauna kit with prebuilt wall panels in a single afternoon.

Economical, relaxing, and healthful, today's sauna is rapidly becoming part of a master bath. Kits, with no plumbing and little carpentry work involved, make installation a snap.

While minimum space requirements start at 4x4′, kits are available in sizes up to 8x12′.

SAUNAS VS. STEAMBATHS

Saunas produce a hot, relatively dry heat from hot, porous rocks. The rocks emit a constant, long-lasting heat that is evenly distributed over the body, causing your body's natural cooling system to perspire. Steambaths are actually cooler, usually 120° F., but feel much warmer than saunas.

Because water vapor distributes heat in a steambath and the air is saturated with water, steam condenses on the body, which inhibits the perspiring mechanism from working effectively. When perspiration cannot evaporate readily, body heat will rise faster, causing you to feel warmer.

Actually, the most important component of any sauna is the heating unit, known as *kiuas* (pronounced kew′ us). The traditional "smoke saunas" still found in rural areas of Finland use the original stone-covered log fire that takes both time and planning to use. Modern electric heating units circulate fresh air by convection, making the heat source clean, and convenient.

Heater installation is simple. No flues or chimneys are required, and its operation is accomplished with a flick of the switch.

Like the traditional smoke saunas, electrical heating units also heat stones which retain and radiate the heat. The stones are stacked in the heater unit—large on the bottom, small on top—with room for air circulation around them. When hit with a scoopful of water, *loyly* (pronounced low′ lou), sauna vapor is produced.

Quarried black peridotite-type igneous rocks used in Finland are available. However, fist-size, round, smooth stones such as those along river banks will also work. Having been previously exposed to the elements, they can withstand the repeated temperature changes of a sauna.

Well-designed, prefab sauna kits can be installed by do-it-yourselfers in a single afternoon.

Selecting A Sauna

Several companies produce sauna kits for do-it-yourself installation; one of the largest and oldest is FinnLeo, offering kits in two basic lines in prices ranging from $1,995 to $4,500 for kits from 4x4′ to 6x8′. The company, through its dealers, offers technical assistance, as well as a long list of sauna accessories. When selecting a kit, consider the type and thickness of wood used, the design of the heaters, and special options, such as deluxe interiors, windows, or all-glass doors.

Because humidity is low in a sauna, it can be made of wood—usually tongue-and-groove redwood, white spruce, red cedar, or hemlock. Timber thickness in kits varies from 5⁄8″ to 1¾″ to 2¼″. White spruce and redwood are especially suitable since they readily absorb moisture, resist warping, and add a pleasant fragrance. Hemlock is said to have health-promoting properties all its own. African abachi wood is popular for benches, backrests, and headrests because it is knot-free and does not splinter.

Periodic scrubbing of the sauna interior with a good brush and mild, natural soap will preserve the natural look and fragrance of the wood. For both safety and maintenance reasons, wall tiles do not belong in a sauna. Painted surfaces are also not advised.

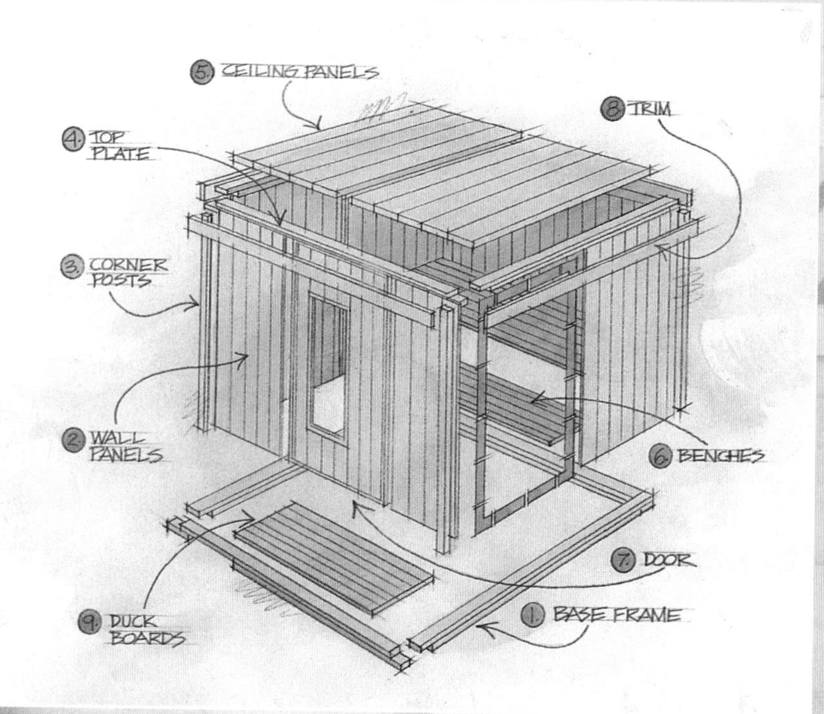

The premarked base frame makes wall panel and door installation, photo above right, exceptionally easy. The main parts of a kit, illustrated at left, include: 1) base frame; 2) prebuilt wall panels; 3) exterior corner posts; 4) top plate to align and lock wall panels; 5) prefab ceiling panels; 6) prebuilt benches; 7) door; 8) trim, and 9) duck boards.

Installing a Sauna Kit

As with any home construction project, check your local building codes for any special building requirements and get any necessary permits before installing a sauna kit. A general requirement for building a sauna is a level, waterproof surface. Any waterproof floor covering may be used because the floor stays relatively cool. Vinyl flooring should be installed first with the structure assembled on top of the vinyl. Ceramic tile and unfinished wood slats (duck boards) can be installed after the sauna is completed. Here is the basic procedure suggested for installing kits from FinnLeo:

Base Frame. The base frame boards are assembled on the floor, making sure the frame is square. At this point, the heater and air inlet locations are selected, and the base frame marked for the location of the air inlet, which should be as near the heater as possible.

Walls. Prebuilt tongue-and-groove panels are set in the base frame. Panel size varies from 1x7′ to 4x7′ in the different price ranges. One of the panels includes electrical conduit that is installed where the heater will be located. Walls are assembled by sliding the wall panels onto the base frame—matching the number at the top of the panel with the number on the base frame. Starting in a corner area, the first panel is installed, then an adjacent panel is positioned to form a corner. To complete the corner, an outside corner post is installed, and, when properly aligned, 3″ screws are used to attach it to both panels.

Additional panels are set into place as marked on the base frame, using barbed wood fasteners to join the tops of the panels. The door panel is installed in sequence, the same as the other panels.

Top Plate. After the wall panels are up, the next step is to assemble and install the top plate or "ceiling frame." The top plate aligns and locks the top of the wall panels, giving the sauna structure additional strength. When assembled, the top plate is guided over the top of the front wall, until it drops inside a notch on top of the wall panels. The exterior of the top plate is set flush with the top of the tongue-and-groove of the interior walls and is permanently fastened to the wall panels with 2″ screws.

Ceiling Panels. Prefabricated insulated ceiling panels are installed by sliding each ceiling panel over the top of the wall panels, until it comes to rest on the top plate. Next, cove molding, with either butt-end or miter joints, is installed at the ceiling/wall junction with 4d galvanized nails. The air outlet vent is then located on the back wall or toward the back of a side wall, and a sliding vent valve is attached to the interior of the sauna. The last step is to install fascia and exterior corner trim.

The Sauna Tradition

The sauna has been part of Finnish everyday life for the last two thousand years. So much a part that Finns would always complete the sauna before the house was built. In Finland, it is considered an ideal place to negotiate, philosophize, or make plans. As such, it is included in the Finnish decision-making tradition, both political and corporate. Saunas also are used for all possible celebrations with family and friends, yet individual tolerances to heat are respected—not everyone goes for a roll in the snow or jumps into an icy lake to cool off.

Although saunas have had a variety of uses—from childbirth to drying wheat and smoking ham—its main function is for bathing and relaxing.

To understand why relaxation is part of the ritual, picture a golden summer evening. You alternate between the sauna and water—a lake, the sea, a river, or stream. Cooling off, you admire the evening, the landscape, or the stars as you sip a refreshing drink. After a light supper, a deep, satisfying sleep is the natural reward of the sauna.

The Finns use the term *sisu* for the special kind of physical and mental energy that is the sauna's gift. Living in a cold climate and what was a forest wilderness, they believe that the sauna has helped

Deluxe sauna interiors include lighting soffits, under-bench trim, and a variety of back and head rests and bench configurations. Accessories of wood, photo next page, include clocks, sand timers, thermometers, hygrometers, and lamp shades.

them endure and prosper through the centuries. Today, the sauna is known to provide more immediate benefits—beyond simply helping one relax strained muscles after a vigorous workout.

Though the feeling of well-being achieved is reason enough to appreciate the sauna, research shows that raising the core body temperature in a sauna acts as a catalyst for several positive physiological changes. The perspiration generated helps rid the body of harmful toxins such as nickel, mercury, and lead absorbed from the environment. Body pores are cleaned and the old, dead skin cells removed, resulting in a more youthful appearance.

Research also shows that weight loss occurs because of the energy it takes to perspire. As many as 300 calories are expended in a typical sauna session, equivalent to running 2 or 3 miles.

Other health benefits of sauna include reduced mental stress, increased resistance to illness, and relief for cold or sinus symptoms. Muscle relaxation can prevent or lessen the severity of an injury or of strained muscles. Saunas also are said to be a good complement to joint-injury therapy and may provide temporary relief from the pain of arthritis and rheumatism.

Sauna Accessories

Necessities include a timing device, a thermometer, a wooden water bucket with wooden handle, a lighting source, and a wooden water scoop. Some kits include these as well as abachi wood benches and duck boards of spruce for the floor.

Amenities to check out (see photo above right) include a hygrometer to track the humidity level, wooden clothing racks, brush sets, loofah sponges, and sauna soap. Note that it is important to avoid metallic objects which can cause burns. Besides a variety of sauna brushes, buckets, and ladles, clockwise are: a sand sauna timer; thermometers; wooden lamp shade; wood thermometer; abachi wood head rest; water buckets of polar pine with silicone sealed bottom; wooden and twig clothing racks, and a "bucket" clock.

Benches. The kit's 2x2″ support rails for the benches are installed on the side walls at 12″ and 30″ heights from the floor. In some designs, longer supports for the lower bench allow the bench to slide in and out for easy cleaning. Better benches are made of knot-free wood and constructed from the bottom so the seating has no exposed fasteners.

Heater. Usually mounted on the door wall, a wood heater guard is attached first to the wall. The electric heater is then hung in the center of the guard, leaving 2″ of space between the heater and guard rail. Electric sauna heaters require a separate 240-volt circuit. Get professional help unless you have experience in electrical wiring.

Heaters are sized according to the dimensions of the sauna constructed. Some heaters, such as those from FinnLeo, have vertically positioned heating elements to provide more contact with the stones. This design results in a softer steam and avoids the "toaster" feeling some

Tips On Enjoying A Sauna

Common sense and "listening" to your body are the primary guidelines for enjoying a sauna. Do what feels good. Some suggestions from FinnLeo include the following:

Dos

• Consult with your physician if you have a history of heart or other health problems.

• Set the temperature between 160° and 190° F. The temperature should not exceed 190° F. (10 to 15 minutes in 180° F. is the norm, while less than 170° F. is usually not enough to produce perspiration).

• Both before and after taking a sauna, drink plenty of water, mineral water, or juice—either fruit or vegetable—to replace lost water and trace elements.

• Clean skin of cosmetics before entering the sauna, and don't apply oils to your skin—oils block your pores and inhibit perspiration. The only exception might be baby oil applied to dry spots such as nose or elbows, a moisturizing cream for the face only, and lip balm.

• Stay in the sauna for 10 to 15 minutes, cool off, and then return to the sauna for another "inning." Repeat several times. Do start slowly and always leave sooner if you are uncomfortable. Because heat rises, begin by sitting lower in the sauna. And remember that the core temperature of the body varies from day to day and with one's level of activity. If it's high to start with, your tolerance to heat will be lower, so don't go strictly by the clock.

• Gently scrub your skin with a loofah or bath brush to rejuvenate it and keep it healthy.

• Experiment with the humidity. Only a sauna allows you to control the amount of moisture in the air. Pour water on the rocks to get the desired effect.

• When you are through with the sauna, clean your skin with a shower or bath. A cool rinse helps close the pores.

• Shampoo and condition your hair, and apply a moisturizer or body oil to your skin after your final shower.

• Have someone available when you are in the sauna in case you fall asleep or need assistance.

Don'ts

• Taking a sauna is like jogging around the block. Persons with a history of chest pain, diabetes, vascular problems, hypertension, obesity, kidney dysfunction, or metabolic conditions should get a doctor's okay first, as well as anyone on daily medication.

• Pregnant women should avoid prolonged exposure to heat. Check with your obstetrician if you are pregnant and want to continue using the sauna.

• Avoid alcohol. Over 90% of accidental burns and the majority of cardiovascular problems occurring in saunas are related to alcohol use.

• Do not take a sauna on a full stomach. Just as for swimming or any exercise, wait at least 30 minutes after eating.

• Specially formulated "fluid-replacement drinks" contain mostly salt and are not recommended.

• Don't wear earrings or other jewelry since hot metal can burn.

Sauna Heaters

The heater design in this illustration has vertical heating elements that allow more rocks to be in direct contact with it. The results are free air flow and fast, effective heating with minimal energy use.

The heater is hung on its wall brackets clear of combustible material. After filling the heater with rocks, the electrical hookups are made.

Heater sizes vary according to the sauna kit's dimensions. For home installations, FinnLeo has four smaller heaters designed for small saunas and tight spaces, from 45 to 150 cubic feet, while four other models accommodate saunas from 100 to 420 cubic feet.

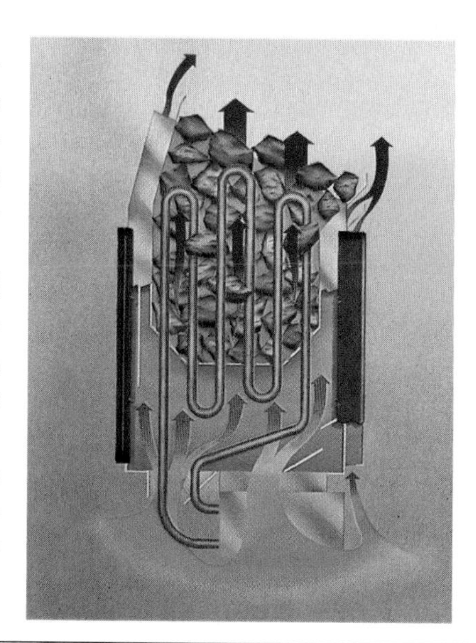

Timers on the smaller heaters can be preset to start the sauna up to 9 hours later. Digital controls allow for 24-hour presetting.

Note: For more information, you can contact FinnLeo, Div. of Helo Saunas and Steam, 575 E. Cokato St., Cokato, MN 55321. Their toll-free number in the USA and Canada is 1-800-882-4352.

MASTERING MOLDING

Some Tricks Of The Trade Can Help You Look Like An Expert

Back in the late 1800's, special wood wall treatments were all painstakingly crafted by hand. But today you can create similar special effects with unfinished wood moldings available from your local building materials dealer.

The area beneath a staircase, for example, is often too easily dismissed with a coat of paint or wallpaper. By adding wood molding, it can be transformed to contribute to the visual interest of your home.

Below the staircase shown at right, simple S-4-S (sanded four sides) molding is nailed to the wallboard to form the vertical and horizontal edges. Then base cap molding is used on both sides of the S-4-S to complete the project.

Wood molding can be used to enhance the beauty of your home in a variety of ways. Below are the basic steps to help you plan, measure, install, and finish molding projects. They come from the experts at Georgia-Pacific Corp. The company also has several helpful brochures available on the use of molding (see end of article).

TOOLS

Only basic tools are needed to install wood moldings. However, better quality tools will make the job easier and will help the results look more professional.

Tools you'll need include an accurate miter box, a backsaw, a 6″ to 8″ coping saw, hammer, nails, nail set, staple gun, tape measure, and goggles. Typically, either 3d (1¼″) or 4d (1½″) finishing nails are used; they should be long enough to penetrate to the wall stud.

To make painting the molding easier, apply a primer coat and a top coat before installing the molding. Then putty, sand when dry, and touch up the nail holes.

MEASURING MOLDING

The first step of a molding project is to determine how much molding you will need. List the molding types you plan to use and then measure the length needed for each type. Always round up to the next full foot to allow for errors.

On ends that will be mitered to fit any outside corner, such as around door and window openings or for picture frames, add the measurement of the width of the molding to each end when figuring the totals.

For example, when working with a 3″-wide molding for a 30″-wide window that will be mitered at both ends, add 3″ to each end for a total length of 36″.

Always mark the molding for a miter cut to allow for the longest point of a 45° angle (Figure 4, next page).

Molding is sold in lengths varying from 3′ to 30′. Whenever possible, try to buy shorter lengths to fit the area. Often less expensive, the shorter lengths also are easier to work with and to transport.

CUTTING

If you have never cut molding before, practice the different cutting techniques on scrap molding.

If you are applying more than one style of molding (creating a built-up application), use scrap pieces to decide how you want the molding stacked or spaced. You can hold the scrap pieces up to the ceiling or on the floor to determine and mark their positioning.

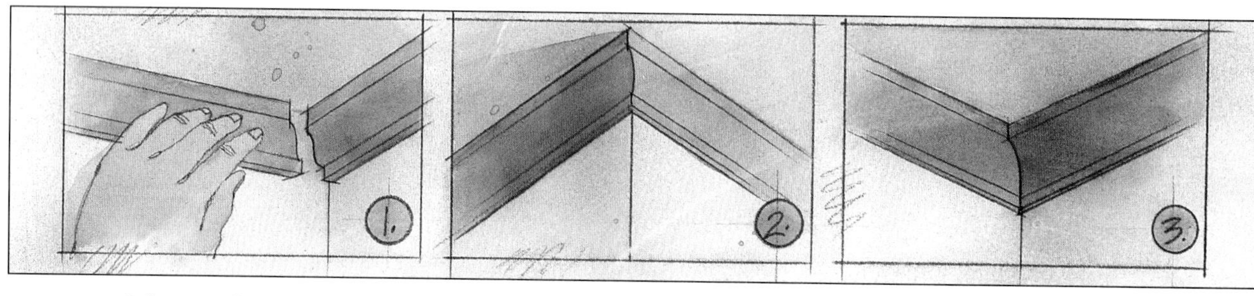

Miter Cuts

The most basic cut used to install moldings is the 45° miter. Miters are used when two pieces of molding meet at an outside corner, an inside corner (when the molding is applied flat to the wall), or around doors and windows.

Copes. The coping technique is used to get the best fit possible when butting moldings at an inside corner. One piece is cut to fit flat to the wall at a 90° angle, and the adjoining piece is sawed to fit the face profile of that piece (Figure 1).

Splices. Splicing is used to join two pieces of molding together, end to end, when a single, continuous piece is not long enough to cover the space. Directions under Base Molding, next page, explain how to make a splice with a scarf joint.

Ceiling Molding

Mitering. Place the molding in the miter box upside down (as if the bottom of the miter box were the ceiling and the back were the wall). Be sure the molding is secure in the miter box; you may want to use a C-clamp with pads. Use long, even strokes when sawing, keeping the blade upright and straight.

Outside Corner Miter. To cut the left-hand piece of molding, as in Figure 2, make a 45°-angle cut from left to right (Figure 4). The piece on the right after cutting will be the left-hand piece of the installed corner joint. To cut the right-hand piece in Figure 2, make a 45°-angle cut from right to left (Figure 5). The piece on the left will be the right-hand piece of the installed corner joint.

Inside Corner Miter. This is used when molding fits flat to wall, as in Figure 3. To cut the right-hand piece of molding in Figure 3, make a 45°-angle cut from left to right (Figure 4). After cutting, the piece on the left will be the right inside corner piece of the installed corner joint. To cut the left-hand piece, cut a 45° angle from right to left (Figure 5). The piece on the right will be the left inside corner piece of the installed corner joint.

Coping. Molding meeting at an inside corner can be joined with a coping joint. The end of one piece of molding (the piece on the right in Figure 1), is cut at a 90° angle so that it will fit flush to the wall in the corner. The left-hand piece is mitered and coped as follows to fit over the right-hand piece.

Sculpting. To cut the left-hand piece, place the molding right-side-up in the miter box, as if the back of the miter box were the wall. Cut at a 45° angle from left to right (Figure 6). The resulting cut exposes the profile of the molding, which serves as guideline for the coping saw.

Follow the profile with the coping saw at a 90° angle to the face of the molding (Figure 7). The resulting cut will be a duplication of the molding pattern which fits over the face of the opposite piece of molding as shown in Figure 1.

Base Molding

To cut your base molding, place the molding right-side-up in your miter box, as if the bottom of the miter box were the floor and the back of the miter box were the wall.

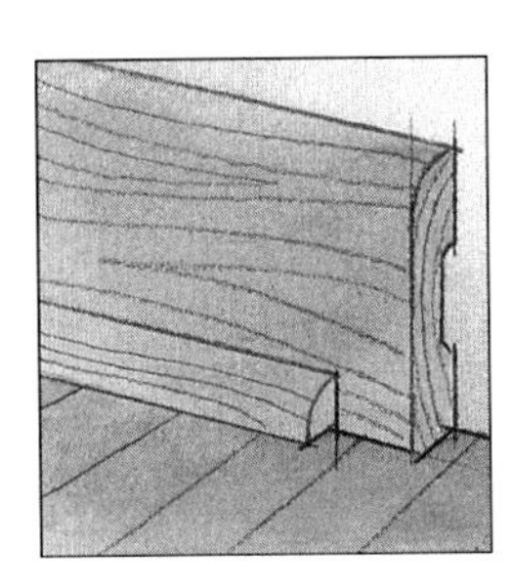

Outside Corner Miter. To cut the right-hand piece of the molding, make a 45°-angle cut from left to right (Figure 4). After cutting, the right-hand piece will be the right outside corner piece. To cut the left-hand piece, cut the molding at a 45° angle from right to left (Figure 5).

Inside Corner Miter. To cut the left-hand piece of molding, make a 45°-angle cut from left to right (Figure 4). The piece on the left will be the left inside corner piece. To cut the right-hand piece, make a 45°-angle cut from right to left (Figure 5). The piece on the right will be the right inside corner piece.

If your miters don't fit exactly, sand the inside edges with 80-grit sandpaper to remove high spots and imperfections. If the joints fit but leave a small gap, it is probably because your saw wavered off the angle; you can fill gaps with wood putty, but they will look better if you resaw them more carefully.

Splicing. Splicing can be used to join two pieces of molding together on a long wall (Figure 8). Position the pieces in the miter box as if the back of the miter box were the wall (Figure 9).

Miter the joining ends at a 45° angle, cutting the left and right pieces from left to right (Figure 10). This allows one piece to overlap the other, making a scarf joint (Figure 8), which is the least noticeable way to join two pieces. Glue the joint so it will stay closed, and nail or staple into place.

Finishing

Generally, it's easier and faster to do the finishing after the molding has been measured and cut, but before it is installed. Sand any rough areas with the grain using 150- to 220-grit sandpaper.

Wipe the sawdust off with a slightly damp cloth. If you are staining the molding, make sure you choose solid molding. Finger-jointed molding can be used if you plan to paint.

Installation

Completely install each molding type, working your way around the room, before installing a second type. Nail the molding into place. If you are using finishing nails, blunt the ends of the nails with a hammer to prevent splitting before driving them into the wood. You can also pre-drill the holes to prevent splitting, or use a nail spinner.

Note: For more information on the uses of molding, contact Georgia-Pacific Corp., 133 Peachtree St. NE (30303), P.O. Box 1763, Norcross, GA 30391. Another good source is the Wood Moulding and Millwork Producers, 1730 SW Skyline Blvd., Ste. 128, Portland, OR 97225.

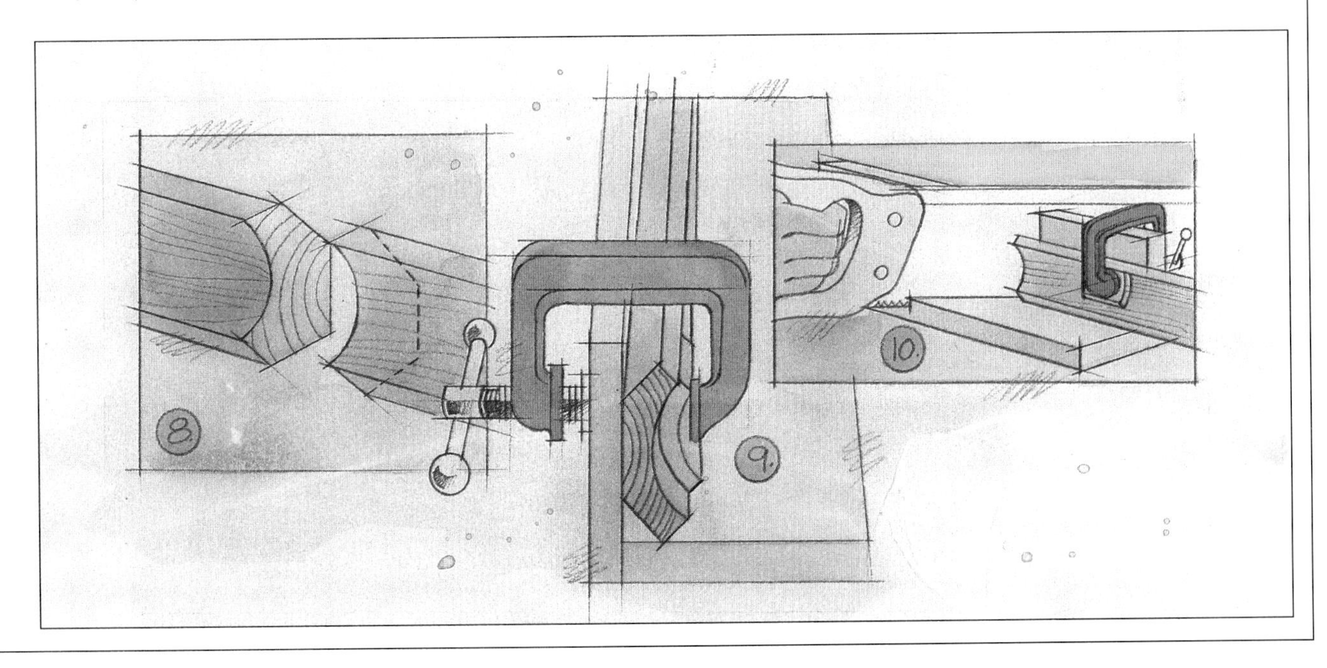

PARADISE OUTDOORS

Inspiring And Practical Project Ideas For Discerning Backyard Builders

Most often with do-it-yourself projects, it is not how hard you work or how much money you spend that counts most, but what you decide to work on. Starting out with good design ideas is the way to get results you'll be proud of when all is said and done.

Outdoor projects are classic examples. You've seen finished decks that still look like a pile of lumber. Well-designed decks, on the other hand, blend in with backyard spaces and greenery. And, by accessorizing the deck with appropriate fences, gates, arbors, and other shade designs, a deck can look like it belongs where it was built.

The key is to think of a deck as part of a larger plan. By starting with a good design and doing much of the work yourself, the cost of creating a backyard paradise can be lower than a run-of-the-mill deck built by a hired contractor. The tri-level deck, built by Brian and Della Zita, photos left and above, is a case in point. When the Zita's bought their home in northern California, the backyard consisted of a metal awning, bare dirt, and a concrete slab. Over the next six months, the couple decided they wanted a redwood deck, plus a trellis to shade the deck and southwest side of the home.

The Zita's 800-sq.-ft. tri-level redwood deck unites the family room and bedroom, and provides space for relaxing and entertaining.

First, Brian built models of the deck and trellis. After getting a bid of $10,000 from a contractor, the couple decided to build the project themselves. Taking a week off from work, they built the deck. The following week, in the evenings after work, they completed the trellis. Total cost: $2,500.

The trellis louvers overhead are redwood 1x6s, attached to 2x8 beams with ¼" dowels. Control rods of 2x2s, attached to the center with eye screws, allow 180° rotation.

The deck was built in three levels; the lowest level covers part of the existing concrete patio. The middle level, 5½" higher, covers the rest of the slab. The upper level outside the bedroom is also built 5½" above the middle level. The lowest level is supported by 4x4 joists on 2x4 blocks bonded to the slab with construction adhesive. The center section rests on 4x4 blocks and 2x8 joists. Pre-cast concrete footings support the upper deck level.

Beams of 2x6s are bolted to both sides of the 4x4 posts, with 2x6 joists resting on them. The 2x6 decking runs at right angles and alternates on each level.

The details give this project a professional look. Trellis posts of 4x4 redwood are built up with 1x2 plant-ons cut from 2x2s. The 2x10 trellis support beams are routed on the bottom and the 1x4s nailed onto the beams help break up their mass and cover bolts. Fascia boards of 2x6 redwood at the base of the deck are routed with a ½" radius to soften the deck's appearance and to allow smooth transitions between deck levels.

For more design ideas on creating the perfect backyard, see the following pages. The photos are from the California Redwood Association, which has several publications for backyard builders. Write 405 Enfrente Drive, Suite 200, Novato, CA 94949, or call 415/382-0662.

The owners of a charming 1930's Craftsman-style shingled house, photos left and below, built this 12x16′ redwood deck of 2x6s to replace an existing one in bad condition. Multiple built-in redwood benches are wrapped around the deck to create a feeling of intimacy, using 3x6s for seats, 3x8s for uprights, and 2x4s and 2x8s for seat backs.

An overhead redwood trellis of 3x8s with 2x3 stringers provides cozy shade. The railings are faced front and back with wood shingles to echo the home's materials; uprights of 1″ copper pipe will weather to a blue-green patina to match the home's trim color.

A handsome, new Victorian-style home, photo above, needed a fence for privacy and to define two separate entries—one for the owner and another for a tenant. The solution was a 6′-high fence of 1x8 redwood with a "dog-eared" top. The fence on the tenant's side is built with 1x8s topped with lattice panels of 1″ redwood lathe. Low rock walls and paths and artful planting add the finishing touches.

Mike and Debbie Mullen of Dallas, Texas had an existing swimming pool built partly out of the ground. To expand their outdoor space, they wrapped this 800-sq.-ft. redwood deck three-quarters of the way around the pool, photos left and below. Decking of 2x6s runs diagonally around the pool and in an opposite diagonal one level up to define the shade shelter area and create a herringbone effect. Brick paving sets off the remaining area.

The shade-sheltered area jogs out from the rest of the deck, and a redwood latticed trellis with curving edges echoes the shape of the decking below. The trellis has 8x8 columns, 6x12 supports, 1x4 lattice, and 2x6 joists. The curving trellis surround is made of 1x2s, 1x4s, and 2x6s, kerfed to achieve the rounded corners.

The Mullens also built a classic arched redwood bridge over a natural stream near the entry of their house, photo right. The bridge is of laminated 1x4 redwood beams, bent and held in place with resin glue before installation. Redwood 2x6s cover the bridge floor; the railings are of 4x4 posts, 2x2 uprights, and 1x4 tops.

Often a key to finishing off a fence is the entryway, photo below. The posts, rails, and beams here are all of redwood, and the fence boards are 1x6s. Structural members and decorative elements of the pergola (passageway) are fashioned from larger timbers. Galvanized post anchors, set in concrete and gravel, support the posts above the soil line. Galvanized nails and stainless steel hardware help avoid staining, which can occur with corrosive hardware.

Dimensional Drywall

Low-Cost Ways To Create Dramatic Curves, Arches, Recesses, And Sculpted Effects

If your home was built 40 or more years ago, chances are you have plaster walls that are surrounded by architectural details like built-ins and molding that give your home a modest, custom-built feel.

But, if you own a newer home, chances are you're surrounded by plain, straight walls that can leave you feeling as though you live in a box. However, you can add true distinction and drama to your home, at an affordable price, through the creative use of gypsum wallboard.

Drywall Sculpting

Gypsum wallboard, or drywall, has been around since the 1920s, but it first became popular (and feasible) for residential use around 1950. Contractors liked it because it is consistent, easy to work with, and easy to finish.

More recently, homeowners are taking a second look at its versatility for small projects as well as major remodeling. With the proper techniques, drywall can be used in nearly any situation that requires an aesthetic touch. Scoring along one side allows moistened drywall to be bent to conform to almost any radius. Slim pieces can follow the contour of most designs. And, using architectural shapes and forms, almost anything possible with lath and plaster can be done with drywall at a lower cost.

When building or remodeling, the focus is often on saving money on "the box," and spending more money on interior detailing. The trick to adding architectural interest to your home using drywall is to think beyond "the box"––those areas of the home which are not exposed.

Drywall is economical, yet also is flexible enough to conform to a wide variety of shapes. Curved walls, arches, and soft corners of drywall can add interest and detail to a home's interior. A wide variety of panels are available:

- Water-resistant drywall, often referred to as "greenboard," is used as a tile substrate in high-moisture areas like bathrooms and kitchens.
- Fire-resistant drywall uses a special fire-resistant core to impede the destruction of walls and ceilings from a fire.
- Foil-backed gypsum board provides a built-in vapor barrier to help prevent moisture from entering the home.
- Portland cement board is a drywall cousin used for high-moisture and high-heat applications. Areas where it is commonly used include tub, sink, shower and steambath surrounds, as well as fireplace chases and mantles.

Installation Basics

Working with drywall is relatively easy. Cutting straight edges and soft arcs is simply a matter of scoring the panel's paper skin, then "snapping" the panel with a quick, firm movement. Lightly sanding the cut edge prepares the panel for installation.

Drywall also can be easily cut for curves and complex shapes. After scribing the arc on the paper skin, a keyhole saw, coping saw, or drywall router can be used to cut the desired shape, or to cut around electrical outlets or ductwork.

Although drywall is easy to work, a little extra care in preparation and installation will boost the quality of the finished project. First, make sure any framing is square and plumb so you will end up with a uniform, ripple-free wall surface. If necessary, use shims or replace any warped framing. Also check with local officials for their recommendations on the installation of vapor barriers before the drywall is attached.

Installing drywall involves fastening the panel to the framing with drywall nails or "buglehead" screws for walls, or fasteners plus drywall adhesive for ceilings.

Screws provide the best grip to resist "popping" caused by wood shrinkage, and they are favored over nails today by most contractors. Fast installation can be accomplished by using electric or cordless drills equipped with clutches designed to sink the screw so its head sets just slightly below the paper without breaking it.

Once drywall panels are in place, joints and inside corners are finished with joint tape and compound. First spread a thin, even coat of compound the length of the joint, then press joint tape in place. Embed the tape with a 5″ drywall knife, then apply a thin coat of compound over the tape. After the embedding coat is dry, apply a fill

(second) coat 7″ to 10″ wide over the taped joints using an 8″ knife.

Then feather the edge of the second coat approximately 2″ beyond the edge of the first coat. After the second coat is dry, apply a thin finish (third) coat over joints using a 10″ knife. Feather the edges of the third coat at least 2″ wider than the second coat.

Nail or screw heads are easily hidden using a couple coats of drywall compound. For outside corners, using a special corner bead can be used to achieve a clean, finished edge. This bead is nailed or taped in place, then multiple coats of drywall compound are used to finish the edge. Metal J-trim or L-trim is often recommended where gypsum panels butt windows or concrete block.

Nearly everyone who has tackled a remodeling project knows that sanding drywall compound can be dusty, but there are ways to minimize the mess. Use only as much compound as is needed, applying thin, feathered coats to cover joints and screw heads. Plastic sheeting helps confine dust to the project space, and window exhaust fans can help clear the air. (Use face masks when dust is in the air.) Where only minimal sanding is needed, you can wet-sand the joints with a sponge to remove high spots and feather the compound flush with the surface.

Regardless of the sanding technique you use, a final wipe of walls and ceilings with a wet sponge will help remove all remaining dust before painting. To get professional results when painting new drywall, use a primer coat to eliminate joint banding and surface differences. Primer coats provide a base that equalizes surface textures and porosities so that finish coats look consistent.

Drywall readily accepts a variety of finishes, from paint to stippled textures to help create a cottage, Tudor, or Southwestern motif.

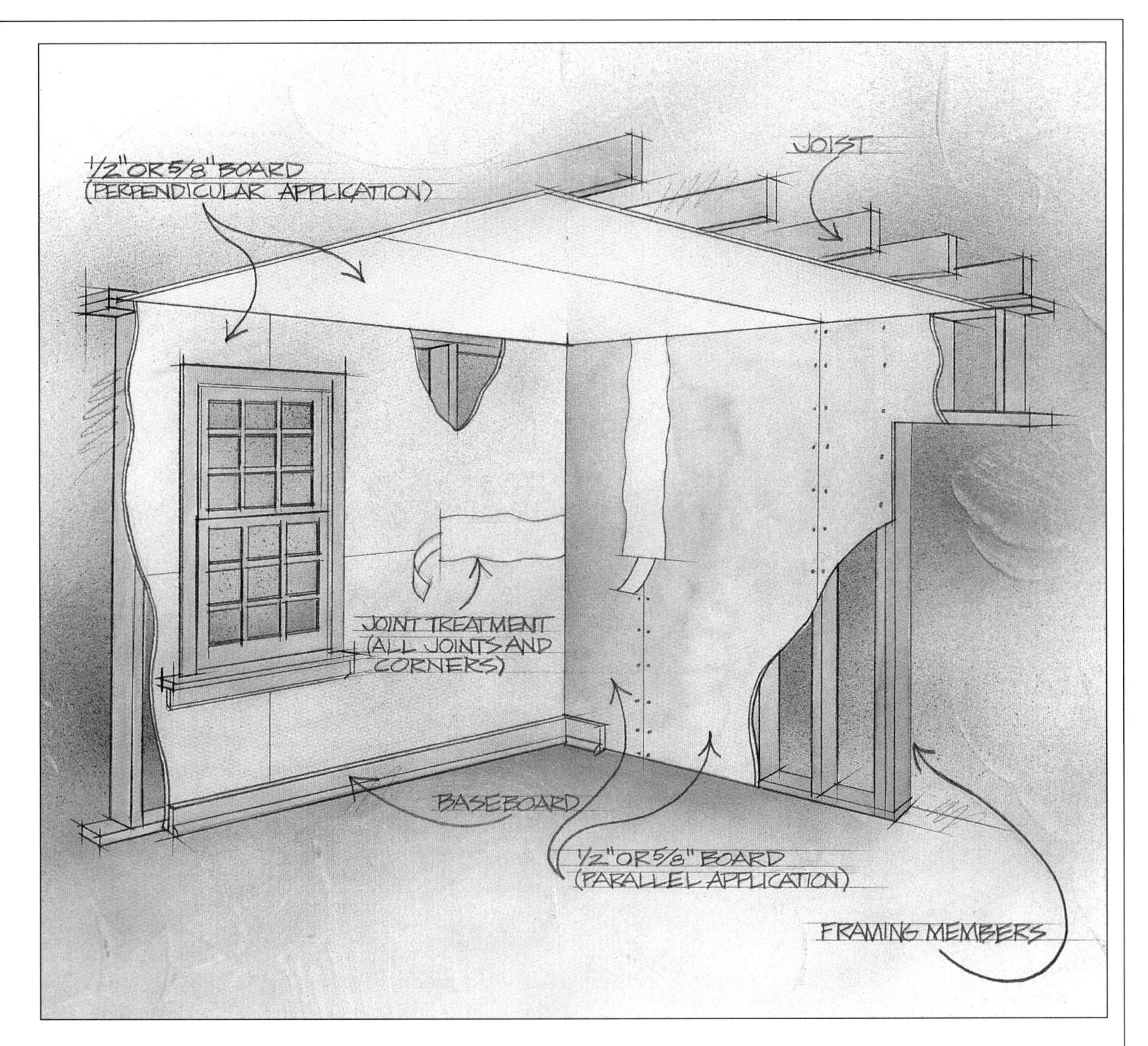

Building Arches

The graceful, flowing lines of arches and soft corners were common in older, lath-and-plaster construction homes. But the shift in the Fifties to contemporary designs saw the emergence of square walls, sharp corners, and crisp details around doorways, and over pass-throughs, or window frames.

Interior arches are often used to reinforce features of the home's exterior. Architects often try to incorporate these same details in doorways, fireplace elevations, or even in an arch over a vanity.

Arches for windows, mirror recesses, and other areas are limited only by your creativity and room dimensions. But when adding an arch to a doorway, be sure to keep enough clearance height for easy passage through the door.

Creating an arch is a simple operation that can be done in a number of ways. One option is to use pre-molded forms which simply attach to the wall surrounding the opening, then fill and feather using joint compound.

A second option is to use conventional framing, plywood, and drywall. An arched wood frame serves as the foundation. Drywall is cut and attached to the framing and shaped to form the arch.

A variety of methods exist for creating the inside curve of the arch. If the arch is gradual enough, you can simply bend and attach the drywall in place.

For tighter curves, you can score the inside surface of the drywall at 1″ intervals and gently snap it to form the arch. Or, you can wet the drywall and bend it to form the arch.

Next, you form and attach the corner bead by clipping it to form a smooth edge, then apply several layers of joint compound to smooth the arch. After a final sanding, the arch is ready for painting.

Curving Walls

A relative of the arch and equally popular among designers today are curved walls and surfaces. Curved walls can be easily incorporated into any home remodeling, and drywall can be an affordable alternative to plaster and wire.

Like interior arches, curved walls are often designed to emphasize the home's exterior features. The feeling of half-round windows, arched entryways, porticos, or bay windows can be carried through to the home's interior with curved dividing walls, half-walls, or even curving entrances and stairways.

A curved wall can be an economical way to expand interior space and add a dramatic design element. You can set off half-round windows with a short, curved divider wall. Or, consider a curved wall in a stairwell for added interest. Just remember that the forms and surfaces inside and outside the home should complement each other. Try to envision a curved wall within the context of the whole home—not just a single room, or part of a room. Also tie-in the curved wall with other aspects of the room, such as flooring, furniture, and accessories.

Supplies to work drywall are relatively inexpensive. It's best to have drywall knives in three widths and a corner knife if doing many inside corners.

The techniques for drywall curves and arches are similar. You can attach 2x4 studs to special flexible metal channels for curved sections. Stud spacing can range from 6″ to 12″ on-center, depending on the radius of the curve. The tighter the radius, the shorter the spacing.

For gentle curves you simply secure the drywall with screws. For tighter-radius curves you can soak the drywall to achieve the desired shape. Manufacturers do not recommend using the soaking technique over larger curves.

Drywall Tools and Supplies

Cutting and measuring tools:
- Utility knife and extra blades
- Metal tape measure
- Marking pencil
- 4′ straightedge or wallboard T-square

Installation tools:
- Screw gun or electric drill
- No. 2 bit for buglehead screws
- Drywall adhesive and caulk gun (optional)
- Keyhole saw, sabersaw, or drywall router
- Carpenter's or wallboard hammer
- Panel lifter (optional)

Finishing tools:
- Tin snips or hacksaw
- 5″-, 8″-, and 10″-wide joint-finishing knives
- Bread pan to hold compound
- 150-grit sandpaper or 220-grit mesh cloth
- Sponge (small-celled polyurethane works best)
- Poly sheeting to seal off work areas
- Window or box fan
- Step ladder

Accessories:
- Portable light extension cord
- Dropcloths
- Safety glasses
- Dust masks

Note: Drywall joint compound is available in ready-mixed and powder form, which must be mixed with water before use. Newer joint compounds offer the convenience of lighter weight, faster application, easier sanding, and reduced shrinkage.

Drywall tape comes in rolls, and you'll need about 40′ for every 100 sq. ft. of wall or ceiling. Corner bead usually comes in 8′ and 10′ lengths. To figure how much you'll need, simply measure all outside corners and arches.

To estimate how many screws you'll need, figure on approximately 1½ lbs. of Type W buglehead screws for every 500 sq. ft. of drywall.

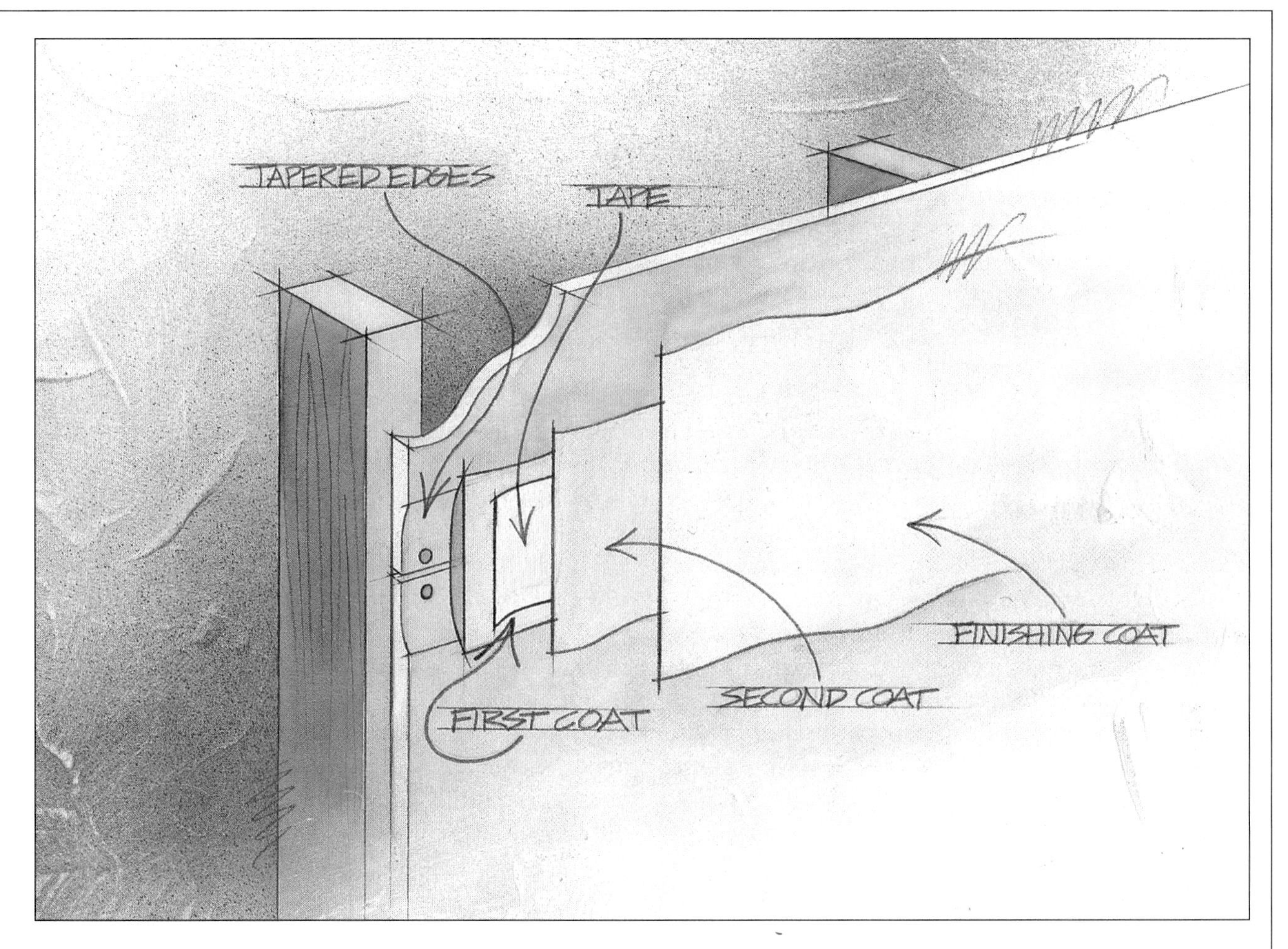

Creating Niches

From a simple storage space to a stunning display, niches are a great way to add function and focal points to a wall, hallway, or stairwell. And, you don't need to limit yourself to a plain, square niche. Using simple framing and drywall, you can incorporate arches or compound angles in the niche.

Constructing a niche is an easy project that can be completed in a few hours, without major mess or disruption to the house. The easiest way to add one in an existing wall is to build it between the framing studs. By using the existing studs for support, you eliminate the need for extra framing. However, you also will be limited to the standard 14½″ width between 16″ wall studs. If you want a wider niche, you will need to cut out and reframe wall studs.

For displays, designers recommend locating the niche at or near eye level. If you want to include lighting, it is a good idea to locate the niche near a switch or outlet so you will have easy access to wiring.

To build a niche into existing framing you will need to add framing to support the base and top of the niche. Once this framing is complete, attach the drywall, then tape and coat the joints with compound. To save space, use thinner ¼″ or ⅜″ drywall. Attach corner bead on all outside corners to provide a clean, ding-proof edge.

To finish the niche, you can paint the drywall to match the existing wall color, or for added detail you might consider a textured finish coat.

Fireplace Chases

Whether remodeling an existing hearth or installing a new fireplace, drywall offers opportunities. With the development of efficient zero-clearance and masonry fireplace designs, homeowners rediscovered woodburning fireplaces. But, often zero-clearance units sacrifice the aesthetic appeal of a traditional brick chase.

You can use drywall to form curves and niches to create a sculpted, Southwestern-style adobe hearth, adding depth and drama with a stippled, textured finish coat. Or, with veneer plasters, you can create a dramatic skip trowel, swirl, fan-shape, or bold texture for a custom, wet plaster look. Veneer plasters cost only slightly more than drywall compound. Plus, you'll save time in sanding and cleanup.

Check local codes and manufacturer's recommendations to determine the clearance needs around the firebox. Use cement board for maximum fire protection around the firebox. Cement board can be finished with ceramic or thin-cut stone tile, thin brick, or other materials. Framing and finishing areas not adjacent to the firebox can be done with regular drywall.

Detailing Ceilings

Easily the most overlooked area of the home for adding drama and detail is the ceiling. But ceilings hold great potential for easy-to-add custom details using drywall.

When used on ceilings, drywall can actually hide a multitude of visual problems—particularly in basement spaces where plumbing and heating vents frequently are exposed. To conceal them, just add simple framing around the pipes or vents, then cover with drywall, tape and finish. Using drywall, it is also easy to add recessed lights to a single wall or around the perimeter of a room. The lighting cans and wiring can be concealed by attaching a soffit box frame to the overhead joists.

Adding one or more layers of drywall on the ceiling or its perimeter also can help define the space. With staggered strips of drywall around the perimeter, you can actually create a raised ceiling effect to define a room without walls. Or, you can use staggered layers to literally create a shadow box to add drama to a chandelier.

Other design opportunities include curved or straight shadow lines, or layers stacked in ziggurat fashion reflecting elements such as a fireplace elevation or other design.

Installing multiple layers of drywall is also simple. Just mark and snap straight edges to size, and cut curved edges with a keyhole saw or drywall router. Then tape exposed edges and screws, cover with joint compound, and feather for a smooth, uniform look. Adding metal-edged trim pieces and using larger-radius corner beads let you add a soft finishing edge to the ceiling.

Anchoring is a key consideration when layering drywall on a ceiling and/or walls. Be sure screws are long enough to penetrate the framing members. For additional insurance, fully laminating the layers together using a setting-type joint compound provides the best results.

Gypsum Panel Coverage Calculator

No. of Panels	Size of Panels 4x8′	4x10′	4x12′
10	320 sq. ft.	400 sq. ft.	480 sq. ft.
11	352	440	528
12	384	480	576
13	416	520	624
14	448	560	672
15	480	600	720
16	512	640	768
17	544	680	816
18	576	720	864
19	608	760	912
20	640	800	960

Note: Add 32 sq. ft. for each additional 4x8′ panel; 40 sq. ft. for each additional 4x10′ panel; and 48 sq. ft. for each 4x12′ panel.

Estimating Drywall

Estimating how much the materials will cost for your drywall project is easily done.

To measure the amount of drywall you'll need, determine square feet by multiplying the length and height of all wall and ceiling surfaces, then subtract the square footage of large openings like doors and windows.

To figure how many sheets of drywall you'll need, simply follow the chart. Drywall panels are available in 4x8′, 4x10′, and 4x12′ sizes.

The idea is to install drywall with as few seams as possible. For smaller remodeling projects, you may be limited to smaller panel sizes. If you have large walls or ceilings to cover, larger panels are preferable; you'll have fewer joints and seams to tape and sand, resulting in faster installation and a more uniform, consistent surface.

Note: U.S. Gypsum Company is a good source for information on drywall applications, including a special do-it-yourself Sheetrock installation and finishing tips brochure. To get a copy, write to the company at 125 S. Franklin, P.O. Box 806278, Dept. 147-4, Chicago, IL 60680-4124.

Another source is the Foundation Of The Wall and Ceiling Industry, a national, non-profit, information center with a full library of books and videos available for 30-day loan and on-staff specialists to answer technical questions. You can call 703/534-1703 between 7 AM and 3 PM ET, or write them for a bibliography of their materials at 307 E. Annandale, Suite 200, Falls Church, VA 22042-2433.

TECH NOTES: SHAPING DRYWALL

Drywall can be formed to almost any cylindrically curved surface, including arches. Panels can be applied either dry or wet, depending on the radius of the curve desired. To prevent flat areas between framing with sharp curves, use closer-than-normal stud and furring spacing.

Curved Walls. Panels can be gently bent around the framing and securely fastened to achieve the desired radius. The chart on the opposite page shows the minimum radius suggested for a dry panel of specific thickness. A panel may be bent to a shorter radius than shown by thoroughly moistening with water (see bottom sketch).

One method to create curves is to use 3½″ steel runners for the wood studs. (See illustration on the next page.) Cut one leg and the web of the top and bottom steel runners at 2″ intervals for the length of the arc. Allow 12″ of uncut steel runners at each end of the arc. Bend the runners to a uniform curve (90° maximum). To support the cut leg of the runner, clinch a 1″ x 25-ga. steel strip to the inside of the leg. Attach the steel runners to structural elements at the floor and ceiling with suitable fasteners.

Position the studs, with the open side facing in the same direction, engaging the floor and ceiling runners. Begin and end each arc with a stud, and space intermediate studs equally as measured on the outside of the arc.

If necessary, drywall panels may be bent to a shorter radius if the face, back papers, and core are thoroughly moistened. The panels must be handled very carefully

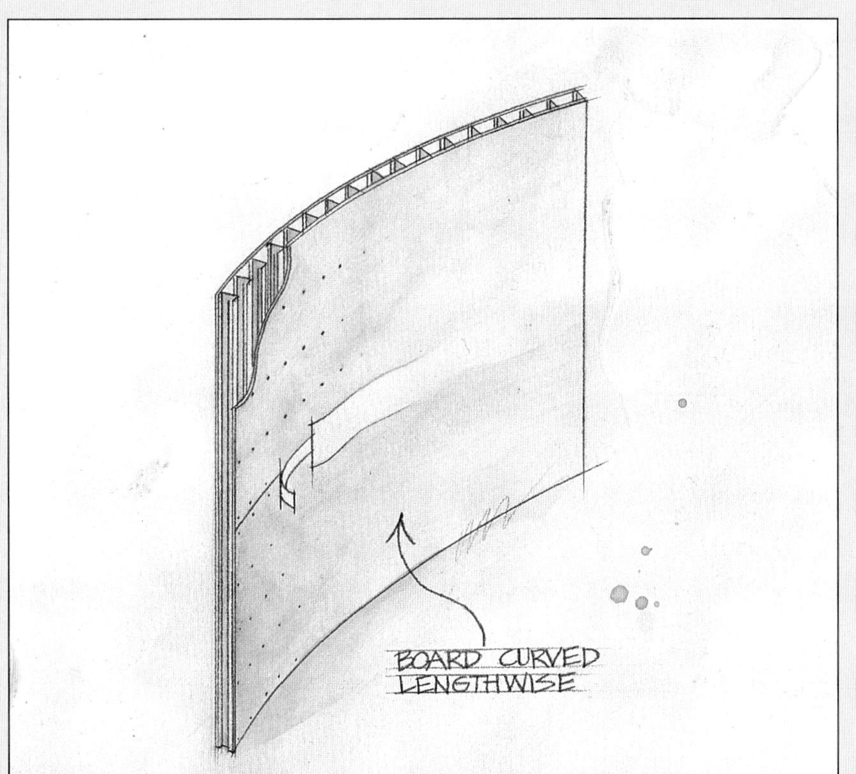

When dry gypsum board is curved lengthwise, the minimum recommended radius is 5′ for ¼″ panels (see chart next page).

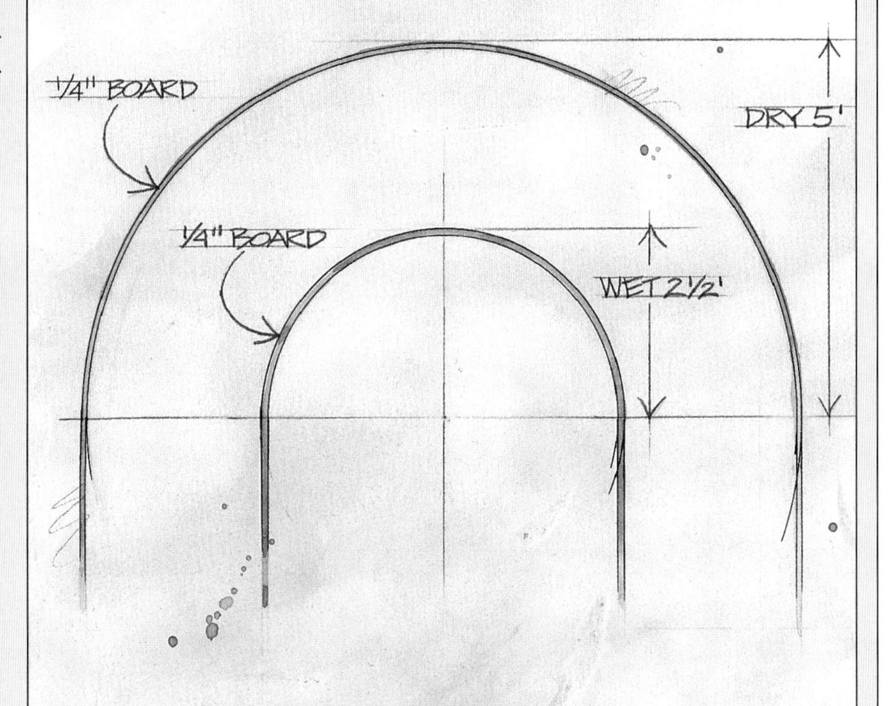

When gypsum board is moistened, the minimum radius can be reduced to roughly half of that recommended for dry panels.

while moist. Upon drying, they will regain their original hardness. You can moisten panels using a short nap paint roller, water pump, or spray gun, applying clean water to the entire face and back surfaces. Do not allow water to stand or puddle. Stack moistened panels on a flat surface and allow to stand for at least one hour.

To apply panels to a concave surface, attach a stop at one end of the curve and push on the other end of the panel to force the center of the panel against the framing. Fasten with nails or screws while working from the "stopped" end, being sure the panel is held tightly against the framing. On a convex surface, fasten one end to the framing with nails or screws and gradually push the panel against the framing and fasten, working from the fixed end to the free end.

Arches. Gypsum board may be applied to the inner face of almost any archway. The panel should be precut to the proper length and width. For sharp curves, the panel can be moistened or the back paper scored across the width using parallel score marks approximately 1″ on-center. Break the core at each cut. Then fasten with nails or screws.

Finishing. To apply joint compound to corners of arches or other curved surfaces, fold the joint tape lengthwise, snip one side of the tape from the edge to the center at about ¾″ intervals. Apply the uncut edge of the tape to the curved surface and the cut half to the flat surface. Then finish as you would for flat applications. Likewise, corner bead may be used by snipping one leg every ¾″, applying the uncut leg to the curved surface and the cut leg to the flat surface.

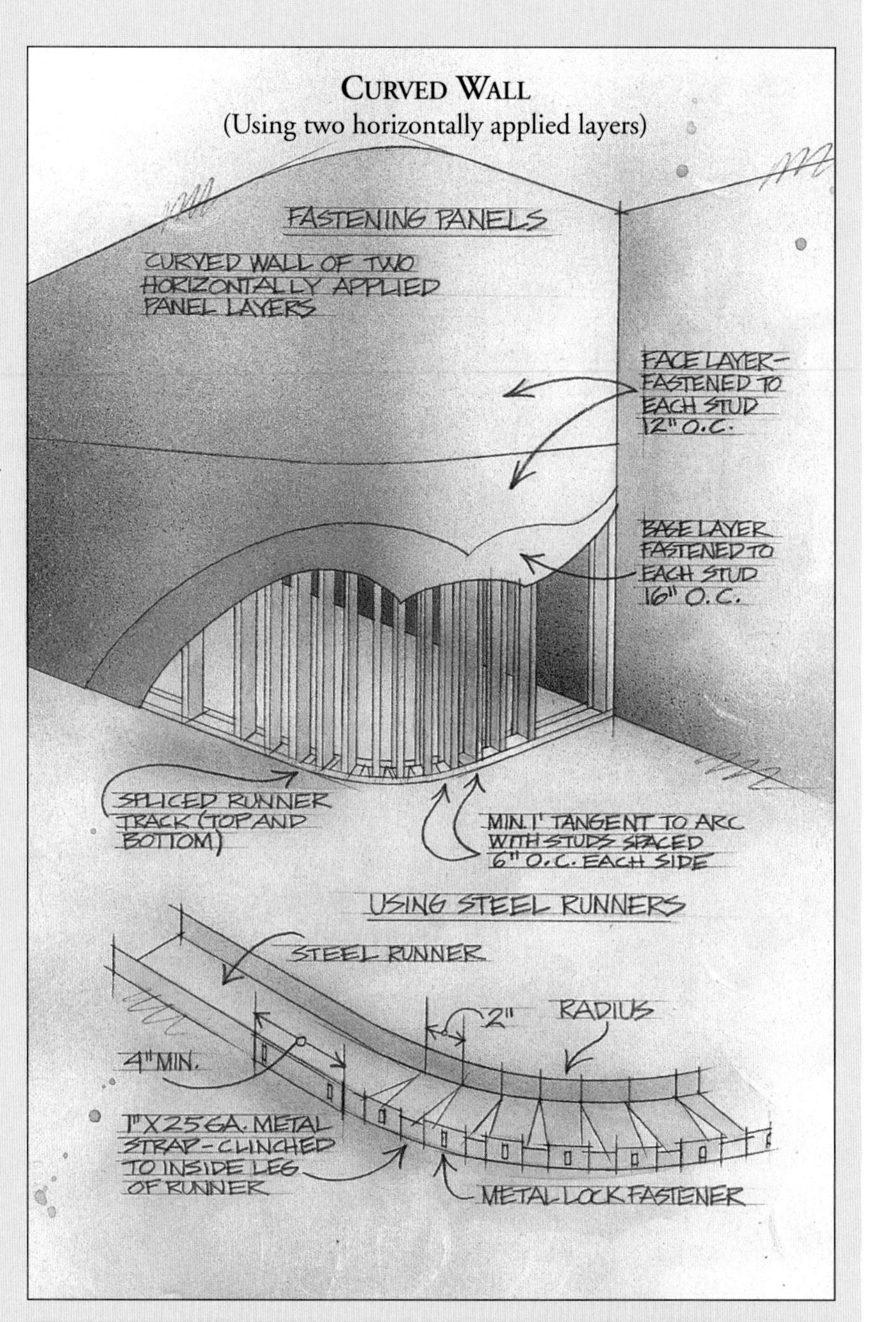

Bending Dry Gypsum Board

(Minimum bending radius recommended for dry gypsum board panels of various thicknesses)

Panel Thickness	Bent Lengthwise	Bent Widthwise
¼″	5′	15′
5/16″	6¼′	20′
⅜″	7½′	25′
½″	10′	Not Recommended
⅝″	15′	Not Recommended

Note: Two ¼″ pieces bent successively may be used to get a final ½″ thickness at the shorter bending radius.

BACKYARD BEAUTY

How To Gain Outdoor Storage Space Without Giving Up Style Or Grace

Most backyards in suburban America have both a fence, for privacy, and a pre-built shed to house garden tools and lawn-care paraphernalia. You know the problem. The shed sticks out like a sore thumb and, more often than not, the fence is of a different material and style.

Therein lies the opportunity. When shed and fence are designed in tandem, as this project demonstrates, the results can be dramatic.

This handsome garden shed is built into the corner of a double-sided privacy fence; both are clad in the same materials to provide a seamless integration. Result? The fence and shed give the impression of a larger yard area. With its doors closed, the shed almost disappears. It even looks good from the street.

The goal of this project, which was co-sponsored by The American Plywood Association (APA), was to design backyard architecture that a homeowner could build while taking advantage of plywood's durability outdoors. "We wanted to show a viable alternative to the pre-built storage shed, and show how storage can be incorporated into an overall plan," explains project architect Steve Mead of Des Moines, Iowa. Though not for the rank beginner, the construction should present no mystery to those skilled in basic carpentry. Inexpensive building materials (see illustration) make the project affordable as well.

By integrating shed, fence, and compost areas into a single flowing design, photo above, you can bypass typical pre-built shed clutter.

The shed is built on a plywood platform 6″ above grade. It uses the two end-posts of the fence, with two of its own, for its foundation. Unlike the rest of the fence, the shed is one-panel thick, finished only on the sides exposed to the street and the yard, and replicates the fence design. Inside, the shed remains unfinished with exposed studs and stiffeners.

Building The Shed

The shed's pyramid roof has 2′ of acrylic skylight near the peak that brightens the interior and also saves on materials. From the eaves up, the roof is covered with 4x8′ sheets of medium-density overlay (MDO) plywood. The 1/8″ acrylic meets and slightly overlaps the finished edges of the MDO panels. Sealed at all joints with silicone, it is fastened to the roof framing with stainless-steel screws.

To build the shed, first make sure the site is level and well drained. The shed can be built on a concrete slab or over a bed of gravel. The first step is building the shed floor. (Treated lumber and treated plywood are recommended.)

Begin by setting the treated 4x4 posts into the ground. Attach the treated 2x6 joists, then install the panels. Once the floor is finished, build the roof frame. The floor provides a level working space off the ground that will not be available once the walls are up. (See illustration for roof framing details; the skylight is optional.)

Once the roof frame is done, set it aside and move on to the walls. Begin with the two walls that adjoin the fence, then build the remaining wall and door opening. Before placing the roof framing, attach all trim, then build and attach the framing for the two fence sections that adjoin the shed. The roof will get in the way if it is installed first.

Now you can build the ramp at the entrance to the shed. The framing is of treated 2x6 lumber, installed using 2x6 joist hangers. Finally, cover the top and ends with 3/4″ preservative-treated plywood.

View from the outside. To properly repel and drain water, both shed and fence use a beveled cap design and siding with tongue-and-groove joints.

Building The Fence

The wood fence provides a barrier to sound and sight that is also attractive and durable. It is covered with Texture I-II (TI-II) plywood siding that resembles lap siding; its uninterrupted mass helps dull sound transmission. "Wood actually absorbs sound better than concrete," says Mead. "It is also more visually appealing."

The fence is supported with pressure-treated 4x4 posts sunk into 4′-deep, 12″-diameter holes filled with concrete. The posts are 6′ on center, a span that allows the fence to withstand winds up to 80 mph.

To create a "good neighbor" fence, both sides of each section are finished with TI-II infill panels; each 4x8 sheet is cut to fit between the posts and then held in place with 3/4″ stops. The 1x4 boards nailed vertically between the two panels give the fence sections stiffness and create dead air space that helps muffle sound up to 40%. To shed water, the siding has tongue-and-groove joints.

To build the fence, first set the posts and install the top and bottom framing pieces. Once a section of fence framing is done, fabricate the panelized center section. Each side requires 1 1/2 siding panels. Remember that the grooved sides of the siding panels should face outward. Also make sure the outside lap on the lapped panel edge points down to shed moisture.

Attach the panels to one another with vertically nailed 1x3 lumber stiffeners. Stagger the panel joints so that on one side the joint is near the top of the fence and on the other side near the bottom. This will increase the fence's rigidity.

Once the panels are nailed together, install a 3/4x3/4″ lumber stop on the fence framing and nail the panelized section in place. Install another stop on the other side of the panelized section. The trim is of chamfered 2x2s and 2x4s and is attached with finishing nails.

It's important to make sure the grooves in the siding panels on the fence and shed match. Before installing the fence sections, make a 4″x8′ story pole from a piece of scrap. Mark the pole to show the location of framing members on both the fence and the shed, as well as the location of the panel grooves on the shed. Use this pole as a guide when trimming the fence panels to help make sure the grooves match.

Note: The American Plywood Association has a full library of plans for other outdoor structures and workshop projects. For a current listing and pricing, write P.O. Box 11700, Tacoma, WA 98411-0700, or call 206/565-6600.

The storage shed, photo above, is suspended above grade while the ramp is built over a bed of pea gravel to drain water. The design also includes an enclosed compost and recycling area with composting bins. It is simply made of fence sections, configured in a rectangle, with a gate added for access.

The walls of the compost area, photo right, match the fence and shed design and also tie into the existing fence post structure. Built to the same elevation as the other structures, the walls of the compost area are kept open at least 3" at the bottom to vent odors and moisture.

TECH NOTES: INTEGRATING A BACKYARD

This backyard plan is both attractive and practical. The fence adds privacy and good looks while the shed and an enclosed storage area hide items like lawn gear and trash cans. The shed has 64 square feet of floor space and is 10½′ high at the peak of the roof. Each fence section is 6′10½″ long and 5′7½″ high. The enclosed storage area shown in the plans is 8′x 6′7¼″, but it can be easily expanded. A gate can be added to the enclosed storage area for security. The amount of fencing required will vary depending on the size of your yard.

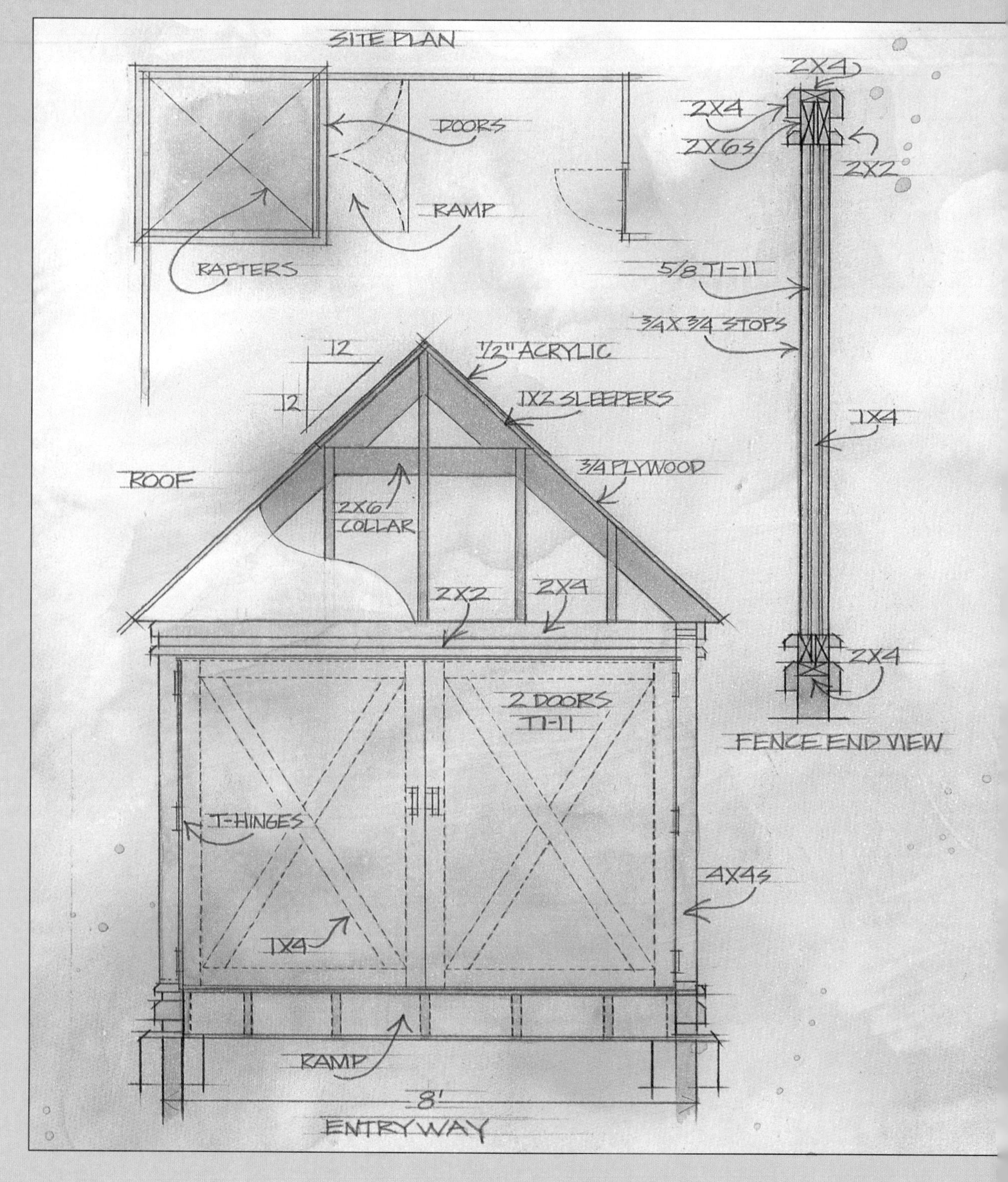

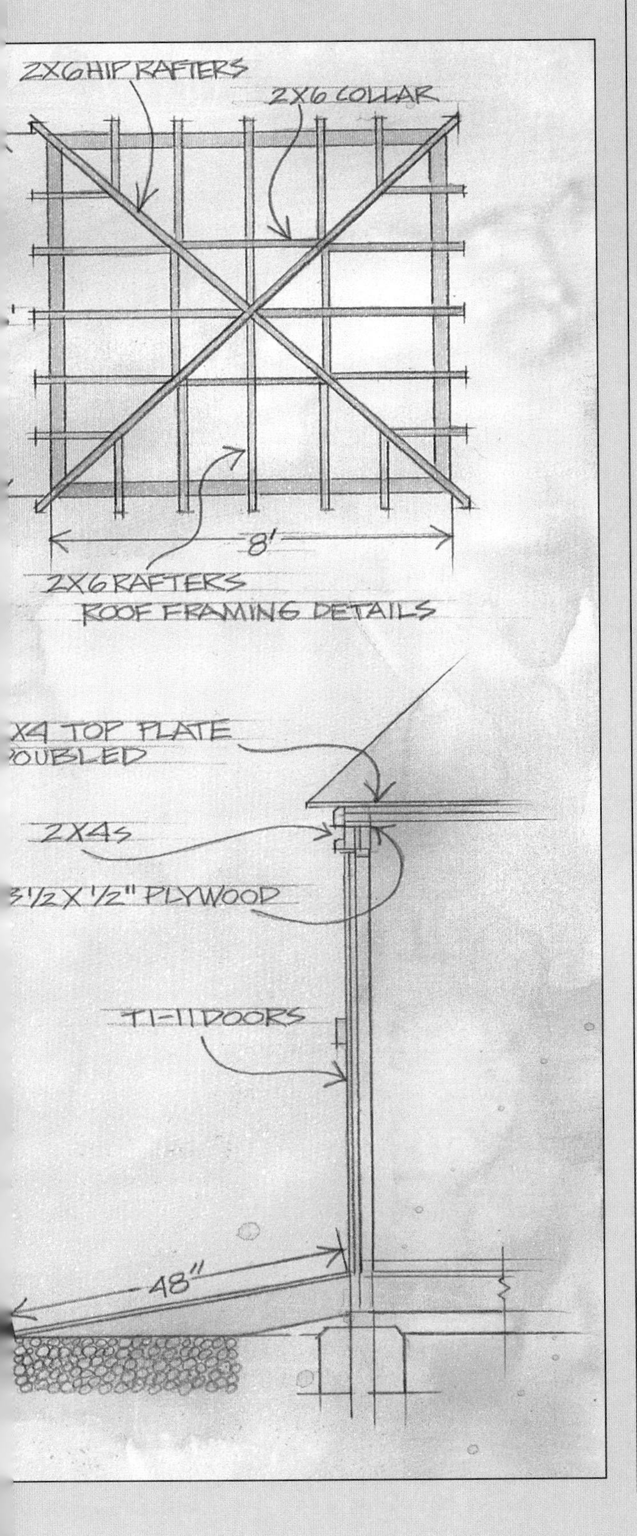

Materials List - Shed

Recommended Panels

3	APA Preservative Treated Plywood, C-D, Exterior panels, with tongue-and-groove edges (for floor and ramp) ¾″x4′x8′
6	APA -rated siding panels ⅝″x4′x8′
4	APA MDO plywood panels ¾″x4′x8′ for roof. (Other types of APA Exterior or Exposure-1 panels may be used if additional roof material is applied.)

Framing

32 linear ft. of treated 4x4 posts
88 linear ft. of treated 2x6 floor joists
128 linear ft. of 2x4 studs
84 linear ft. of 1x3s
46 linear ft. of 2x2s
168 linear ft. of ¾x¾″ lumber
24 linear ft. of 1x5 lumber
52 linear ft. of 1x4 lumber
332 linear ft. of 2x6 lumber
10 linear ft. of 1x2 lumber

Other Materials

5 lbs.	16d galvanized box nails
1 tube	Silicone sealant for edges of skylight
1	Lock hasp
2	Barrel bolts
3 sets	6″ T-hinges

As required: 2x6 joist hangers
2 sheets ⅛″or 3⁄16″ clear plastic, 36x72″ for skylight

Materials List - Fence

Per 6′ section of fencing (finished on both sides)

Recommended Panels

3	APA -rated siding panels ⅝″x4′x8′

Framing

14 linear ft. of 2x6 lumber
14 linear ft. of 2x4 lumber
14 linear ft of 3x½″ lumber
16 linear ft. of treated 4x4 posts
46 linear ft. of ¾x¾″ lumber for stops
30 linear ft. of 2x4 for trim
24 linear ft. of 2x2 for trim

Other Materials

1 lb. each of 16d and 5d galvanized finish nails
2 lbs. 16d galvanized box nails

Do-It-Yourself Improvements

REAL GRANITE

The Earth's Oldest Natural Material Offers New Options For The Kitchen Remodeler

You can spot the quarries from five miles away in central and southwestern Minnesota, like giant circus tents without their canvas. Close by, you first hear the whistle, then the blast of dynamite that jars the ground for a half-mile around.

What is being extracted at these sites is granite. Pushed through the earth's crust some two to four billion years ago, it is the oldest rock in the world. Though granite has long been quarried for monuments, building blocks, and road building materials, today the slabs being loaded onto railroad cars could be headed for a familiar destination—your kitchen.

Recently, sales of granite for use in kitchens has skyrocketed. But leading designers aren't puzzled about the trend. They say the interest in granite is a logical offshoot of a movement toward the use of more organic materials, particularly in the kitchen. Granite's grain patterns and depth make it especially compatible with the organic look of materials such as hardwood floors or cherrywood cabinets.

Earth-natural granite is a luxurious choice for kitchens as shown here, plus baths and other areas of the home. The color of granite can range from black to reddish to charcoal, with each slab containing its own unique patterns and grain lines.

Besides countertops, granite is also becoming a prime candidate for backsplashes and floors, says Mary Jane Pappas, head of Pappas Design in Minneapolis. She advises that the selective use of granite in a kitchen can help stretch limited budgets while still delivering a "high-end" look.

Natural granite has a variety of colorings, from deep black to rose, peach, and mahogany. Some granite might be of a mahogany hue with subtle hints of blue, peach, or red. Another might be predominately black with flecks of taupe.

These shadings offer builders and remodelers flexibility in design and colors. "I've always loved the blacks and the charcoals," Pappas says. "Sometimes I'll use different shades of granite with a striking white kitchen. The result is stunning, almost jewel-like. And there really aren't any granite colors that are dated; the subtle hints of other colors in many of the granites allow for a variety of color scheme changes down the road."

Pappas points out that not every surface of a kitchen needs to be covered with granite. One technique is to use it as a focal point on an island, breakfast nook, or backsplash, then complement the stone surface with neutral-colored accents. Or, a small slab of granite, set into a tile countertop, is an ideal food preparation or kneading surface.

Pappas also likes to use squares of thin granite tile as part of a ceramic tile pattern. The rich grain and pattern of the granite against a solid-colored tile provide drama and elegance.

Granite can be surprisingly affordable, costing about the same as synthetic solid-surface materials on a square-foot basis, and in some cases, even less. And it's virtually indestructible.

"Granite also has a toughness that surpasses any other countertop material," says Jacob Abrams, an interior designer who works extensively with stone. "I've seen everything from bacon-grease vinaigrette and swordfish marinade to household lubricants spilled on granite. They simply wipe up, leaving no stain. Even foods like cranberries and Dijon mustard won't stain this material."

It also resists scorching and blistering. Hot frying pans and casserole dishes set directly on granite countertops leave no marks. Peggy and Dennis Doyle of suburban Minneapolis agree.

They installed granite on counters, island, and wet bar in the home they recently built. "You can't dull or scratch the finish," says Peggy. "It could literally outlast the rest of the home."

Peggy notes that marble countertops can stain easily, while those of synthetics and laminates can be prone to scratches, blisters, and cracks. "My two preschoolers have written on the counters with pens and crayons, and whacked on them with toys. But nothing has hurt them so far."

Most of all, the Doyles say they prize the natural look of granite. "Our home sets in a gladed natural setting near the Minnesota River. With granite, we were able to accent the beauty of our home's natural setting. The polished countertops reflect the sky and trees like a mirror, literally bringing nature right into our kitchen."

Installing larger granite countertops can be a do-it-yourself project if the weight is manageable. Most countertops 1″ thick will weigh about 5 lbs. per square foot. Smaller surfaces are no problem, as well as projects such as tiling with thin-set granite. Like other solid-surface countertops, once the base cabinets are installed, precise measurements are made before the order is placed. The countertops are usually installed without any construction adhesive, and silicone caulking seals the joints.

Note: For more information, you can contact the Cold Spring Granite Company, the world's largest granite supplier, by writing 202 So. Third Ave., Cold Spring, MN 56230-2593, or by calling 800/328-7038 or 612/259-3400.

Granite counter surfaces can be used throughout a new or remodeled kitchen, photo above, or they can be used an elegant accents, as shown below.

Tech Notes: Installing Granite Countertops

Granite slabs for countertops can measure up to 4½′ wide and up to 8′ long. Large island counters, however, can sometimes be made from a single piece of granite, providing the slabs are large enough and the finished slab can be brought into the home.

Should more than one slab be needed, the pieces are matched for color and grain consistency, then cut to butt squarely against each other. All cutting and polishing is best done at the factory, rather than on the project site, because factories with modern equipment are able to cut to within 1/16″ to allow tight fits. On all slabs ¾″ to 2″ thick, the industry fabrication tolerance is +⅛″ to -1/16″.

If you are installing new kitchen cabinets, the general procedure is to first install the wall cabinets, then the base cabinets. Before beginning the project, check to see if the walls of your kitchen area are out of square.

A good way is to use the principle of the 3-4-5 method. From a corner, mark a distance of 36″ along one wall, then a distance of 48″ along the second wall. The distance between these two marks should be 60″.

If the distance between the marks is more than 60″, the wall is "out of square, in favor"; if the distance is less than 60″, the wall is "out of square, out of favor."

With "in favor" situations, any gap behind the cabinets will be at the opposite end of the walls from the corner. In this case, it's best to install cabinets so the gap won't be exposed at the end of the cabinet run and will be hidden by the countertop, as shown below. With "out of favor" situations, any gap will be widest in the corner. This can shift the position of sink base cabinets. It's best to adjust the cabinets to keep the sink aligned with any window in front of it.

Before installing cabinets, also check the floor by placing a level on a longer straight board and sliding it perpendicular to the wall along the floor. Mark the high points onto the walls. If you have a standard 8′-high ceiling, mark the walls from the high points, drawing one horizontal line 34½″ up on the wall for the top height of the base cabinets, and another line 84″ up for the top of the wall cabinets.

After installing the wall cabinets, start with the base cabinets in one corner. Install a corner unit, drilling ⅛″ holes through the top back rail until you hit a stud. Then use No. 8x2½″ screws to secure the cabinet. Add a cabinet on each side, then the remaining cabinets. When joining front cabinet frames, you can get a more professional look by removing a door and hinge, then drilling and inserting screws under the hinge plate. This hides the screws when the door is replaced.

Also remember to level the base cabinets. As they are installed, check for level front to back and along the front edge. If the front frame is not plumb, use shims below the cabinet. Shims also can be used between cabinets and wall to keep back rails from bowing.

When installing granite slabs as countertops, in most cases a silicone bond, plus the weight of the granite, is all that is needed to anchor the pieces in place. Joints can be sealed with silicone to produce tight seams and prevent food, liquids, or other material from seeping between the slabs.

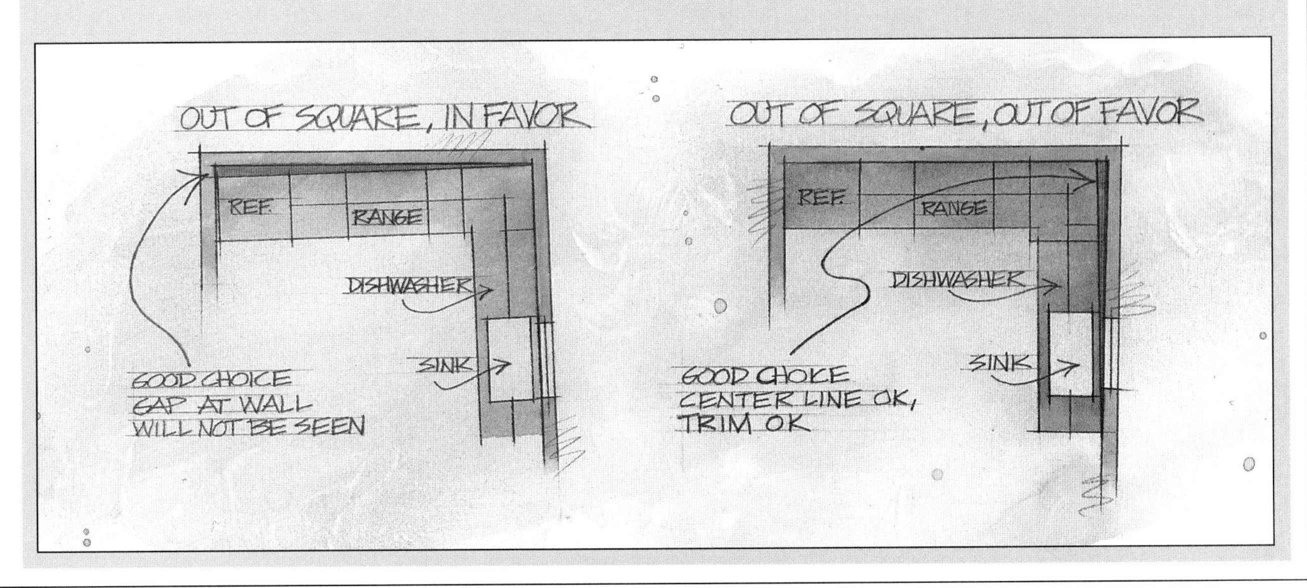

CONCRETE PAVERS

A Simple, Elegant Way To Heighten Your Home's Curb Appeal

You spend time and money to keep your home and lawn in tip-top shape. But viewed from a distance something is missing overall; it still has that tract-house aura.

The answer may lie in dressing up the hard, flat surfaces of asphalt or plain concrete—what architects call the "exterior hardscape"—that make up a large part of your home's total picture. By using interlocking concrete pavers to replace part or all of these surfaces surrounding your home, you may discover you've supplied the missing link to curb-side elegance.

Installing concrete pavers is a perfect do-it-yourself project. Individually, they are light and easy to handle, and with a typical compression strength of more than 8,000 pounds per square inch (psi), they are sturdy enough to be used on airport runways for 747s. Modern pavers also boast a low water absorption rate (less than 5%) to eliminate freeze-thaw problems.

As the photos show, the texture and patterns give pavers visual superiority over plain, hard surfaces. Pavers are prime candidates for driveways, sidewalks, terraces, garden paths, pool decks, even roof-top gardens. Many of these shapes and patterns interlock to combine greater visual appeal with superior traffic strength.

What does it cost? Depending on where you live, the material cost of pavers might run about $1.85 per square foot, not counting labor. That square-foot cost also doesn't count any special edging, such as the pre-made PVC edge restraints. The edging from Pave Tech Inc. comes in 10′-long sections for straight or curved edges.

Most sources of pavers handle the edging plus other required products and tools, and also will advise you throughout your project. The biggest variable in the procedure is in the thickness of the base; for a surface for light vehicles or people, a base 4″ to 6″ thick might be sufficient while a driveway subject to heavy vehicle traffic will require a base of 8″ to 12″ thick.

Most often areas to be paved are excavated. However, it is possible to use pavers as an overlay on existing concrete and asphalt. When this is done, the existing surface must be in relatively good condition. Any potholes must be filled with compacted aggregate and any large cracks filled. A 1″ layer of bedding sand is spread over the surface after first laying down a filter cloth to keep sand from seeping into cracks or holes in the old pavement.

The easiest paving project is a walkway or patio. The Tech Notes that follow list the materials and tools needed, plus a method of squaring up any area.

Paver installation consists of excavating, compacting the area, installing and compacting a base, installing edge restraint, adding a sand bed, laying the pavers, installing edging, compacting the pavers, sweeping sand between joints, and a final compacting.

Thornton

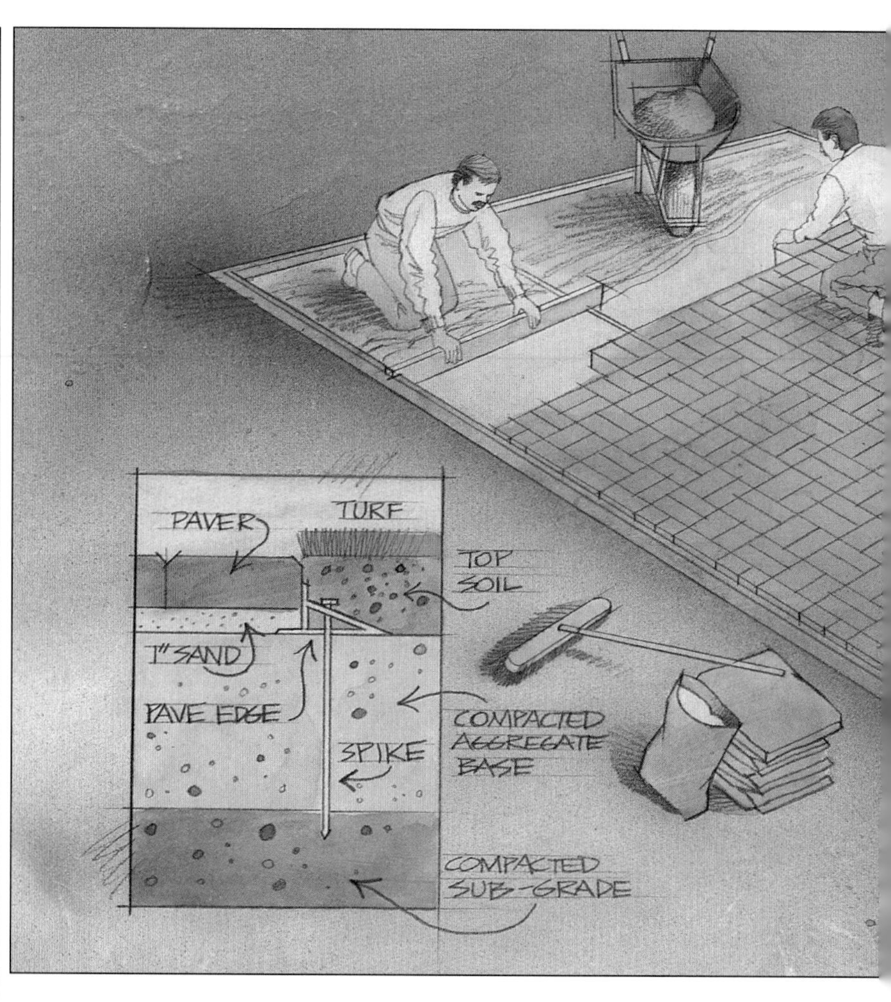

Excavation. Before doing any digging, call your local utility companies to locate any underground lines.

Using a flat shovel, cut evenly to remove sod/dirt to a depth of at least 7⅛″ to allow room for 2⅜″ paver, ¾″ of compacted sand, a minimum of 4″ of compacted crushed stone base (more if the soil is very soft).

If the house is newly constructed, there probably will be settling next to the foundation over time. In this case, increase base thickness to 6″ (or a total excavation of 9″) within 2′ of the new foundation. Note that the excavation should be 6″ wider on the sides where a purchased edge restraint is to be used.

Base Preparation. The more time and effort you put into preparing the base, the better the results and the longer it will last. Use either ¾″ or ½″ graded base material that includes sizes down to fine dust. This material is easier to compact and will give a tight, close-knit surface.

Compaction is important, and it's best to use a 4- to 5-hp plate compactor available at rental centers. First, run the plate compactor over the excavated area. (Make sure no soil gets stuck to the bottom of the plate tamper.) Each pass should overlap the previous one by about 4″. Next, spread the gravel base material out evenly in about 2″ layers. If the material is dry and dusty, use a garden hose to lightly wet it down. This helps the gravel compact faster and makes it easier to rake smooth.

Starting around the outer perimeter, use the plate compactor and again overlap each pass about 4″, working towards the center. Make at least two complete passes for each layer. Use a hard-tooth garden rake to smooth out any unevenness, turning the rake upside down for final smoothing.

When finished, the base should be very smooth and flat. If you were to put a straight edge flat on the surface, there should be no more than ⅜″ maximum gap anywhere along the straight edge and the base. Pay attention to sloping to make sure of proper runoff. It's best to plan at least ¼″ per foot drop; do not exceed ½″ per foot.

Sand Bed. It is important to keep the sand dry. Always keep it covered in case of rain. Also, don't attempt to level any area or surface irregularities with the sand. This will result in an uneven surface and unwanted settling.

Lay screed guides (1″ electrical conduit, 1″ strips of wood, or other suitable rigid 1″ guide) 4′ to 6′ apart and parallel. First use a shovel to spread the sand evenly over the area. Work from side to side to screed a 10′ section of sand. Then use a 6′ to 8′ 2x6 to strike off any excess. Don't walk on or work from the screeded sand, and don't worry about voids that the screed guides have left after you have removed them. You can fill them with sand and trowel them smooth as you lay the pavers.

Laying The Pavers. For small areas, start from a permanent edge, such as the house, driveway, or a piece of edging. Lay the first paver starting from either side. (As you start laying pavers, work from right to left, then left to right and so on, one row of pavers at a time.)

Set the pavers lightly onto the sand; never press or hammer them in. If using edging, allow 6″ on the open sides for later installation. If you begin with edging as a starting point, run a string line across the front of the laying edge every 4′ or so. If there are some pavers lagging behind, go back three to four rows and use a small prybar to pry the pavers forward until they are in line again. Don't worry too much about gaps at this point; they will even out during tamping later.

Set the pavers hand-tight, but don't use a hammer to adjust the pavers or set them. If you are doing the project over a couple of days, cover the entire area with plastic overnight if rain is expected. Remember to stop laying pavers at the 6″ extended base area where edging will be installed later.

Cutting Pavers. You will need to cut pavers if you have to go around a post, where you come up against an existing structure, or where a radius is desired. Mark any stones to be cut with a crayon or chalk and allow for up to ¼″ gap between the stone and the edge. This will be filled with sand later. You can use either a diamond-blade mason saw or a paver splitter.

Finishing Up. After you have laid all pavers and installed perimeter edging, you are ready to complete the project. Note that during this step the pavers will settle down ¼″ lower during compaction (if the proper 1″ loose screeded sand has been used). This should be their final height.

First sweep off any debris or loose sand that may be on the pavers. Then, using a vibratory plate compactor, make at least two passes over the pavers. Starting around the perimeter and working inward, overlap each pass 2″ to 4″. Make the second pass at a 45° angle to the first pass. The first pass of the compactor will level all the pavers, compact the sand bed, and force sand up into the joint.

Repeat the passes if the pavers are not yet level and flat. Then, using a dry, coarse washed sand for the joints, spread a thin layer over the surface. (Always make sure the jointing sand is kept dry.) Use a stiff-bristle street broom to sweep back and forth over the entire area until the sand has stopped falling into joints.

Alternate between tamping and sweeping as you continue to work the sand into the joints. When no more joints open up as you make passes with the compactor and broom, you are finished compacting. Sweep up all excess sand and backfill edges with top soil and sod or seed. (If you are using seed, it is best to also use one row of sod along the new pavers.) Lastly, be sure to water freshly seeded or sodded areas regularly.

Note: A source of pavers is Uni-Group U.S.A., 4362 Northlake Blvd., #109, Palm Beach Gardens, FL 33410, or call 407/626-4666. Write Pave Tech Inc. at P.O. Box 31126, Bloomington, MN 55431, or call 800/728-3832. A third source of paver information is the Interlocking Concrete Paver Institute, 1323 Shepard Dr., Ste. D, Sterling, VA 20164, or call 800/241-3652.

Tech Notes: Paver Project Planning

To get started, first measure the area that you intend to pave. Determine its square footage by multiplying length by width, then add 5% for breakage and cutting. Measure the lineal feet of open edges, such as those not up against a permanent structure, like a house, etc. This will be the lineal footage of edge restraint required.

Draw your plan on a piece of paper showing all important dimensions. Take this plan to your supplier to help determine the proper amount of materials needed to complete your project.

You can use the 3-4-5 triangle method to determine a perpendicular line. Then run parallel lines from the perpendicular line to establish a boundary. Place stakes every 4′ to 6′ and at the corners. These stakes should be 8″ outside of the planned edge of the pavers.

Note: You can check to make sure an area is square by making sure both sets of cross corners measure the exact same distance.

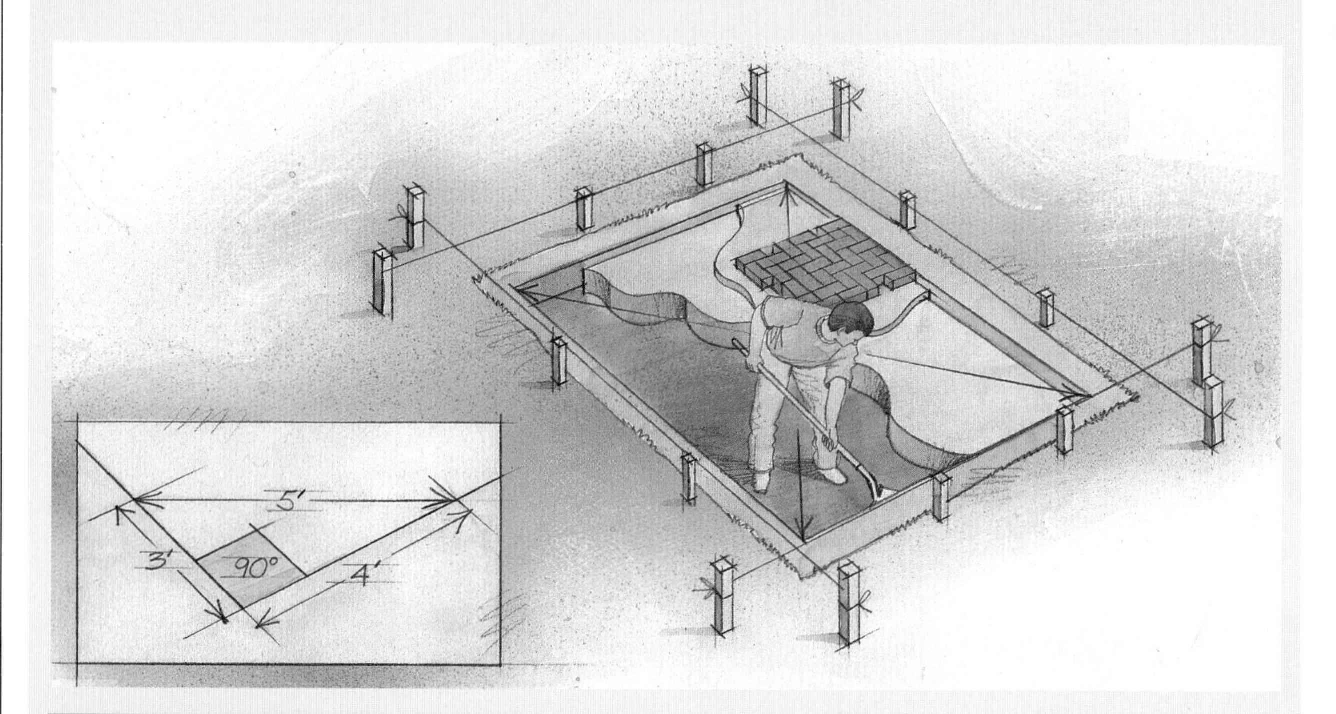

Materials Needed

- **Base material** (Doublecheck with your supplier. It should be ¾″ or ½″ gravel, including particle sizes down to fine dust. A 1″ depth of compacted base weighs approximately 1,200 lbs. per 100 sq. ft. It is best to add another 5% to 10% for edges and miscellaneous areas.)
- **Sand** (Coarse concrete sand, enough for 1″ loose depth. This sand at this depth will weigh about 900 lbs. per 100 sq. ft. It is best to also figure an extra 10% to use for jointing sand.)
- **Pavers**
- **Professional Edging**
- **Steel Spikes** (10″ long x ⅜″ diameter)

Tools Needed

- Wooden stakes
- 3- to 5-lb. hammer
- Sand screed guides (1″-dia. pipe, wood, etc.)
- Wide-blade mason's chisel
- Stiff bristle street broom
- 2x4s or 2x6s, 6′ to 8′
- Level, 4′
- Mason's string
- Chalkline
- Flat shovel
- Wheelbarrow
- Garden rake
- Measuring tape, 25′
- Small prybar

Rental Items

- Plate compactor, 4- to 5-hp (not a jumping jack)
- Block/paver splitter
- Mason's diamond saw

HOME PLUMBING

Once Forbidden Territory, It's Now Fair Game For Home Do-It-Yourselfers

A homeowner, by choice or not, usually ends up with a more intimate knowledge of plumbing than might be desired. But today plumbing doesn't have to mean spraying pipes, flooded basements, bruised knuckles, and ultimate defeat. More and better plumbing materials, along with an admirable attempt by suppliers to take the mystery out of plumbing projects, are all making home plumbing fair game for do-it-yourselfers.

There is no one big secret for working on anything related to the plumbing system, but there are many techniques that can make plumbing projects easier and more fool-proof. For most homeowners, however, the challenge of plumbing projects is more of learning what not to do in attempting repairs.

Usually big pipe wrenches aren't needed for most home plumbing projects. A minimal tool kit for plumbing should cost you less than $50.

The first lesson is not to let little problems grow into big ones. Second, when you are going to do the repairs yourself, don't start cutting into the system until you have figured out what you are going to do and how you are going to do it. Third, forget about the idea that you need to use big pipe wrenches and lots of muscle. In most cases, you will do more harm than good.

Plumbing, like other mechanical systems, will eventually wear out. Once or twice a year, visually check the whole system in your home. If you have little problems, such as drips, fix them right away. When a two-handled faucet starts to drip, fix it as soon as you can. Otherwise, you will be turning down the handles harder to stop the water. In time, the screw holding the washer will gouge a hole into the faucet seat. Then, instead of just a washer, you need to buy and install a complete faucet.

TACKLING PLUMBING

What plumbing projects can a homeowner attempt? There are no hard-and-fast rules. It gets down to what is the cheapest way, which includes the value you put on your free time. If you tackle small repairs, certain approaches can help keep you out of trouble. Here are some examples:

• Once you break into a plumbing system, try to have everything you'll need. Go over the project three or four times and write down the necessary purchases. Then gather up all the supplies in one trip, even if you have to go to several stores.

Compare the new parts next to the old parts to be sure that you have everything you will need before you start disassembling the system.

• Buy a couple of pipe wrenches, and make sure they are not too big, preferably not more than 14″ long. Try not to force anything. Sometimes homeowners shut off the water service to the house, but can't get it turned back on. Usually this is because they have turned the valve down so hard that when they try to open it up, the threads strip on the inside.

• If you are cutting out a section of old galvanized steel pipe, arrange to have a helper available. While you cut, your helper can hold onto the pipe to prevent it from shaking.

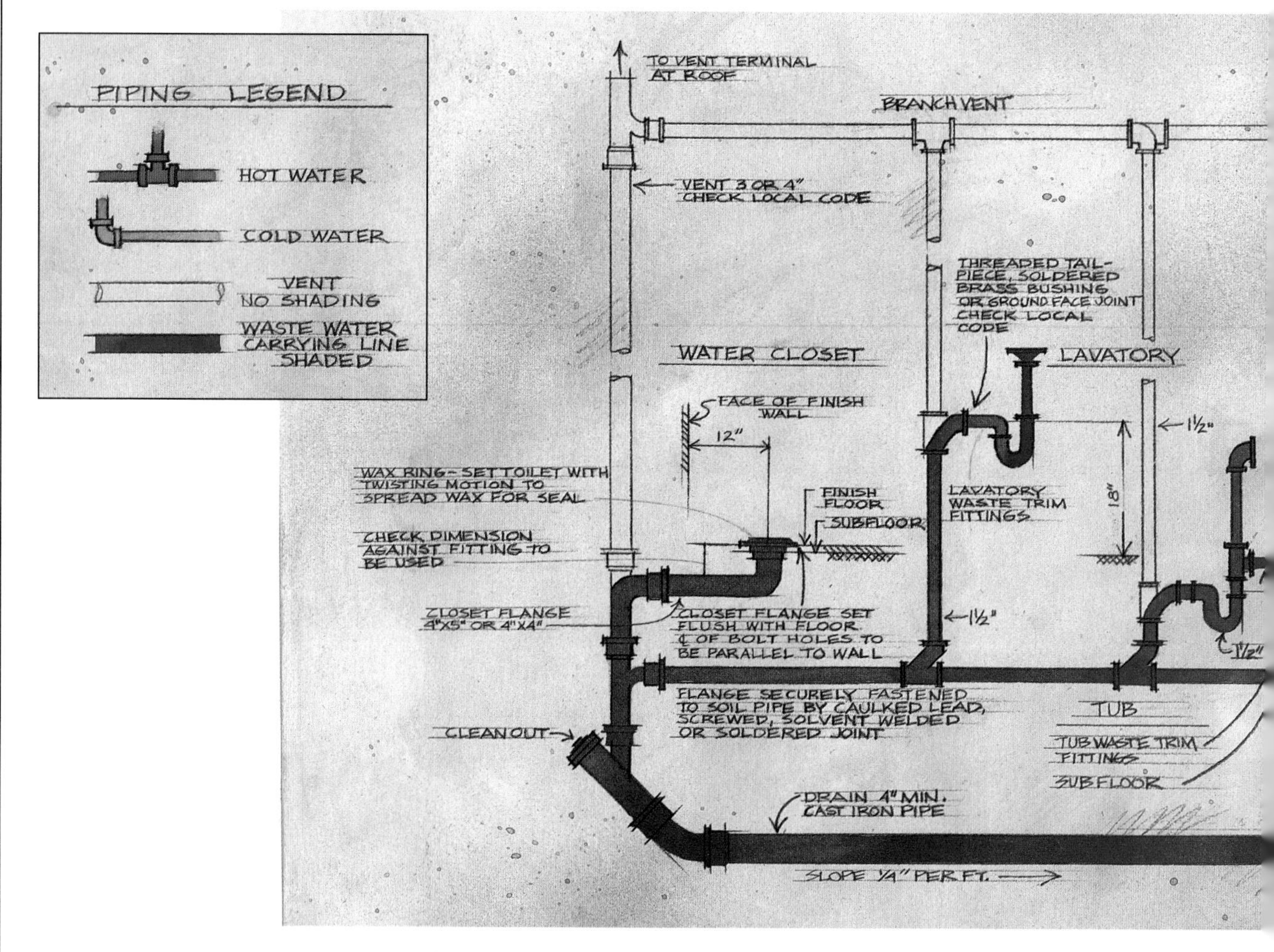

Excess shaking may break joints farther down the line and your small project will turn into a big job.

• If you are replacing steel pipe, measure the length between the fittings, then add ½″ extra for threads on each end to go into the fittings. This is for supply pipe that is either ⅜″, ½″, or ¾″ in diameter. For 1″-diameter pipe, allow ⅝″ for threads; for 2″ pipe, allow ¾″. Have the threading done at a hardware store or home center that offers the service. You can use a union fitting to get the pipe back together.

• To get leak-free threaded joints, a good procedure is to use both Teflon tape and pipe compound. Put the tape on first, in a clockwise direction going with the threads. Then put compound over that. However, don't use tape where small bits of it could break loose and jam up delicate control mechanisms, such as next to a dishwasher or directly in front of a water pump with a pressure gauge.

• When soldering copper pipe, make sure fittings are clean inside and out. You can use emery cloth or sandpaper, but what also works well are green Scotch-Brite pads. They don't shred if they get wet, as sandpaper will.

And watch that you don't overheat a joint. Play the torch over it only until the solder starts to run, then quit heating it. If the joint is too hot, the flux burns and prevents the solder from sticking.

• It is hard to solder copper joints if there is moisture inside. Make sure that all moisture is out of the copper pipes before you attempt to solder them. For any soldering work, wear gloves, long sleeves, and eye protection. Wear a cap, as well, if you are soldering overhead.

• If you regularly have a problem with frozen pipes, the best solution is to cut a hole on the inside of the wall near the pipe and cover it with a louvered register. This way, heated air from the house can keep the temperature of the pipe above freezing. There are different ways to thaw pipes, but a regular small hair dryer can work well.

• For plugged drains in the home, professional plumbers generally recommend using only small snakes that you can buy at a hardware store. If they don't do the job, call for help. Liquid drain cleaners can be hard on pipes and traps; try not to use them if you can avoid it.

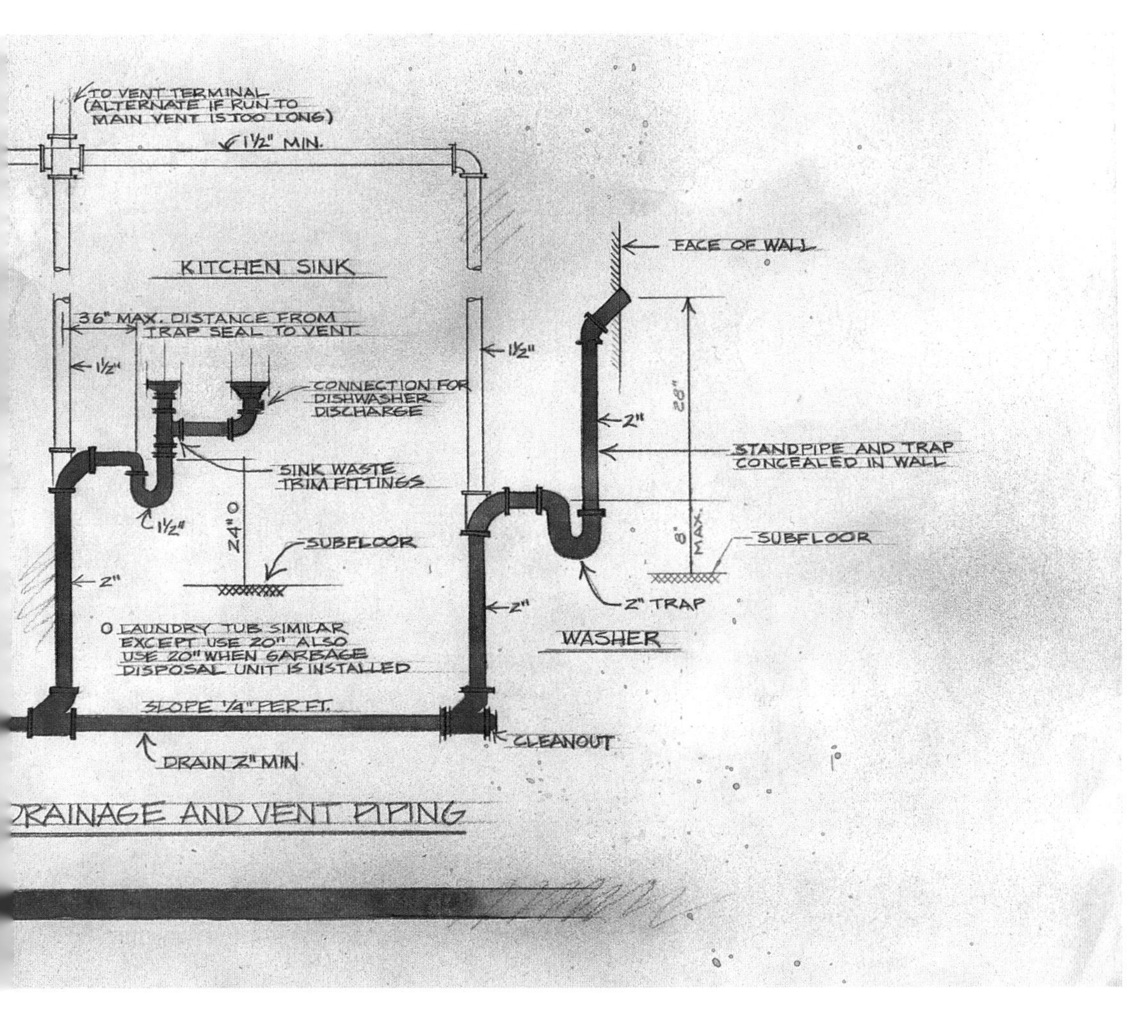

Replacing Plumbing

Often a homeowner can replace the components of a plumbing system, but it will take you longer than a professional. For example, it might take you a weekend to install a water heater, while a pro might be able to do it in less than an hour. Deciding whether to hire a plumber or to do the work yourself boils down to whether you have time and how quickly the problem must be fixed. Here are some ideas for determining what needs to be replaced and when.

Water Heaters. One rule of thumb is to replace a water heater if it is 10 or more years old, especially if there is carpeting in the basement which can present a mess after accidental flooding. Some water heaters will plug along for 30 years, but others may need replacement in as few as seven years. When heaters die, 90% of the time it is because the tank starts leaking. The rest of the time, it generally is the controls that go out.

It is hard to tell how old a heater is by looking at it. But if a heater starts rumbling, beware. That's a sign there are deposits on the bottom that could pop the glass in the tank within a year. When you replace a heater, make sure that you don't get the hot and cold lines mixed up. It happens more often than you might think.

Some professionals use the thermocouple to gauge whether a gas heater should be replaced. The thermocouple is a small tube leading from the gas control to near the burner. It should last as long as the tank. Sometimes it goes out on a heater that's only five years old if it was out of adjustment. But usually when a thermocouple goes bad it is a sign the heater should be replaced. When a heater is replaced, an approved Temperature/Pressure relief valve must be installed within the top 6″ of the tank.

Faucets. If a faucet goes bad after about five years, it may be wise to replace it. Often a defective faucet has dripped for months, and cranking the handles down harder has probably damaged the insides. But if it is a quality faucet, such as a Kohler or Moen cartridge type, it could very well be worth fixing.

It is easier to get replacement seats for faucets if you know the name of the faucet manufacturer. If you need a new faucet, invest in

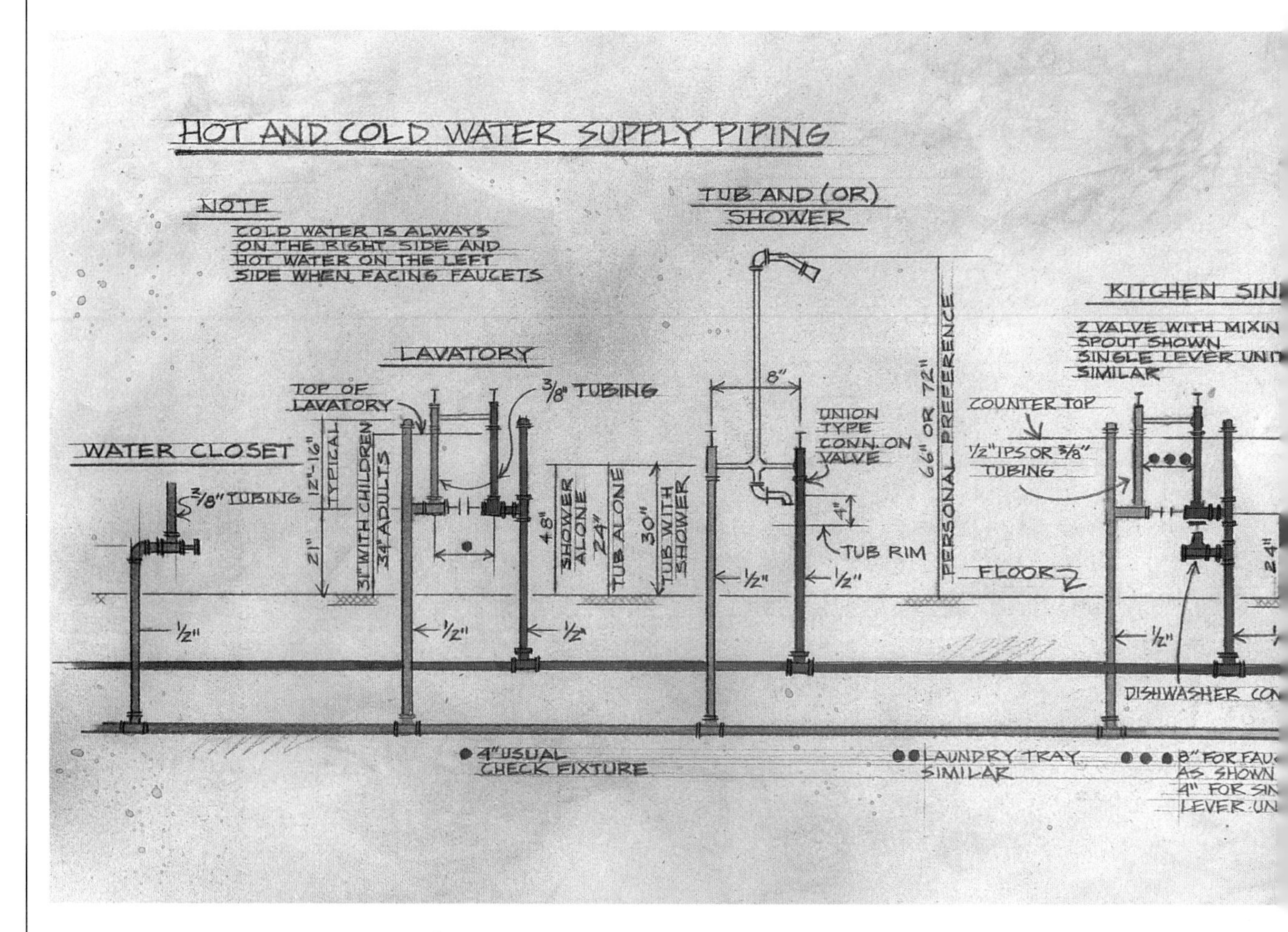

quality. A higher-priced faucet could last three times as long as a cheap one. A quality faucet will save you the cost of a second and third faucet, plus the cost or time to install them.

Be cautious of replacing a faucet if you don't have stop valves underneath. Stop valves allow you to isolate a fixture from the system and still have water in the rest of the home. Without stop valves, if something goes wrong with your project, you won't be able to turn the main water valve back on. Consider having a plumber install stop valves, or do it yourself when you can do without water for a while.

Toilets. Toilets rarely need to be replaced. Most replacements today are the older versions with a flush elbow connecting a tank on the wall to the bowl. Parts are hard to find for this type, but fairly easy to find for the rest. If you install a toilet, be sure to get the wax ring under the base set straight, otherwise it will leak. Don't forget that the parts inside a new toilet are loose and have to be tightened up before you turn on the water. And remember that you may be tampering with older pipes filled with debris. Flush out the supply pipe before installing new parts to avoid having problems.

Supply Pipes. If the pipes in your house are 30 or more years old, corrosion can build up so the flow is only about half of what it was when the pipes were new. You can't tell just by looking at the pipes. Hot-water pipes will usually have more corrosion inside, though they might look better on the outside than cold-water pipes, which get discolored because of condensation. Look for the worst condition where there is a galvanized-to-copper transition.

Using Plastics

Whether replacing pipes or installing an entire new system, newer plastic plumbing components make almost any do-it-yourselfer a potential plumber. They are easier to use, don't require special tools, and mistakes are easy to correct. In fact, with some homework, you could plumb the water supply system for a home in one or two days using plastics.

With plumbers charging around $50 an hour, you can save a bundle by doing the work yourself with plastics. Professional plumbing

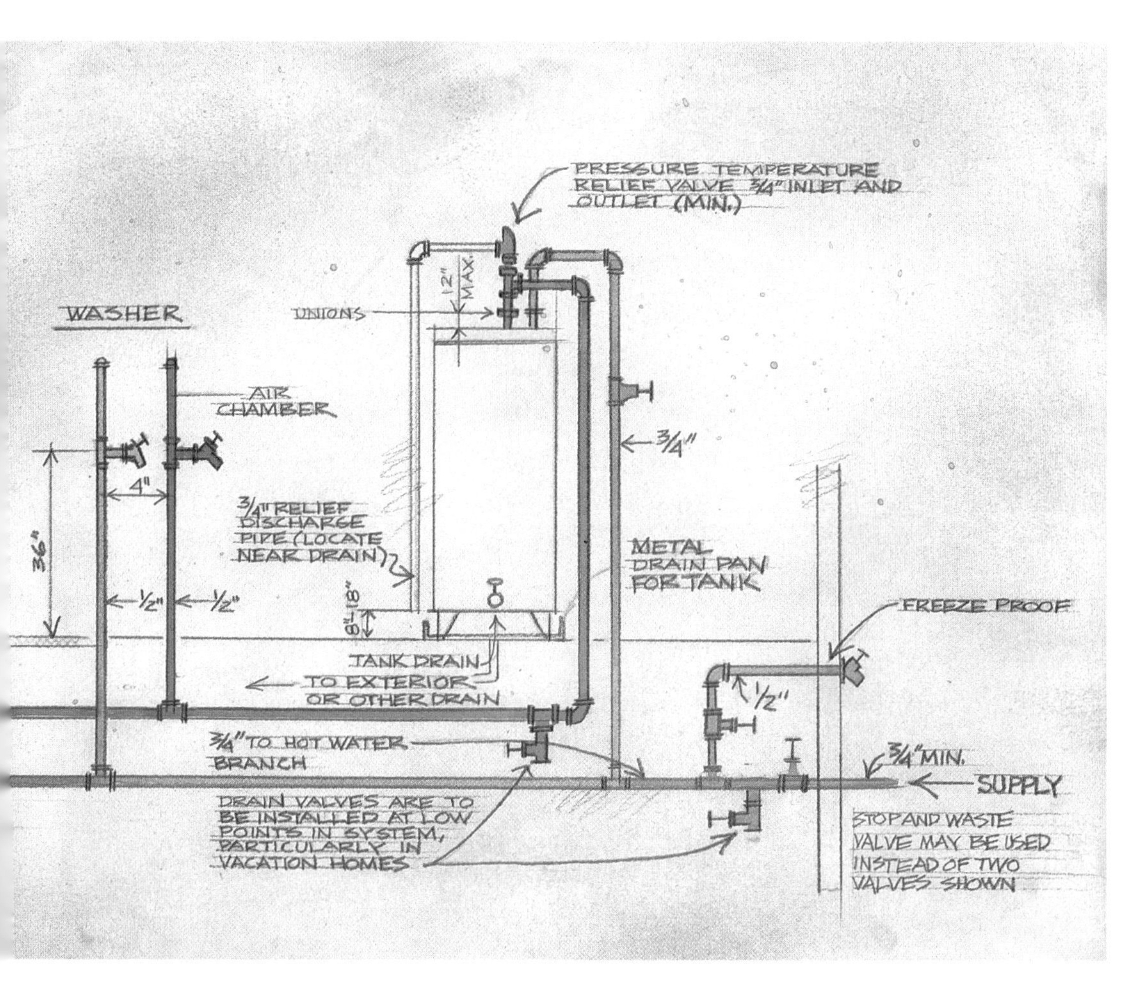

charges typically include 25% for materials and 75% for labor.

Plastics displacing traditional plumbing materials include CPVC (chlorinated polyvinyl chloride), PVC (polyvinyl chloride), ABS (acrylonitrile butadiene styrene), and PB (polybutylene). CPVC is used for rigid hot- and cold-water lines, while PVC and ABS are most often used for drain-waste-vent and sewer piping. PB is used for flexible hot- and cold-water lines. Both CPVC and PVC are joined with two-step solvent welding; ABS joins with one-step solvent welding, while PB joins with mechanical couplings.

Plastics have been approved for use in plumbing systems by all six regional plumbing codes in the country. In fact, in some states such as California almost all plumbing work (including professional jobs) is done using plastic components. Before you start any project, however, check first with local officials on the off-hand chance that there may be restrictions in your immediate area.

Plastic materials offer many other advantages for do-it-yourselfers. Using special adapters, you can also tie plastics in with metal plumbing materials. But whether you are planning an addition, a repair, or even a new installation, plastics are also cheaper.

Fewer Tools. Plastics join with either solvent welding or simple mechanical fittings. That means you don't need traditional tools, such as power hacksaws, threading dies, pipe wrenches, or soldering equipment. With CPVC, for example, all you need is a hacksaw, a knife, a rag, cleaner, and solvent cement. (A power mitersaw can work well for cutting plastic pipe.)

Fast Connections. The solvent welding used with CPVC and PVC is almost as simple as using model airplane cement. You just cut the pipe to length and use a knife or reamer to remove any burrs. Then you wipe the outside of the pipe, and the inside of a fitting, with cleaner/primer. Next, you apply the solvent cement and press the fitting into place, slightly turning the joint to spread the cement. In 30 seconds you have a leak-free fitting that will never come apart. With PB, you just push the tube full-depth into the fitting and hand tighten.

Correctable Mistakes. With CPVC, it is easy to cut out any mis-

Notes On Drawings

1. Cast-iron pipe is shown for all underground piping. Cleanouts are to be provided at all changes in direction of drain lines.

2. The pipe sizes shown are minimum; systems are frequently installed with 4" main stack and house drain and 2" for other lines.

3. The kitchen and/or laundry areas may connect directly to the house drain. (The house plan layout will determine pipe location and point of connection.) They may use a separate vent stack if the distance to the main stack is excessive.

4. Support drain lines at 5' intervals (maximum) with strapping material, hangers, or other means. Stacks are to have support at the bottom or be secured in the wall.

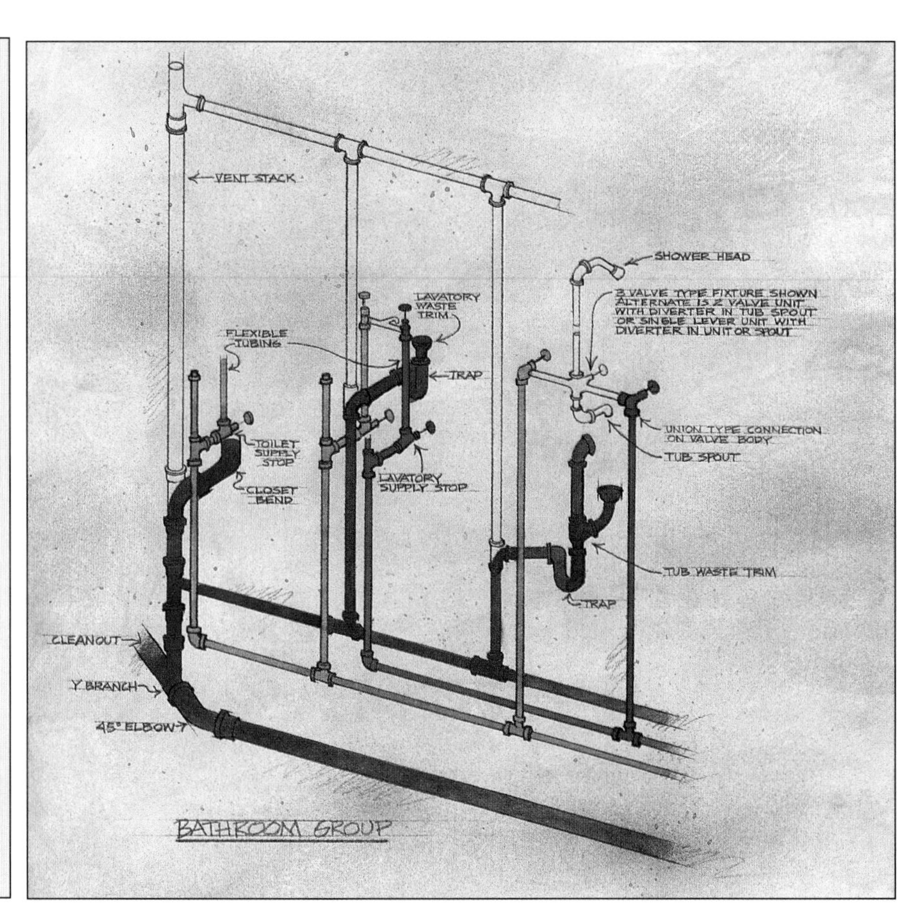

takes and use inexpensive couplers to install a new section. Unlike threaded steel pipe which requires straight-arrow alignment, you can easily make slight bends with flexible CPVC pipes (technically called tubes) to get to the next fitting. Mistakes can be redone in minutes.

Longer Life. Because plastics like CPVC are not susceptible to corrosion, these piping systems will last much longer than metal before having to be replaced because of corrosion buildup inside the pipes.

Other advantages over metal pipe include more thermal resistance, which helps eliminate sweating of cold-water pipes, and less noise from water hammer.

You still need to map out your plumbing system, of course, the same way you would when using any other piping material. Actually, the hardest part is learning about the plastics available, and what is used where.

Choosing Materials

While PVC and PE (polyethylene) can be used for cold water pressure lines outdoors, only CPVC and PB can handle hot water lines indoors. Whether you use CPVC or PB on the supply side of your system, instead of either galvanized steel or copper, can be a matter of personal choice, what is readily available, and the codes where you live.

The two cost about the same per foot, however, CPVC is more rigid while PB is flexible. If your installation is mostly straight-line runs, you might use CPVC because its solvent-welded fittings are cheaper than the mechanical fittings of PB. But if the system requires going around many corners, if you don't have many fittings, and if your plumbing codes allow it, you may be better off with PB.

On the supply side, both CPVC and PB work well at water heaters and softeners with proper transition fittings. You may occasionally need metal piping in situations that require firm mechanical support, such as when piping to a bathtub. On the waste side, both PVC and ABS in Schedule 40 replace cast iron and copper. Where both are available, PVC is the material of choice since it is tougher and more chemical resistant.

While ABS is used more on the West Coast, PVC accounts for more than 90% of the plastic drain-waste-vent (DWV) systems now being installed. Be aware that you can find PVC in two versions. Both versions have 3″ inside diameters, but one version has thinner walls. This thin-wall version, called Schedule 30 In-Wall, can be installed inside the width of a normal 2x4 wall instead of requiring a 2x6 wall, or a furred-out 2x4 wall.

Both PVC and ABS may also be used for underground drain piping. These are thinner-walled lines used for storm drains and septic system piping. RS (rubber-styrene), which joins with one-step solvent welding, is sometimes used for this purpose as well. However, underground drain pipes and fittings should not be used for assembling a DWV system inside the home.

Sink traps are also available in plastic. PP (polypropylene), one of the toughest plastics available, is a choice material for traps. You can also find traps of PVC, some with ABS slip-joint nuts. But be aware that ABS is susceptible to stress cracking when it contacts animal fats or vegetable oils; don't use plumber's putty or silicone rubber sealant on the ABS nut.

Before deciding to install a plastic system, or to repair your existing plumbing system with plastic, it's best to find a source of supply nearby. Try to find a dealer who keeps up-to-date on plastic plumbing, stocks a complete line, and can help you plan your project. A good dealer can save you hours of research, help you find the right parts, and help you with any nagging questions. Here are some guidelines that may help you in making an installation:

Supply Lines. Water supply lines are generally ¾″ for main lines and ½″ for branch lines. Keep in mind that CPVC and PB pipes used on

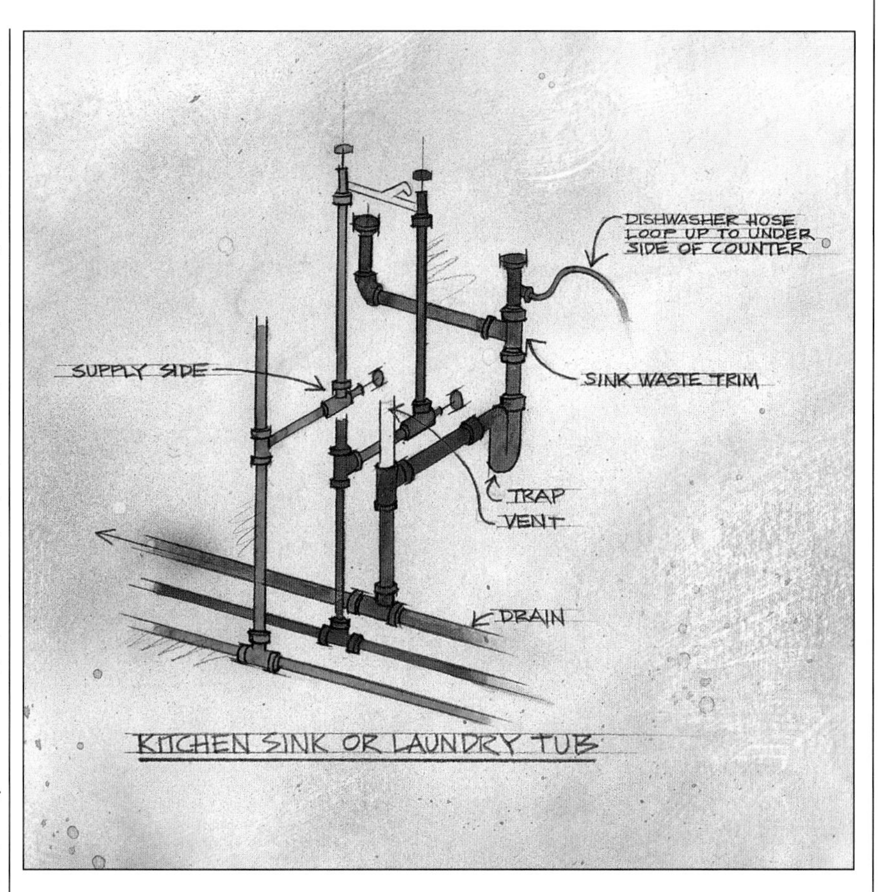

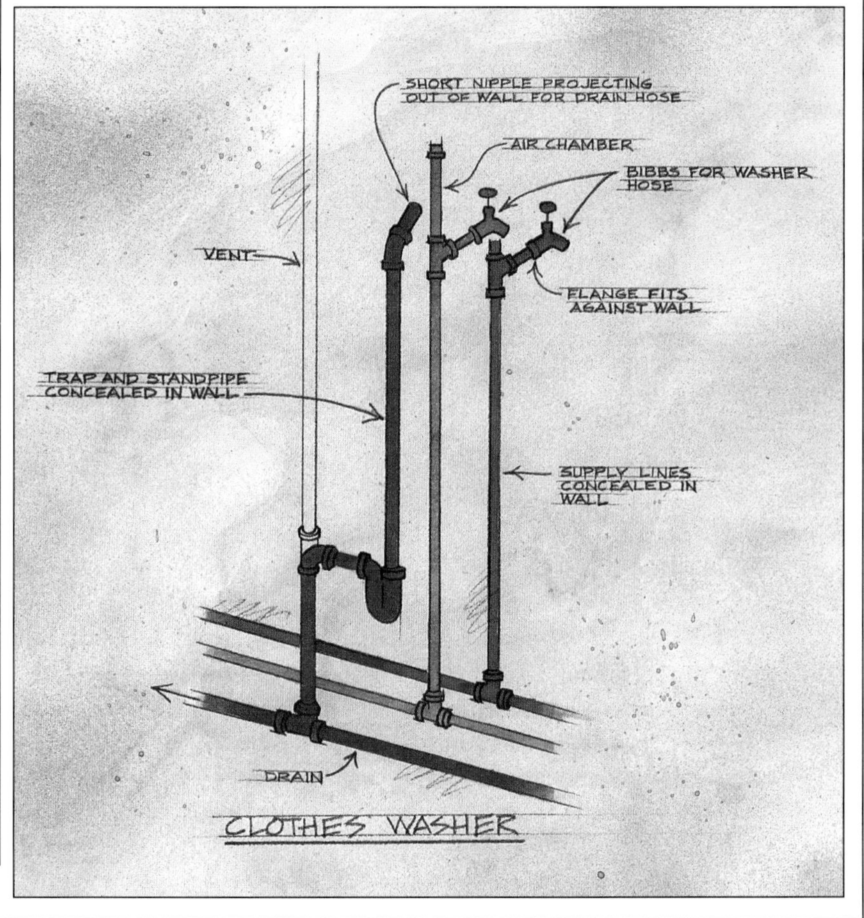

Shown here, the simple three-step process of using solvent cements to join CPVC.

the supply side are sized nominally by their inside diameters, but are measured exactly by their outside diameters, like copper tubing. However, PVC pipe used on the waste side is measured nominally by inside diameter, like iron pipe. A ½″ pipe is therefore somewhat larger than a ½″ tube.

Compatibility. Try to make sure all the materials you buy, including solvent cement, are compatible. It's easier to stick with one brand of materials, if you can, so all the fittings will fit and the solvent cements will be correctly matched. (It pays to read the directions the first time around. One solvent cement, for example, may be needed for CPVC on the supply side, while another is needed for the PVC used on the waste side. Or use an all-purpose solvent cement that works with all four solvent weldable plastics.)

Standard Stamps. Like with other items you buy, check the pipe and fittings to make sure that a manufacturing defect hasn't slipped through the inspection process.

The pipe and fittings should have an ASTM number, which means the product meets the standards of the American Society for Testing and Materials. Water supply pipes also should have NSF-pw stamped on it. This indicates the National Sanitation Foundation's approval for potable water use.

Final Flushing. Studies show plastic plumbing to be safe from a health standpoint. (In fact, increased concern has surfaced in regard to the leaching of lead from metal plumbing systems.) But one important precaution to take with plastic is to flush out any possibly toxic solvent vapors from the system after it is completed. This is done easily by flushing water through the system a half hour after the last joint is solvent-welded. The vapors will dissolve in the water and be carried away.

To flush the system, open all faucets, then slightly open the main valve. When water comes out the lowest faucet, slow it to a trickle. Then move on through the installation, closing other faucets the same way. Let the faucets trickle for about 10 minutes, wait for about a half hour, then repeat the procedure two more times.

After the third flushing, close all faucets, pressurize the system and open and close all faucets fully to get rid of any debris. Flush the toilet, too.

Getting More Help. Don't be wary of working with plumbing officials in your area. Their job is to help you make sure your installation is done correctly and safely. Show them your plans and take out a permit, if required. If inspections are needed, consider them added insurance that your plumbing job will be done right.

To plan out and do major plumbing work in your home, you will need more complete and detailed information. A helpful source is a special five-page, blueprint format summary of critical plumbing diagrams (of the kind shown here) from HomeStyles Plan Service Inc., 275 Market St., Suite 521, Minneapolis, MN 55405 (612/338-8155). The cost is $12.50, plus shipping and handling.

Note: To get a head start on plastic plumbing projects, the book, "Do-It-Yourself Plumbing ... It's Easy With Genova," is helpful. It shows how to plumb a whole house or addition, build a sewer-septic system, or install a sump pump using plastic materials. To order, send $9.95 plus $.50 handling to: Genova, Inc., 7034 E. Court St., Davison, MI 48423 (add sales tax in Michigan).

A preassembled roof truss is a framework of dimensional lumber and metal plates which rests on the exterior walls. The top provides a surface for the roof, while the bottom provides the surface for the ceiling below.

TRUSS RAFTERS

Raising The Roof Can Be Fast And Simple Using Made-To-Order Factory Trusses

It used to be that building rafters was what separated the men from boys on a construction site. A good carpenter, steel square and pencil in hand, would earn his salt by being able to determine exactly where and how to turn a pile of lumber into precisely cut and fitted rafters.

Today, however, building rafters on site is mostly a relic of the past. Most new homes and garages are now built using what are called plated wood trusses, special-ordered from assembly plants which build them to your specs and deliver them right to your project site.

Prefabricated wood trusses make framing much easier for the do-it-yourself builder. By capitalizing on the rigidity of the basic triangle, they gain enough strength to handle loads over long spans without extra beams, supports, or load-bearing walls underneath.

Compared to building rafters from scratch, trusses go up fast; there is less chance for costly errors, and there is less waste. Plus, they allow a building to be rapidly enclosed which helps avoid lost time due to bad weather.

A crew of three or four, for example, might be able to install roof trusses for a double garage in as little as a couple of hours. It might take only a day to top off a new three-bedroom home with attached double garage, as shown in the photos on these pages.

The two most critical steps in using truss rafters are 1) specifying exact dimensions for the trusses needed for your project, and 2) installing the trusses properly and safely. Pre-built roof trusses are engineered for specific load requirements for the area where they will be used. They are built with both live and dead loads in mind. Live loads include wind and snow, while dead loads include the materials used on the roof and the inside ceiling.

There are many types and shapes of roof trusses, the most common being the W or Fink truss (see Tech Notes) which normally uses 2x4 members for spans of 24′ to 32′. Other types are known by names such as King Post, Modified King Post, and Howe trusses. Trusses are available in shapes other than triangular, such as scissors (or vaulted ceiling) trusses, used for higher-than-normal ceilings; mono trusses (or half trusses), used for single slope roofs; or hip trusses, used for hip roofs.

You can also order special trusses to use, for example, where a fireplace intersects the truss span inside the home. The permutations are almost endless; if you need it, it's likely they can build it.

Roof trusses might each weigh about 90 lbs. for a 20′ span, on up to about 170 lbs. for a 32′ span. The easiest trusses to work with are the triangular gable trusses. When ordering, major considerations include 1) the roof pitch you want, and 2) how the gable ends and soffit areas will eventually be finished off.

Roof pitch refers to the slope of the rafters; it is the rise of the rafter (top chord) in relation to half of the truss length. For example, the most common roof pitch is 4/12. This means the roof will rise 4″ for each horizontal foot of length, or 2′ for every 6′ of run. Likewise, a 3/12 roof will rise 1½′ for every 6′.

The truss rafters here are being set over a two-car garage attached to a new home. A gable-end truss is set in place first. Then top plates are marked for 24" on-center, photo bottom left.

Trusses are individually raised and nailed into place, photo right, checked for level, photo below, and then stabilized with temporary braces.

Check your plans, if you have some, or else consult a supplier regarding pitch options, and also how to precisely measure for the width of your roof trusses.

Generally for a wood frame building, trusses are ordered so that the bottom chord extends just to the outside edge of the top plate on each side. What is called "truss span," however, does not include the amount of overhang, which is measured as the horizontal distance from the bottom chord to the bottom edge of the rafter (top chord). The ends of the rafters can be untrimmed, square cut, or plumb cut.

For a gable roof, special "gable-end" trusses are usually used at each end of the building, and "common" trusses are set 24" on-center between them. The way gable-end trusses are configured will depend on whether you will be using horizontal or vertical siding, among other factors. Also, depending on how you want to finish off the gable ends, you might need either a "drop bottom" or "drop top" gable-end truss. With either one, the height of the truss will be 3½" lower than the common trusses, allowing you to build a ladder-like overhang panel.

Overhangs and soffit returns can be handled more than a half-dozen ways, depending on the width of the overhang and the type of walls. Discuss all of the options with your supplier.

Note: For more on how to handle, install, and brace truss rafters, a good source is the Truss Plate Institute. Write to 583 D'Onofrio Drive, Suite 200, Madison, WI 53719, or call 608/833-5900 for a list of available publications. For tips on crew sizes and truss data, write the Wood Truss Council of America, 5937 Meadowood Drive, Suite 14, Madison, WI 53711, or call 608/274-4849.

TECH NOTES: USING TRUSS RAFTERS

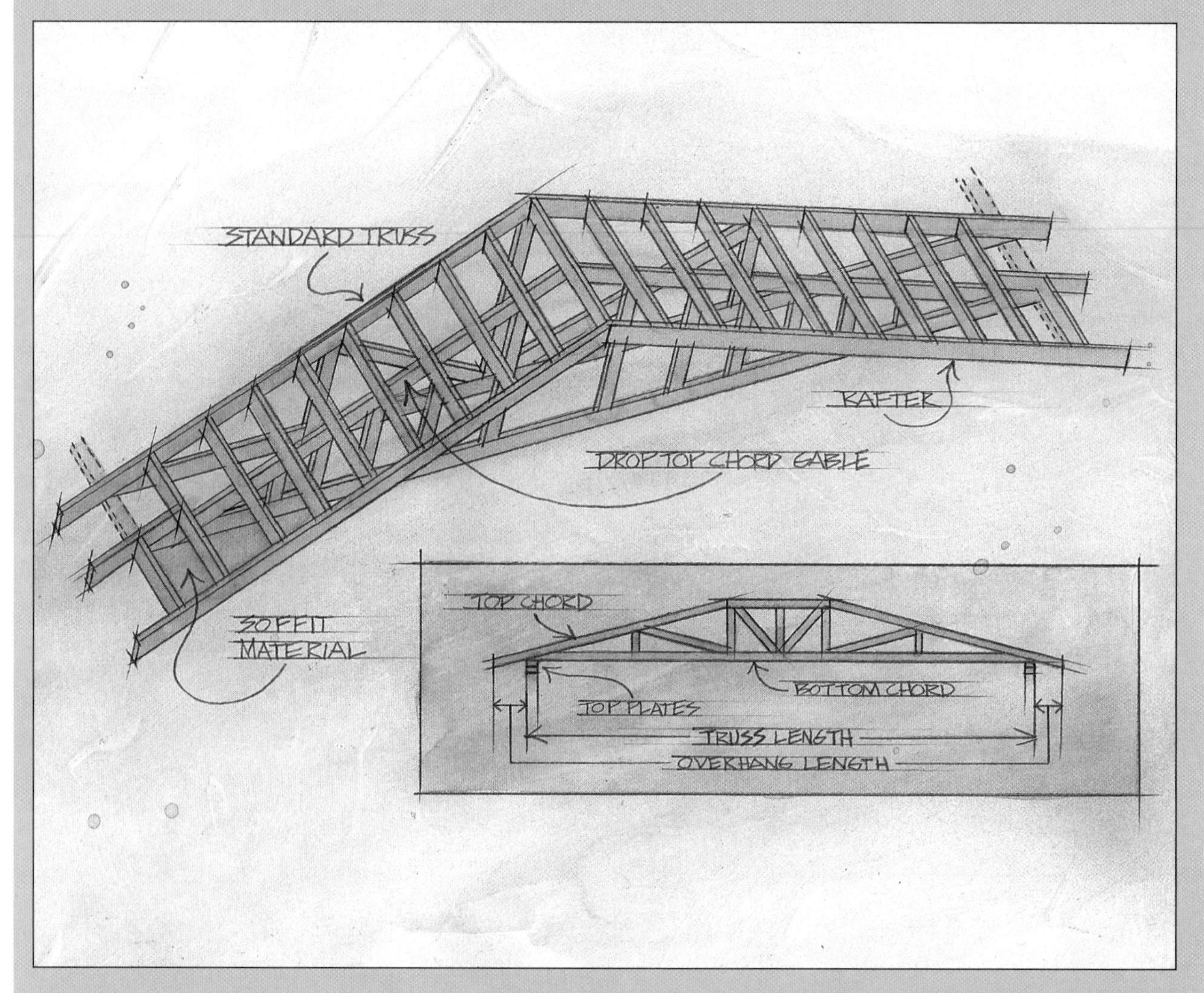

To prevent accidents, specialists strongly recommend that, before any truss installation takes place, you read document HIB-91, Commentary & Recommendations for Handling, Installing & Bracing Metal Plate Connected Wood Trusses, by the Truss Plate Institute (address previous page).

To get trusses into place on larger homes, cranes are often hired to get the job done within an hour or so. On one-story structures, such as a garage, it pays to assemble several helpers and have sturdy ladders and/or scaffolding in place. Two people can push the trusses up while two others on the building pull them up onto the walls. Wear good work gear and pay attention to the weather; don't work when lumber is wet and slippery.

The basic steps of installing trusses varies slightly among professional crews, and with the size of the project. With gable trusses, one way is to first nail a couple of guide boards onto the end walls of the building. Then move a gable-end truss to the end of the building, tip it into position, and toenail into place with two 16d nails on each end. Then do the same at the opposite end of the building.

Next, nail a chalkline from one gable truss peak to the other and draw it tightly into a straight line. Mark out centers 24″ apart along the top plates. Then tip up one truss at a time, making sure the peak is exactly under the chalkline, and toenail into place. As the trusses go up, pre-marked 1x4s can be fastened near the ridge as spacing guides.

All trusses should be securely braced both while being set in place and after the installation. It is most important to temporarily brace the first truss at the end of the building. Your supplier will be able to give you exact recommendations for bracing the trusses you will be using.

Carpenter Lore

A Sampling Of Slick Tricks
For Beginning Builders And Remodelers

If you watch a professional framing or finishing a house, you may quickly figure out that most of the work boils down to measuring, cutting, positioning, and fastening.

Mistakes anywhere along the line can cost time and money. But learning a few tricks of the trade can reduce "do-overs" and make the project more efficient, with more satisfying results. To give yourself a head-start, check out the following ideas. They capsulize the best of the procedures, double-checks, and shortcuts used by the old-timers.

There is more to raising walls, above, than meets the eye. Tricks used by professionals help get them up plumb, square, and true.

Buying Lumber

Some of the wood in the piles at lumberyards or home centers may carry large knots, or be splintered, rotted, or even infested with insects. The most common defect, however, is that some boards are not straight and true. Some may have crowns, meaning they are curved on their narrow-edge surfaces. Others may be bowed—they are curved on their wide surfaces. Others may be warped or twisted.

When selecting lumber, keep in mind that a bowed stud is better than one with a crown. Although a bowed stud is not as strong as a straight stud, it will stay inside the

Cutting boards between two sawhorses is easier if you use a couple of 2x8s or 2x10s for support. Set your blade to cut just a fraction deeper than the board you are cutting.

plane of a wall. A crowned stud, on the other hand, will cause problems when drywall or paneling is attached.

Using Saws

A common problem for beginning do-it-yourselfers occurs when the buckling of a board being cut on sawhorses causes the saw to bind or kick back. To prevent binding when making a cut in the center of a board, you can use one or two 2x8s or 2x10s on the sawhorses as a work surface. Put the board to be cut on the supports, and set the saw so the blade cuts just a fraction deeper than the board's thickness. The supports will get nicked slightly, but you can use them over and over.

Cutting Angles

Building projects often require that several cuts be made at the same angle, such as when cutting rafters. To get the correct angles without a lot of repetitive measuring, you can make a simple jig that will serve as both an angle guide and cutting guide.

To make the jig, find a straight piece of 1x2 and a scrap piece of plywood that also has a straight edge. Nail the 1x2 across the plywood at the angle you need. Then position the angle guide on the board and push a circular saw along the edge of the plywood.

Sorting Lumber

Sort studs into three piles: straight, slightly curved, and everything else. When building the various parts of a wall, you can pull from these piles, according to your needs.

Try to pull from the "straight" pile for framing around the doors and windows to later avoid trying to install straight window or door frames in crooked openings.

Wall intersections are less critical than doors and windows; here you can pull from the "slightly curved" pile. You may be able to straighten these studs somewhat by toenailing one stud to another. Put the studs from the "everything else" pile deep inside the walls, between the corners and the door and window openings, where they won't cause problems.

Using Bowed Boards

There are ways to use slightly bowed or C-shaped boards. If you want to nail a bowed board so that its edge or surface is straight, don't start by nailing it at both ends. If the board is bent, you will never get the bend out of the middle, at least not without excessive force. Instead, nail down one end of the

To cut a number of pieces of lumber at the same angle, you can make yourself a simple angle guide from plywood and a 1x2.

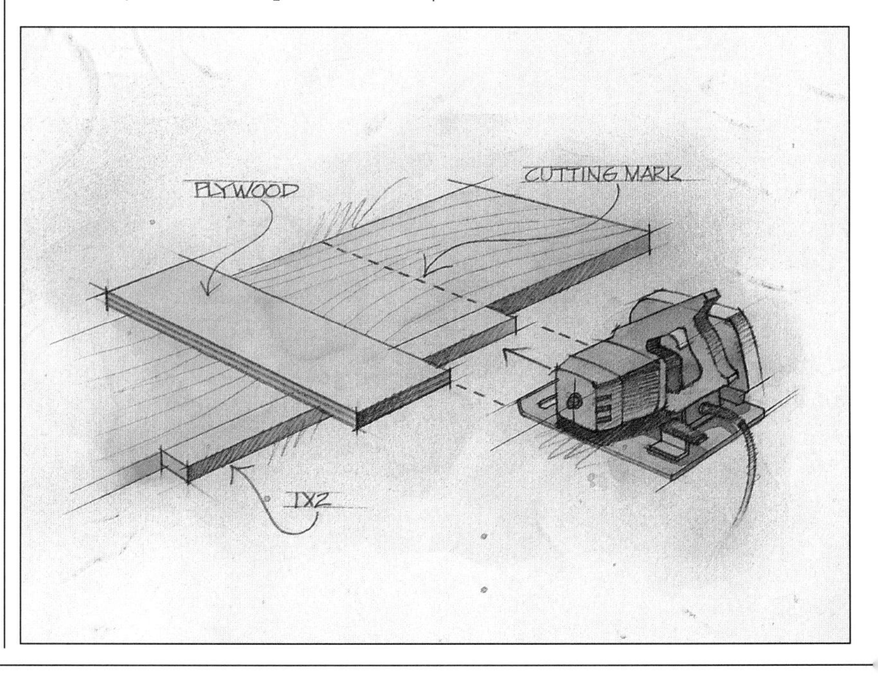

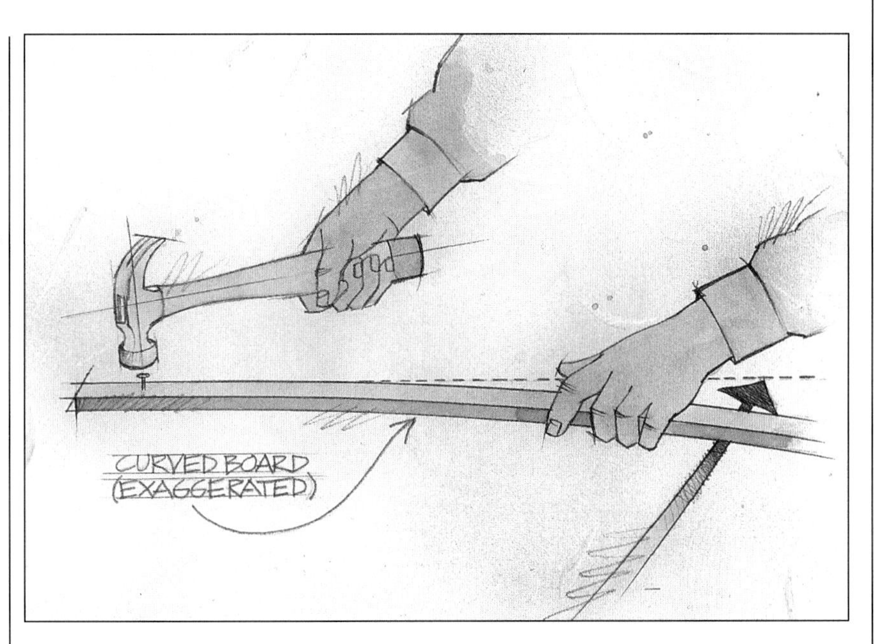

Sometimes C-shaped and S-shaped bowed boards can be salvaged. Nail them flat by alternately driving nails and pulling the board back into a straighter position.

board, then move down a couple of feet, pull the board in the direction opposite to its curve, and drive the second nail. Work down the board, pulling and nailing.

If the board is bent in more than one direction (S-shaped), start by pulling it in one direction. Then, after driving in a few nails, pull it back in the other direction. In some cases, a board's curve can actually help, for example, when using a curved stud at the end of a partition wall. Position the stud so it curves inward, toward the rest of the wall. Then, when you nail the stud to an adjoining wall, the curve will pull the two walls together.

Muscling Lumber

Let's say you are working on a deck where the ends of some joists extend a couple of feet beyond a beam, but the very ends of the joists are slightly unlevel. Nailing the header on directly would leave some ends up and some down. One way to solve this is to nail the header to the first joist. Then, if the next joist is low, pull the header down to nail it. If the third joist is higher, pull the header up to nail it. The header will pull all the joist ends into line.

Or, say you have two joists running along the side of a stairwell, but one is higher than the other. Here is one way to make the two joists level with each other: Pound a 16d nail straight down into the lower joist, then hook the hammer claws around the nail and pry as if you are going to pull the nail out. The top of the hammer will force the higher joist down. While holding it there, have someone else drive nails horizontally through both joists to pin them flush.

Raising Walls

When lifting a wall into position, the bottom of the wall can slip across the floor deck, or even fall off. A solution is to position the wall as it lays flat, then drive duplex nails through the bottom plate of the wall into the floor. The nails will pin the bottom of the wall where you want it. The duplex nails will bend as you raise the wall and will pull out of the floor just as you get the wall vertical. Then simply pull out the double-headed duplex nails.

Cutting Plywood

Plywood tends to splinter when cut with a circular saw. This can be a nuisance in finish work when you

Two parallel boards that are not level with each other can often be muscled into position by driving a spike into the lower board, then pulling to force the second board into position.

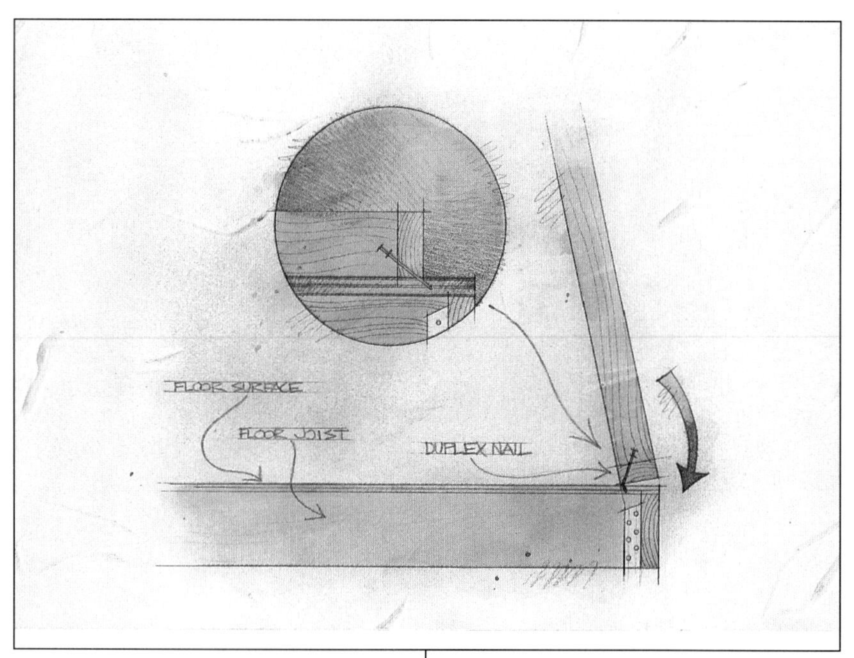

To keep walls from sliding, you can tack the bottom with duplex nails. They'll bend as you raise the wall. After the wall is up, pull them out.

want the surface to be free of flaws.

There are several ways to combat splintering. One way is to adjust the saw so that the blade extends only about one tooth's length below the bottom of the sheet. This makes the teeth come up through the wood at a shallower angle, which creates less splintering.

Another approach is to turn the plywood over and cut along the back surface instead of the front. Any splintering will be on the back, where it won't be visible. With this method, however, all cuts must be reversed. For example, if you want to take 3″ off the right-hand side of the sheet, you have to remember to make the cut on the left-hand side, because you are cutting on the back. This method can get confusing if you are cutting out a complicated shape. An alternative is to cut on the front surface, but with a piece of scrap wood on top of the plywood. The scrap will help prevent splinters because it presses against the plywood.

Squaring Walls

The best time to square a wall is while it is still lying flat, before it is lifted up into position. To make sure it is square, measure the wall diagonally. Assuming that the top plate is as long as the bottom plate, and that the ends of the wall are equal to each other, the wall will be square if the diagonal measurements are equal. Adjust the wall until these measurements are the same. To keep the wall square while tilted in place, attach the sheathing to the wall while it is still flat. If that will make it too heavy to lift, an alternative is to attach temporary diagonal braces before you raise the wall and put the sheathing on.

Lifting Walls

To be sure the wall will be positioned correctly before lifting the wall, snap a chalkline on the platform to show where the inner edge of the bottom plate will go.

Stand the wall up, adjust, and nail down the bottom plate. Then secure the wall with wall-to-platform braces. The braces will hold the wall until you have all the walls in place and firmly anchored at both the bottom and top.

Use duplex nails on the braces for easy removal. Also, if possible, extend some of the braces to the ground outside of the platform. This makes the interior less cluttered so

Squaring up a wall before raising it is done by measuring the wall diagonally from corner to corner. When both diagonal measurements are equal, the wall should be square.

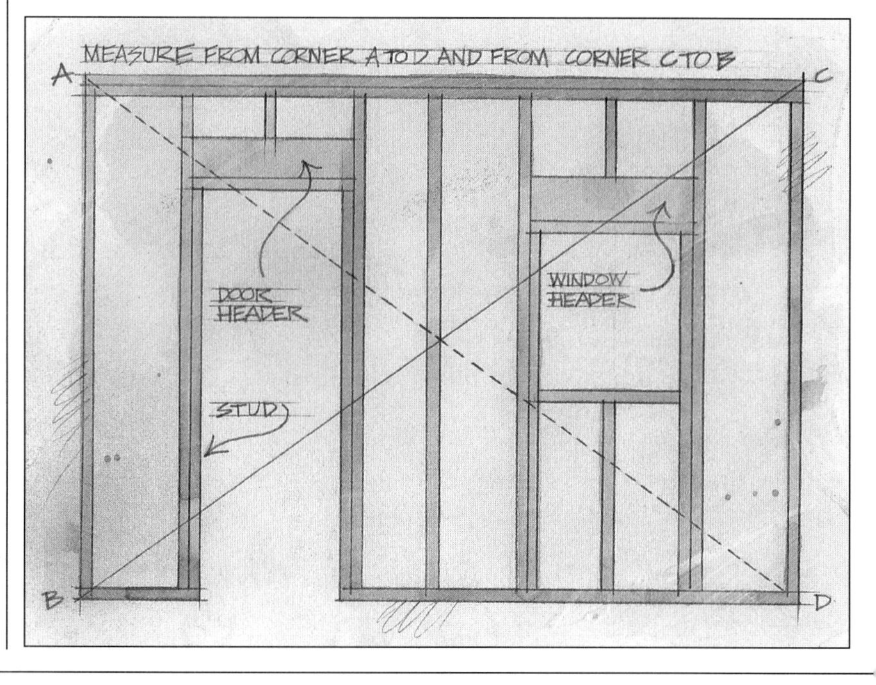

If you don't want to attach sheathing before lifting because of the weight, you can steady a wall temporarily with diagonal braces.

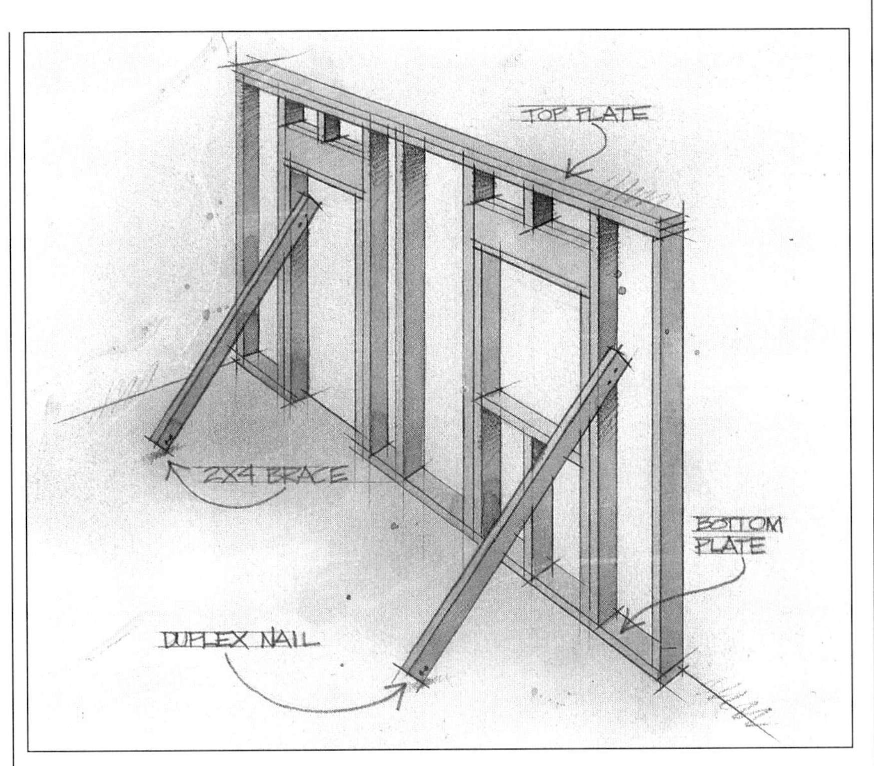

you can move around more easily.

Plumbing Walls

Making sure walls are straight will simplify all subsequent work, from hanging doors to hanging wallpaper. You can check a wall for plumbness with a plumb line, or use a carpenter's level together with a long, straight board that has identical blocks attached at its ends.

The blocks will hold the wood away from the stud being checked and give you an accurate reading even if the stud is slightly warped. Check for level both on the fronts and sides of the studs, and adjust the wall as necessary by repositioning the braces.

Besides getting a wall plumb, you also need to get it straight. Make sure the bottom plate lies along a pre-marked chalkline so you will know the bottom of the wall is straight. Have another person eyeball the top plate while you push or pull with braces to get the top plate straight.

And, to be sure that the top of the wall is straight, attach equal-sized blocks to the inner edges of the top plate and stretch a string between the blocks (see illustration on the next page). Then check all along the top plate with another block cut from the same stock. If the third block fits in snugly every-

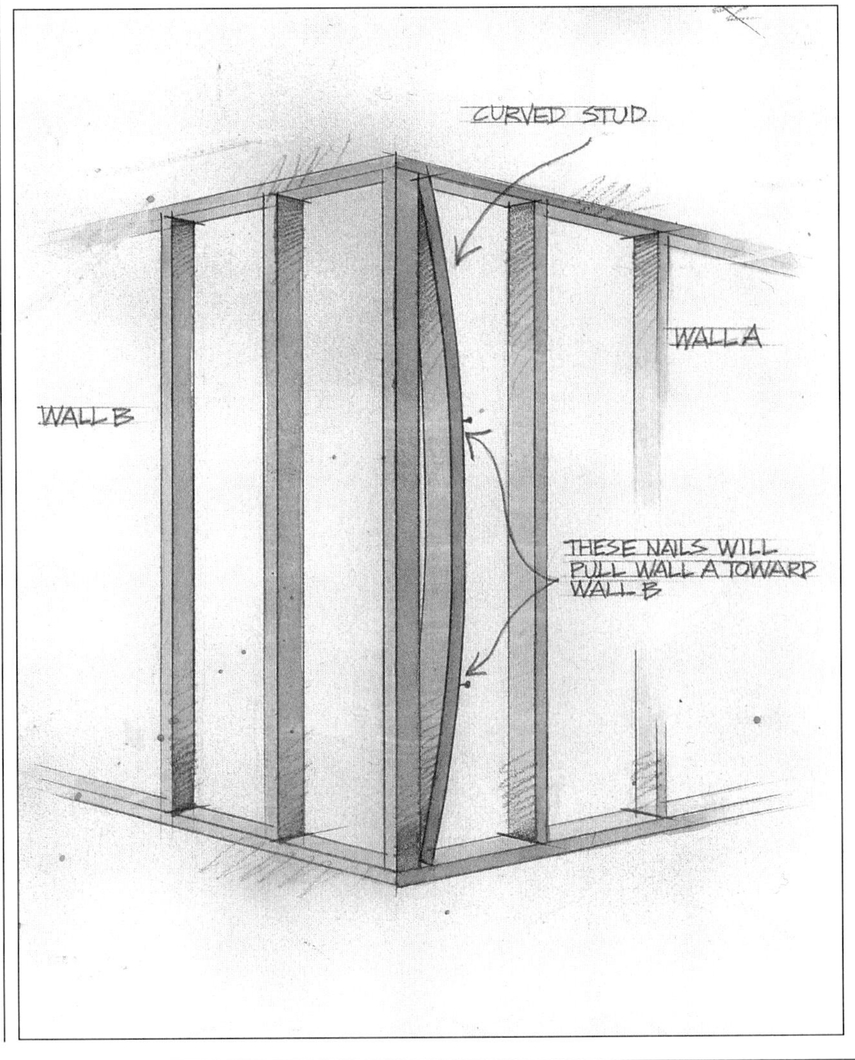

A bowed board can be used at the end of a wall, with the curve bending away from the adjoining wall. Nailing the stud will help pull the two walls together.

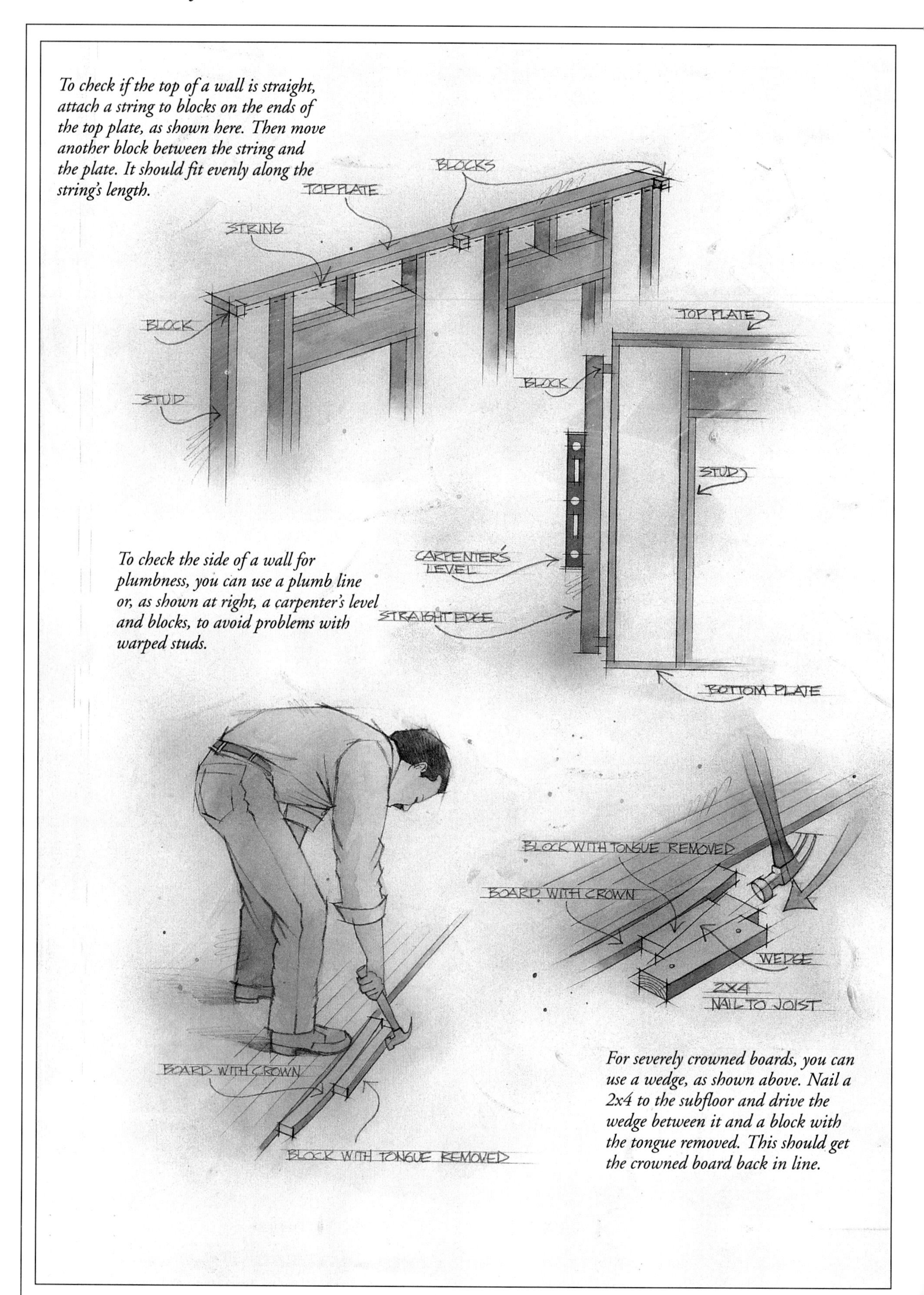

To check if the top of a wall is straight, attach a string to blocks on the ends of the top plate, as shown here. Then move another block between the string and the plate. It should fit evenly along the string's length.

To check the side of a wall for plumbness, you can use a plumb line or, as shown at right, a carpenter's level and blocks, to avoid problems with warped studs.

For severely crowned boards, you can use a wedge, as shown above. Nail a 2x4 to the subfloor and drive the wedge between it and a block with the tongue removed. This should get the crowned board back in line.

where along the plate, you know it is straight.

Installing Wood Floors

When installing floor boards, you will find that some, inevitably, will be bent. You can push on the edge of a 4″ board to straighten it out, but this is more difficult to do if the board is 6″ wide. One way to straighten up tongue-and-groove boards is to use a power nailer. Available from rental companies, you slug this tool with a mallet. It will pull most boards into line, provided they are not severely bowed.

Hitting a tongue-and-groove board directly with a hammer can break off the tongue or mar the surface. Instead, saw the tongue off a block of scrap tongue-and-groove, position it on the board you want to straighten, then hit this block with the hammer. For severely crowned boards, nail a 2x4 at an angle on the subfloor with duplex nails driven into the joists beneath the subfloor. Then drive a wedge of 2x board between this 2x4 and the tongue-and-groove block you have positioned on the crown. The wedge will push the block, and the block will push the tongue-and-groove board into line.

Tip: Unless you buy quality flooring boards, you may find that some will be of slightly different widths. If one board is wider than the other, it will jut out farther, making it difficult to get a good fit when you install the next row. Measure each piece to be sure that pieces of equal width butt together.

Fitting Baseboards

To get tight-fitting joints where baseboards meet in the corners, try this technique: Cut each piece just slightly longer than the bottom of the wall to help get a snug fit with no gaps at the ends of any piece. For the first piece, cut both ends square. Then use a block plane to trim the ends to fit the irregular angles you will probably find in the corners. Initially cut the molding long enough so that, after you have trimmed the ends, it will still be about 1/32″ longer than the wall. When using square stock, you can cut all the pieces the same way you cut the first one.

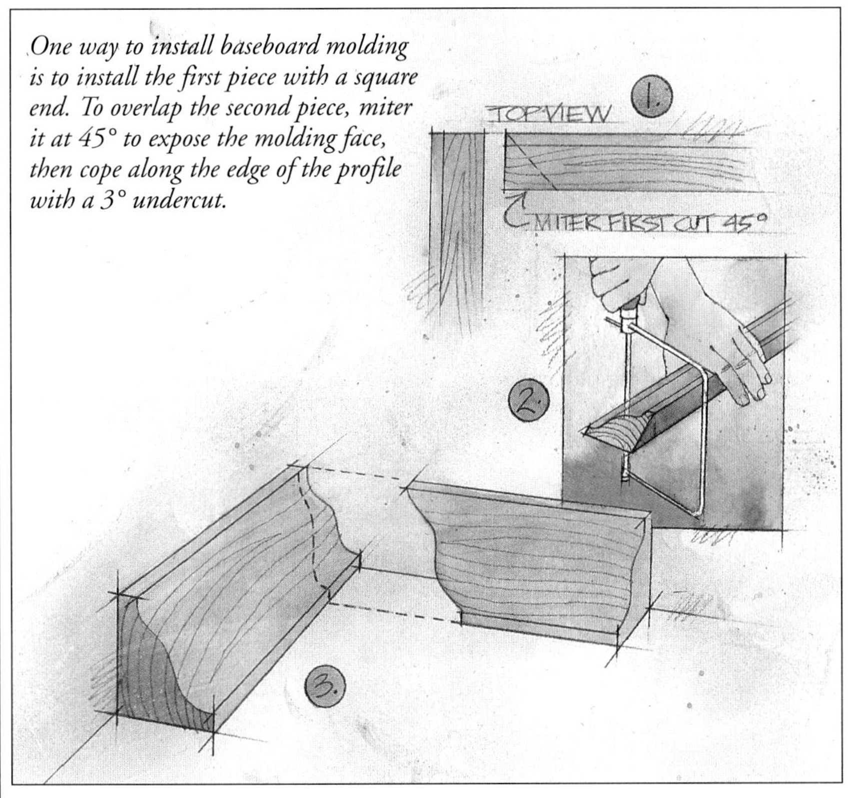

One way to install baseboard molding is to install the first piece with a square end. To overlap the second piece, miter it at 45° to expose the molding face, then cope along the edge of the profile with a 3° undercut.

For decorative molding, a good approach is to cut the pieces so they overlap in the corners. Install the first piece the same way as for square stock, cutting each end square. For the succeeding pieces, make both mitering and coping cuts. With a miter box, cut the end of the second piece of molding at a 45° angle to expose the profile of the molding's face. Then use a coping saw and follow the edge of the profile, undercutting about 3°.

The undercutting will create enough leeway so you can fit the piece into the corner, even if the corner is slightly more or slightly less than 90°. Because the pieces overlap, there won't be a visible gap. You don't have to miter and cope both ends of the molding, just the end that will butt against another piece of molding in the corners. Proceed around the room, cutting and installing each piece of molding in succession.

When nailing the molding, make sure the nails are driven into solid wood. The top row of nails should go into the wall's bottom plate. If the molding is higher than the bottom plate, locate and nail the molding to the studs. If floors are uneven, there may be some gaps between the bottom of the molding and the floor. You can cover these by installing toe molding: narrow, flexible strips of wood that are placed at the bottom front edge of the molding. Have someone stand on the toe molding to bend it flush with the floor, then nail to the floor.

ROOF RESCUES

Do-It-Yourself Reroofing Can Become An Opportunity In Disguise

If the roof on your home is overdue for replacement, deciding to do the reroofing yourself can lead to a double payback.

First, you can save big money by doing it yourself; typically about half the cost of hiring roofers is for labor. If the bid is for $3,000, for example, you can figure roughly $1,500 will be for the labor. Second, boosting the curb appeal of your home with a handsome new roof also will pay off at resale time.

According to nationwide surveys, the typical homeowner can recover from 46% to 100% of the cost of a new roof for a 25-year-old home when selling. The percentage will vary depending on the condition of the original roof.

Of course, the best time to reroof is before it becomes a necessity. Leaks can lead to severe structural damage to the house, stained ceilings, ruined floors, and expensive repairs. If your roof is more than 15 years old and you notice signs of wear (cupped, curling, or missing shingles, or worn-off granules collecting at the base of rain gutter downspouts), it may be time to replace your roof.

When selecting new shingles, remember that the secret to good design is balanced color, texture, and pattern. For best results, consider all of the features of your home's exterior.

DECIDING TO REROOF

Reroofing can be a challenge, but it's not as difficult as it might look once you know the proper techniques. And, the money you can save by doing it yourself will compensate you well for your efforts.

When reshingling, use good work practices. Follow the manufacturer's instructions when using power tools, adhesives, and finishing materials. Also wear goggles when using power tools or a hammer.

Another option to consider is to buy your own materials and hire a contractor to install them. One advantage to this approach is the ability to get the exact color, style, and quality you want, rather than something "almost like it" from the contractor's offerings. Plus, you may be able to save some money by buying the materials yourself.

Should you do it yourself or hire a contractor? If you are handy with tools and enjoy the work, by all means consider tackling the job yourself. Applying a new roof is within the realm of the do-it-yourselfer, particularly on a one-story home with a low-pitched roof. Just try to schedule your project for dry weather and make sure you have both the time and the proper tools to complete the job.

One factor in the decision is the number of layers of shingles that have already been applied on the roof. Generally, depending on your local building codes, if there are two or less layers, and you have a single-story home with a moderately pitched roof, you won't have to remove the existing shingles, and the job should be relatively safe. Beyond basic tools and the willingness to use proper precautions, patience is all that is required. If your home already has more than two layers of shingles, you can still reroof yourself. However, the old roofing must be removed before new shingles can be nailed down.

As for shingling styles to choose

from, so many types are currently available there is no need to settle for humdrum roofing.

Selecting Shingles. Today's shingles fall into two categories: *standard three-tab* and *architectural.* Architectural shingles are top-of-the-line products designed to give rooflines the visual appeal of wood shakes without the disadvantages of wood roofing. The deep profile and substantial "heft" of architectural shingles create an interplay of light and shadow that enhances your roof's visual impact.

Three-tab shingles are the traditional choice for cost-effective, quality roofing. Available in colors to enhance any exterior scheme, three-tab shingles combine durability and good looks at competitive prices.

Also available are fiberglass-based shingles, which offer self sealing, wind resistance, and a Class-A fire rating. The self-sealing feature helps a new roof stay flat and effective for years. After the shingles are nailed to the roof, a factory-applied adhesive strip on each shingle warms with the sun and bonds firmly to the overlapping shingle.

Other Decisions

If it is time to reroof your home, consider residing and adding (or upgrading) insulation at the same time. There are several advantages to this approach.

First, it is easier to pick complementary materials for the entire house when you choose roofing and siding together. Second, you will only have to face the clutter and cleanup of remodeling once. Third, you may save on delivery costs, labor costs (if you are hiring a contractor), and detail work like painting the trim or installing new gutters by combining your projects.

And, finally, upgrading the energy efficiency of your home makes good sense and is particularly easy to do when you are getting ready to reside. Just install the insulation first, under the new siding. You will enjoy increased, year-round comfort, lower heating and cooling bills, and increased value when you are ready to sell your home.

If you hire a contractor for roofing, or other jobs, keep the following suggestions in mind when making the selection:

- Always ask for references and always check them. Look at the contractor's work yourself whenever possible to be sure it meets your standards.
- Check with the Better Business Bureau to see if any complaints have been filed against the contractors you are considering.
- Will all the workers be bonded, licensed, and insured? This is an essential, since on-the-job injuries or damage to either your property or a neighbor's can create major problems.

Ask for proof of insurance before

A roof makes up a good part of your home's curb appeal, as shown on this home outfitted with Georgia-Pacific's Summit® Roofing. Before reroofing, consider making other improvements at the same time.

anyone starts work. (Keep in mind that homeowners' policies do not necessarily cover damage caused by contractors or subcontractors.)

- Make sure the contractor's bid includes debris cleanup and a specific completion date.
- Get more than one written estimate for every job. Three is a good number; four or more is better. Beware of extremely low and extremely high quotes.

Once you've chosen your contractor and the crew has started work, try to avoid making changes to your original plan.

Roofing Terms

Course: Each successive row of applied shingles, beginning with number one at the eaves.

Coverage: The degree of weather protection offered by a roofing material (single, double, or triple coverage).

Deck: The roof surface or platform to which roofing materials are applied.

Drip Edge: Weather-resistant metal edge installed along eaves and rakes to facilitate shedding of water at the edges.

Eaves: Parts of a roof that project beyond or overhang the face of the wall at the lower edge of the roof.

Exposure: Exposure to weather as measured by the distance from the butt edge of one shingle to another.

Felt: A building paper composed of a strong, tough base saturated with asphalt.

Flashing: Strips of metal or roofing material used in making watertight joints on a roof, especially in valleys or where inclined and vertical surfaces intersect.

Gable: The end of the building wall which comes to a triangular point under a sloping roof. Also, a type of roof.

Hip: Any external angle formed by the meeting of two sloping ends of the roof, from the ridge to the eaves. Also, a type of roof.

Rake: The inclined edge of a sloped roof over an end wall.

Ridge: The apex of the angle formed by a roof, or the peak where the common rafters meet.

Soil Stack: A plumbing vent pipe that penetrates through the roof.

Square: The amount of roofing material required to cover 100 square feet (10x10′) of roof surface.

Valley: An internal angle formed by the intersection of two slopes in a roof.

The tools needed for reroofing are relatively inexpensive, if you don't already have them. Priorities should include adequate, safe ladders, and goggles.

Finishing right begins with starting right. Take extra care at the beginning of the project, following the manufacturer's instructions.

Getting Started

Installation instructions are printed on the back of shingle bundles from most suppliers. Reading them before you start work is a good double-check on procedures.

Determine Roof Slope. "Slope" is the rate at which a roof rises for each foot of horizontal run. For example, a roof that rises 5″ vertically while covering 12″ of the house beneath is said to have a slope of 5/12 or 5″ per foot. A roof with a slope between 4″ and 6″ per foot is easiest for a do-it-yourselfer to install.

Roofs with a slope of less than 2″ per foot require special roofing techniques best left to a professional. Roofs with a slope of over 6″ can be dangerous for do-it-yourself installers to work on. It's best to hire a contractor if your home falls into either of these categories.

Estimate Shingle Coverage. Shingles are sold in squares—each square covering a 100-square foot (or 10x10′) area. If you have a simple roof with unbroken planes, such as a ranch-style house, estimating the amount of roofing you'll need is a simple process.

Measure each roof section along the eave and rake (the inclined edge of a sloped roof over an end wall). Multiply the length of the eave times the length of the rake to

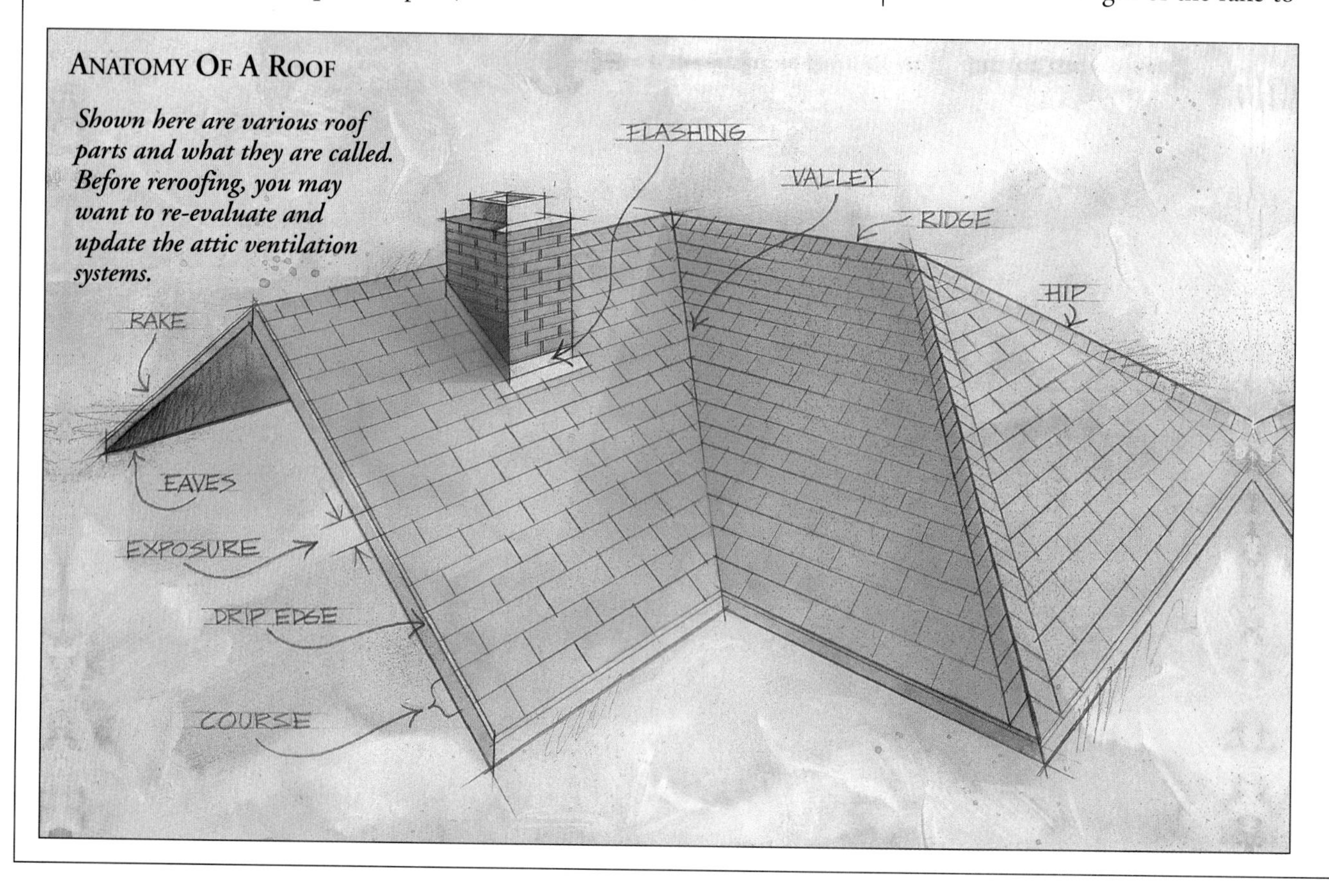

Anatomy Of A Roof

Shown here are various roof parts and what they are called. Before reroofing, you may want to re-evaluate and update the attic ventilation systems.

get the square feet. Add the various areas you've measured; then allow an extra 10% for waste. Divide the total by 100 to find the number of squares you will need.

Roofs with dormers, extensions, and other architectural features are more complicated to measure. Consult your shingle supplier for more help and advice.

Roof Inspection. The first step in reroofing is to inspect the old roof for damage. Brittle, cupped, or curled shingles with most of the granules worn away are ready for replacement. Pull out or nail down any protruding nails and replace any missing or broken shingles. Replace the drip cap, if necessary, and sweep the roof clean of debris and loose granules.

If you need to remove the old shingles, start at the roof ridge. Work your way down, prying out the nails while you tear the shingles away with a flat-bladed shovel. Pull out remaining nails and old flashings with a hammer, and repair the decking wherever necessary.

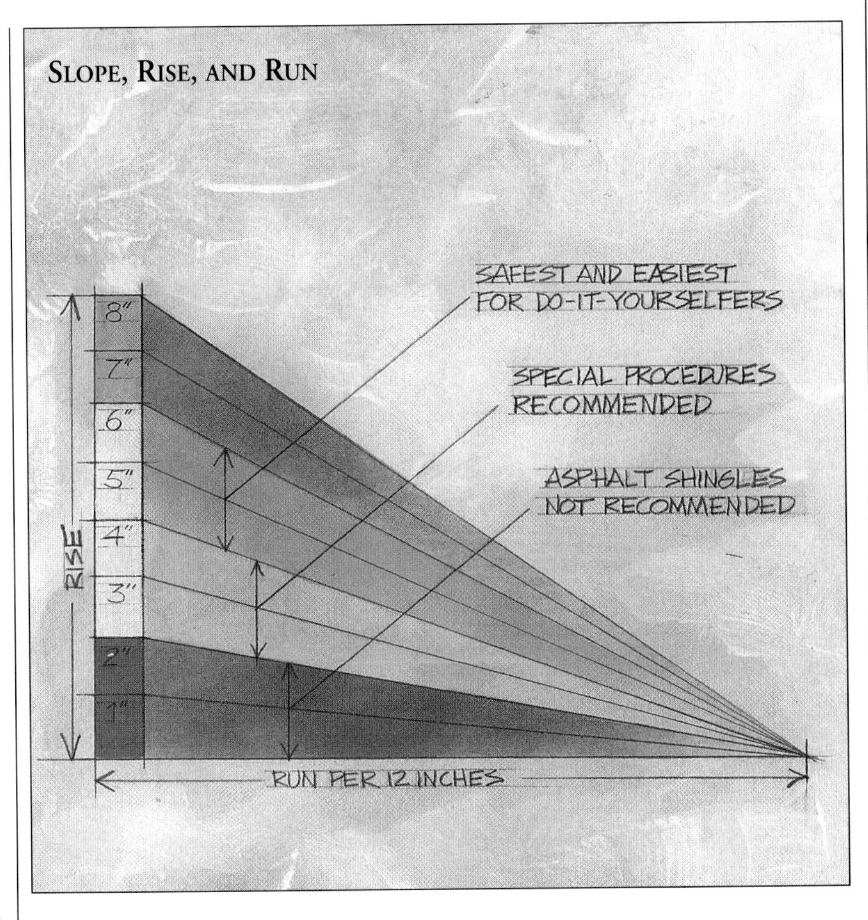

ROOFING TIPS

Safe work habits are of utmost importance when installing a new roof. Always wear rubber-soled shoes and work only on a completely dry roof. Wear a well-secured safety harness or rope and keep extra tools and shingles out of the work area when not needed. Warn others to stay away from the grounds beneath the eaves.

Use an extension ladder at least 2′ longer than the eave height, and make sure the ladder has safety feet which grab and hold firmly. (Never use a ladder near power lines.) The ladder should be tied off at the eaves and at the ground to a stake.

Roofing Tools. You probably have many of the tools you will need. They include a broom; carpenter's apron; caulking gun; chalk line; chisel and saw; flat-bladed shovel; hammer or roofer's hatchet; ladder and scaffolding; putty knife, pointed trowel, or brush; safety goggles and rope; tape ruler, and utility knife.

Underlayment. If you have stripped off the old shingles, apply saturated felt underlayment over the wood deck before applying new roofing. Allow a 2″ horizontal overlap and a 4″ vertical overlap where edges of underlayment meet. Use only enough nails to hold the felt in place.

Install non-corrosive drip edges along eaves and rakes to help shed water at the roof edges. The underlayment goes under the drip edge at the rake and over the drip edge at the eave line.

Valley Flashing. If you use roll roofing for flashing material, cut a strip 18″ wide and lay the mineral surface down in the roof valley.

Tack in place with nails. Cut a second strip 36″ wide and lay it mineral surface up on top of the first strip. Install metal valley flashing if you will be using shingles with a Class-A fire rating.

Other Flashing. Apply non-corrosive sheetmetal flashing anywhere the shingles contact an abutment such as a chimney, vertical wall, stack, or vent. Seal the flashing with asphalt plastic cement.

Applying Shingles. The same basic procedures are used for most conventional roofing shingles. Some special types, available in limited geographic regions, require a slightly different installation. Check with your dealer or home center, or refer to the shingle package for specific instructions.

- Prepare a starter course to run the length of the roof by cutting the tabs off of the full-sized strip

Valleys, hips, and ridges take special procedures (see opposite page). Keep personal safety the foremost priority, using ropes as needed for insurance.

shingles. Be sure the starter strip is positioned with the adhesive strip face up along the eaves. Trim the top of these pieces so the starter course will fit snugly against the bottom of the existing second course. When cutting shingles, cut them from the back side. This will make the cuts easier and more accurate, and your knife blades will last longer.

• There are three different methods for applying tabbed strip shingles—the 6″ method, the 5″ method, and the 4″ method. These correspond to the amount of shingle width removed from each successive course to get the desired pattern, since varying the width of the first shingle in the first few rows prevents the cutouts in one course from lining up directly over those below. For illustration purposes, let's look at the 6″ method.

Each succeeding course after the first—and up to the sixth—starts with a shingle 6″ narrower than the preceding one. The first course starts with a full-width shingle. The second starts with a shingle that has had 6″ cut from the end. The third starts with a shingle 12″ narrower and so on through the sixth course, which starts with a shingle that has had 30″ removed. Adjacent shingles in each course are all full-width. Start the seventh course with a full-width shingle and repeat the pattern.

• Apply shingles horizontally across and up the roof, cutting them to go around obstructions like vents and chimneys. Use a liberal coating of asphalt cement to seal gaps between cut-out shingles.

Nailing Patterns. Use 11-gauge or 12-gauge hot-dipped galvanized roofing nails. Make sure they are long enough to penetrate all roofing materials and into the deck at least ¾″. Use four nails per shingle (one 1″ back from both ends and one ⅝″ above each cut-out slot). Do not nail into or above the self-sealing strip, and avoid breaking the asphalt surface of the shingle when you drive the nails.

Valley Shingling. Snap two chalklines along the valley from the ridge to the eaves. They should be 6″ apart at the ridge and spread ⅛″ per foot until they reach the eaves. For an open valley, position a shingle over the chalkline (don't fasten it yet) and mark the top and bottom where the chalkline appears. Remove the shingle and cut between the marks using a straightedge and a utility knife. Trim the upper corner of the shingles to direct water into the valley, then apply asphalt cement beneath valley shingles to form a waterproof seal.

For a woven, or closed valley, lace the shingle courses across the valley with a 12″ overlap. Use the vertical and horizontal chalklines on either side of the valley to maintain proper alignment.

Hips and Ridges. For reroofing, completely tear off the old hip and ridge shingles. Trim the top course of new shingles where they intersect at hips and ridges. Make new hip and ridge capping by cutting full-sized shingles into equal thirds.

Snap chalklines along the length of hips and ridges. Start from the bottom end of a hip and bend the caps over the center line. Nail once on each side and apply asphalt cement on the bottom and edges of the end cap to seal out water. Apply the ridge caps the same as hip caps, but orient them away from the prevailing wind.

Note: A good source for additional information on do-it-yourself reroofing is Georgia-Pacific. Check with local suppliers, or write the company at P.O. Box 105605, Atlanta, GA 30348-5605, or call 1-800/447-2882.

Tech Notes: Reroofing Procedures

You can roof over old shingles if 1) there are one or two layers of shingles, 2) the deck is sound and solid enough to hold nails, and 3) there are no large areas of damage. You must rip off the old shingles if 1) there are more than two layers of shingles already applied, 2) parts of the roof deck are rotted, warped, or damaged, and/or 3) there are large areas of damage.

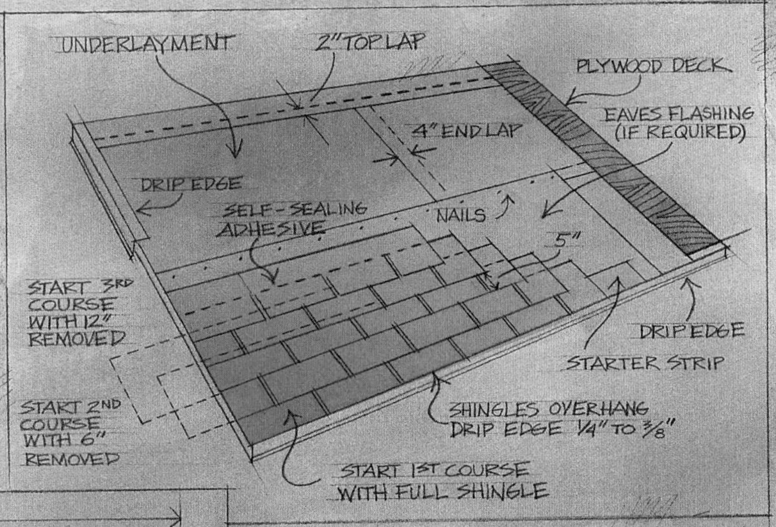

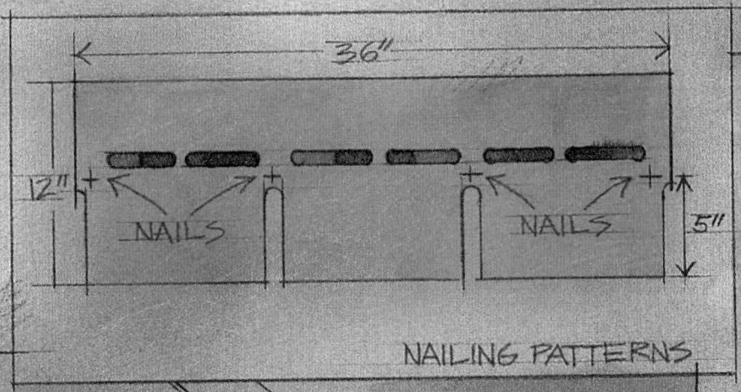

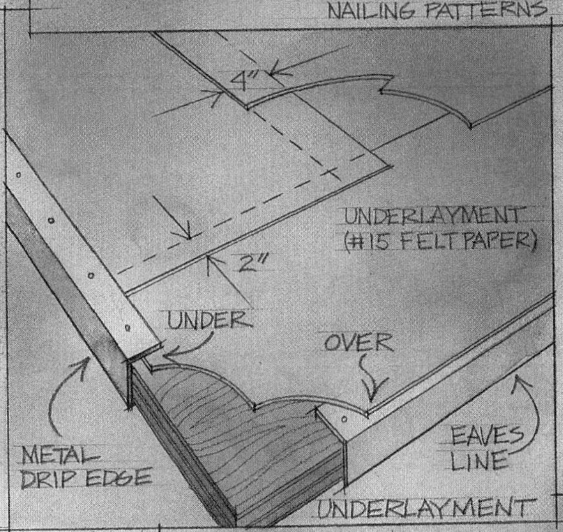

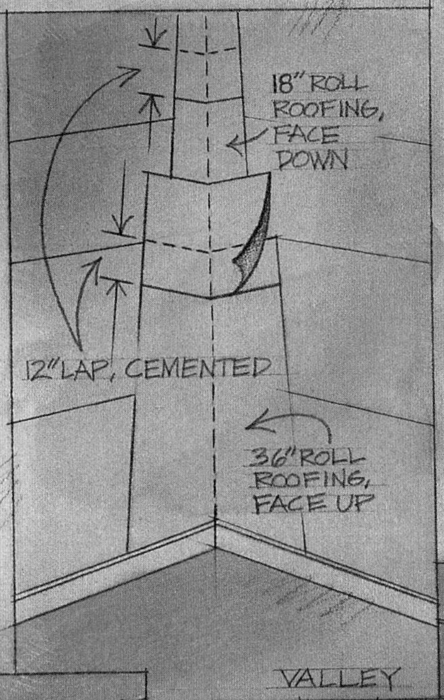

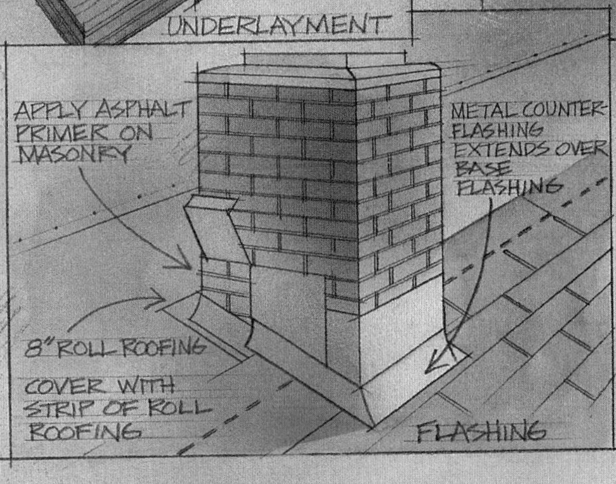

ATTIC VENTILATION

Ridge Vents Provide Attractive Relief From Attic Ventilation Problems

Inadequate attic ventilation can cause a myriad of problems for a home. If your present vent system is not doing the job, or if you are about to reroof, it will pay you to consider updating it.

A good system will balance the attic's inside temperature with outside temperatures. In summer, it removes heat that can distort and destroy roof shingles and cause premature deterioration of roof boards, sheathing, siding, and insulation. It will also reduce your air conditioning costs.

In winter, a good system helps prevent several problems. First, it reduces moisture condensation on roof sheathing, trusses, floorboards, and rafters. This moisture contributes to wood rot, mildew, rusting fasteners and metal elements, and makes insulation less effective. Also, by helping keep attic air temperature from rising higher than outside air, a good venting system helps reduce ice dam problems.

There are two basic types of ventilation systems—active and passive. Active mechanical systems include wind turbines and power vents. Ridge vents fall into the second category, generating ventilation passively. Ridge vents can be made of metal or plastic. Of the plastic varieties, some have a baffle on the interior or exterior and can't be cut lengthwise for narrower ridge caps. A new option is to use a flexible, mat-like material, which can be cut to fit ridge caps of any width.

Providing venting with the new fiber undershingle ridge matting is an excellent alternative to other types of devices. Research shows that, when installed with proper soffit venting, a 32′-long section of this type of ridge venting can equal one 1,120 CFM power vent, five turbine vents, or 12 roof louvers of 45 sq. in. each.

While all ventilation systems are designed to reduce heat and moisture, research has also shown that ridge vents can do a superior job of moving air throughout the attic. A wind turbine, for example, generally only draws from an area within a 5′ diameter of its position.

A subtle appearance is a desirable feature to look for when selecting a ventilation system; ridge vents integrate visually into the roof line. Because the shingle cap for the fiber mat ridge vent is made of the same roofing material as the rest of the roof, it blends in well. It also can eliminate the hodge-podge of mechanical devices often added piecemeal to increase ventilation.

The illustration shows how the Cobra Ridge Vent from Cobra Ventilation Co. works. The design has proven so successful that the technology and trademarks were recently acquired by GAF Building Materials Corporation.

The Cobra system uses fiber and polymer matting made mostly of recycled material that is easy to handle, installs quickly, and has a low profile when installed. A retrofit to an existing roof can be done in an afternoon.

The mat material comes in 20′ and 50′ rolls to accommodate the typical 40′ to 50′ installation.

The undershingle design of the vent fits any pitch roof (from 3/12 to 20/12) and installs without end pieces, connectors, fabrics, or the need for special tools. It also works well with cedar, composition, metal, and tile roofs. The matting is almost indestructible, and has no external baffle to trap dirt, snow, or insects.

To install the system, a 2″ slot is first cut on each side of the roof ridge, leaving a 6″ section at each end of the ridge uncut. The cut is made only through the sheathing, not the roof trusses. For homes with a ridge board, a 3½″ slot (1¾″ on each side) is cut. Next, the ridge vent material is applied along the entire length of the ridge, also covering the 6″ uncut sheathing areas on both ends. Joints are simply cut square and butted tightly without connectors.

The final step is replacing the shingle cap with 2″ roof nails directly over the ridge vent matting. A minimum of ¾″ is left for the matting between the roof and the shingle cap, which should just snug the venting material against the ridge.

Note: For more information about the Cobra Attic Ventilation System, write to Cobra Ventilation Co., Inc., Subsidiary of GAF Building Materials Corp., 1361 Alps Rd., Wayne, NJ 07470. Or call 800/688-6654.

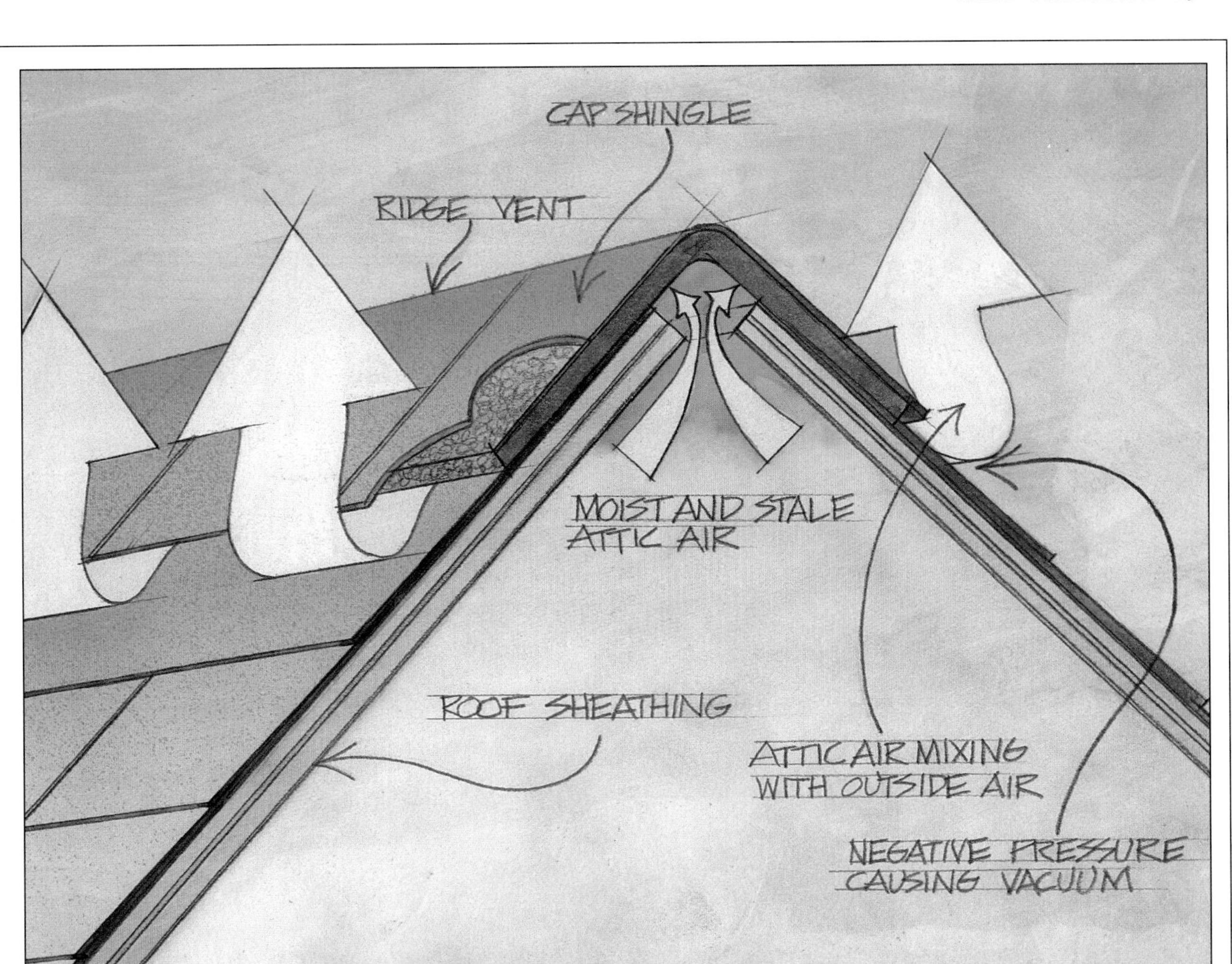

The Cobra system uses a mat-like material over the ridge. In conjunction with soffit vents, the system provides energy-conserving, passive attic ventilation. Air traveling across the roof creates negative pressure at the ridge line, drawing stale or moist air out of the attic through the ridge vent. At the same time, fresh air is drawn into the attic through the soffit vents, equalizing temperature and pressure inside the attic and out.

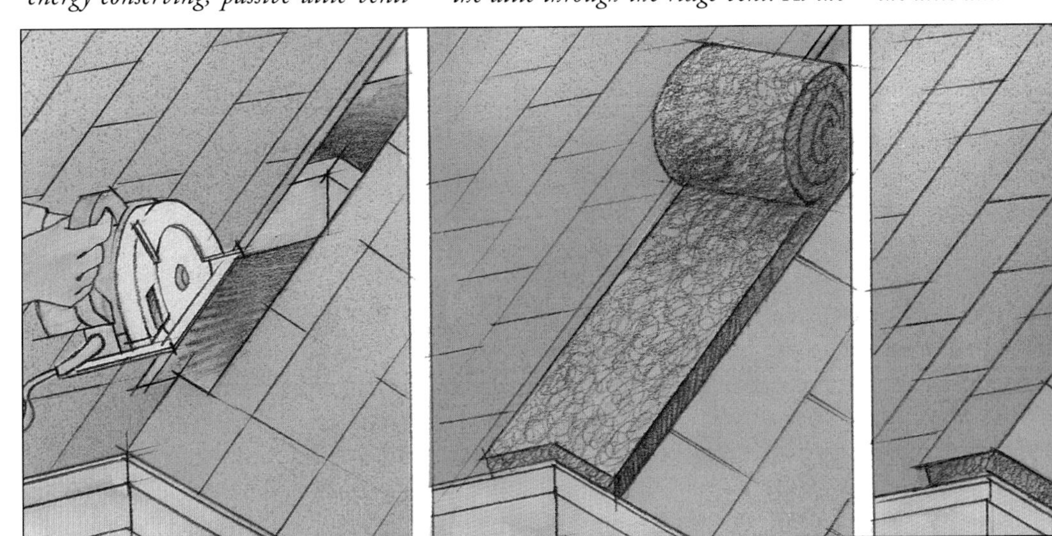

1 The first of three basic installation steps is to cut a slot in the ridge through the sheathing.

2 After the slot is cut in the ridge, the coil of vent material is unrolled over the entire roof line.

3 The final step is to nail shingles over the matting until they both fit snugly against the roof.

Painting Shortcuts

Some Easy Ways To Take The Pain Out Of Home Painting Projects

On a pleasure scale from 1 to 10, a holiday in the Caribbean would be a 10 for most of us, watching TV might be a 6, cleaning out the garage a 3. But painting might rank a 1—possibly a 2—for occasional painters.

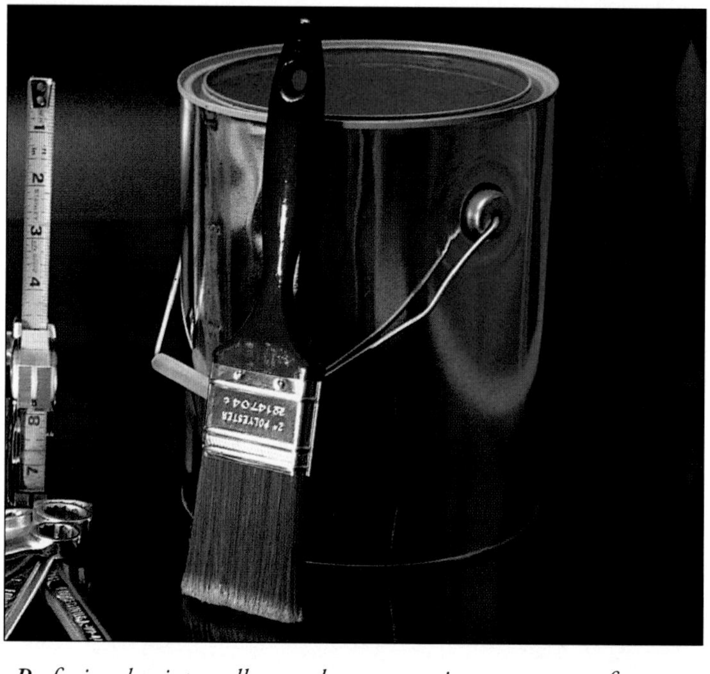

Many homeowners groan at the thought of painting because the job can be messy, expensive, time-consuming, and frustrating. Yet a painting project successfully completed can generate a good amount of personal satisfaction. The key is to learn the basics of painting, then do everything you can to minimize the drudgery.

To start, don't get your mind in the wrong gear and think that the job is mainly applying the paint. The truth is that planning and preparation account for most of the work, so set your expectations accordingly. Once you get into the project, there are several ways to save time on preparing surfaces, on cleaning up, on repainting, plus some tricks to keep from spending more money than necessary to get the job done.

Professional painters all agree that preparation can account for up to 80% of the time spent painting. Taking the right shortcuts can save you time without sacrificing the quality of your work.

Cutting Prep Time

Getting all chalking, flaking, or peeling paint off the surface you are about to repaint is a must. On the outside of the house, consider using your garden hose or a rented pressure washer. Unless you are using latex, wait until the surface is completely dry before starting to paint. If you have mildew problems, use a bleach solution (one pint per gallon of water), to kill the mildew and bleach out the stains. If you don't kill mildew, it can grow under the new coat of paint.

Inside the house, you can use shellac to seal water stains. Waterborne stains will bleed through latex paint. (If you try to just use latex to cover a water stain, you still may be at it after 15 coats.) Shellac dries quickly.

Use alcohol, not mineral spirits, to clean shellac from your brushes.

Remove the wall items you don't want painted, such as electrical plates. This is quicker and easier than trying to mask everything with tape. Then cover up what you can't remove. For example, tie garbage bags over fixtures such as chandeliers. Use care when painting around exposed wiring.

Glass can slow you down. Some do-it-yourselfers don't bother covering glass, believing it is faster to scrape the paint off later. You can stick wet newspapers on glass, but they can dry out and fall off.

A better solution is to use dry newspaper over glass, applying masking tape around the edges.

Minimizing Cleanup

Try to avoid unnecessary cleanup when your painting is interrupted or finished. Line roller trays with plastic; you can even slip a plastic garbage bag over the tray. A lining not only makes cleanup easier, but also prevents the high pH of latex paints from interacting with the aluminum tray. If you use plastic lining, buy a grid-like roller screen that fits inside the tray over the plastic. The screen will keep the plastic from wrinkling and the

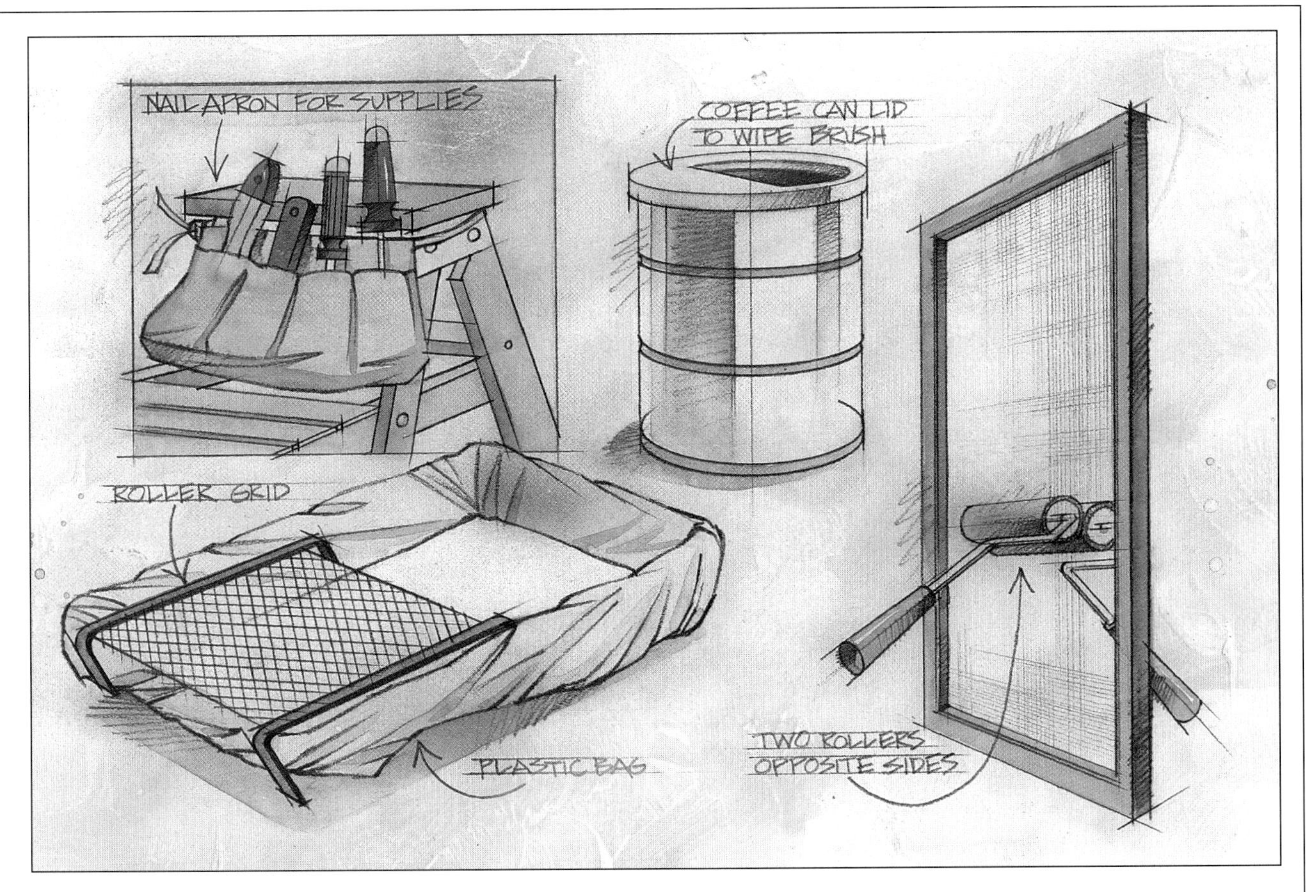

roller from slipping.

Put paint tools and trays inside a garbage bag to keep them from drying out if you stop painting for a few hours or overnight. Small plastic sandwich bags work great for brushes and also help them keep their shape. For rollers, you can use Ziploc storage bags, plastic wrap, or large, plastic food-storage bags.

To speed brush cleanup, try not to get the bristles wet beyond about half of their length. When painting overhead, paint will drop down into the brush. To remove this paint, wash the brush, then comb it out with a bronze wire brush, the kind used for cleaning barbecue grills.

A trick for cleaning rollers is to roll off any excess paint on a scrap of gypsum board; you will be able to use the same scrap board for years. Then clean the rollers using the stream of a hose nozzle. By turning the hose on full blast and directing the spray to the side of the roller, it will almost spin itself clean.

Preventing Spatters

One thing professional painters learn early on is that it is easier to cover up than to clean up. When mixing paint, prevent spattering by putting the can inside a cardboard box or a garbage or grocery bag. Any flying paint will be neatly confined. To prevent paint from running down the side of the can, you can buy special plastic lid devices that fit over the rim. You can also fashion your own by cutting a semi-circle in a coffee can lid to within about one inch of the edge. Then use the inside edge to wipe your brush.

Buy plenty of drop cloths. Canvas lasts longer than plastic and soaks up paint, but 3-mil plastic works fine. Make "paths" with newspaper to and from the work area so paint sticking to your shoes won't be dragged through the house. Also get enough masking tape. You are buying it to save time, so buy a good brand that is at least an inch wide. If tape comes in contact with some paint solvents it can glue itself to the surface. Pull it off as soon as the paint has set. Between jobs, store tape in the refrigerator to prolong its life, or at least keep it out of direct sunlight.

To clean solvent-borne paints off your hands, try ordinary salad oil. (Solvent-borne paints include oil-based paints, varnishes and urethanes.) Salad oil will take the paint off and won't irritate your hands like other solvents. It also can help you remove solvent-borne paint spilled on wood finishes that are sensitive to other solvents.

Saving Paint Time

There is no point in painting if it isn't absolutely necessary. For example, if you have small water stains on a ceiling, experiment to see if you can remove them without painting. Mix up a water-bleach solution and apply it with a small spray bottle, using normal safety precautions. The stains may disappear, saving you a

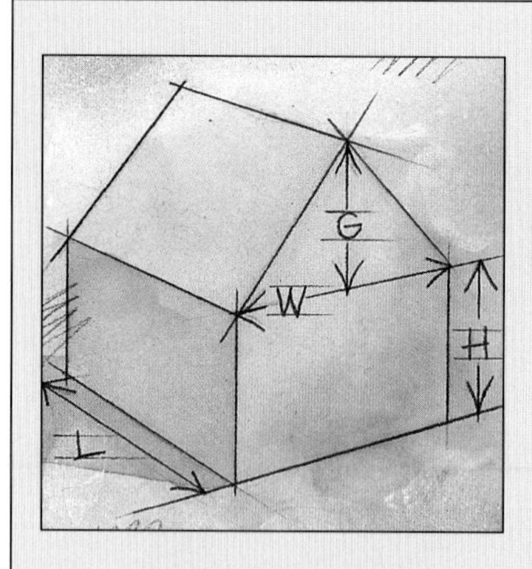

Calculating Paint Coverage

Making Calculations. To calculate how much paint you will need to cover the exterior of your home, consider three factors: 1) the total square footage to be covered, 2) the number of coats you plan to apply, and 3) the condition of the surface to be painted.

• To figure the square footage, add up the area of the sides, the gable, and any overhanging eaves. For the sides, multiply the length of your home (L) by the height at the eave line (H) in feet. This will give you the area of one side in square feet. Repeat this calculation for each of the sides, then add up the total for all the sides.

• To figure the gable areas, multiply the width (W) by the height (G) and divide by two to get the area of one gable. Make this same calculation for each gable and add up the totals.

• To figure the area under overhanging eaves, if any, multiply the length by the width to get the square footage of this area.

Once the above calculations are made, add the total square footage for the sides, gables, and overhanging eaves (don't forget to include the areas of any dormers). This will be the total square footage of the exterior. Next, subtract the areas that won't be painted, such as windows, brick or stone work, and fireplaces, to get the total square footage. Divide that figure by 400, which will give you the approximate number of gallons you will need for an average one-coat application.

Making Adjustments. While most exterior paints will generally cover up to 400 square feet per gallon for one coat, adjust for factors like surface porosity. If the surface is rough or porous, add 20% to the total gallons figured. Likewise, if the siding on the home is narrow (4″ to 5″), add 10% more. For any corrugated surfaces of either metal or fiberglass, add 33%. If the paint will be the first coat on concrete block, double the figure. If power equipment will be used, also consider the waste factor (see article).

paint job. Here are some other shortcuts that can save on painting time:

• Lay screens on top of sawhorses to confine splattering while you are painting them. Or use two sponges, pads, or rollers at the same time directly opposite each other on each side of the screen. You also can set boards across the second rung on a stepladder to support screens or storm windows while they are being painted.

• Attach a carpenter's nail apron to the top of your stepladder to store small painting supplies such as putty, nails, or screws that you may need while painting.

• Quart-sized or smaller paint cans are hard to carry and easy to tip over. To avoid these problems, put the small can inside an empty gallon can. It will be easier to carry and, if it spills, you can pour the paint back into the little can.

• If you are looking to really speed up interior home painting projects, buy or rent a power roller. Some do-it-yourselfers find that with a power roller they can paint a living room, dining room, hallway, and bedroom all in one day.

Trimming Paint Costs

There is no need to throw away expensive solvent after only one use. Pour it into a metal can and cover it. After the paint particles settle out, pour off the clear solvent for reuse. You can do this a number of times. Occasionally rub some of the solvent between your fingers. When it begins to feel sticky, throw it away.

Brushes can be expensive to replace. If you have brushes that are dried out and hard, try soaking them overnight in water-washable paint remover. Then clean and comb them out with a bronze wire brush. This overhaul works best with brushes that have been used with oil-based paints.

When storing paint, blowing into the can before sealing will increase its shelf life. The carbon dioxide in your breath reduces the oxygen level that causes paint to skin over. You even can throw in a small chunk of dry ice to increase the carbon dioxide level. But don't blow into cans of moisture-cure urethanes (most of today's polyurethanes) because your breath also contains moisture.

Another trick for storing paint is to use plastic wrap. Push it into the can, down to the paint, and seal it around the edge with your finger. If paint does get lumpy, strain it through old nylon stockings or pantyhose. Just hang the nylon above an empty can and pour the paint through it.

If you want to keep full cans of paint for long periods, store the cans upside down for a month, then right side up the next month, then upside down, etc. This will move the paint's pigment back and forth and keep it from settling out.

When should you throw paint out? Some corrosion-inhibiting pigments can react with paint over time, turning it into a semi-solid gel. Once this happens, the paint is finished. Also, once latex paint freezes and looks like cottage cheese, you may as well throw it away and save your time.

Avoiding Do-Overs

There are several tricks that you can use to avoid the headache of repainting a newly painted surface.

When using latex, for example, be sure the temperature is above 50° F. (Latex won't form a film at lower temperatures.) With solvent-borne paint, be sure the temperature is at least 5° F. above the dew point. If it's not, water may condense on the surface as it cools while the solvent evaporates. This can result in uneven color.

Painting over new galvanized metal can be a problem. If possible, let the metal weather for a year. The next best alternative is to treat it with a preparation material such as Galva-Grip. Never use solvent-borne paints such as alkyd resins. They will turn into soap on a galvanized surface and lose their adhesion. Use an acrylic or vinyl-acrylic paint instead.

When buying brushes, get nylon bristles for latex. (The high pH of latex will ruin expensive hog-bristle brushes.) Good nylon-bristle brushes can be used for solvent-borne paints, but hog-bristle brushes are best if you can afford them. Also, don't be casual about buying roller covers. Spend the extra money and get quality covers with a nap length to match the surface.

One fear many do-it-yourselfers have is that they will buy more paint than they need. As a result, they often end up a little short.

Assume that almost all paint will cover about 400 square feet per gallon at a normal 4-mil thickness. Latex goes on so easily it is tempting to stretch it too much. For example, you could cover 700 square feet per gallon, but you will need to put on a second coat to complete the job.

The approximate coverage you can expect is usually listed on the paint can label. Adjust these figures for the application method you are using. For brush or roller applications, the waste factor will be about 10% of the paint; with airless sprayers, it will be about 20%, and with air sprayers about 40%. Also keep in mind that rough, textured, or porous surfaces will take more paint than smooth, sealed areas.

Note: For more tips that can save you time and help you do a better job of painting, see Do-It-Yourself Hints, page 144.

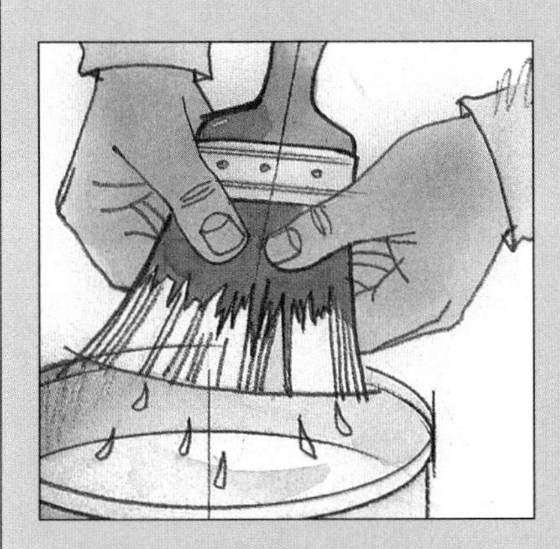

Tips On Cleaning Up

It's best to clean up your painting equipment as soon as you are finished with it. Following is a good general procedure to use:

- To clean brushes used with oil paints, work the appropriate paint solvent into the bristles. Squeeze out as much paint and solvent as possible. Repeat this procedure until all the paint disappears. Give the brushes a final rinse in clear solvent, then wash them in soapy water, rinse, and allow to dry. To preserve the shape of a brush, carefully wrap it in heavy paper.
- To clean brushes used with water-based paints, follow the same procedure, but substitute soapy water for the solvent.
- To clean rollers used for oil paints, remove the roller from the handle and submerge it in paint solvent. When most of the paint has been worked out, wash it in a mild detergent solution, rinse in clear water, and hang up to dry. Use solvent to remove any paint from the handle.
- To clean rollers used with water-based paints, substitute soapy water for solvent.
- Use the correct solvent to clean up equipment. Check the can label. Generally, use mineral spirits for alkyd enamels, acetone for epoxy paints, lacquer thinner for lacquer, water for latex paints, mineral spirits or turpentine for oil paints, alcohol for shellac, and mineral spirits for varnish. Use all appropriate fire, ventilation, and safety precautions. Most solvents except water are flammable, poisonous, irritating to the skin, and produce hazardous fumes. Lacquer thinner and acetone also may damage finishes and dissolve plastics.

Project Helpers

A Half-Dozen Ways To Save Time, Money, And Effort On Your DIY Projects

It's a very good time to be a do-it-yourselfer. Innovative products are coming out of the chute at an exponential rate each year.

Just 20 years ago, for example, plastic plumbing (see page 61) was unfamiliar to many homeowners. Today, plumbing racks are filled with plastic parts that almost make pipe wrenches obsolete.

The annual crop of new products cuts a wide swath, ranging from laser levels (see page 183) to the new slide compound miter saws that are giving radial-arm saws a good run for their money. If you walk into a home center every six weeks, it's likely that you will make a new discovery. But not all the innovations are coming from large corporate R&D departments.

A good example is Gary Green, the owner of Performax Products. In tech school, the idea flashed in his head that there had to be a better way to sand large, flat wood glue-ups. About 10 years ago, he perfected an ingenious, revolving drum attachment for the radial-arm saw that did the trick. He went on to develop stand-alone floor-model sanders, and today his new, smaller bench-top version (see photo below left) is selling like hot cakes.

When looking for ways to ease project work, here's a tip: Don't overlook items hidden away on store shelves without a whit of promotion.

One such item is the nail spinner (under $8) which can make driving brads almost fun. You simply chuck it into your drill, insert a brad, and spin it home. A nail set finishes the job. Besides eliminating blue thumbs and marred work, the spinner makes it much easier to get professional-looking results—which should be the true test of any new do-it-yourself product you buy for your toolbox or shop.

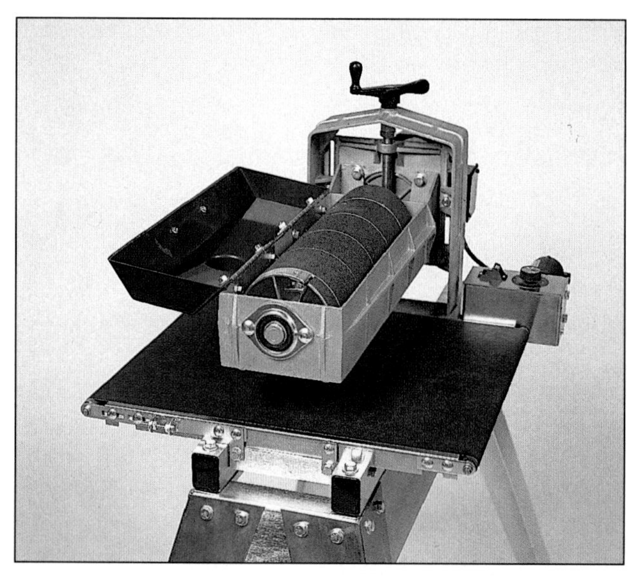

Power Sanding. *This new bench-top sander produces results comparable to industrial-size sanders at a fraction of the cost. The Performax 16-32 mounts on either bench or stand, and its open-end design allows sanding flat stock as wide as 32" in two passes. An abrasive conveyor belt feeds stock through its 5x16" revolving drum which sands to a thickness uniform to .010". Tension rollers allow sanding small or thin stock at a rate of 0′ to 10′ per minute. Multiple cut-outs can be sanded at one time. Write Performax Products, 12211 Woodlake Dr., Burnsville, MN 55337.*

Computer-Age Bits. *Lab tests show that new TurboMax drill bits can drill 1⅓ times as many holes as its leading competitor 28% faster, thanks to computer technology. Computers helped design a special Jet Point tip with sharper, longer-lasting cutting edges, special shoulders for cleaner exit holes, and self-centering points for clean, fast starts. The bits, three years in development, are ground with CBN super-abrasive and have flatted shanks for better chuck grip. They are available in 29 sizes, from 1⁄16" to ½", at tool outlets. Write the Irwin Co., P.O. Box 829, Wilmington, OH 45177.*

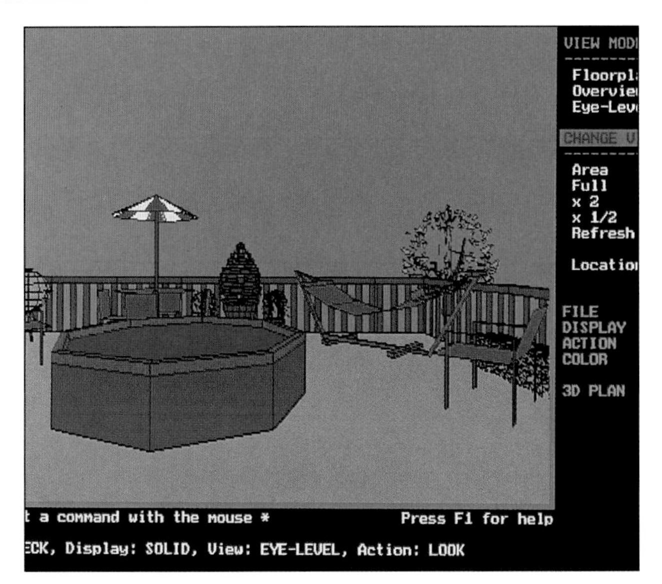

Do-It-Yourself Designs. *Plug this software into a PC and in 30 minutes you can be turning out computer-aided designs for home projects accurate to 1/16". New HomeStyle Release 2 software from Autodesk offers programs for kitchen and bath, decks, and landscapes. Each has a 3-D viewer so you can "walk through" your design before building. The series includes 550 pre-drawn symbols like walls, doors, and furniture. Once a plan is done, the software generates a "shopping list." Programs cost $69.95 and use an IBM PC/XT/AT or compatible computer. Write Autodesk, 11911 North Creek Parkway S., Bothwell, WA 98011.*

Project Camera. *Equipped with two lenses, close-up and 4' to infinity, this JobPro Polaroid has many uses, including project design. Just a few ideas: Identify broken, missing, or unknown parts; keep a record of open walls to show plumbing, wiring, ducts, or buried cable; or create design sketches of remodeling and landscaping ideas you have in mind. By enlarging a picture of the major elevations about five times at a copy center, the bare outlines of the structure will show up without the confusing detail of the original picture. Then, on the photocopy, sketch your proposed design over the basic structure. Available at home centers nationwide.*

Curved Molding. *Curved walls used to be a major obstacle to molding projects. These curved moldings solve the problem. They also are ideal for half- and quarter-circle windows or any radius or curved situation, such as arched drywall projects. Made of high-quality polyester resin, they can be painted or stained to look exactly like wood. Oak graining is also available. Pre-curved molding is made to match all moldings patterns made by Ornamental Mouldings. Write them at 1907 Nuggett Road, P.O. Box 4257, High Point, NC 27263, or call 800/779-1135.*

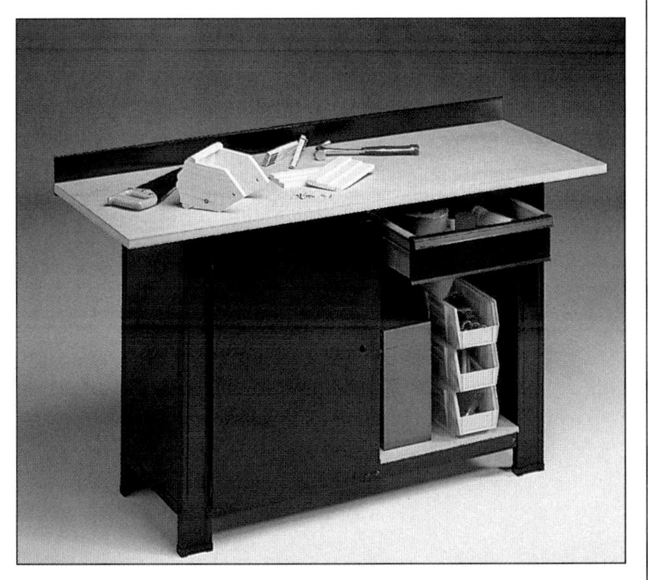

Instant Workbenches. *Help for setting up shops is available with two new workbenches from Hirsh Co. For serious do-it-yourselfers and commercial workshops, the deluxe model comes with a 1"-thick particle board worktop measuring 24x60". The legs of the bench are tipped with rubber non-skid feet. The bench also has a knock-out electrical outlet for power tools. A second, lower-priced bench is also available. The benches join Hirsh's Iron Horse line of benches, saw tables, and shop accessories. At local retailers, or write Hirsh Co., 8051 Central Park Ave., Skokie, IL 60076.*

Do-It-Yourself Investments

OLD HOUSES

Do-It-Yourself Restorations Take Time, Patience, And A Love For The Past

Buying a Victorian or other vintage home is a major decision that impacts not only where you will live, but also your lifestyle. With a stroke of a pen on the purchase agreement, you can be committing yourself to a line-up of do-it-yourself projects that can seem virtually endless.

But if you love the craftsmanship of yesteryear, fixing up an old house may be exactly what you should do. And you won't be alone. Thousands each year make the commitment to love, honor, and fix up structures erected dozens of years before they were born. Asked why they do it, most will answer: "Because they just aren't building them like they used to."

One place where old-home restoration has continued at a fever pitch over the years is Eureka Springs, a town of 2,000 in the Ozark Mountains of northwestern Arkansas. Because it looks much the same as it did 100 years ago, it attracts over a million visitors each year. While less ambitious tourists browse the shops and sip coffee in the cafes, the more energetic clamber up daunting stone streets to admire elaborately painted, lovingly renovated old houses that hug the surrounding hillsides.

Whining saws and clanging hammers echo up and down the valleys as homeowners and inn-keepers (over 100 B&Bs) continue to resurrect history. Some 60 natural springs here had long been known to the Crow, Choctaw, and Osage tribes before adventurer Dr. Alvah Jackson began spreading the word that one of the springs contained magically healing waters. In an age without aspirin or antibiotics, its gurgling pools began attracting relief-seekers by the thousands and the construction of homes, hotels, spas, and stores proceeded at a frantic pace.

Newly-named Eureka Springs became a honeymoon retreat as well as a medicinal spa. New rail service from Missouri and Oklahoma cut through the rugged terrain to reach a trolley line connecting the spas and hotels to various springs. But, unlike other areas of the New West, no sod or log homes appeared here. The settlers included many who had tasted the refinements of city life. With the help of skilled carpenters, masons, and craftsmen from all over the world, they tucked quaint cottages and massive mansions into the hills that slant steeply upward from Spring Street, the town's main thoroughfare.

Today, a century later, a good share of these buildings are listed on the National Historic Registry. But renovating old houses continues to be a major obsession for do-it-yourself homeowners and a cadre of local craftsmen in Eureka Springs, one of whom is Darrell Hoover.

A master carpenter with 20 years experience, Hoover has renovated more than a dozen old houses in the area. "I sometimes wonder how the old-timers did what they did with such primitive tools," Hoover muses. "The results they got with just hand tools are amazing. They didn't have computer printouts or sheaves of blueprints either. Those guys just started to work!"

Tommy Joe Jackson, a journeyman carpenter who has gained a reputation around Eureka Springs for fearlessly walking open rafters, agrees. "Actually the most important skill you need in restoring any old house is patience. Even with modern tools and materials, nothing can take the place of careful work."

Useful advice on renovating Victorian houses is often elusive, observe these craftsmen; vintage houses can be downright quirky, often reflecting the eccentricities of earlier owners. That doesn't stop those knee-deep in restoration projects from offering opinions, however. Some will tell you that many renovations begin as a love story: You see the house and you fall in love with it.

"That's a dangerous way to start out," observes Jo Kennedy, an Oklahoma-raised architect with 30 years experience under his belt. Before buying a building, he suggests it's definitely good procedure to have it checked out by a contractor, builder, or engineer—or all three. He also advises prospective owners to dig into the history of the house by talking with neighbors and previous owners. "Check with the local library and city offices. Even local bankers may have records of earlier renovations of that house."

How much of the restoration can a do-it-yourselfer hope to do? Kennedy says that if it is your first

home, or if you are adding rooms, changing the exterior, or doing anything requiring the approval of local officials, it will probably pay you to hire a general contractor. But if you have some experience, you might opt to act as your own general contractor and subcontract out parts of a major project.

After drawing up plans and getting needed approvals, get bids from subcontractors for plumbing, framing, electrical, drywall, and carpentry. Most subcontractors will provide bids on either a fixed price or a time-and-materials basis. In either case, have them provide a written list of the materials to be used.

Temporary worker's compensation insurance will cover anyone you hire on an hourly basis. But make sure that subcontractors provide you with documented proof of liability and worker's compensation coverage.

The Queen Anne Mansion, photo above, was originally built in Carthage, Missouri in 1893. It was completely disassembled, moved, and rebuilt in Eureka Springs 10 years ago (see following pages). The 12,000-sq.-ft. structure is now a bed and breakfast.

Eureka Springs renovator Priscilla Bowie offers more advice: "As a do-it-yourselfer, you have to be realistic about what you can do," she says. "What you can't do is best left to the experts."

She has been a major force behind the renovation of some of the town's most charming and lavishly decorated B&Bs, among them a "painted lady" once owned by Pearl Tatman, MD, one of the first women physicians in northern Arkansas.

When starting a renovation project using professionals, Bowie suggests you be sure to make space available for stacking lumber and supplies. Also have a first-aid box and a telephone available, and even a rented chemical toilet if it will save time.

"You can help keep costs down by providing cleanup help and trash removal," she adds. "If you plan to live in your house while renovating it, store as much furniture as possible during the project. But remember that it may be necessary to bring large pieces, such as wardrobes and oversize beds, back into the house before the doors and windows are set back in place."

She adds that renovations are much more involved than building a deck. "Plan for as much balance in your life as you can during such extended projects, and figure that even then you will end up working evenings, weekends, and holidays. As a rule of thumb, expect projects to take double or triple the time you originally planned. Renovating an old house is definitely an undertaking for the brave and the patient."

The Ultimate Restoration

The star renovation of Eureka Springs, the Queen Anne Mansion, was originally built in Missouri by wealthy furniture manufacturer Curtis Wright for $22,000. In 1984, every section and piece of the house was numbered, charted, and disassembled for the move orchestrated by master engineer Clay Russell. The mansion required 37 trips in a low-boy truck, and three loads in a covered van. Its roof, of Belgian Gray slate from Pennsylvania, challenged the most fearless of roofers. Finish carpenters, photo left, from as far away as Washington and Michigan, along with six local carpenters, devoted over 15 months to restoring the first two of its three stories.

The original turrets, photo below left, used a series of inside beams, like a ship's hull. Each beam was scored, then soaked to make it flexible, a technique used by old-style wheelwrights. The roof gables of the mansion, photo right, were kept intact during tear-down. The home's hand-carved interior woodwork of oak, cherry, walnut, and poplar, includes seven fireplace mantels and five pocket doors.

Mapping Out The Project

Marvin Hawkins, a Kansas native, is the building inspector and code enforcement officer in Eureka Springs, Arkansas. He offers some ideas on developing a strategy for renovating an older house:

A first priority is to bring that house up to electrical or plumbing code. Rewiring an old house can be a big undertaking. Also, installing safe, efficient mechanical systems—such as the heating and air conditioning—should be a top priority. A potential problem with older houses is the connection between the house and the city sewer lines; work with local building and waterworks departments to check this out. When renovating an old house, plan your attack. The checklist, at left, shows a typical sequence.

Remember that wet paint and sawdust don't mix. Preplanning won't prevent all conflicts or delays but it should help remind you to order critical items, such as special windows and antique plumbing or light fixtures, so they will arrive on time and not hold up the main project.

Flow Sequencing

- foundations and masonry
- framing
- plumbing
- major electrical work
- roofing
- insulation
- doors and windows
- drywall
- electrical fixtures
- finish carpentry
- siding
- final plumbing
- decorating

HOMESTEAD HERITAGE

European Craftsmen Volunteers Help Restore An American Pioneer's Home-Building Project

Not all homes being restored in America are Victorian mansions. Across the country, efforts are being made to preserve all types of architecture. Recently, for example, a homesteader's farmhouse built in the mid-1800s in southeastern Minnesota was resurrected through an international effort involving teams of volunteers from the tiny country of Luxembourg.

Over a period of three years, from 1988 to 1991, groups of master craftsmen used up their vacation time to help preserve a remarkable relic of America's immigrant past—a stone farmhouse built in 1857-59 in a valley of the Whitewater River near the community of Elba.

The home, long abandoned and often vandalized, was physically a wreck but historically a gem in the rough. With 2′-thick stone walls, hand-hewn timbers, square shuttered windows, and unusually low doors (less than 6′), it was a prime example of the kind of homes pioneer immigrants had left behind in the old country.

Begun in 1857, the year John Marnarch and his family immigrated from Luxembourg to these rolling hills, this type of massive, fortress-like house had been built in his homeland since the 1700's. Houses like it are still common there, but in America the style presents a rare type of architecture.

The restoration began when the building came to the attention of the Luxembourg Ministry of Cultural Affairs. In response, the Luxembourg Heritage Society, a nonprofit group, evolved to help preserve early buildings constructed by Luxembourgers in this country. Volunteer craftsmen were enlisted for the project from those who had helped restore about 4,500 other structures in that country over the past dozen years.

Donations from individuals in both Luxembourg and America helped to fund the project, and the townspeople from Elba contributed labor and hospitality as well—all in the effort to preserve a unique piece of international history.

Often pressed for time to protect themselves from the elements, early pioneers usually abandoned European building techniques for more expedient methods. Fortunately, John

Marnarch, previously a stone mason by trade in Europe, saw no reason to change the way a house was built, even if it was located on the new American frontier.

The interior of the home he built also reflected his European heritage, including the stucco/whitewash finish on the walls and the finishing of the wood trim, originally waxed or oiled, then painted with robin's egg blue oil paint.

Two stories high, the structure was built in stages, with a low jerkin roof (a gable with pitched ends) covered by hand-split cedar shingles. In conjunction with the thick limestone walls, John and his son Nickolas used post and beam framing to support roof and floors, all connected by pegged mortise-and-tenon joinery.

The lumber for the framing was hand-sawn from oak trees on their land. Hand-hewn timbers used for indoor window casings still show the original adze marks.

The goal of everyone involved in the restoration, which included the Minnesota Historical Society, was to authentically replicate the condition of the home as it was built, when stagecoaches regularly kicked up dust on the Oronoco Trail just a few short paces away.

The first crew of European craftsmen made major progress in their first three weeks on the project in 1988. Because the west wall was in danger of collapsing, it was dismantled to the first floor level and rebuilt before the rafters and roof were restored.

With reconstruction underway, there were some surprises. Unknown until the craftsmen arrived, the west wall was in danger of collapsing. Before the roof could be restored, the wall had to be dismantled to the first floor level and rebuilt.

Under the home's jerkin style roof, an attic window provided ventilation for the crops that were stored there. A unique feature of the attic was the floor. A 2"-layer of cement was poured over the heavy timbers and planks, most probably to protect the home below if the attic or roof caught fire.

Luxembourg volunteers had repaired all of the exterior surfaces in their first three weeks, including reconstruction of the top half of the west wall, new rafters and roof, new door and window units, and a new coat of stucco/grout sheathing the limestone.

Reinforcing concrete belt-girders are now concealed within the wall's stone coursing to stabilize the structure.

The next job was to repair the exterior surfaces and finish them with new stucco/grout. New doors and windows that had been handcrafted back in Luxembourg were installed next, followed by a new cedar shingle roof. The attic presented a problem, however. A 2"-thick layer of cement had originally been poured there over mud and straw to serve as a place for flailing grains, drying corn, and storing the crops—a practice common in the old country. (It is also thought that the cement attic floor served as a fire barrier in the event that the roof or attic were set fire by Indians.) To prevent further structural damage, most of the cement floor had to be removed.

The original builder of the house is long gone, buried in a plot down the road at Elba in 1900. But Guy Thomas, a contractor and restoration specialist from Luxembourg City who led the first team of ten craftsmen, is convinced the restoration was worth it. After all, he observed at the time, letting a historic structure like this disintegrate would be like throwing away a classic Bentley or Rolls Royce.

The home's floors of wide planking were nailed with cut nails to heavy timber framing. The lean-to at the back of the house, shown above, served as a summer kitchen for the pioneer farmers.

Hand-hewn timbers, below, still visibly bear the marks of the adze that John Marnach used to fashion the window casings of his home.

AN OLD-HOUSE INSPECTION CHECKLIST

Old houses hold many secrets—some of which are better discovered before you sign a purchase-and-sale agreement. This checklist, prepared by the editors of the *Old-House Journal,* takes you step-by-step through a rational evaluation of a home's structure.

It is not meant to take the place of a professional inspection, but it can help you eliminate a few potential purchases yourself. It can also be used for annual maintenance checks by making multiple copies for future use.

When setting out on an inspection, bring a flashlight, a small magnet, a plumbline (a string with a small weight will do), a pen-knife, a marble, binoculars, pad, pencil, and copies of these pages.

Whether you begin with the exterior or the interior of the house doesn't matter, as long as you correlate what you see on the outside with what you see on the inside, and vice versa. As an example, the sagging ridgeline of the roof should prompt you to look closely inside the attic where you may discover missing collar beams.

Give each individual category a grade, from A through F; then assign overall grades to each part of the house. Average these to come up with a final grade. It is impossible to assign an absolute grade in each case—it really comes down to a judgment call. For example, an asphalt-shingle roof in tip-top "A" condition may get a "B" for its relatively shorter life-span.

Don't worry about the absolute value of the grade you assign. More important is your consistency in using the same criteria from house to house. If you are consistent in your grading, the relative value assigned to each house will tell you how they compare with each other.

Note: If you are serious about renovating an older home, the Old-House Journal is an excellent resource. Besides bimonthly issues ($24 per year) the magazine also offers back issues and an extensive offering of helpful books (including Old-House Journal Yearbooks and OHJ Catalogs). For more information, write them at Two Main St., Gloucester, MA 01930 or call 508/283-3200.

EXTERIOR

I. Roof

A. Roofing Materials

1. Type of roof (arranged in approximate order of longevity): slate, copper, ceramic tile, tar and gravel, asbestos tile, wood shakes, wood shingles, galvanized steel, asphalt shingles, and roll roofing.

Note: A sound, tight roof is the first line of defense against the number one enemy of an old house: water. If the roof is in bad shape, you should plan on repairing—or replacing—it right away. Binoculars give you a good close-up view.

2. Pitched Roof: Any sign of missing, broken, or warped shingles or tiles? (This could mean roof will have to be replaced soon. It can also mean that there is water damage inside.)
3. Asphalt Shingles: Are the mineral granules getting thin? Do the shingle edges look worn?
4. Asphalt Shingles: Does roof look new but lumpy? A new roof may have been applied directly over old shingles, with no way to tell what sins may have been covered over.
5. Flat Roof: Any sign of bubbles, separation, or cracking in the asphalt or roofing felt? (Roofing should be flat and tight to roof; it shouldn't feel spongy underfoot.)
6. Any sign of ponding water–either actual water or water marks? (If so, there may be structural deflection in the roof.)
7. Any sign of rusty, loose, or missing flashing around chimneys and valleys? (Flashing is the weakest part of any roof. Copper is the best flashing and will show a green patina.)

Roofing Materials Grade ____

B. Chimneys

1. Is the masonry cracked or crumbling? Is the parging (if any) cracked or peeling?
2. Do the old chimney flues have a tile lining? (If not, they could be a fire hazard in conjunction with wood-burning fireplaces.)
3. Is the chimney leaning? (If so, it may have to be rebuilt.)

Chimney Grade ____

C. Roof Structure

1. Does the ridge or any other part of the roof sag? (This could be normal settling that comes with age, or a result of rotted rafters or other structural problems. Check further!)
2. Is paint peeling badly on the cornice, especially the underside? (This can be a sign of a roof leak that is spilling water into the cornice.)
3. Are the gutters loose, rotted, or missing?
4. Is the attic ventilated with a soffit vent, gable vent, ridge vent, or other type of vent?

Roof Structure Grade ____

OVERALL ROOF GRADE ____

II. Walls

A. Structure

1. Do exterior walls seem plumb? (If you can't tell by eyeballing them, check with your plumb line. Out-of-plumb walls can indicate serious foundation problems.)
2. Sight along exterior walls. Any sign of major bulges? (This could signal major structural flaws.)
3. Do doors and windows line up squarely in their frames? (Out-of-square doors can be a sign of foundation trouble.)
4. Does the siding undulate? (This can indicate differential settlement.)

Wall Structure Grade____

B. Water And Termite Damage

1. Any signs of veins of dirt on exterior walls? (These can be termite mud tunnels. Look for them on foundation, steps, and cellar walls, as well as under porches. Always make purchase contingent upon a termite inspection!)
2. Does wood near the ground pass the "pen-knife test"? (Probe with a pen-knife to test for soundness. Check areas such as cellar window frames, sills, siding, porches, and steps.)

Note: Unsound wood can be caused by either termites or rot. Rot can be arrested by eliminating the source of moisture. Termites call for chemical warfare. If you're at all unsure about the cause of bad wood, call in experts.

3. Is all exterior wood at least 6″ to 8″ above the ground? (If not, you have an inviting target for termites and/or rot.)
4. Is there any vegetation close to the house? (Vegetation holds moisture in wood; be sure to check behind it for rot.)

Water/Pest Damage Grade____

C. Siding, Trim, And Finishes

1. Are there many loose, cracked, or missing clapboards? (This is an open invitation to water and rot.)
2. Are shingles thick and well nailed? (Thin, badly weathered shingles may have to be replaced.)
3. Do shingles have a natural finish? (Natural finishes are easier to re-apply to shingles than paint.)
4. Is decorative woodwork firmly attached to house and tightly caulked to prevent water penetration?
5. Is exterior paint fresh and in good condition?
6. If paint is not new, is it powdering and chalking to a dull, powdery surface? (Chalking paint requires a little extra preparation before repainting.)
7. Is paint peeling, curling, and blistering? (This could be a water problem, either a leak or lack of sufficient vapor barrier.)

8. Are there open joints around door frames, window frames, and trim? (These will have to be caulked.)

9. Are joints between dissimilar materials (e.g., wood and masonry) well protected with flashing or caulk?

10. Is there mold or mildew on siding or trim, especially on north side or other shady areas? (This would indicate a moisture problem.)

11. Has any of the original trim or siding been covered over or replaced with vinyl or aluminum siding? (If so, it could hide rot or other damage underneath.)

Siding/Trim/Finishes Grade____

D. Doors And Windows

1. Do the doors and windows fit properly?

2. Is any of the wood rotted, especially sills and lower rails?

3. Are the doors and windows weatherstripped?

4. Is the glass intact and properly glazed?

5. Are there storm and screen windows/doors in serviceable condition?

Doors/Windows Grade ___

E. Foundation And Masonry

1. Any signs of cracks in masonry walls? (Horizontal or hairline cracks in mortar are usually not a problem; cracks that run vertically through bricks may be more serious.)

2. Is mortar soft and crumbling? Are bricks missing or loose? (Loose masonry is vulnerable to attack by water; having a masonry wall repointed with fresh mortar is expensive.)

3. Are any bows or bulges apparent along walls?

4. Has masonry been painted? (If so, it will have to be repainted about every five years, or else stripped–a major task.)

5. Any sign of spalling, cracking, or crumbling of stonework? (This can be expensive to repair.)

6. Is there an adequate (continuous) foundation, or is the building resting on posts or masonry piers? (A continuous foundation lessens the likelihood of differential settlement.)

7. Is ground water and downspout water properly diverted away from building with correct grading and splashblocks under leaders?

Foundation/Masonry Grade ____

OVERALL EXTERIOR WALLS GRADE ____

INTERIOR

I. CELLAR

A. Foundation

1. Is there a dug cellar with wood sills resting solidly on a masonry foundation well above ground level? (Some old structures have "mud sills": heavy beams resting directly on the ground. These eventually have to be replaced, a major undertaking.)

2. Is mortar in foundation soft and crumbling? (This isn't necessarily serious as long as there is no sign of sag in the structure; ditto for foundation walls laid dry without mortar.)

3. Are there any vertical cracks in the foundation wall? (This could be serious, or it could be from settling that stopped ages ago. Have an engineer check it out.)

Foundation Grade____

B. General Condition

1. Does the cellar smell damp or moldy? (This may indicate moisture problems.)

2. Do sills (the wood beams at the top of the foundation walls) show signs of rot or termites? (Probe with pen-knife.)

3. Any sign of dampness on the underside of floors around pipes? (If leaks have gone undetected for some time, there could be wood rot.)

4. Does basement show signs of periodic flooding? (It is a good sign if current owner stored important tools and papers on the cellar floor. Bad signs: rust spots, efflorescence or mildew on walls, material stored on top of bricks to raise it above floor level.)

5. Any signs of sagging floors, cracked headers or beams, rotted support posts, or jury-rigged props to shore up weak flooring?

6. Is there asbestos board on ceiling? (It is usually identifiable by embossed pattern/texture and manufacturer's name in face of board. If it is there, it must be removed at considerable cost by a licensed asbestos-removal contractor.)

General Basement Grade____

C. Heating Plant

1. Was heating plant originally designed to burn coal? (If so, it is probably more than 30 years old, and may be a candidate for replacement; old converted boilers are usually leaky and inefficient.)

2. Is the fuel tank inside or outside; what is its capacity; what is the condition of the fuel lines?

3. Is boiler encased in an asbestos jacket (whitish-gray, cloth-covered material similar to crumbly cardboard)? Are heating pipes encased in this material? (If so, asbestos may have to be removed by licensed removal contractor.)

4. Does heating system operate satisfactorily? With the owner's permission, run this test:

a. Turn on emergency switch.

b. Move thermostat setting above room temperature.

c. Boiler/furnace should fire immediately after burner kicks on, without any loud initial rumbling or back puffing. Heating plant should run steadily and cleanly; intermittent firing or smoking are not good signs.

d. Look for any obvious blockage or leakage in breaching (flue pipe which leads to chimney).

e. Heat should be evident at hot-air registers in a matter of minutes (forced-air systems).

f. Radiators should warm up in about 15 to 20 minutes (hot-water or steam system).

g. All pipes in a steam system should be pitched back to the boiler; otherwise, system will knock and bang where pipes are improperly pitched.

h. Look for signs of leakage on heating pipes.

i. If you are still unsure about the condition of the heating system, have a heating contractor inspect it and test its efficiency.

5. Is the yearly heating cost reasonable for your budget? (Ask to see a season's heating bill, if possible.)

6. Is domestic hot water heated by boiler or separate hot-water heater? (The best system has the boiler heating water in the winter, and a separate water heater for summer.)

7. Is the capacity of the hot-water heater at least 40 gallons? (This is the minimum required for a family of four.)

8. Are there signs of leakage (rust spots) on the tank?

9. Is the flue in good condition?

10. Are either the hot-water or heating systems multi-zone? (Important in a two-family house.)

Heating Plant Grade ____

D. Plumbing

Check whether the water is supplied from city main, deep well, or spring. If the supply is from a well, it is best to have the water tested; if from a spring, it will probably be necessary to drill a well.

1. Is the water main coming into the house made of lead? (If so, it may have to be replaced.)

2. Is the main shutoff valve functional?

3. Type of distribution piping (arranged from best to worst): copper, brass, galvanized iron, or lead. (Lead pipes should be replaced to eliminate health hazard.)

Note: Use a magnet to test for iron. Detect lead by scratching pipe with a pen-knife to see if it is soft and silvery. If the pipes are brass or copper, look for bluish-green stains, which can indicate that the pipe doesn't have much life left.

4. Is there a gas smell in the cellar? (If so, inspect gas main and distribution pipes for leaks.)

5. Is sewage disposal tied into city sewer? (If you have an on-site system, find out if it is adequate by talking to the last person who serviced it.)

Note: Waterfront properties sometimes dump raw sewage directly into the water. Make sure it is possible to install a legal septic system, and find out what it would cost.

6. Are the waste pipes in good condition and properly pitched? (Look for evidence of leakage, especially at joints. Look for patches or other makeshift repairs. If waste pipes look heavily rusted, tap pipe lightly with a hammer. A ringing sound means the pipe has some life left in it; a dull thump means it is almost rusted through.)

7. Is there a dry well or sump pump in the cellar? (This can indicate water problems in the cellar.) Where does the sump pump discharge? (It should discharge into a sewer, or well away from the house.)

8. Is there a trap and vent where the waste pipe exits to prevent the sewer gases from entering the house?

Plumbing Grade_____

E. Electrical

A 100-amp electrical service is usually the minimum for the average single-family house. A modern panel box will have the rating marked on it. An old fuse box with only three or four fuses may mean there is only 30- to 50-amp service.

Note: Many city codes require that wiring be shielded in flexible cable or rigid conduit, whereas non-urban areas often permit unshielded cable. Get familiar with your local electrical codes, or bring an electrician when you inspect the house.

1. Is power brought in overhead rather than underground? (If so, look for trees or other hazards that could cause problems.)

2. What is the general condition of wiring and the level of competency of the installation? (If there is frayed insulation or exposed wiring, or if the wiring appears to be haphazard and amateurish, have an electrician look at it.)

3. Are all connections made in fully enclosed junction boxes? (This is an essential safety consideration.)

Electrical Grade ____

OVERALL CELLAR GRADE ____

II. FINISHED SPACES

A. General Conditions

1. Are there any signs of damp plaster? (This means leaks, either from roof or internal pipes. Check especially top-floor ceilings, the inside of exterior walls, and ceilings and partitions under the bathrooms.)

2. Is there any loose plaster on the walls or ceilings? (Cracks in plaster are par for the course, but plaster that crumbles or flexes when you push on it will have to be replaced.)

3. Is there a noticeable bounce to the staircase when you jump on it? Are there any noticeable gaps between treads, risers, and stringers? Is the stair pulling away from the wall? (Substantial vibration may mean costly structural problem.)

4. Is flooring original and in good repair? (Floors covered with carpeting or linoleum can harbor many problems, especially if you want to restore the original flooring.)

5. Do floors have a pronounced sag or tilt? (Simple test: Place a marble on the floor and see if it rolls away. If so, the cause could be a serious structural flaw or just normal settling.)

6. Do floors vibrate and windows rattle when you jump on floors? (This indicates inadequate support. Among possible causes: undersized beams, inadequate bridging, cracked joists, or rotted support posts in the cellar.)

7. Windows: Do sashes move up and down smoothly?

8. Do window frames show signs of substantial water leakage? (Look for chipped and curling paint at the bottom of sash and sills. Although quite unsightly, this can be cured with caulk, putty, and paint.)

9. Are bath tile and grout in good condition? (Missing caulk or grout around the edge of a tub can cause damage below.)

General Finished Grade ____

B. Fireplaces

1. Do active fireplaces have an unobstructed flue running all the way to the roof?

2. Does the firebox have a firebrick liner with a 1½′ hearth in front?

3. Is there an operable damper?

4. Is the flue lined with a clay-tile liner to prevent fire and fume leakage into the building?

Note: All of the above are essential for a safe, efficient wood-burning fireplace.

5. Is the fireplace in good cosmetic condition?

6. Clean and inspect all flues and chimneys before using any fireplaces or woodstoves.

Fireplaces Grade ____

OVERALL FINISHED GRADE ____

III. Mechanical Systems

A. Heating

1. Are there enough radiators or diffusers to heat all of the rooms adequately? (Sometimes additions or alterations are made without upgrading the heating system.)

2. Is there evidence of water staining around radiators? (This can indicate radiator leakage.)

3. When you shine a light into the hot-air register, is there any evidence of deteriorating ductwork?

4. Are the steam radiators dead level or pitched toward the condensate return pipe? (A radiator pitched away from the return will usually be noisy.)

Heating Grade ____

B. Insulation

1. Is any sidewall insulation evident? (Look near electrical outlets or other openings into sidewalls.)

2. Type of insulation (arranged from most problem-free to least effective): fiberglass, rockwool, cellulose, foam.

Note: It may be difficult to detect sidewall insulation. Ask the owner, if possible, ask for work receipt.

Insulation Grade ____

C. Plumbing

1. Is there adequate water pressure at the tap? (Inadequate pressure may mean the pipes are full of rust and scale.)

2. Does the water look rusty or smell unpleasant? (If this isn't city water supply, find out what is causing it.)

3. Do toilets or faucets run continually? (If water is allowed to run long enough, it will wear out the fixture and begin eroding the waste pipe.)

Plumbing Grade ____

D. Electrical

1. Are there enough outlets (at least one per wall)? Are they grounded?

2. Do the outlets in the bath have GFCI (ground-fault circuit interrupter) receptacles? (No unrenovated old house will have this type of outlet, but should be added for safety.)

3. Is any surface wiring or regular extension cord tacked to the wall? (These are hazardous conditions.)

4. Are there any pull-chain fixtures? (It is expensive to install wall switches to these fixtures. Note that pull-chain fixtures are not to code in most instances.)

5. Is there a functioning exhaust fan in the kitchen?

Electrical Grade ____

OVERALL SYSTEMS GRADE ____

IV. Attic

A. General Condition

1. Any leaks (such as dark water stains) on the underside of the roof, especially around chimneys, valleys, and eaves?

2. Is the attic adequately ventilated? (Check especially for signs of mildew on underside of roof boards.)

3. Are there any broken or missing collar beams?

4. Are there any cracked or sagging rafters?

Attic Condition Grade ____

B. Insulation

1. Is loose-fill insulation visible between attic floor joists? (This is the best place for attic insulation.)

2. Has insulation been blown into sidewalls? (You may have to take the owner's word for this. In cold weather, you can check wall insulation by feeling the inside of an exterior wall and comparing with the temperature of an interior partition; they should feel about the same.)

Insulation Grade ____

OVERALL ATTIC GRADE ____

FINAL HOUSE GRADE ______

Cinderella Saws

A New Miter Saw Might Be The Next One To Buy For Your Home Workshop

Judging by the talk in power tool circles, the sales of new miter saws are blossoming like the first crocus of spring.

Just within the last dozen or so years, home workshop enthusiasts began to quietly adopt this motorized version of the miter box as part of their shop tool arsenals. Today power miter saws, including the newer slide compound versions, are fast becoming standard fare on tool-buying menus.

Early miter saws got the nickname of "chop saws" because they were built like a circular saw without a sole plate, hinged at the back so they could be pulled down to "chop" a board.

From this humble beginning, today's slide compound miter saws represent the top of an evolutionary chain of engineering improvements. They provide four separate actions (see illustration) which offer clues on how the saws evolved to this pinnacle of sophistication.

The first step in the evolution of the basic chop saw was to attach the power head unit (motor and blade) on a lazy-Susan-style turntable so it could be swung left or right while the fence remained stationary to allow miter cuts. A second step was to arrange for the motor/blade to rotate, allowing a beveled cut.

At this point, the saw's blade could be pulled down to chop, swung side to side for mitering, and also could be angled to make compound miter cuts. This meant that a board could be cut at an angle across its face surface, plus the blade could be adjusted so the cut edge could be made at a beveled angle.

At this stage of development, the saw truly could be called a compound miter saw. But engineers evolved the tool still one step further by putting the power unit on a sliding arm (or arms) so that it also could slide back and forth over the workpiece. With this addition, the saw could cut compound miters on wider pieces of wood and now had evolved to the status of a true slide compound miter saw.

A whole new category of shop saws, light-weight compound miter saws, like this 3-hp Sears 10" model, offer presicion complicated cutting, along with new levels of personal safety.

Miter saws excel at jobs like framing or installing flooring, siding, or cabinets. On the surface, the slide compound saws appear to offer stiff competition for traditional shop saws, such as the table saw and the radial-arm saw. However, even the most expensive miter saws can not rip stock lengthwise. So, for most of the workshop tool buyers, a miter saw serves a supplementary function, with enough advantages to claim a spot in the workshop.

Professional woodworker Russ Barnard observes that, because of their relatively low cost, he could see one or even two miter saws in the well-equipped shop, even if they are used only occasionally at specific locations for basic cut-off work.

Newer miter saws offer excellent guards that move up and down, or collapse as the blade is pulled down

The illustration, right, shows the basic actions of miter saws. You can buy saws with only actions #1 and #2, actions #1, #2, and #3, or actions #1, #2, #3, and #4. Slide compounds offer all four.

into the work. They also offer electronic braking of the blade which stops it almost the instant the switch is released. But perhaps the biggest advantage of the saws is their portability (often less than 50 lbs.) which makes it easy to bring the saw out to a project. (Unfortunately this also makes it easy for your brother-in-law to throw it into his car trunk to work on his project two states away.)

Once you start looking at miter saws, you'll see that the fixed-head saws that offer only mitering (refer to actions 1 and 2 in the illustration) will range from about $125 to $175; compound miter saws (actions 1, 2, and 3) will run from about $175 to $250; and slide compound saws (actions 1, 2, 3, and 4) can cost from about $400 to over $900.

Besides weight differences, you'll find minor variations in the safety features, plus differing design approaches to handles, switches, fences, adjustment controls, and dust collection systems, as well as slight differences in the "feel" of the various models.

Miter saws most often come equipped with combination carbide blades which you may want to replace if you are doing fine woodworking. While miter saws can be found with 6½″, 8¼″, 10″ or even 12″ steel or carbide blades, the 10″ is most common. Because of their sliding action, blade size on slide compound saws is not as critical to the width of cut as it is on non-sliding saws. Most slide compounds with a 10½″ blade will crosscut a board at a 0° setting (straight) at least 2½″ thick and 12″ wide. Set at a 45° miter, the maximum width of cut generally will drop down to around 8½″.

Slide compound saw motors will range from about 9½ to 15 amps. If you plan to use a saw mostly for complicated cuts in thick stock, you will appreciate the most power you can find. Besides motor size, carefully compare the blade size and type, the miter and bevel ranges, the detents for miter and bevel stops, and the accessories that come as standard equipment. Accessories available may include extension guides, work vises, and workstands.

Slide compound saw manufacturers, such as Makita, advise that all work should be clamped to the table before making cuts, so check the vises supplied and how they are used. Extension guides may be worthwhile if you will be doing much on-site cutting of longer boards with the saw. For a miter saw's "home" spot in your workshop, you either can provide a cut-out in a workbench, or build raised supports off the sides of the saw if it is set on top of the workbench.

Howard Silken, Florida power tool specialist and inventor, advises you remember that even slide compound miter saws are "dedicated tools" designed for specific operations. Besides not being able to rip, slide compound saws can't cut panels and they are not designed to take attachments. This means miter saws can't be used for shaping, panel raising, mortising, grooving, rabbeting, beveling, sanding, grind-

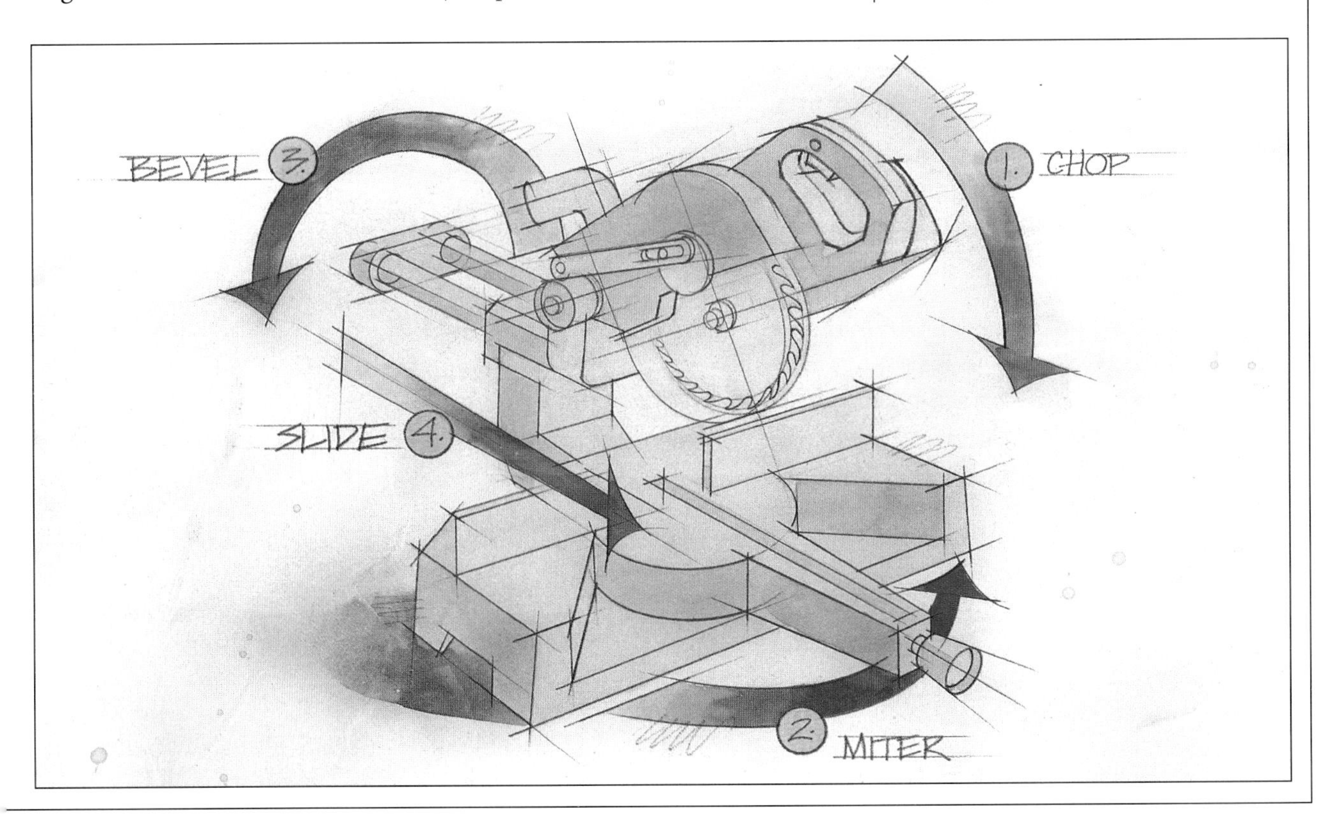

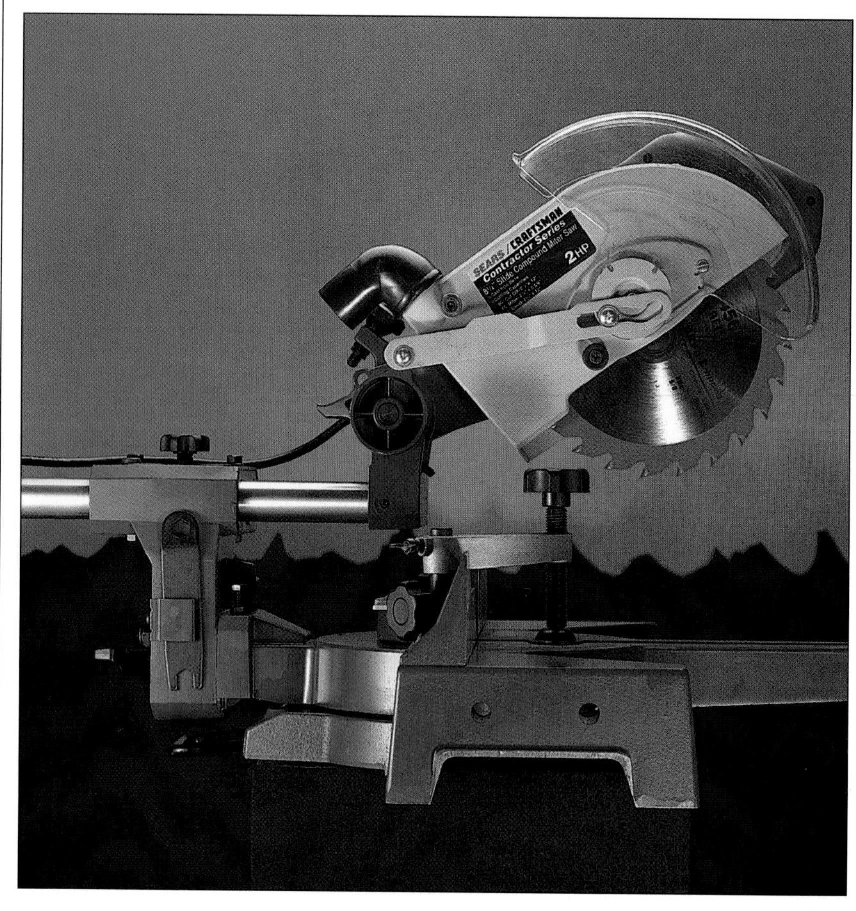

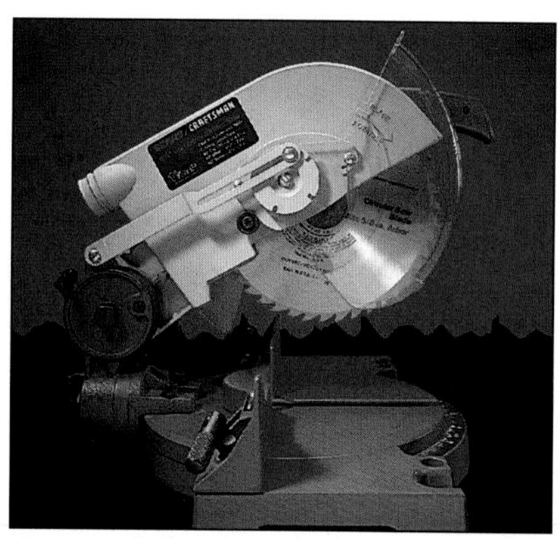

Among slide compounds highly touted are the Sears 2-hp, left, and the Makita LS1011, below. Non-sliding saws, like the Sears 1½-hp above, cost much less.

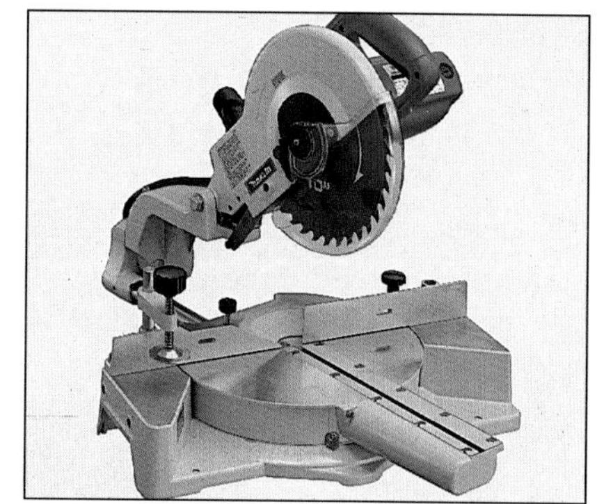

ing, polishing, and other operations that can be done either on a table or radial-arm saw.

He observes that slide compound saws can dado to an extent, but the length of the dado is limited and the operation might be better called "notching." Slide compound saws, like radial saws, tend to "climb." Climbing is when the blade propels itself into the cut as you pull it toward you. It can be reduced on the radial saw by adjusting the drag on track bearings. To help avoid this problem on slide compound saws, manufacturers advise making all cuts by first pulling the saw forward, placing the board against the fence, then making the cut by pushing the blade into the work. This procedure is safer, but can cause more splintering on the board surface.

Manuals for slide compound miter saws offer charts and tables for cutting various types of molding (see next page). On some saws, like the Makita LS1011, this critical data is summarized on a handy stick-on label on the saw.

Silken points out that power brakes on wood-cutting tools have substantially cut down on serious accidents. While brakes on miter saws can stop the blade in a few seconds, all blades act as flywheels and the larger the blade, the more difficult it is to stop.

If a radial saw were braked too fast, the blade would tend to keep rotating after the motor stops. The blade's rotation is the same as is used to remove the retaining nut. After a few stops, this can loosen the retaining nut and the blade can come off. (This is another reason why you should never run a radial saw without the guard on it.)

On most miter saws, Silken observes that the blade is keyed to the jackshaft of the saw by a square, diamond, or "D"-shaped hole. When the jackshaft stops, the blade stops. Some also use special threaded blade retainer bolts that tighten under load. However, they do not eliminate the flywheel effect. Every time you stop the saw, the blade wants to continue to spin. This action puts great pressure on the corners of the blade hole. So if you own, or will be buying, a miter saw with a fast-acting brake, periodically check the condition of the jackshaft driver.

Note: For more about miter saws, two excellent articles include "A Buyer's Guide To Sliding Compound Miter Saws," Mar./April 1993 American Woodworker (33 E. Minor St., Emmaus, PA 18098); and "A Survey Of Compound Miter Saws," Aug./Sept. 1993 issue of Fine Homebuilding (63 S. Main St., P.O. Box 5506, Newtown, CT 06470).

Tech Notes: Using A Miter Saw For Moldings

The miter saw's main purpose in life is the tricky business of cutting trim and molding. Some manufacturers, such as Makita, go to great lengths in their manuals to simplify the process. The following is an excerpt from the manual that comes with the Makita LS1011 slide compound saw equipped with a 10″ blade and 12-amp motor:

Compound cuts on crown and cove moldings can be made with the molding laid flat on the turn base. There are two common types of crown molding, and one type of cove molding (shown below): 52/38° wall angle crown molding, 45° wall angle crown molding, and 45° wall angle cove molding.

There are crown and cove molding joints to fit "inside 90° corners" (#1 and #2) and also "outside corners" (#3 and #4). When cutting crown and cove moldings, set the bevel angle and miter angles as indicated in the first table and position the molding as indicated in the second table.

For example, when cutting 52/38° crown molding for the left-hand side of an inside corner (see position #1 in the drawing), use the following procedure:

- Tilt and secure the bevel angle setting to 33.9°.
- Adjust and secure the miter angle setting to 31.6° RIGHT.
- Lay the crown molding with its broad back surface down on the turn base, with its CEILING CONTACT EDGE against the guide fence on the miter saw.

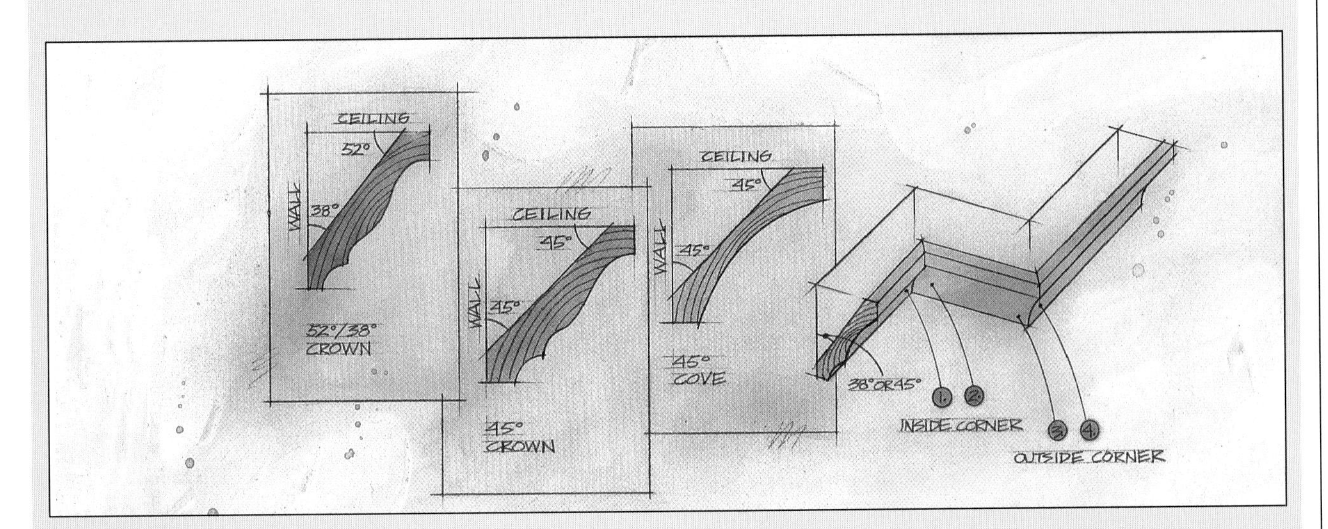

Bevel And Miter Angles

Position		Bevel Angle		Miter Angle	
		52/38° type	45° type	52/38° type	45° type
For inside corner	1	33.9°	30°	Right 31.6°	Right 35.3°
	2			Left 31.6°	Left 35.3°
For outside corner	3				
	4			Right 31.6°	Right 35.3°

Molding Positions

Position		Molding Edge Against Guide Fence	Finished Piece
For inside corner	1	Ceiling contact edge should be against guide fence	Finished piece will be on the left side of blade
	2	Wall contact edge should be against guide fence	
For outside corner	3		Finished piece will be on the right side of blade
	4	Ceiling contact edge should be against guide fence	

Shop Kids

Learning How To Work With Kids In The Home Workshop Is Worthwhile

Some people say that a shop is no place for kids, that it's too risky, too much mess and bother, and it's not worth it.

But there are others who believe that if you have a workshop and children you care about, you might be missing a once-in-a-lifetime opportunity if you lock the shop door on them. They say shop projects are a good way to nurture the creative process in young minds, and instill a valuable sense of pride and accomplishment. In your home workshop kids can gain an appreciation of how technology works, as well as the value of patience, planning, thinking, learning from mistakes, and sticking with a project until it is done.

Children who show an interest in shopwork present a gold mine of opportunity. Welcoming them into the workshop and encouraging their creative efforts can pay off in several ways.

Welcoming kids into the shop is a great way to show them how to use their hands, and that there is more to life than sitting in front of a television set. Working on shop projects can give kids a new direction. It also can help them associate with adults and their friends on a whole different level and can actually change their lives. Once kids find they can make something by themselves, they experience the pride of accomplishment.

Those who have worked with kids in the shop say that the best time to get children involved is between the ages 6 and 12. But, they caution, there can be more to working with kids than meets the eye. Some approaches can turn them off cold to the idea of working on shop projects; other approaches can keep them safe, interested, and enthused.

Which tools kids are allowed to use calls for individual judgments. Small children may be limited to making things out of scrap wood and glue and using sandpaper. As they get a little older, let them use a hammer, pliers, small hand planes, and small twist drills with larger bits.

Be cautious about letting them use sharp tools, like saws or chisels, until they get older. For the most part, ordinary hand tools are fine for kids, but you might consider buying a light hammer (about 10 oz.) that they can handle well. Also make sure you have a good handsaw for them. It can be a turn-off for kids to attempt to use a tool that doesn't work for them.

At about 10 years of age, they could be ready to start using a small power drill or a jigsaw. But age isn't the only factor; you have to judge their strength, height, and maturity. One good rule of thumb is that if they have to stand on a box to use a tool they are too young to use it. (If they slip off the box, they could fall into the tool.)

Kids in their early teens might be ready to use power tools like a bandsaw, radial-arm saw, or drill press, but it depends on their maturity more than anything. As you provide close supervision with all larger power tools, the most important thing to teach them is respect for the tools.

Taking time to make kids comfortable in the shop is worth the effort. Consider making pint-size workbenches, such as the one on page 138, so they won't have to stand on a box to reach yours. Even a couple of sawhorses and an old

"Shopwork can help kids to feel good about themselves and to appreciate the work of others."

door will work.

Also consider making them their own pegboard holders so they have a place to keep their own tools. Insist that if they use a tool, they put it back when they are done with it before doing anything else.

Also agree that once they start a project, they will finish it. Some woodworking dads charge their kids 50 cents a day to use the shop to help them understand that tools and materials are not free. One way to encourage the completion of a project is to say that you won't charge them for the materials once the project is done. Try to minimize competition among kids in the shop and try to suggest projects that get them thinking for themselves. Some other soft touches:

Encourage Originality. Shoot to use shop projects as an antidote for the tremendous pressure kids are under today to conform. Tell them that they can't copy projects from others. If they insist, try to have them alter the design or construction in some way to make the project their own.

Ask for Drawings. Make them draw out what they want to build. This helps them learn to communicate on paper. Also insist that they mark all boards with a pencil to show where they want that board to be cut, instead of just showing you with their fingers.

Don't Push. Don't force kids to work in the shop, and don't force projects on them. If the kids are bored, don't make them stick with it. The more athletic kids may leave the workshop, run around and scream outside, but they will eventually be back to where something is going on.

Avoid Criticism. Whether it is a drawing or a finished project, never criticize. Tell them to do as well as they can, and let them explore and make mistakes. When they make a mistake, try to show them it is not a problem but an opportunity to learn something.

Overall, the key is to get children's interest first, explain the safety factors, then work on the refinements later. Let them go at their own pace, and try to work with them as an equal instead of as a teacher. Also learn to listen to what kids are saying.

Working with kids in a shop is an opportunity for parents to help them develop their self-esteem and personal confidence through creative projects. Sooner or later, kids will find they have unique abilities that are purely their own. As a result, they will not only start feeling good about themselves, but also will begin to learn to appreciate the work of others.

Starter Shop Rule Suggestions

Because shops have inherent risks and dangers, it is a good idea to start off with basic ground rules. Following are some to consider applying to every child entering your home workshop.

1 All tools are on loan for their proper use. This rule will helps prevent arguments over who gets to use which tool and helps kids understand that the tools are not toys.

2 No throwing, no running, and no fast moves in the shop. Make an agreement that rough-housing is for playing outside, and also that no tools will go out the shop door.

3 No switches are touched or turned. Explain that switches are off limits; however, show kids the function of each larger tool, its dangers, and where they can safely stand when tools are operated.

4 The code words are "Take It Easy." With this rule, if you see kids working too fast or roughly in the shop, you can simply ask what the code words are to remind them.

5 No new tool is used without permission. Until kids are about 16, it is best not to allow them to work with shop power tools unless closely supervised.

6 All kids should wear eye protection and tucked-in, short-sleeved shirts. Also insist that they put long hair up in a hat, away from machinery, and that they don't wear jewelry.

WASTE DISPOSERS

Advice On How To Remove And Replace Yours When It Goes On The Blink

The evening before Thanksgiving, everything is going fine getting the big meal started. Twelve famished relatives are expected, and then the sink starts backing up. The waste disposer has quit.

A quick phone call to an appliance dealer reveals you might have to pay top dollar for a new disposer, plus $75 for the installation. But the problem is that they can't intall it until the following Thursday. Another call to a home center informs you that plenty are in stock, and some are even on sale. You decide you could replace it yourself.

Should you start ripping it out right away?

Replacing an existing waste disposer (also called a garbage disposal) can be relatively easy, provided everything else involved goes well. The problem is primarily one of timing; whenever you start dismantling older plumbing, it's best to allow plenty of leeway, including an extra hour or two to make unscheduled trips to buy parts, should it become necessary.

It's also preferable to tackle the replacement during daylight hours. You'll be able to see better under the sink, especially if you need to turn off all the power using the main shut-off switch.

Rather than starting the project with time limits, you will be better off scraping by until after the holiday, then tackling the replacement when you have a full day free of distraction, a day when the stores are open.

The tools needed are minimal; you probably have all you need except perhaps some plumber's putty in case you need to install a new mounting ring. Extra trips to the home center, however, may be necessary to buy new drain pipes and connections. Often you won't know what you need until you are in the middle of the project.

Where to begin? The easiest project is a direct replacement, using a new unit of the same dimensions. If you upgrade to a bigger, better (and more expensive) disposer, you will most likely have to alter the drain pipe arrangement.

Most newer units have the same type of mounting system. If the unit you are replacing is less than 12 years old, chances are good that you will be able to use the old mounting assembly, unless the rubber shield inside the strainer assembly is worn out, or unless you want to update it.

Before leaving to buy a new disposer, double check to see if the old unit is not dead, but just overloaded or simply jammed. If the disposal is jammed, then first try to find the cause and, if possible, remove the blockage with tongs. Wait five minutes, then push the small red re-set button on the bottom of the unit.

If the disposer still doesn't work, do some further checking at the service panel. Check for, and replace, any blown fuse, or reset any circuit breaker that has been tripped. If, when you flip the wall switch on for a second, the disposer buzzes, but still won't move, try to unjam it by turning off the switch and inserting the disposer's service

A defunct waste disposer, like a dishwasher, can leave a kitchen limping. Besides a new unit, you'll need only minimal tools and supplies to make the replacement.

wrench into the hex-shaped hole at the bottom. (If you can't find the wrench, use a 1/4" Allen wrench.) Work it back and forth until the disposer moves freely for a complete revolution. Make sure the motor has cooled down, then remove the wrench, press the re-set button, and turn on the wall switch for a second or two.

If it still doesn't work, you can take more aggressive measures. Sometimes a small object, such as a bobby pin, paper clip, or fruit pit can cause a jam so tight the service wrench can't handle it. Insert a prybar into the disposer so the end is alongside the grinding protrusion near the outside edge of the grinding disc. (Before applying pressure, check that the bar is on the correct side of the protrusion so the disc will move in the normal direction.)

If these emergency measures don't work, replacement may be the only answer. If you plan a direct replacement, take the critical measurements as shown in the drawing. Also make a sketch and measure the rest of the drain piping. Take along a tape measure and, at the store, check the old disposer measurements against the display models. If units aren't on display, ask if you can open a box to look at the owner's manual which will likely list the measurements for all models from that manufacturer.

The first decision is which model to buy; prices may start as low as $40 and increase to $175 or more. Warranties for low-end models will generally be one year, and increase by an additional year for each model up the line.

However, before you leave the store, think through another decision: whether you plan to add a P-trap immediately next to the disposer that will then be connected to the main drain pipe assembly under the double sink. The main drain pipe should already have a P-trap installed.

Your old disposer may be simply connected to the main drain with a straight horizontal pipe. Manufacturers recommend the extra trap, which connects directly to the discharge tube at the side of the disposer. Once you have the new unit and other plumbing supplies you think you'll need, you are ready to clean out under the sink and get to work. If the cutting elements on your old disposer were worn and not grinding well, the drain line may be partially blocked. If there is a chance of this, you can use a drain auger to clean out the pipe.

Removing. Before starting the job, turn off the electrical power at the service panel. Use a pipe wrench to disconnect the drain line from the disposer, and a screwdriver to disconnect the clamp holding the dishwasher drain tube. Next,

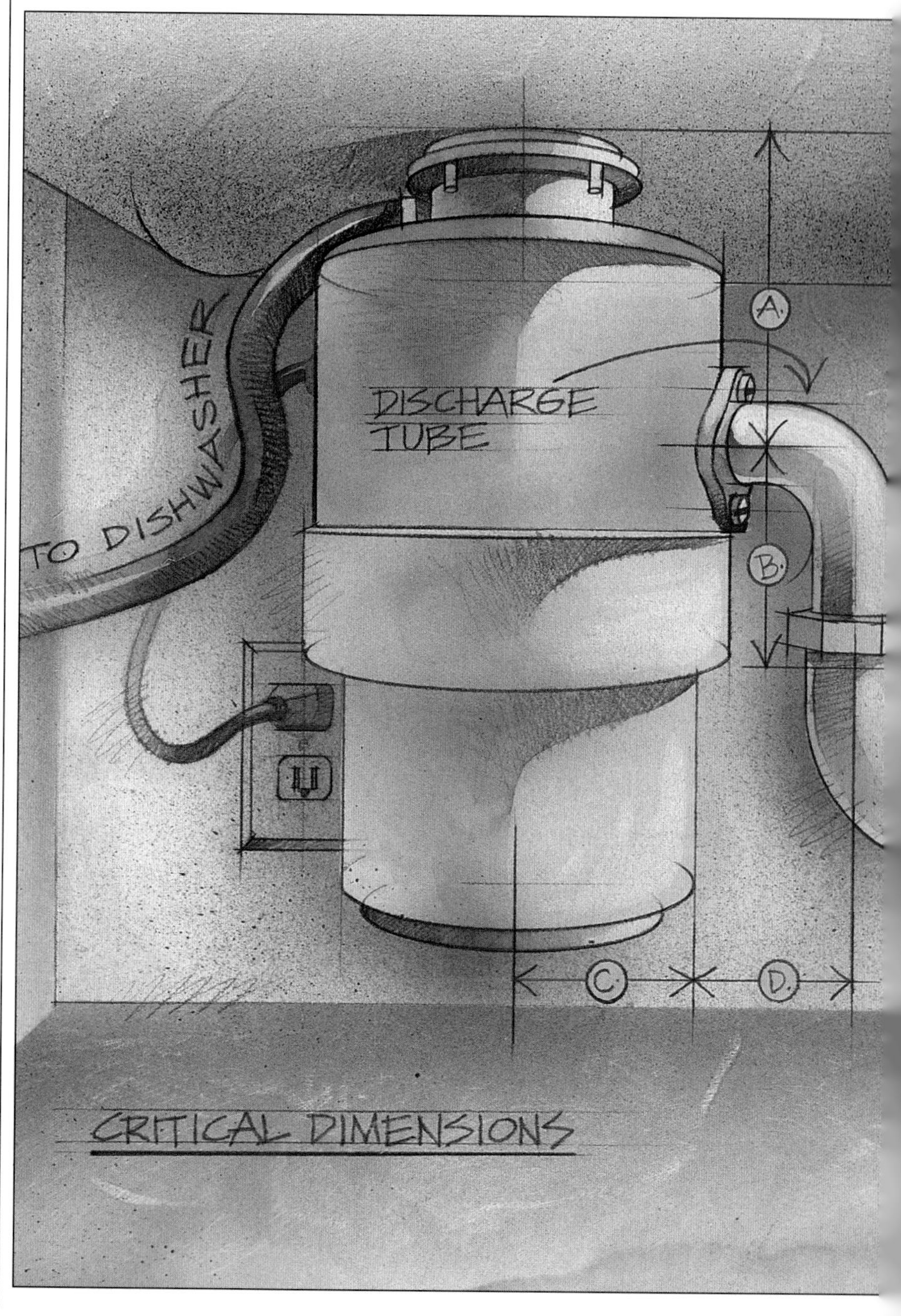

disconnect the old unit from the mounting under the sink. If your new disposer has the same mounting, you can leave the old assembly in place. Insert a screwdriver into the right side of one of the mounting ring lugs at the top of the disposer. Then turn the mounting ring counterclockwise until the lug lines up with one of the sink mounting assembly screws.

(Caution: The old disposer will fall when released, so be prepared to hold it up or else prop it up with something sturdy.)

Once the old disposer is unhooked, turn it upside down and remove the electrical plate. Make sure the power is off. Remove the ground wire, then the electrical wire nuts from the wires. Separate the disposer wires from the cable wires, then loosen the cable clamp and remove the cable. The old disposer will now be free and can be taken out and discarded.

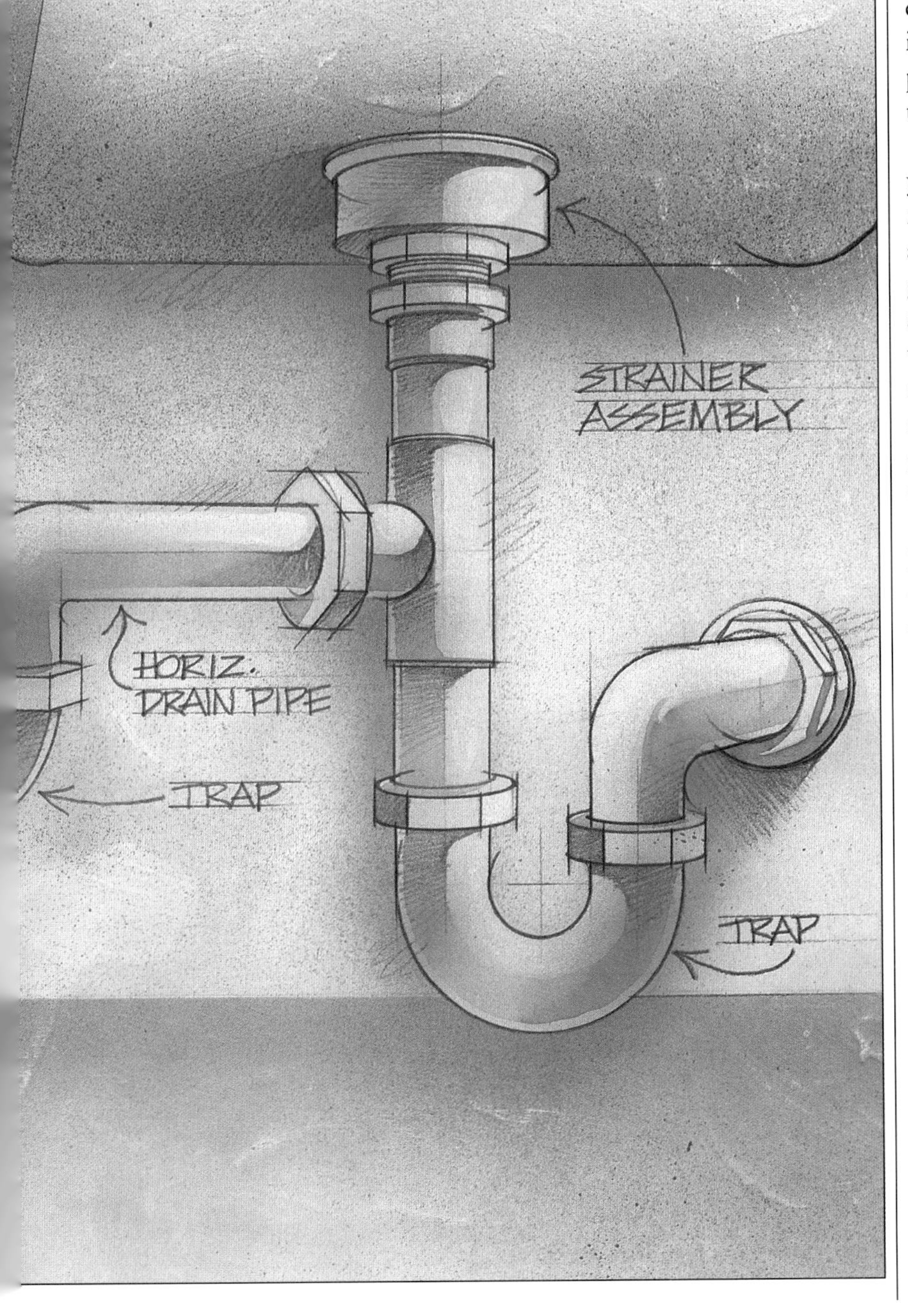

Rewiring. To install the new disposer, first make the electrical connections. (If you need to replace the mounting assembly under the sink's opening with the new one that came with the disposer, instructions included will tell you how to do it.)

Manufacturers recommend running single 15- or 20-amp 120-volt circuit to the disposer. Reconnect the wires from the switch to the new disposer (white to white and black to black) using electrical wire nuts. Wrap the connections with electrical tape and push the wires inside the housing. Check for proper ground, then replace the electrical cover.

Note: If the wiring system in your home is older and the cable running to the disposer has a metal exterior, the unit should be grounded, provided the entire system is grounded to a metal cold water pipe. If not properly grounded, an electric shock hazard may exist. Don't reconnect the electrical power at the main service panel until a proper ground is made.

If the circuit is of plastic-covered, Romex-type cable with black (hot), white (neutral) and bare (ground) wires, simply attach the bare wire to the green ground screw on the unit. If there isn't a ground wire in the cable, buy a length of copper wire at least the size of the other wires, and attach one end to the green ground screw on the unit. Then attach the other end of the ground wire to a metal cold-water pipe using a UL-listed ground clamp.

Don't ground to a gas supply pipe. Also make sure the pipe used is continuous metal from the sink to the ground. If any non-metal pipe is used in your home water connections, or if plastic pipe is used in the water supply piping, you will need a qualified electrician to install a proper ground. If you have a water meter, also check to see that there is a wire that goes across it. If there is no wire, the cold-water pipe may not be grounded. In this case, and for any other electrical questions, seek help from qualified local experts.

Remounting. After the wiring is done, lift the new disposer so its three mounting ears are lined up under the ends of the sink mounting assembly screws. Then, while holding the unit in place, turn the ears to the right (clockwise) until all three are engaged in the mounting assembly. At this point the disposer will hang by itself. The ring can be locked later, after the plumbing connections are made.

If the old disposer had a straight horizontal pipe running from it to the main drain pipe, and you don't plan to add a second trap, you can reconnect it. If the old unit had a trap next to it, or if you are installing a new trap, the next step is to attach the discharge tube to the new disposer.

On some models you first insert a rubber washer in the discharge opening, then slide a metal flange over the discharge tube and tighten it in place using bolts. On other models, a gasket is first installed onto the flat lip on the discharge tube. Then a metal flange with a hook on one side and a bolt hole on the other is placed behind the gasket to fasten the tube.

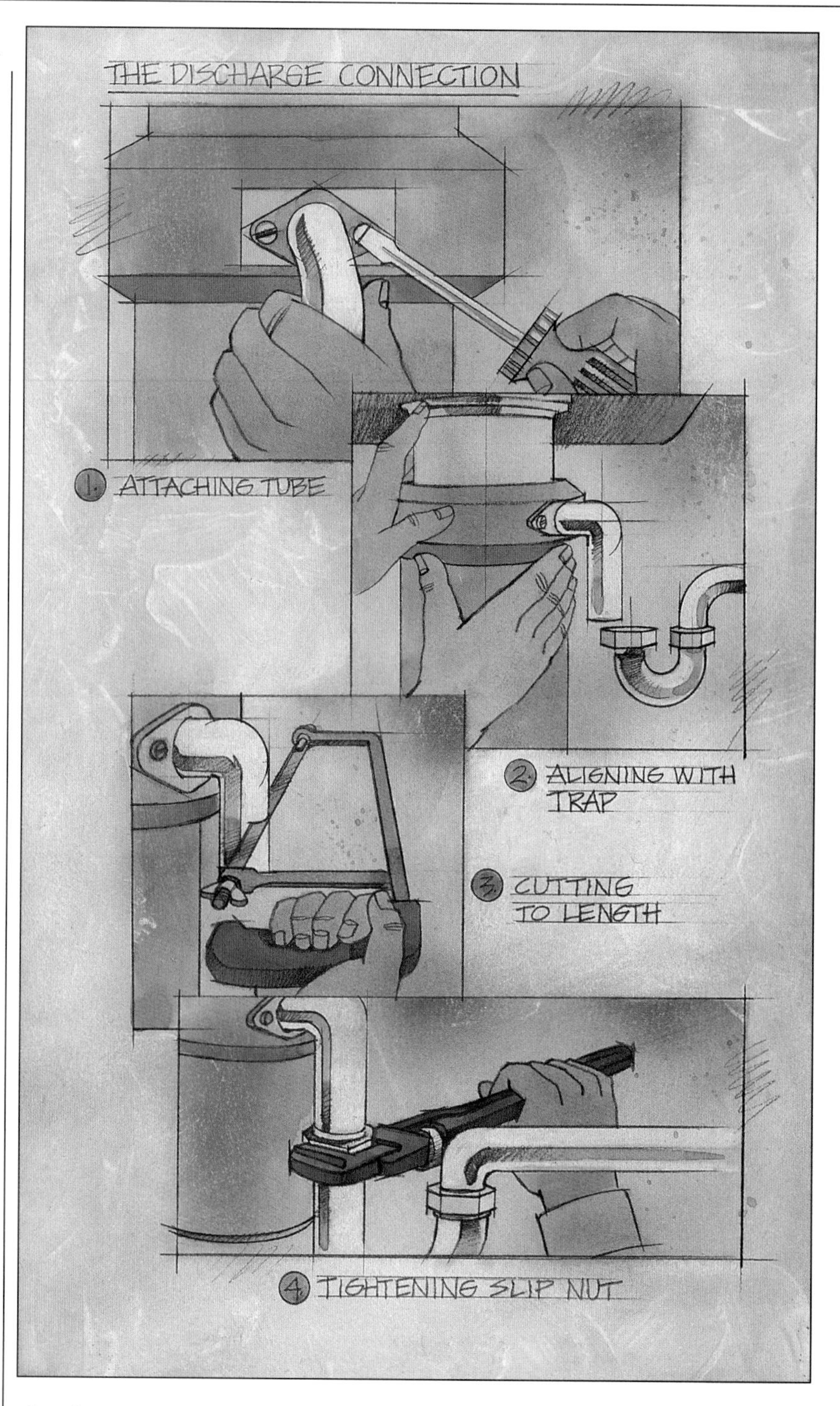

If the new discharge tube is too long to allow the trap to come up high enough, just cut it to length with a hacksaw. If it's too short, buy a drain trap extension that includes a slip nut and add it on. When connecting the drain system, it's a good idea to check the condition of all the pipes and replace those in questionable condition. After reconnecting the rest of the drain piping, lock the disposer into position. Put a screwdriver into the left side of one of the mounting ears at the top of the disposer, then turn to the right until the unit is firmly locked.

The last step is to check for leaks. Slowly run water through the unit. Next, put the stopper in seal position and fill the sink with water. Pull the stopper and let the water run out. If there are no leaks, the installation is complete.

Keep in mind that with continuous-feed disposers, cold water should be run at full flow whenever the disposer is used. To avoid blockages, always turn on the water full force before starting the disposer. and continue to run the water after grinding to flush all material away.

WONDER TOOL

The Router Can Catapult Your Shop Projects Into Professional Ranks

Router expert Patrick Spielman is convinced that the router is a low-cost tool anyone can learn to use and the key to making your home projects look more professional. Good routers start as low as $75 and major brands incorporate most of the features you will need.

The portable router has become a must-buy tool for even the sparest of home workshops. Routers use high speeds, ranging from about 8,000 to 25,000 rpm, to produce a very smooth cut which usually requires little or no sanding. A router can both cut and shape, and also can do the work of a lathe or shaper. It can be used for beading, fluting, grooving, routing, and carving on the surface of a board or panel, as well as for other decorative inlay work. With accessories, it can make dovetail joints, rabbets, dadoes, and tenons, or it can be used to trim laminates and veneers, to mortise door hinges, or for planing.

The motor housing has handles and a base which rests on the work, or it can be fastened to the underside of a router table. Handles can be of the arm, D, or knob type. A collet holds the router bits. If possible, buy a router that accepts bits with both ¼″ and ½″ shanks which are less likely to bend. The motor, usually from ⅓ to 1½ hp, is adjustable within the housing to control cutting depth. Depth adjustment may be accomplished through rack-and-pinion, spiral, ring, or plunge mechanisms.

Plunge routers, which make cutting in the middle of a surface easier, have become popular. Plunge depths can range from 1⅜″ to 3″. Higher horsepower and variable speed control, available on many routers, are valuable when cutting with bits over 1½″ in diameter in tough materials.

An important design consideration is the switch type and location.

The router, some shop owners say, is the handiest tool they own. It typically ranks right after drills and circular saws in tool sales volume.

TECH NOTES: TIPS ON PUTTING A ROUTER TO WORK

■ CONSIDER A TABLE

When you buy a router, also consider buying a router table or building your own. (Plans are available through companies and publications.) A table with a router attached to its underside effectively becomes a stationary shop tool. Router tables can be found for as low as $50 and many incorporate safety features such as see-through swing-away guards and hold-downs for edgework.

■ HOLDING SMALL PIECES

For edge-routing, you need to keep work from slipping and causing kickback. One of the best, quickest ways to hold pieces too small for clamps is simply to fasten them with hot-melt glue onto a larger piece of scrap plywood clamped to your workbench. The trick is to use short beads of the glue. It will hold, but not penetrate, so it can be cleaned up with a chisel. On other work you can use router mats, which resemble carpet padding, or rig up a frame-type holding fixture.

■ SURFACING SET-UP

Routers can be used to level rough-cut slabs, but this can be difficult if you don't set up correctly. Build a box frame (see illustration above) and attach an extended base to your router. This can be just a board long enough to fit over the frame on all sides. The box will keep the router bit at a uniform level above the work if the wood is secured so it doesn't move. You also can make the ends of rough-cut logs perfectly flat and parallel by using a box frame built up so that the log can stand on end.

Switches can be rocker, slide, toggle, or trigger types. Better routers have precision adjustment for depth control, a light to illuminate work in progress, and a dust pick-up attachment. Accessories worth looking at include edge guides, guide bushings and adapters, and guides for cutting circles and curves. Routers can weigh as little as 5½ lbs., or as much as 12 lbs.; more horsepower generally adds more weight. Light-duty routers will cost about $75 or less, while heavy-duty models may cost $275 or more.

Once you get a router, advises Spielman, locate a local service that can sharpen your carbide router bits. The shop should also be able to re-tip carbide bits and sell you ball-bearing guides. Above all, he emphasizes, the idea is to enjoy producing work with the router. Wear goggles or a full-face shield, and good hearing protection.

Try to keep the base waxed and free of pitch and gum. You can use lacquer thinner on a small cloth (with good ventilation) to clean your bits, or keep your bits in a jar of all-purpose household cleaner, such as Fantastik, to dissolve pitch and grime. If you prefer not to fish for bits in a jar, keep router bits in a drawer, all standing on end.

Always unplug the router before making adjustments or changing bits. After making adjustments, first trigger the router for a quick rev-up. If anything is wrong, you will find out before beginning work. Always start the router in the air, not in the work. If you lay it on the

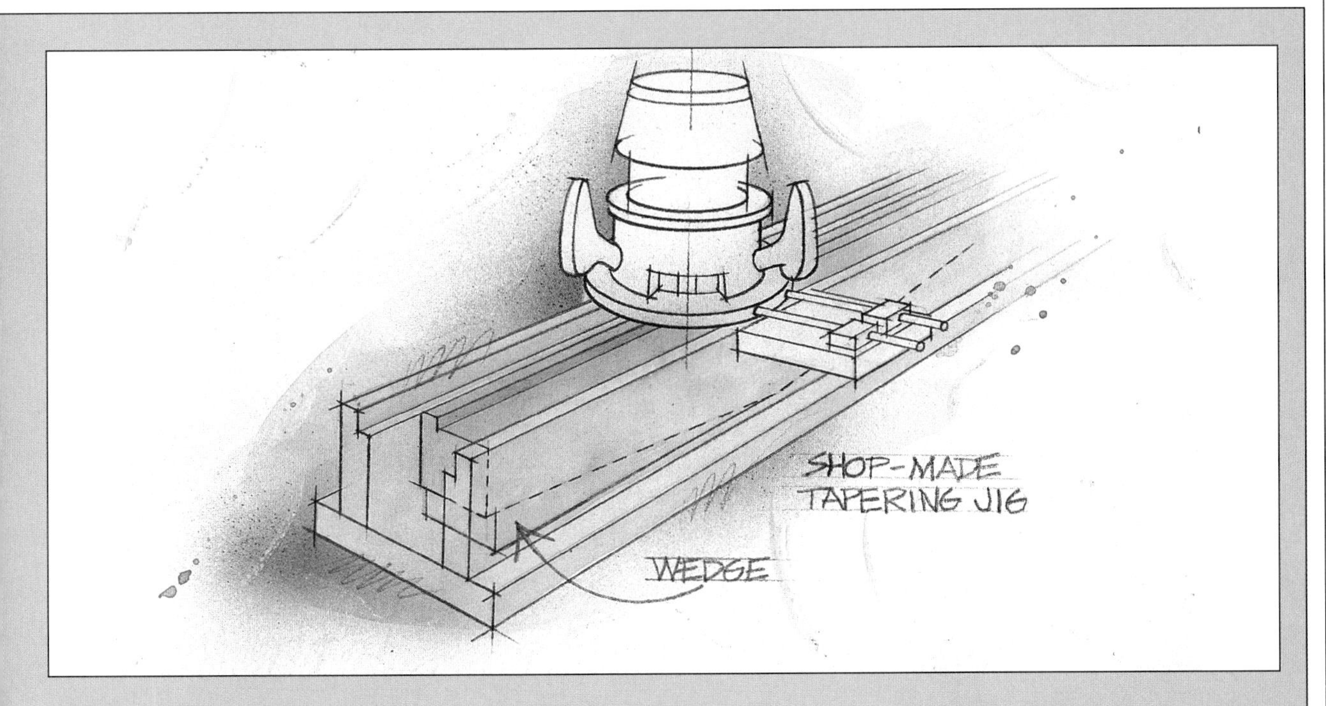

■ Rabbeting Shortcut

Routers are great for machining joints and construction details. Basic case and box construction requires various rabbet joints (cutting out a section on the edge of the material). For many jobs, you can make the rabbet cuts for the box bottoms and cabinet backs after assembly. You can use a ball-bearing-guided rabbeting bit that leaves the inside corner rounded. These can then be chiseled square, or the corners of the bottom or back can be rounded to fit.

■ Router Tapering

You can set up a similar device with wedges to make taper-cut surfaces, as shown in the illustration above. Mark the small end of the piece with layout lines, and wedge the piece up until the bit matches the lines at both ends of the tapered surface. Then run the router over each of the four tapered surfaces. The same kind of device can be used to cut flutes or other surface decoration into the tapered surfaces.

■ Freehand Routing

Once you learn to use the router freehand, you will find less need for templates and patterns. Start on scrap and make sure you can see the bit and the area around the cut. Remove the sub-base of the router to open up the viewing area, or buy or make a clear plastic sub-base. Proper position is important: Clamp the work well in from the edge of the workbench so you have to reach for it. This forces you to put your arms on the bench and/or the work (if it is large).

work, you will be trying to cut in only one revolution instead of several thousand. Don't try to work very small pieces, especially on a router table. Secure small pieces for edge routing with clamps, nails, or hot-melt glue. To avoid splitting on edge work, do the end (across the grain) edges first. Then do the sides.

Experiment on scrap pieces to find the right feed rate. The feed rate on end grain will be slower than that with the grain. Feed the work against the rotation of the cutting blade, which is clockwise as viewed from above the router. This means moving the router counterclockwise around the work on the outside edges, and clockwise around the inside edges. Don't use the wood to stop a coasting blade. Let the router stop by itself, up and away from the wood.

Also find ways to control dust and chips. Breathing sawdust is unhealthy. Sawdust also hinders accuracy by building up under the router, or between the router and a straight-edge or stop. Investigate router vacuum attachments, or rig up your own system.

Router owners seem to agree that Patrick Spielman's *The Router Handbook* is the benchmark router reference book; it has sold over a million copies. A new, expanded paperback edition, called *The New Router Handbook*, is just out. The $16.95 book is available at woodworking and book stores, or it can be ordered from Sterling Publishing Co., Two Park Avenue, New York, NY 10016.

SEARS / CRAFTSMAN
8¼" RADIAL SAW
10"
Direct Drive
10 15 20 25 30 35 40 45
DANGER
2.5HP

Shop Spaces

A Sampling Of Ideas On How To Set Up A Workplace Of Your Own

Most experienced do-it-yourselfers will tell you that setting up your own home workshop can be a life-long pursuit, a slow but steady accumulation of tools and know-how over many years.

However, if you have always wanted to set up a workshop of your own and never had the time or money, it is never too late to start, advises a new 192-page handbook published by Meredith Books.

Called *The Home Workshop Planner*, the colorful guide was assembled by how-to editor Gene Schnaser, with the help of major tool companies and more than a dozen home workshop experts. Russ Barnard, a veteran fine woodworking specialist, served as technical editor.

Improvising and adapting are keys to setting up a dream workshop like this one, says Russ Barnard, who helped design five levels of ideal home workshops for the new book.

Achieving the shop of your dreams, according to the book, involves four basic stages: 1) selecting the workshop space, 2) physically setting it up, 3) equipping it with appropriate tools, and 4) learning the basic techniques that will help you get the most from your investment.

Studies show that roughly 45% of workshops are set up in garages, about 30% in basements, and about 25% in separate buildings. Often a low-cost way to find shop space is to add on to the front or back of a single-car garage, or to double its width by cutting it in half lengthwise, moving one side over, and then filling in the middle.

A full complement of major workshop tools can cost $6,000 or more. However, functional shops can be assembled for $1,500 or less.

Where to start? The space you allot for tools will depend primarily on two factors: the space available in the area you choose, and the largest boards you would like to handle without moving tools. For average woodworking, the longest boards handled generally will be 6′ or 8′, and the largest sheet or panel will be 4x8′. You can allocate tool spacing to accommodate these sizes, or you can cut materials down before they are brought into the shop.

The floor plans on the following pages show a sampling of the diverse workshop arrangements possible; they confirm that no matter what kind of space you have available, something can be done with it.

Besides the layouts shown here, *The Home Workshop Planner* also includes specific floor plans, designed by Russ Barnard, for five home shops of increasing complexity:

1) an 8x12′ Start-Up Workshop you could set up in a basement room or on a garage end wall. Total tool budget is under $500;

2) a nice 14x20′ Homeowner Workshop that could either be in the basement or in a single-car garage using a tool budget of less than $1,500;

3) a nicer 22x24′ Woodworker Workshop set up in a large basement room or in a two-car garage with a tool budget of about $3,750;

4) a 24x32′ Craftsman Workshop, best set up in a three-car garage or in a separate building using a tool budget of about $7,750; and,

5) a 26x36′ Professional Workshop best set up in a separate building with a tool budget of $15,500.

A good way to think about a workshop investment is to compare it to buying cars. An adequate workshop might cost about the same as a decent used car, while a top-of-the-line shop with the best of everything, fully equipped with accessories, might cost about the same as a quality new car.

The new guidebook provides extensive tool and accessory buying menus that recommend specific tools for each workshop and show what they cost. Spaces are also provided so you can draw out your own shop arrangement and pencil in your own tool-buying budgets.

Russ Barnard emphasizes that planning a workshop often requires a "best information at the time" approach. "While it is difficult to foresee the future," he says, "the best way is to start now, plan out as much as you can, and keep your plan as flexible as possible."

He suggests considering the workshop as a major tool in itself, one with many components that can be arranged one way, tested, then rearranged and refined several times over the years ahead. "A workshop is a means to an end, not an end in itself. Like a car, consider it a vehicle to help you get where you want to go. The goal is to have a shop that serves your needs efficiently, safely, and conveniently."

Note: "The Home Workshop Planner" also contains special sections of buying tips for all major shop tools, including stationary (floor-model) tools, benchtop tools, combination tools, portable power tools, as well as what to look for when buying used shop tools. The book, priced at $24.95, is available at bookstores, home centers, and woodworking supply stores. If you can't find a copy, you can write Meredith Books, 1617 Locust, Des Moines, IA 50309-3400.

Of the hundreds of suggestions in *The Home Workshop Planner*, Barnard says one stands out as most important: If you don't start projects out right, you can't finish right.

"As soon as you can possibly afford it, get the tools that can help you size and true up lumber, such as a planer and jointer. By having this equipment, you will be able to wait to bring dimensions down to size as a final step, allowing you to keep lumber oversized throughout the gluing process so you don't have to worry about clamp marks and glue spills."

Another major guideline is to keep as many work surfaces as you can at the same height, matched to the height of saws, planers, or jointers. "Keeping assembly benches and worktables all at this height," says Barnard, "will eliminate the need for extra outboard support when handling long pieces of lumber."

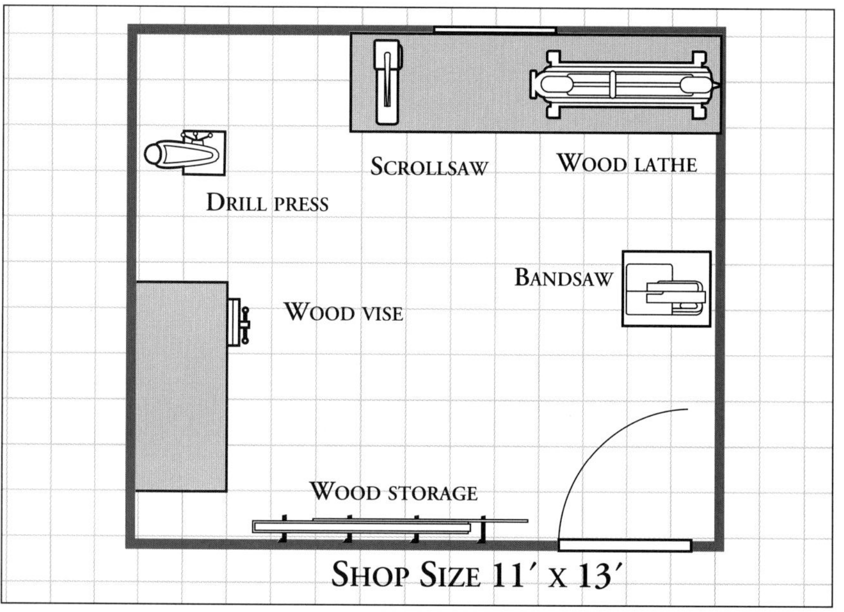

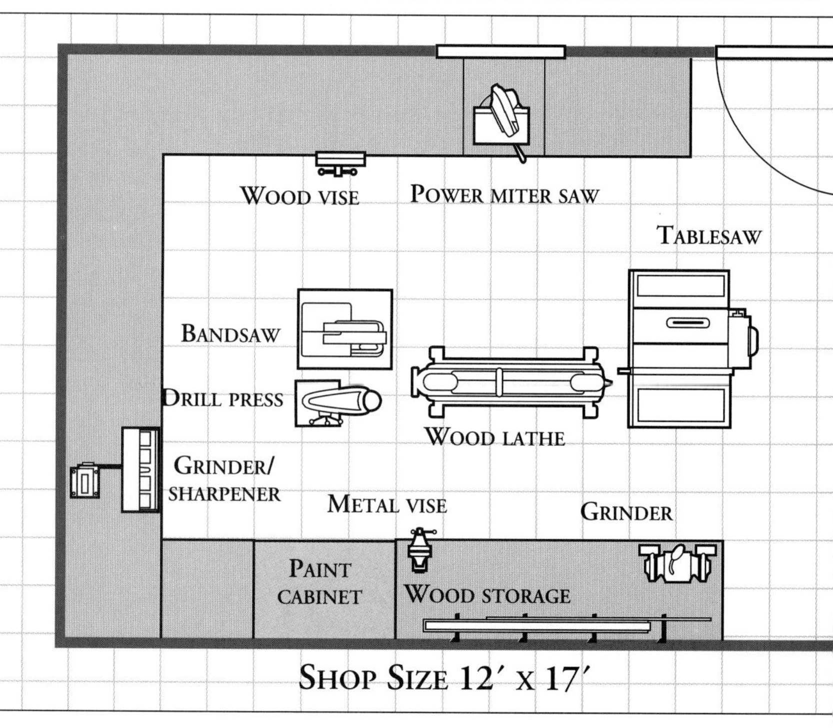

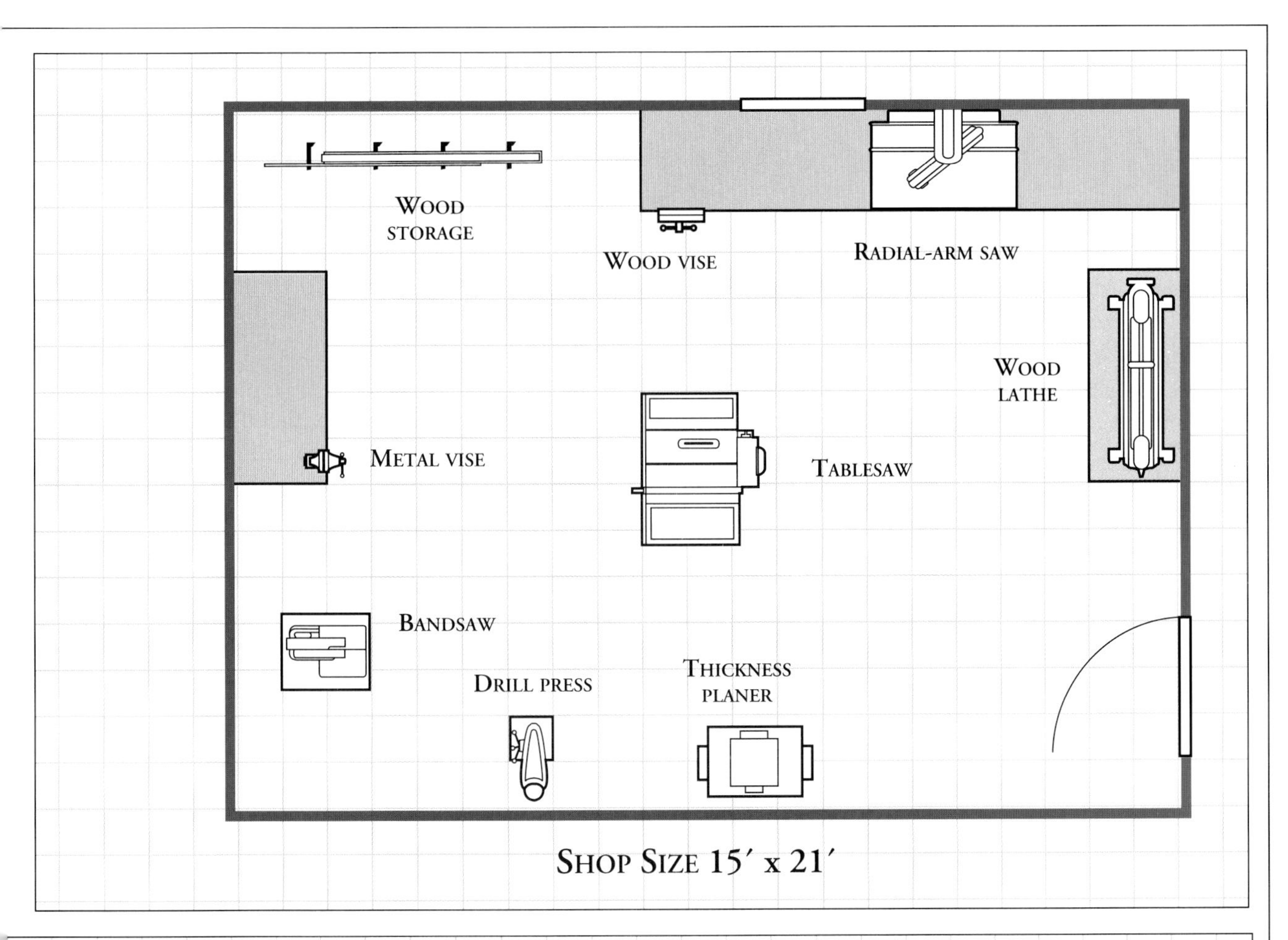
Wood storage
Wood vise
Radial-arm saw
Wood lathe
Metal vise
Tablesaw
Bandsaw
Drill press
Thickness planer
Shop Size 15′ x 21′

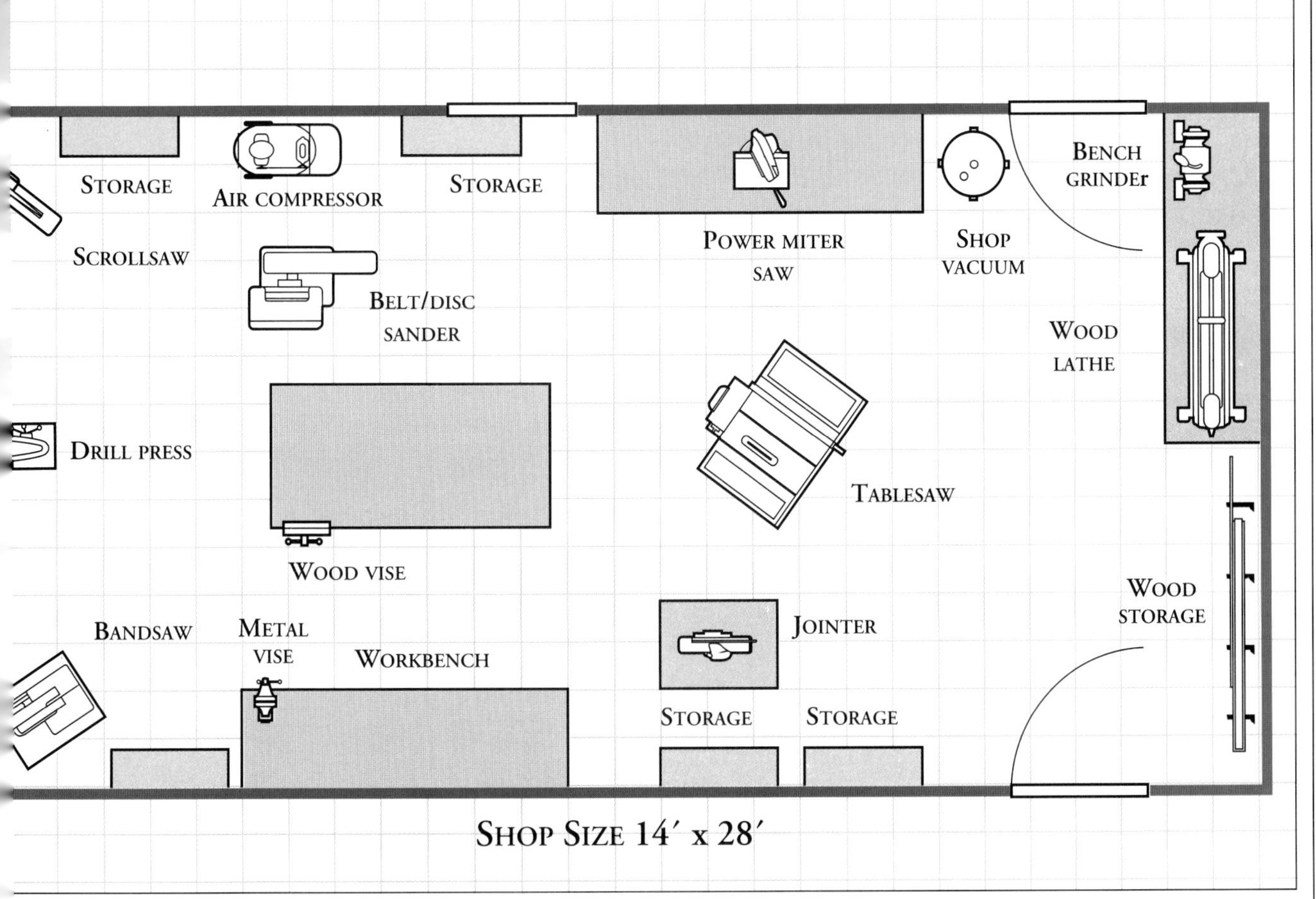
Storage
Air compressor
Storage
Power miter saw
Shop vacuum
Bench grinder
Scrollsaw
Belt/disc sander
Wood lathe
Drill press
Tablesaw
Wood vise
Wood storage
Bandsaw
Metal vise
Workbench
Jointer
Storage
Storage
Shop Size 14′ x 28′

MULCHING MOWERS

How To Make The Most Of The New Approach To Lawn Maintenance

Go looking for a new lawn mower and you'll quickly discover that lawn care has entered a new age. Today more than 75% of the lawn mowers being uncrated are specifically designed to excel as mulching machines, and dealers will give you a long list of reasons why mulching makes sense.

Should you believe them, or is this mulching business just another gimmick to make older lawn mowers obsolete?

Actually, the idea of mulching lawn mowers has been around for a few decades; some were produced as early as the 1960's. However, in quest of the perfect lawn with the "vacuumed-look," homeowners continued to opt for mowers with bagging attachments.

Bagging grass survived as a common practice until about 1980, when 70% of the country's landfills reached maximum capacity. Lawn clippings and leaves were accounting for as much as half the waste sent to landfills during the growing season, and 18% year-round. When it became illegal to dump yard waste in many areas, mower manufacturers dusted off the concept of mulching, and gave it serious engineering attention.

The latest mulching mowers, often with the help of computers, have reached state-of-the-art performance. New research has debunked the myth that mulching contributes to thatch problems, as well as uncovering several side benefits. Research also shows that there are things you can do as a homeowner to get the most from mulching technology.

First, some background. Grass clippings account for 75% of total yard waste, while leaves make up about 20%. Lawn care experts now admit you don't have to bag grass clippings to have a beautiful, healthy lawn. In fact, returning clippings to the lawn naturally fertilizes it and even can make it more resistant to disease.

The experts figure that grass clippings can contribute from 25% to 30% of your lawn's fertilizer needs, allowing you to skip one or even two applications.

By leaving mulched grass on the lawn you also will finish mowing jobs faster. In a Texas study, homeowners using mulching mowers spent 38% less time, compared to those who had to stop every few minutes to empty grass clippings from bags.

Another advantage of mulching is that it helps conserve water—the clippings shade the soil from the sun and help cut evaporation loss. Clippings also decompose into water-absorbent humus.

When mulching mowers first appeared, many homeowners questioned the concept, believing that leaving grass on the lawn would contribute to thatch. Thatch is a layer of roots and stems that grows between the grass and the soil and is difficult for soil microbes to break down. However, agronomists at major universities agree that's not the case. "Finely chopped clippings contribute virtually nothing to the thatch

Keys to mulchers: 1) The specially designed blades produce a powerful vacuum action on the surface of the grass for a clean cut; 2) special deflectors, or kickers, deflect clippings back to the blade where they are cut and recut into tiny particles; 3) the blade fans help circulate clippings, reducing power demands while improving cutting action even in deep, wet grass; 4) the resulting tiny grass particles decompose quickly, feeding the lawn and slowing evaporation of soil moisture.

ayer," says Bill Pound, grass specialist t Ohio State University.

Clippings, on the other hand, are oughly 85% moisture and are rapidly lecomposed by natural organisms. Agonomists say that the leading cause of hatch build-up is over-fertilizing, either y an over-zealous lawn owner or by ggressive lawn services who pump on xcess nitrogen to keep grass as green as ossible.

If you have a conventional mower esigned for bagging, you might be empted just to remove the bagging atachment to leave clippings. While this voids bagging, engineers say the results von't be as good as with a mulching nower.

A mower designed specifically for nulching will cut grass slivers six to ight times before finally leaving them n the lawn. Replacing the blade on your older mower with a specially designed mulching blade is a half step, but still gives you only part of the technology.

The illustration shows how advanced mulching mowers work. Engineers who design Toro and Lawn-Boy mowers note that better mulching mowers have more horsepower to handle the increased chopping load, a longer sharpened blade edge to cut more grass with each rotation, and fans on the blade to help force cut grass back through the blade more times. The underside of a mulching mower's deck is deeper and is designed with deflectors which kick grass stems back into the blade. Engineers are now finding that increasing the size of the deflectors helps the mower cut grass blades more finely with less power.

Even with a new mulching mower, engineers suggest you take extra measures to help the mower accomplish its task. Because mulching takes more power, make sure the engine is running at top horsepower. Change spark plugs, oil, and air filters each year, or more often, if necessary. Also take the time to regularly clean out the debris from under the deck. *Be sure to remove the spark plug wire to prevent accidental starts.* And, because mulching mowers depend so heavily on the blade to work their magic, pay extra attention to its condition and sharpness.

Mulching mower blades should be touched up or sharpened twice as often as older, conventional mower blades. *Read the owner's manual for advice, and take all safety precautions.* You can sharpen your own blade with a bench grinder or portable sharpener.

With either, make sure the blade is balanced by hanging it by the center hole on a nail. Both sides of the blade should remain level. If one side of the blade drops down, sharpen that side more until the blade returns to balance. An easier option is to buy an extra blade, and leave one blade at the service shop for sharpening while you use the other.

Because of their vacuum action, mulching mowers generally tend to leave heavier tracking patterns in the lawn. To avoid this, vary the pattern of cut by starting alternatively on opposite sides of the lawn, or by cutting the lawn first in a square pattern, then diagonally.

Engineers also say that cutting height is more critical when using mulchers; some companies are now incorporating cutting-height charts on one of the mower wheels to eliminate the guesswork.

Tech Notes: Managing For A Healthy Lawn

Below are common questions about mulching mowers and lawn care. The answers come from engineers at Toro, a leading mulching mower manufacturer. For more specific questions, check with a local dealer, write the company at 4649 W. 77th St., #179, Edina, MN 55435, or call 800/321-8676.

Is there a general rule-of-thumb on how often to mow? Regular mowing with a sharp blade is essential to maintaining a healthy, beautiful lawn. Mow often enough so that no more than one-third (about 1″) of the vertical grass height is removed with each cutting.

Is there a difference among the mulching mowers on the market? Tests show some mowers do a more complete and consistent job of cutting and recutting grass blades into finely chopped clippings. This means the clippings are deposited out of sight into the remaining grass to help speed decomposition.

What's the advantage of leaving the grass clippings on the lawn? Finely-cut clippings provide three significant benefits. First, they shade the soil surface and reduce moisture loss. Second, they provide a good source of plant nutrients, such as nitrogen, phosphorus, and potassium. Third, the finely-cut clippings help cool the soil and maintain a uniform temperature.

By returning nutrients to your lawn, mulching can replace one or two fertilizer applications.

Are there times when lawn clippings should be removed? There are a few instances when it may be a good idea, such as when the lawn must be mowed when wet, when the grass is so tall that the clippings may not be distributed evenly, or when the mower is unsafe to operate without a bagging attachment.

How does mulching affect lawn fertilizing? Over-fertilizing can lead to thatch problems. Fertilizers containing slow-release nitrogen will provide a more moderate, uniform grass growth. (Examples include sulfur-coated urea, urea formaldehyde, IBDU, or natural organic fertilizers.)

It's best to apply smaller amounts more frequently. Because clippings contain 1% to 2% nitrogen, they can provide up to 30% of a lawn's fertilizer needs.

Can a mulching mower also be used for leaves? It can be used to cut and recut a light layer of leaves into small pieces that are returned to your lawn.

After you mow, check the shredded leaves on your lawn to be sure that no more than half the grass blade is covered. If you can't see the grass underneath, mow the lawn again with the bag on and compost the contents. Mulching can reduce 10 bags of leaves to only one.

What's the best way to water a lawn? A lush, healthy lawn results from correct watering, feeding, and cutting. Water deeply and less often, but don't overwater. During dry periods, lawns need at least 1″ of water every five to six days.

How many times should a lawn be fertilized? For best results, fertilize three times a year. The most important time is in the fall to help leafy materials decompose, and the lawn resist winter stress.

Using controlled-release fertilizers will give your lawn both immediate and long-term feeding. This type of fertilizer also reduces the likelihood of run-off that can pollute lakes and rivers.

Thatch is a layer of roots and stems, caused by over-fertilizing and improper mowing and watering, that builds up between the grass and the soil.

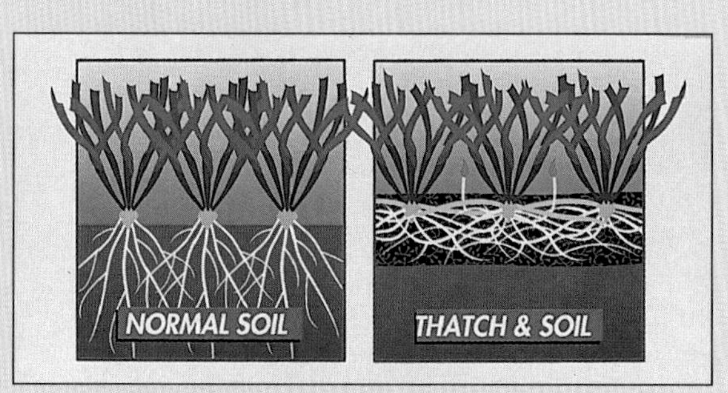

According to university agronomists, the fine clippings from mulching mowers do not cause thatch, but decompose rapidly to feed the grass and keep it healthy.

WORKBENCHES

Hard-Working Shop Helpers You Can Build With Just Basic Hand Tools

The center of activity in most any home workshop is the basic workbench. If you don't have one, or if you need extras, you can easily build your own. The plans here, from The Stanley Works, show how to make both adult and child-size versions.

The benches use common materials available at your local lumberyard or home center. You won't have any problem if you have a basic knowledge of woodworking tools and techniques. And, if you want more specific instructions, you can order a helpful video to guide you through the building process (see end of article).

You can perform all operations with basic hand tools; if you are an average do-it-yourselfer, you should have no trouble building the benches exactly as shown. If you're a more advanced woodworker, you may want to incorporate a few touches of your own.

To make building these benches more convenient, buy large stock, especially the 4x8′ plywood sheets, where you can have it ripped to size. You'll get a straight, true cut and the pieces will be easier to carry home.

Some lumberyards and home centers offer this service for a small charge. Be sure to watch the cutting and check the final measurements. And don't forget the oldest piece of advice in woodworking: Measure twice, then cut once.

ADULT WORKBENCH

Begin by double checking your purchases against the hardware and materials lists.

1. Lay out the legs. You'll work them in mirrored pairs (a pair for the left side, a pair for the right side). Begin by marking each of the four 32½″-long 4x4s with its position (LF, LR, RF, RR). Mark each side A, B, C, and D (Drawing A). Start with the LF and LR legs (Drawings B and D). Near the bottom of each leg you'll make a dado (a U-shaped cut wide enough to accommodate the lower stretcher). Lay it out by measuring 5½″ up and 9″ up from the bottom on all four sides of each leg. Square the lines with a try square. Set your

Building a good workbench is an investment in the future. With vises, work surface, and both under-bench and pegboard tool storage, each of your projects in days ahead will be easier to work on. The Stanley workbenches in this section are designed to be built by those with a basic knowledge of woodworking tools and techniques, but you can do all the construction with basic hand tools.

marking gauge for ¾″ and scribe four depth lines between the squared lines. Scribe two on the B side, two on the C side of LF, one on the A side and B side of LR.

The top of each leg requires a rabbet (an L-shaped cut along the top end of each leg) to accept the top stretchers. Measure 3½″ down from the top of leg, square the line on all four sides. Scribe the end of the leg, parallel, ¾″ in on side B (for the side stretcher), 1½″ in on side A (for the front stretcher). Before you cut, make sure your dado and rabbet marks are on the correct sides. Repeat for the second pair of legs (Drawings C and E).

2. Make dado cuts. Use a backsaw or dovetail saw and be sure to cut inside all the lines. On each dado, cut down to the scribed ¾″ depth. Before removing the material, turn the leg and cut to depth on the other side. To speed removal of material, make several additional parallel cuts into the material to be removed, then use a ¾″ chisel to complete and smooth the bottom of the cut.

3. Cut a rabbet on top of each leg, repeating the dado procedure exactly (cut to scribed depth on one side, turn the leg, and cut to depth on the other side before removing material).

4. Mark, square, and cut four 25″ pieces of 1x4 for the side stretchers (Drawing F).

5. On the two top side stretchers, locate the points for screw holes. Measure in 2½″ from each end, and square the line. Along the line, mark points at ¾″ and 2¾″ (Drawing F).

6. Locate the points for screw holes on the bottom side stretchers (Drawing F). Measure in 1⅜″ from each end, square the line, and mark at ¾″ and 2¾″.

7. Assemble two pairs of legs by attaching the top and bottom side stretchers. Predrill for 2″ #10 flathead Phillips screws.

8. Cut 2x4 front and back stretchers. Cut four 58½″ lengths.

9. Stand two leg units on the floor, put a top stretcher in position between them, clamp with a bar clamp at both ends. Measure in 2½″ from each end (including side stretchers), square the line, measure and mark points at 1″ and 2½″ (Drawing F). Use a ⅜″ bit to drill at each point. Drill through the stretcher and the leg. Secure with 4½″ carriage bolts, nuts, and washers. Tighten securely. Repeat for the bottom stretcher on the same side (Drawing F). To prevent splintering of the stretcher, clamp a piece of scrap wood to the opposite side of the joint from which you'll start drilling. Drill through both the leg and the stretcher into the scrap. Repeat this for the top and bottom stretchers on the other side.

10. Add a ¾″-square cleat (bot-

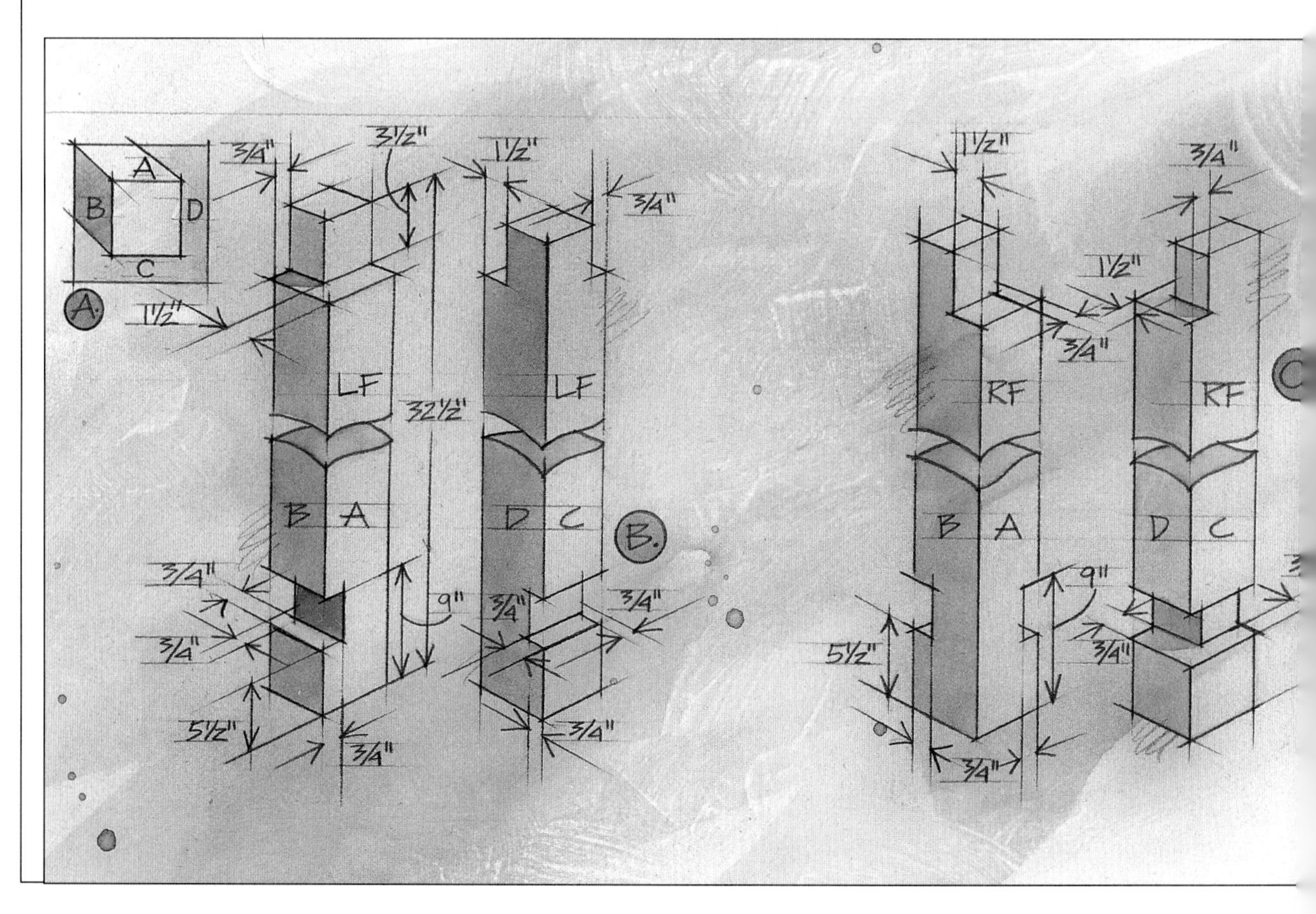

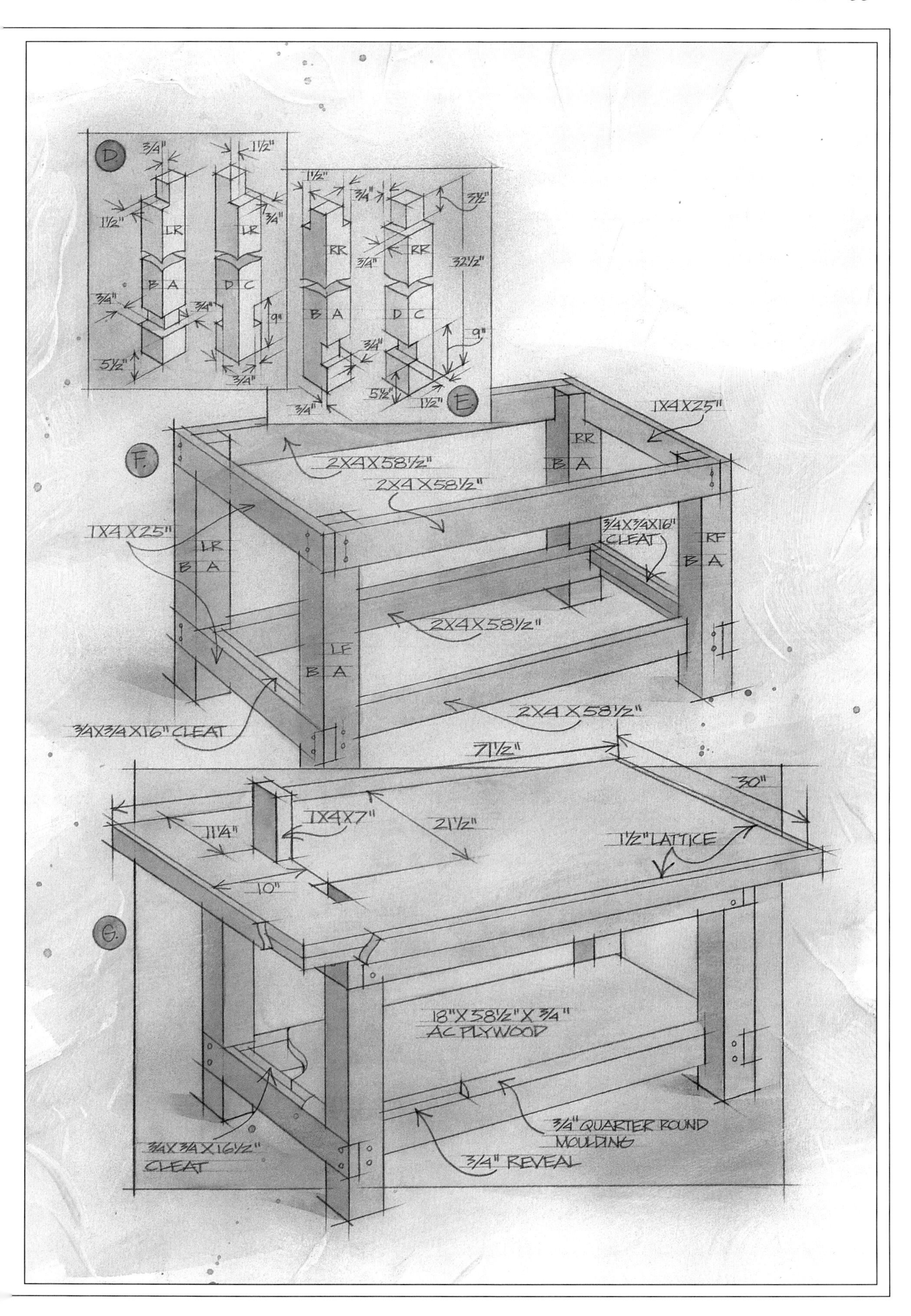
D
3/4"
1 1/2"
1 1/2"
3/4"
LR
LR
B A
D C
3/4"
3/4"
9"
5 1/2"
3/4"
1 1/2"
3/4"
3 1/2"
RR
RR
3/4"
32 1/2"
B A
D C
9"
3/4"
5 1/2"
1 1/2"
E
3/4"
1X4X25"
F
2X4X58 1/2"
RR
B A
2X4X58 1/2"
1X4X25"
3/4X3/4X16"
CLEAT
LR
B A
RF
B A
2X4X58 1/2"
LF
B A
2X4 X58 1/2"
3/4X3/4X16" CLEAT
71 1/2"
30"
1X4X7"
11 1/4"
21 1/2"
1 1/2" LATTICE
10"
G
18"X58 1/2"X 3/4"
AC PLYWOOD
3/4" QUARTER ROUND
MOULDING
3/4X3/4X16 1/2"
CLEAT
3/4" REVEAL

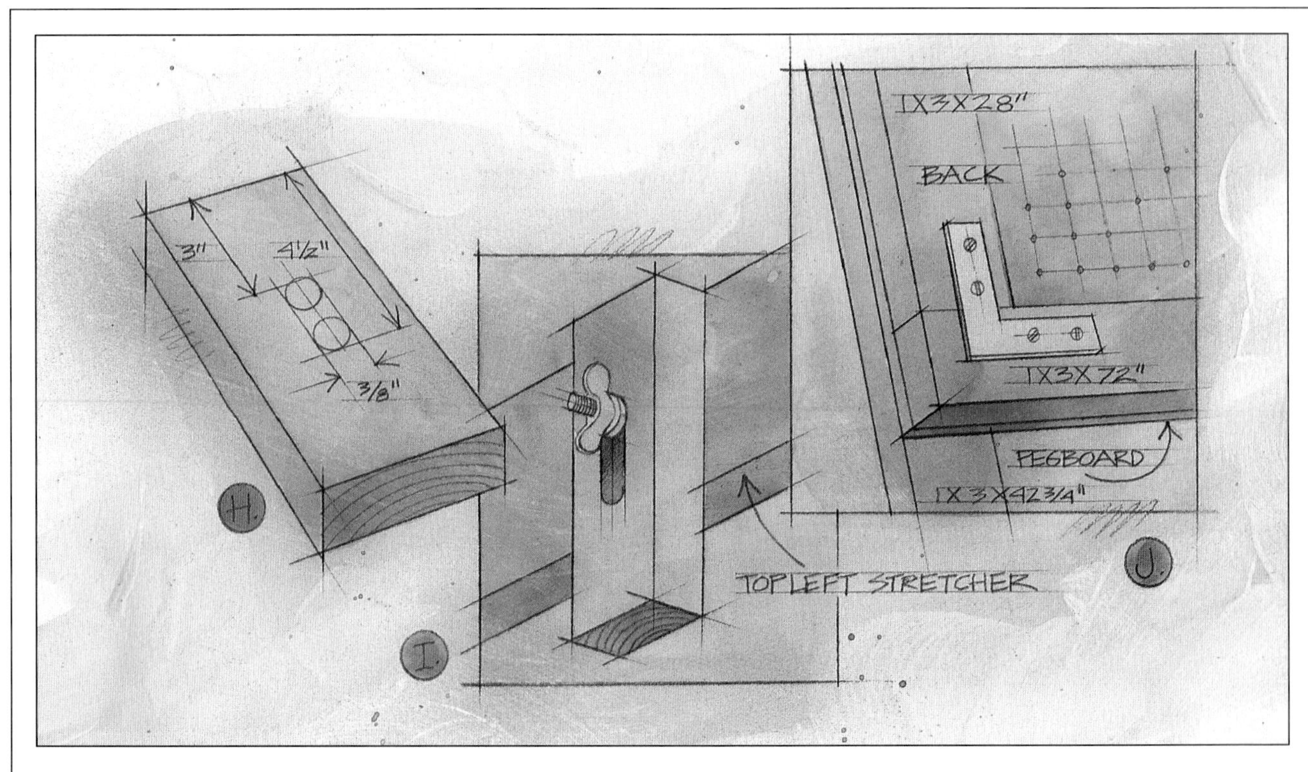

tom shelf support) to the inside of each bottom end stretcher (Drawing F). Cut two pieces 16½″ long. Predrill for 1¼″ #8 screws. Locate the first screw 3″ from one end; the others at 3″ intervals. Repeat on the other cleat, making sure you start marking screw locations from the same end. Glue and screw flush with the top of the stretcher to complete the frame.

11. Make the bottom shelf. Rip an 18x96″ (8′) piece from each of two sheets of ¾″ AC (good one side) plywood. Crosscut one to 58½″.

12. Install the bottom shelf. Drop it onto bottom side stretchers, making sure it is centered between the ends, resting on the ¾″ cleats; check for a ¾″ reveal on all sides (Drawing G). Predrill for #8 screws on all sides, 6″ on center. Secure with 1¼″ #8 flathead Phillips screws. Trim with ¾″ quarter-round molding cut to fit. Glue and tack with 1¼″ brads.

13. Cut and fit the work surface. This design features a double-thickness top for extra strength and stability. (This also makes it easy to replace the top layer if it wears or is damaged.) Use the two pieces of ¾″ AC plywood left after ripping the two 18″ pieces in Step 11. Crosscut both to 71½″ long. With the

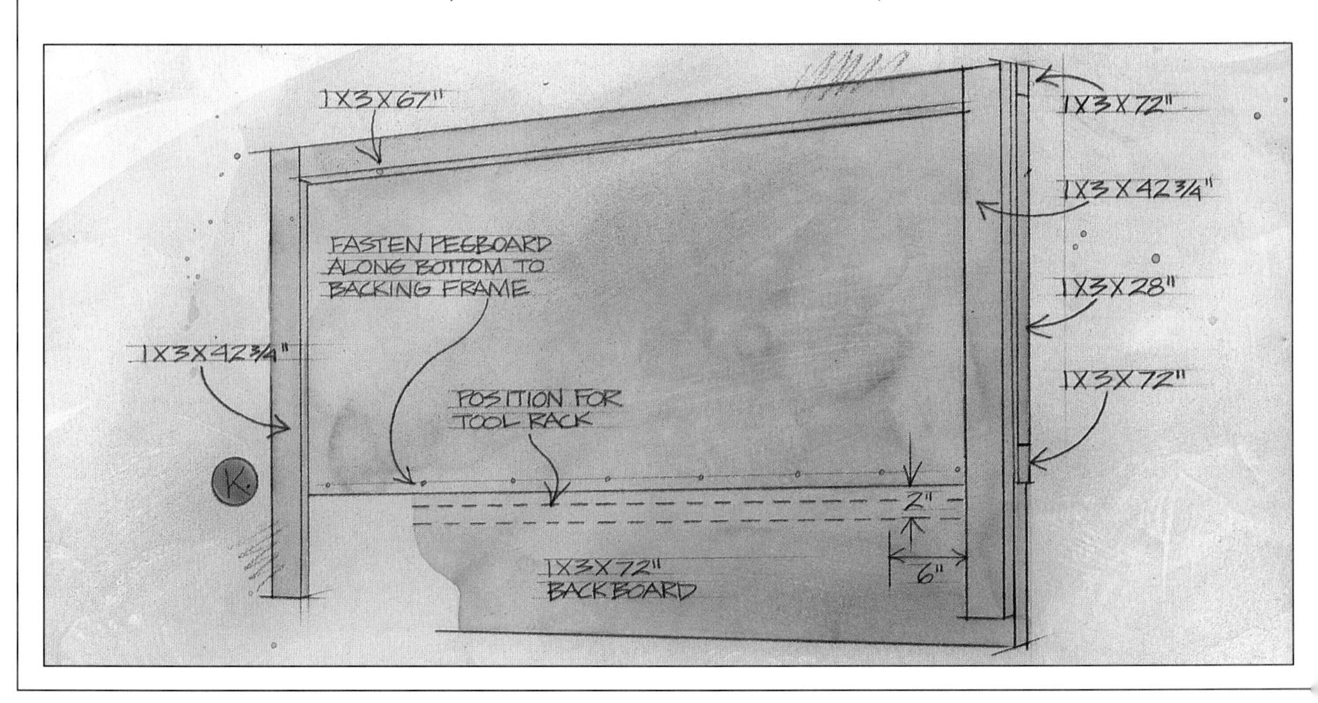

smooth-sanded surfaces facing down, stack the two pieces squarely and clamp firmly on at least two sides. Drill and screw with 1¼″ flathead Phillips screws, 6″ on center around the perimeter and lengthwise up the center.

14. Cut slots for the bench stops. Set the completed work surface, top (good side) up on the completed bench frame (Drawing G). Position the top flush against the back legs and stretcher with a 10″ overhang on the left end. Measure in 10″ from the left side. Use a framing square to square a line from the front to the back of the bench top (Drawing G). Measuring from the back, mark points at 11¼″ and 21½″. Those points mark the back edges of both slots.

Cut two 7″ bench stops from a 1x4. Stand a stop on end at the 11¼″ mark. Seen from the top, the back right corner of the stop should be square with the line and the 11¼″ mark. Use a sharp utility knife to scribe around the base of the stop. Repeat the same procedure at the 21½″ mark.

Using a ¾″ bit, drill four holes within each scribed rectangle. Be sure to stay within the scribed lines. Drill completely through the bench top. Use a ¾″ chisel to remove the remaining material. (To avoid splintering the bottom surface, place a piece of scrap stock under each slot before drilling and chiseling.) Make sure the corners of the slots are square. Test fit both stops. If necessary, carefully chisel out any additional material until the stops glide freely in the slots.

15. Cut bolt slots in the stops (Drawing H). Find and mark the center line on both stops. Along that line, measure and mark 3″ and 4½″ from one end. At both points, measure 3/16″ on each side of the center line. Square all four lines to

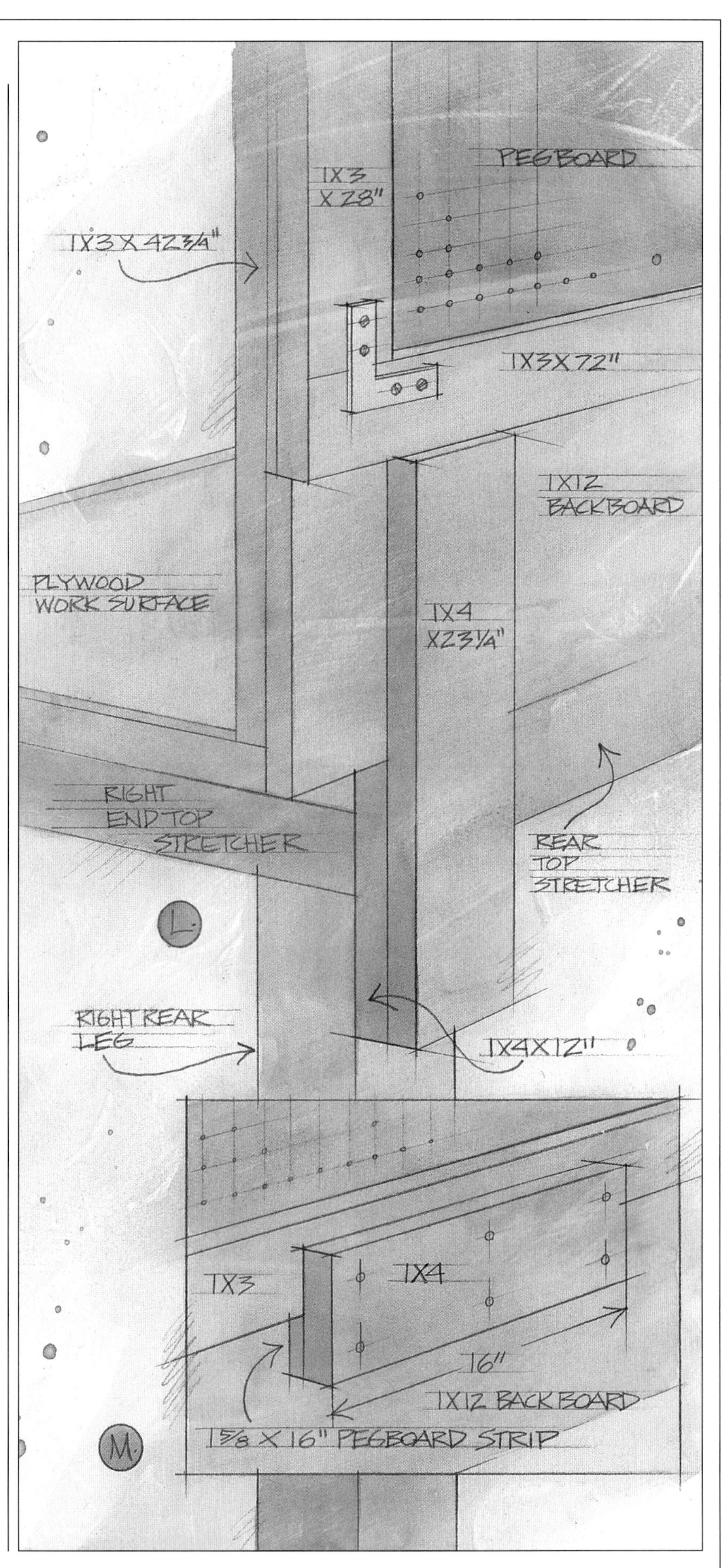

form a rectangle. Use a 3⁄8″ bit to drill holes at each end of the rectangle, clamp the stop to the bench, and use a coping saw to remove the remaining material. Test-fit a 5⁄16″ carriage bolt in the slot. Repeat for the second stop.

Place both stops in their slots, flush with the top surface. This helps locate the top when attaching it to the frame.

Safe completion of the next steps requires at least two adults. Do not attempt to lift the completed frame or assembled bench without adult help.

16. Attach the work surface to the frame. Place the top, good side down, on sawhorses. Place the completed frame, upside down, on the top of the work surface. The stops should project up through the left side of the underside of the bench top. Align the frame flush with the back edge of the bench top. Slide it to the left until the legs are flush with the stops. This eliminates crawling under the bench and holding tools above your head to attach the top to the frame. If you prefer, you may stand the frame on the floor and set the top on, taking care to align it properly with the bench stops and back legs.

Use eight 3″ corner braces and screws to attach the frame to the bench top. Place three braces along the inside of the front stretcher, three on the inside of the back stretcher, and one on the inside of

Recommended Tools	Stanley Catalog Number
Tape measure	33–425, 33–116, or 33-310
Try square	46-502
Framing square	45-300
T-bevel	46-825
Marking gauge	47-064
6″ Quick-Square ® tool	46-050
Mallet	57-522
Claw Hammer	51-490
Phillips or cordless screwdriver	64-830/75-040
Adjustable wrench	87-368
Crosscut saw	15-528 or 15-336
Ripsaw	15-527
Dovetail or backsaw	15-140/15-332
Coping saw	15-106A
Block Plane	12-116
Chisels—1″ and 3⁄4″	16-216/16-212
Cordless drill or bit and brace	75-040/02-660
Screw-Mate® for #8 and #10 screws	04-622/04-623
Powerbore bits 3⁄8″, 1⁄2″, 3⁄4″, 1″ (set)	04-001
3″ C-clamps (4)	83-156
Bar clamps (4)	83-157
Utility knife	10-099
Nail set	58-230
Carpenter's glue	

The Stanley Workbench

Materials List	Hardware	Quantity
2 sheets 3⁄4″ AC plywood (top surface)	11⁄4″ brads	54
1 sheet 1⁄4″ pegboard (tool hanger rack)	Flathead Phillips screws	
1 12′ 4x4 (legs)	3⁄4″ #8	13
2 10′ 2x4 (front and back stretchers and back supports)	11⁄4″ #8	94
2 10′ 1x4 (side stretchers)	11⁄2″ #8	38
1 3′ 1x12 (tool rack base)	11⁄2″ #10	12
4 12′ 1x3 (tool rack frame and tool shelf)	2″ #10	16
16′ 3⁄4x3⁄4″ (bottom shelf cleat)	3″ #10	4
28′ 3⁄4″ quarter round (shelf molding)	Carriage bolts, nuts, and washers	
1 12′ 1⁄4x13⁄4″ lattice (banding for bench top)	5⁄16x41⁄2″	16
	5⁄16x5″ bolt w/wing nut and washer	1
	5⁄16x2″ bolt w/wing nut and washer	1
	3″ corner braces w/screws (Stanley #CD997-R)	8
	3″ flat L-braces (Stanley #CD999-R)	4
	31⁄2″ (16d) finish nails	2

each end. If you inverted the bench for this procedure, stand it upright on the floor.

17. Drill the left top stretcher for stop bolts (Drawing I). Set the stops flush with the bench top. Mark hole locations through the stops at the tops of the slots. Drill holes with a 3/8″ bit. Secure the front stop with a 5″ carriage bolt; the back stop with a 2″ bolt. Insert the bolts from the inside of the stretcher, then add the washers and wing nuts.

18. Measure and fit the 1¾″-wide lattice trim on the bench top (Drawing G). Attach the end pieces first, shave down to 1½″ with a block plane, then measure the front strip to overlap the end pieces. Glue and nail in place using 1¼″ brads every 6″. Plane the front strip down flush with the top.

19. Assemble the pegboard back. Crosscut the pegboard to 72″ (6′) long, and rip to 33″ wide. For the back side of the frame, cut two 72″ pieces and two 28″ pieces of 1x3. Also cut two 42¾″ pieces and one 67″ piece for the front frame. Lay the four back frame pieces on a flat floor and assemble with four flat L-braces, one at each corner. Make sure the side pieces butt inside the top and bottom pieces (Drawing J).

Lay one 42¾″ piece on each end of your new workbench. Place the 67″ piece between them and butt squarely. Secure each corner with a 3½″ (16d) finish nail. Lay the pegboard on top, squaring it flush with the top corner joints. Then lay the completed back frame assembly squarely on top of the tool pegboard. Note: The two 42¾″ front frame side pieces will extend well below the bottom of the pegboard and back frame.

Check for a flush fit on all sides and corners. Clamp on at least two sides. Predrill for #8 screws on all sides, approximately 6″ on center. Drill from the back, through the back frame and pegboard, into the front frame. Fasten both frames and the pegboard together using 1½″ #8 flathead Phillips screws. Fasten through the bottom edge of the pegboard into the back frame using ¾″ #8 screws (Drawing K).

20. Make the backboard/tool rack. Crosscut the 1x12 pine to 72″. Crosscut a 1x3 to 60″. Mark the center line on the 1x3. Starting from each end, mark 10 points 2″ on center. Working from each end, drill two ½″, five ¾″, and three 1″ holes at marked points (20 holes). You may have specific needs that require fewer holes or different sizes; feel free to mark and drill as you prefer. To prevent splintering, clamp a piece of scrap stock to the bottom of the 1x3 before drilling. Mark the front corners for rounding, then round off with a coping saw.

Position the tool rack on the 1x12 backboard, 2″ down from the top and 6″ in from each end. Mark the bottom and end lines. Remove the rack, center, and mark the screw locations every 12″, starting 2″ in from one end. Drill through the backboard from the front. Reposition the tool rack and attach it from the back with 1½″ #8 screws.

21. Attach the backboard/tool rack to the framed pegboard assembly (Drawing K). Use 1¼″ #8 screws to attach the backboard to the backs of the front frame side pieces. The 1x12 should extend 1½″ below the front frame side pieces. Square a line parallel to the backboard bottom, ¾″ up. Predrill for #10 screws 6″ on center, starting 2″ from one end. This completes the pegboard back.

22. With a helper, lift the completed back assembly onto the workbench, making sure it is flush with both ends of the bench. Attach with 1½″ flathead Phillips screws. (Caution: At this point, the pegboard back will support itself, but not a load of heavy tools. You must add the support braces as described in Step 23. If the bench is placed against a wall, you may want to secure the back to the wall at several points, in addition to using the required braces.)

23. Assemble and attach the back support braces (Drawing L). Cut two 23¼″ and two 12″ pieces of 1x4. Stack a 12″ piece on top of a 23½″ piece, butt one end, then predrill and screw together with two 1¼″ #8 screws. Place over the backboard and leg, flush with the sides of the leg, making sure the brace top butts against the bottom of the back pegboard frame. (Carriage-bolt heads will prevent the brace from fitting flush with the leg.) Hold the brace firmly against the leg, strike with a mallet in the approximate position of the bolt heads. Remove the brace, make sure the two bolt head impressions are visible. Use a 1″ bit to drill ¼″-deep holes to accommodate the bolt heads. Predrill for #10 screws for the leg attachment points, and #8 screws for the backboard points. Attach the brace to the leg with 3″ #10 screws, and to the backboard with 1¼″ #8 screws.

24. Add the center support. Cut a 16″ piece of 1x4 and use two ¾″ #8 screws to attach a 15/8x16″ strip of scrap pegboard, making sure it is flush with the bottom edge. Attach it to the backboard, centered, by butting it to the lip formed where the pegboard frame projects over the backboard. Use 1½″ #8 screws (Drawing M). The workbench is now complete. Just sand a few edges, and you have a bench that you will be proud to own.

A Child-Size Workbench

This workbench is an ideal gift for any young woodworker. Building the bench also is a great opportunity for a child to learn the basics of carpentry. Remember, though, to keep the child's age, size, strength, and skill level in mind. Don't overestimate the child's ability to work with tools. Make sure you share the rules of good woodworking. And always have an adult on hand to supervise. It's safer—and a lot more fun—if you work on projects together.

Building the child-size version of the Stanley Workbench involves many of the same tools and procedures used to build the full-size workbench.

1. Lay out the legs. Work them in mirrored pairs (a pair for the left side, a pair for the right side). Mark each of the four 27¼″-long 2x4s with its position (LF, LR, RF, RR). Mark each side A, B, C, and D (Drawing A). Start with the LF and LR legs.

Near the bottom of each leg you'll make a dado (a U-shaped cut

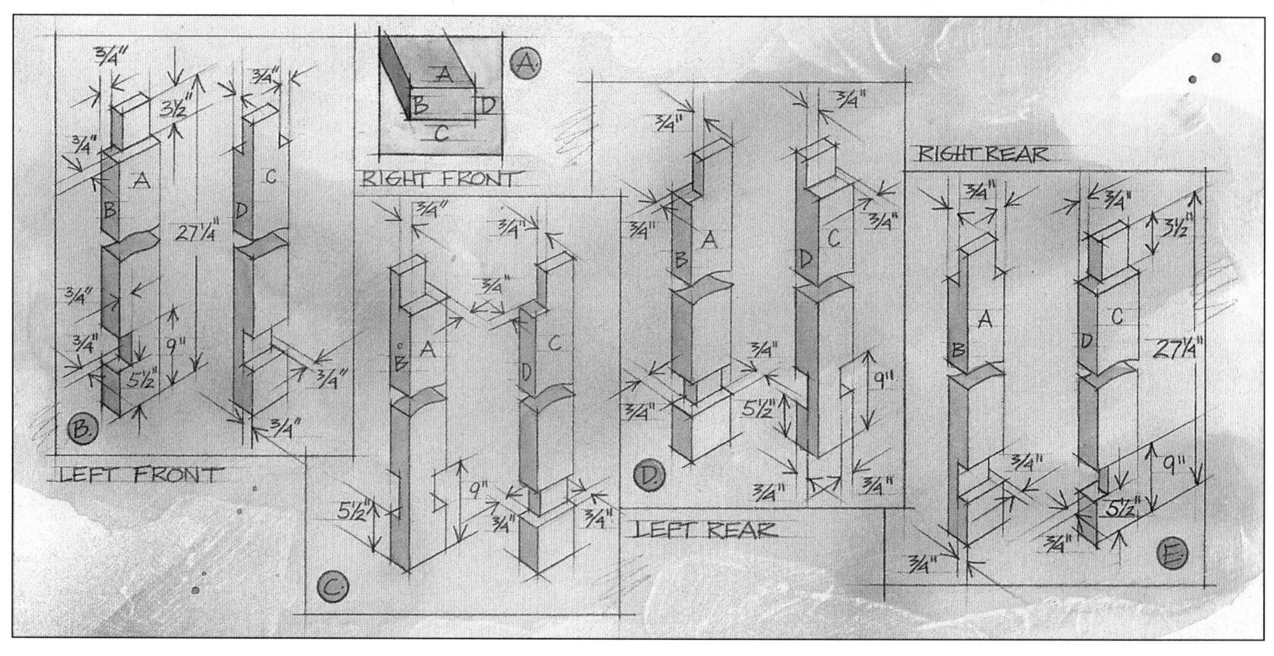

wide enough to accommodate the lower stretcher. Lay it out by measuring 5½″ up and 9″ up from the bottom of the leg on all four sides of the leg. Square the lines with a try square. Set your marking gauge for ¾″ and scribe four depth lines between the squared lines. Scribe two on the B side, two on the C side of LF (Drawing B), and one on both the A side and the B side of LR (Drawing D).

The top of each leg requires a rabbet (an L-shaped cut along the top end of each leg), to accept the top stretchers. Measure 3½″ down from the top of the leg and square the line on all four sides. Scribe the end of the leg, parallel ¾″ on the B side (for the side stretcher), and ¾″ in on side A (for the front stretcher).

Note: Pay close attention to drawings B, C, D, and E. Before you cut, make sure your dado and rabbet marks are on the correct sides. Repeat the procedure for the second pair of legs (Drawings C and E).

2. Make dado cuts. Use a backsaw or dovetail saw and be sure to cut inside all lines. On each dado, cut down to the ¾″ scribed depth. Before removing any material, turn the leg and cut to depth on the other side. To speed removal of material, make several additional parallel cuts into the material to be removed, then use a ¾″ chisel to complete and smooth the bottom of the cut.

3. Cut the rabbet on top of each leg, repeating the dado procedure exactly (cut to the scribed depth on one side, turn the leg and cut to depth on the other side before removing material).

4. Mark, square, and cut four 18½″ pieces of 1x4 for the side stretchers.

5. For the top side stretchers, on two pieces measure in 1″ from each

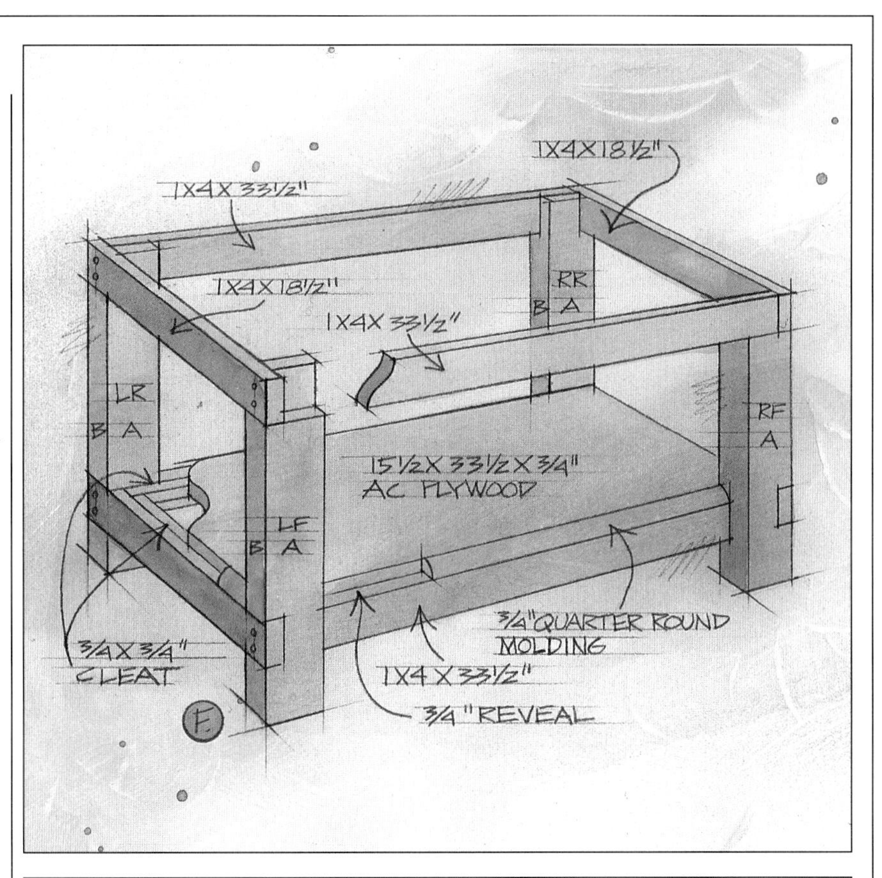

The Child-Size Stanley Workbench

Materials List

1	10′ 2x4 (legs)
2	10′ 1x4 (frame)
1	4x4′ sheet ¾″ AC plywood (bench top and shelf)
1	3x4′ sheet ¼″ pegboard (tool hanger rack)
1	4′ 1x12 (backboard)
	10′ 1x2 (pegboard frame and tool rack)
	10′ ¾x¾″ (bottom shelf cleats)
	10′ 1x3 (tool rack and back braces)
	7′ 1″ wide lattice trim

Hardware	Quantity
1¼″ brads	30
Flathead Phillips screws	23
1½″ #8	8
1½″ #10	4
1¼″ #10	8
¾″ #8	32
2½″ #10	56
3″ corner braces w/screws (Stanley #CD997-R)	6
3″ flat L-braces (Stanley #CD999-R)	4
2½″ (12d) finish nails	2

end and square the line. Along the line, mark points at 1″ and 2½″ (Drawing F). Predrill for 1¼″ #10 flathead Phillips screws.

6. The other two pieces are the bottom side stretchers. Measure in ½″ from each end, square the line, mark and predrill at 1″ and 2½″.

7. Assemble two pairs of legs by attaching the top and bottom side stretchers. Use 1¼″ #10 flathead Phillips screws (Drawing F).

8. Cut four 33½″ lengths of 1x4 for the front and back stretchers.

9. Stand two leg units on the floor, put a top stretcher in position between them, clamp with a bar clamp at both ends. Measure in 1″ from each end of the 1x4—do not include the thickness of the side stretcher. Square the line, measure and mark points at 1″ and 2½″, and predrill at each point through the stretcher and into the leg. Secure with 1¼″ #10 flathead Phillips screws (Drawing F). Repeat for the bottom stretcher on the same side. Repeat for the top and bottom stretchers on the other side.

10. Make the bottom shelf. Cut a 15½x33½″ piece of ¾″ AC (good one side) plywood.

11. Add ¾″ square cleats (bottom shelf supports) to the inside of the bottom stretchers (Drawing G). Cut two pieces 33½″ long for the front and back, and two pieces 14″ long for the ends. Predrill at 6″ intervals. Glue and screw flush with the top of the tool stretcher. Use 1¼″ #8 screws.

12. Install the shelf. Drop it onto the cleats attached to the bottom side stretchers. Mark the screw locations at 6″ intervals, making sure the screws do not interfere with those used to secure the cleat. Predrill for #8 screws. Secure the shelf with 1¼″ #8 flathead Phillips screws. Trim with ¾″ quarter-round molding cut to fit all four

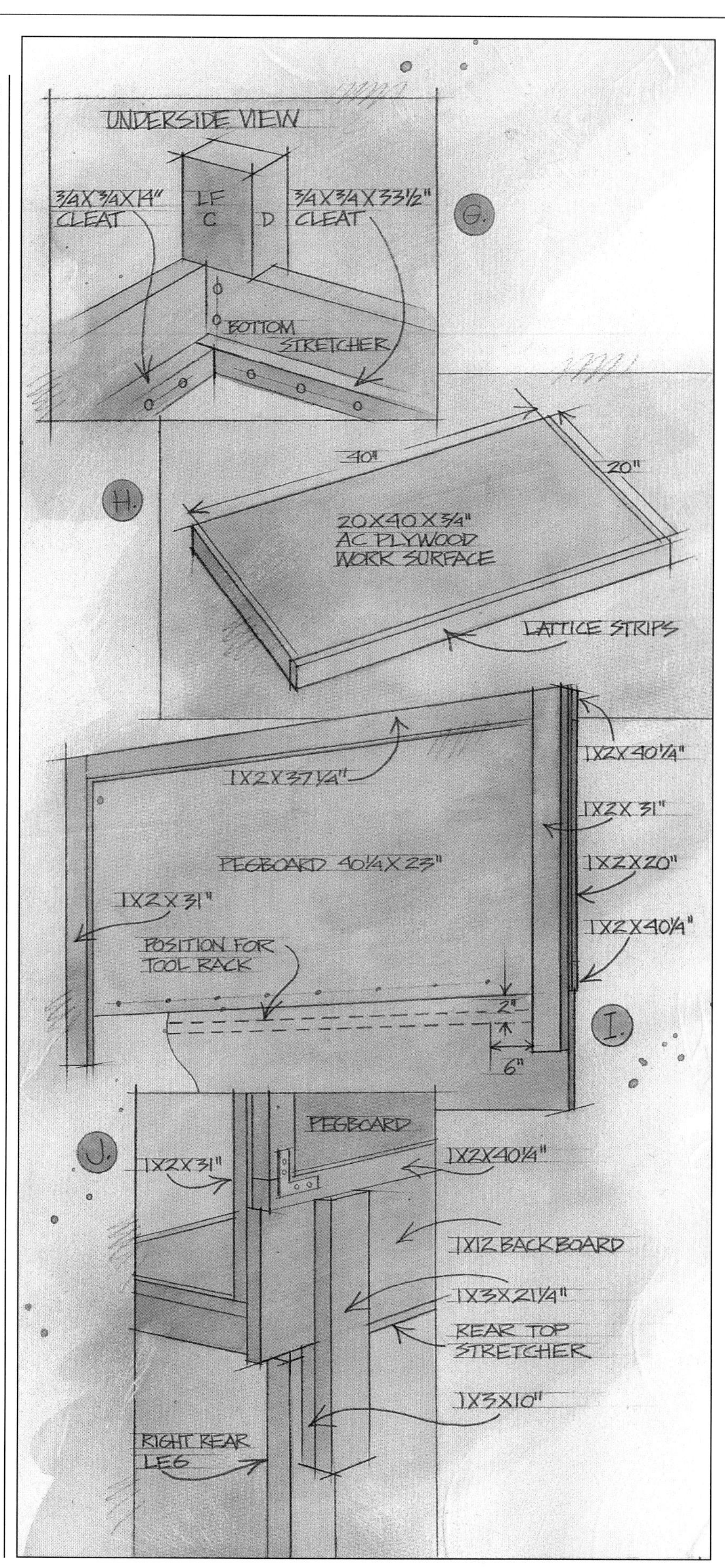

sides (Drawing F). Glue and tack in place with 1¼″ brads.

13. Cut and fit the top. Rip ¾″ AC plywood to 40″, then crosscut to 20″.

14. Attach the top to the frame. Place the top, good side down, on sawhorses. Place the frame, upside down, on top and align it flush with the back edge of the bench top and center it. Use eight 3″ L-brackets and screws to attach the frame to the bench top. Place three brackets along the inside of the front stretcher, three on the inside of the back stretcher, and one inside each end. Stand the bench upright on the floor.

15. Measure and fit the ¾″ wide lattice trim on the bench top (Drawing H). Attach the end pieces first, then measure the front strip to overlap the end pieces. Glue and nail using 1¼″ brads every 6″.

16. Assemble the pegboard back (Drawing I). Crosscut the pegboard to 40¼″ long, then rip to 23″ wide. For the back side of the frame, cut two 40¼″ pieces and two 20″ pieces of 1x2. Also cut two 31″ pieces and one 37¼″ piece for the front frame.

Lay the four back frame pieces on a flat floor and assemble with four flat corner braces, one at each corner. Make sure the side pieces butt inside the top and bottom pieces (Drawing I).

Lay one 31″ piece on each end of your new workbench. Place a 37¼″ piece between them and butt them squarely. Secure each corner with a 2½″ finish nail. Lay pegboard on top, squaring it flush with the top corner joints. Now lay the completed back frame assembly squarely on top of the pegboard.

Check for a flush fit on all sides and corners. Clamp on at least two sides. Predrill for #8 screws on all sides, approximately 6″ on center, drilling from the back, through the back frame and pegboard, into the front frame. Fasten the frames and pegboard together using 1½″ #8 flathead Phillips screws. Fasten through the bottom edge of the pegboard into the back frame using ¾″ #8 screws.

17. Make the backboard/tool rack. Crosscut the 1x12 pine to 40¼″. Crosscut a 1x3 to 33″. Mark the center line on the 1x3. Starting from each end, mark five points 2″ on center. Working from each end, drill one ½″ hole, three ¾″ holes, and one 1″ hole at the marked points (10 holes). You may have specific needs that require fewer holes or different sizes; feel free to mark and drill as you prefer. To prevent splintering, clamp a piece of scrap stock to the bottom of the 1x3 before drilling. Mark the front corners for rounding, round off with a coping saw.

Position the tool rack on the 1x12 backboard, 2″ down from the top and 3⅝″ in from each end. Mark the bottom and end lines. Remove the rack, center, and mark screw locations every 12″, starting 2″ in from one end. Drill through the backboard from the front. Reposition the tool rack and attach from the back with 1½″ #8 screws.

18. Attach the backboard/tool rack to the framed pegboard assembly. Use 1½″ #8 screws to attach the backboard to the backs of the front frame side pieces. The 1x12 should extend 3½″ below the front frame side pieces. On the back side, square the lines parallel to the bottom of the backboard ¾″ and 2″ up. Predrill for #8 screws, 6″ on center, starting 5″ from one end. This completes the pegboard back.

19. With a helper, lift the completed back assembly onto the workbench, making sure it is flush with both ends of the bench. Mark the screw locations on the back stretcher through the predrilled frame. Remove the assembly, drill #8 pilot holes as marked. Reposition the frame, and attach with 1¼″ flat Phillips screws.

Caution: At this point, the pegboard back will support itself, but not a load of heavy tools. You must add the support braces. If the bench is placed against a wall, you may want to secure the back to the wall at several points in addition to using the required braces.

20. Assemble and attach the back support braces (Drawing J). Cut two 21¼″ and two 10″ pieces of 1x3.

Stack a 10″ piece on top of a 21¼″ piece, butt one end, predrill and screw together with 1¼″ #8 screws. Place this over the backboard and leg, flush with the sides of the leg, making sure the brace top butts against the bottom of the back pegboard frame. Predrill for #10 screws for the leg attachment points, and for #8 screws for the backboard points. Attach the brace to the leg with 2½″ #10 screws, then attach to the backboard with 1¼″ #8 screws. The bench is now complete.

Note: You can watch the construction of the full-size workbench and a set of professional sawhorses in the Stanley Workbench video (available in ½″ VHS only). It's 28 minutes long and filled with helpful details and construction hints. Watch it before you begin work, then leave it in your VCR to refer to as you begin each step. To order a copy, send your name, address, and a check or money order for $14.95 to: The Stanley Works, Advertising Services, Box 1800, Dept. WBB, New Britain, CT 06050. Please make payment in U.S. dollars and allow four to six weeks for delivery. Offer good while supplies last.

Do-It-Yourself Achievements

Do-It-Yourself Hints

Some Good Ideas Can Help You With A Lifetime Of Home Projects

If Academy Awards were given for the best solutions to project challenges around the home, chances are you might be able to offer a candidate or two. Most of us discover good project hints as we go along, and let it go at that. Others make a special effort to search out and accumulate better ideas. They are the hint hunters of the do-it-yourself world.

If you fall into this category, you might trace your enthusiasm for do-it-yourself projects to someone who sparked your interest in using tools and materials in your younger years. It might have been a relative who demonstrated the practicality and enjoyment possible by working with your hands. Or, it may have been a neighbor, a high school instructor, or a kindly carpenter on your first job.

Those who have had such a mentor in their past are blessed. But anyone can become a hint hunter, and, with a little effort, can build up project know-how over the years to near-professional levels.

Books, magazines, special classes, woodworking clubs, and watching professionals work also can help propel your project skills to new heights. If you subscribe to several how-to magazines, they will become more valuable if you make it easier to retrieve information from them. Invest in special binders in which to store the publications, and make a special place for them in your workshop. But, before filing issues away, take the time to tape a blank sheet of paper on the cover and list the items of interest to you. The listing will help you retrieve information quickly when you need it.

Over time, you will learn to winnow out the best ideas from various sources. When you discover a valuable tip, it will serve you for the rest of your life. A good way to remember handy hints is to categorize them in your mind in "clumps" or "bunches." Here are a few examples.

One of the most basic of handy hints is to use the best tool for the job. Improvements, like the metal strike caps on these Stanley chisels, help them do better work and last longer.

Starting Fasteners

You'll find one problem area that attracts handy hints is that of starting screws or nuts in hard-to-reach places. (Often, a number of alternatives are needed because only one might work in a particular situation.) A way to start a screw or nut in a hard-to-reach place is to double a piece of tape with the sticky-side out and put it on the end of the screwdriver or nut driver (even chewing gum is worth a try). By placing the screw or nut on the sticky material, you will be able to drive the fastener without holding onto it.

If you are trying to start a screw in a tight area, you also can try putting a small piece of paper over the screwdriver blade. The paper may give enough hold so the screw will stick for a "no-finger" operation.

Another method is to wrap soft wire or even roll solder around the screw near the head to position it until it gets started. After it starts, you simply pull the wire away. Yet another trick is to wrap tape, sticky side out, around your finger. Then stick the screw or nut to the tape, and you can position it with one finger.

Loose Screws

Solutions also accumulate for the challenge of fixing loose screws.

For instance, one way to repair loose screws in wood is to remove the screws and insert toothpicks (or burned wooden matches) with a coating of wood glue into the holes. Cut the matches or toothpicks flush with the surface and put the screws back in. (This trick also works with loose finishing nails in furniture.) Another method is to remove the screw, fill the hole with glue, and push the screw back into the hole. When the glue sets, back the screw out and the glue will have formed a threaded insert in the wood.

Still another way to tighten a loose screw is to put plastic wall anchors into the holes. When you put the screw back in, it will tighten and hold solid. If you don't have plastic anchors on hand, try dropping a very small screw into the hole upside down. When you reinsert the original screw, the little screw will provide grip for the threads of the larger screw.

Stubborn Fasteners

A common problem is a screw that refuses to back out. One solution is to use a soldering iron to heat the head. After heating, allow the screw to cool, and chances are it will have broken out of its "set."

Another familiar problem is the fastener that constantly vibrates loose on machinery or tools. If a bolt keeps vibrating off, take the nut off and wrap nylon fishline around the threads, then put the nut back on. The line will lock it in place. (You can use fishline with screws, too, by putting a piece into a hole and then re-driving the screw.)

Many handy hints collect around problems such as bashing your thumb or marring wood when using small finishing nails. A solution is to use what is called a nail spinner. Or, if you don't have one, you also can start small finishing nails through one of the holes in a piece of pegboard. Then you just lift the pegboard and use a nail set to finish driving the nail.

If you become a true hint hunter, you will find that good hints keep you enthusiastic throughout a project. A good collection of hints also can help you avoid projects that injure, projects that are poorly executed or never completed, and even projects that never get started. Stay on the lookout for hints that help you keep your mind in sync with what you want to accomplish. A sharp, uncluttered mind is probably the best tool you can bring to any project.

Meanwhile, review the following offerings. Try them out and add the best to your own personal collection. Some will certainly save you time, money, or frustration over the years ahead.

Starter Ideas For Hint Collectors

Price Sticker Solution

To remove stubborn price stickers from tools and other shop items, try nail polish remover. WD-40 also loosens stickers on many surfaces.

Sandpaper Press

To keep sandpaper discs from curling, make a simple press to keep them flat. Use ¼″ plywood or paneling sections slightly larger than the discs. Draw diagonal lines from the corners to find the center, then drill a ¼″ hole there. Make two. Put a ¼″ bolt through one, lay the paper on it, put the other on top and fasten with a wingnut. The sandpaper will stay flat.

Easy-On Apron

Tired of fumbling to tie a nail apron behind your back? Do what the pros do. Tie it on backwards, with the back to the front, then slip it around so the nail pockets are to the front.

Buying Tools

Because of market competition, you won't go wrong most of the time if you buy according to a tool's price. Generally, manufacturers have a reason to charge more for a product. If you're pondering whether to buy the $500 or the $750 tool, go with the more expensive. If you buy the cheaper one, you may end up kicking yourself, and its shortcomings may grow in your mind every time you use it.

Moving Tools

If your stationary tools don't have a stand with casters, you can make one from double ¾″ plywood, large enough to accommodate the tool legs. Put casters on one end and attach 2x4 stock at caster height on the other end.

Protecting Ladders

Don't paint ladders; the paint may hide cracks which warn you of unsafe conditions. Instead, if you need to protect from weather, use a clear water repellent such as those sold for wood deck protection.

Tool Check-Out

To check out a major shop tool you want to buy, rent it from a rental store. You can check its features and determine if they are what you expect. You can also confirm that the tool will do the job and which accessories are worth buying.

Cheap Shaping Discs

Drywall sanding screen, or similar abrasive screen, can be cut to make heavy-duty discs for smoothing or shaping with a Moto-Tool. The discs can be cut to fit the tool or job. They are long wearing and you may like them better than the discs which are commercially available.

Buying Saws

When selecting a tablesaw, heavier is better. Heavier saws have less vibration, less run-out, and usually better accuracy of fence and miter gauge alignment. Professionals look for a heavy, rigid tool. If you see a low-priced saw, pick it up. If it feels light, don't buy it.

Bandsaw Buying

Safer than the tablesaw for ripping and most other kinds of cuts, a powerful and well-tuned bandsaw can do nearly everything a tablesaw can do. Buy the deepest-throated, most powerful bandsaw you can afford, and learn to operate the tool properly.

Essential Tools

A jointer is a necessity in a shop, probably one of the two essential stationary tools, the other being a good saw. The longer the bed of the jointer, the flatter the cuts it will take. A surface planer is another tool worth adding if you are serious about woodworking.

Extension Cord Knot

Use one half of a square knot to tie extension cords together so they don't pull apart. Tie just as if you were tying your shoes, except instead of making bows, plug the cords back together.

Homemade Drill Box

Instead of buying a drill box, you can make a simple rack for bits from a block of hardwood. Drill the holes with the bits you plan to store. Tack the drilled block to the wall and store the bits with their points down. Lubricate the inside of each hole with a few drops of oil to protect against rust.

Plane Shelves

Special shelves help keep carpenter's planes organized. But, before mounting such a shelf, rout a groove ½″ deep into its top surface. Position the groove where the blade will rest when it is on the shelf. The groove will provide a slot for the blade and you won't have to retract it for storage.

Chuck Key Holster

A solution to a lost drill chuck key is to make a special holster for it. The next time you need to replace an end on your round extension cord, save the outer plastic cover. Cut around the interior wires and pull the outer cover off. Take this tube, about 1½″ long, and attach it to your drill's power cord with plastic electrical tape. As you begin taping, compress the tube slightly and tape from end to end. When you finish taping, slide the chuck key into its holster; it shouldn't fall out.

Drill Press Oiler. Keeping an oilcan close to your drill press is handy. Find another can and cut two small slits in the upper part to accept a worm-gear hose clamp. Slip the clamp strip in one hole and out the other, then around the post of your drill press about 5″ down from the upper assembly.

Storing Sanding Discs

To store sanding discs, saw a round cake pan in half and smooth the cut edges so they aren't sharp (tape will also work). Then attach one of the half-moons, open side up, on a wall of your shop by nailing through the rim of the pan. Each half will provide an excellent rack to store discs so that they are handy, visible, and protected.

Labeling Shop Items

Apply three labels equally spaced around cans or holders containing nuts, bolts, screws, or nails that will be set on a shelf. This allows you to identify the contents regardless of how they are stored. For square containers, put labels on each of four sides. It's a one-time job that will pay off for years.

Dust-Proofing Tools

To keep tools in the shop dust free, use plastic trash bags upside down over your equipment when not in use. If you take time to do it, whenever you go to use the tools, they will be as clean as you left them.

Hand Saw Storage

Make a protector for the teeth of an occasionally used hand saw from a piece of tongue-and-groove flooring as long as the saw blade. Rip the flooring lengthwise, leaving an inch-wide strip, including the groove. Fit the saw's blade into the groove and hold the strip in place with rubber bands. The strip protector will keep the saw teeth from getting nicked.

Steel Chip Collector

Steel chips on tables in a wood shop can imbed themselves in wood surfaces and be tracked out of the shop by shoes onto carpets. Use a large magnet inside a plastic bag to catch metal chips when you bore holes in metal. Simply turn the bag inside out to pull the chips off; they stay in the bag to be transferred to the garbage.

Sizing Drill Bits

To help size drill bits, try this trick:

If you need to clean your leather tool belt, rub with linseed oil and vinegar, half and half, then polish with a soft cloth.

Measure the bolt or dowel that will fill the hole with a Crescent-type wrench. Then select the bit that fits between the jaws of the wrench.

Equalizing Wood

If you are about to start a carving or turning project, don't take wood at cold or sub-zero temperatures into your shop with high heat and low humidity and immediately start working it. Give the wood a chance to equalize with your shop's heat and humidity, preferable two weeks or longer.

Temporary Sealer

Don't start a project such as a large bowl turning or a carving and leave large areas of end grain exposed to heat and low humidity. If the project can't be completed and the final finish applied, always apply some kind of temporary sealer, such as paste wax, shellac, lacquer, etc., which can be easily removed before finishing.

Low-Cost Cooling

If you don't have an extra air conditioner and you have your own well, consider cooling your shop with a salvaged car radiator. Mount on a wooden frame, then adapt garden hose to both the inlet and outlet hoses. Run cold water into the bottom at a trickle, and out of the top to a drain. Use a floor fan behind the radiator to blow out the cool air.

Shop Work Prices

If you do shop work for hire, first make sure a customer agrees to either a time and material cost (with changes possible as the work progresses) or a set cost for the project based on a plan drawing they approve. This prevents complaints after the project is done when you present the bill. The agreement should be solid and up-front so both you and the customer know what to expect.

Cheaper Wood

If you shudder when looking at the price of good wood, maybe you're not going to the right lumberyard. You can get great oak 3x3s in 4′ lengths from companies that receive shipments of heavy equipment. The lumber is used for shipping flats, and you can make beautiful oak furniture from this free lumber.

Self-Supporting Tape

If you are frustrated with measuring tapes which fall or bend, you need a wider tape. Buy a 25′ carpenter's version which generally is 1″ wide and strong enough to take long measurements without flopping.

Fine Measurements

For greater accuracy when cutting wood, mark your measurements with the sharp edge of a utility knife blade. Such markings will give you more precision than those made with a pencil.

Metal Starter Holes

If you are cutting out a large opening in a piece of metal, try making a starter hole with a sharp chisel instead of drilling one. The starter hole will be ragged, but it is faster than drilling.

Which Side Up?

When sawing wood, keep the good side down when using a portable circular saw or saber saw. For hand saws, scrollsaws, bandsaws, circular tablesaws and radial-arm saws, keep the good side up. The principle to remember is to have the tooth of the blade first break through the back side of the board or panel.

Cutting Habits

You learned in Scouts never to use a knife to cut towards yourself, but just watch someone cut a box open. Cut away from yourself or at least from side to side. Hunters often get deep cuts because they keep the knife in their hand while pulling on a hide or moving a piece of meat. The cuts are serious because of the power behind them. Lay knives and sharp tools in a safe place when not in use, and be extra careful when tired, excited, or in a hurry.

Parallel Lines

If you need to draw many closely spaced parallel lines in a hurry, get some masking tape and a number of pencils. Tape the pencils together, side by side, and draw the lines with one of the pencils up against a firmly held straightedge. All the lines will be parallel. For closer spacing, angle the row of pencils.

Sheathing Cuts

Professional carpenters know this, but if you are working on a once-in-a-lifetime construction project you may not. If you are putting up sheathing of the fiberboard variety, you can save time by making your cut marks with a chalkline instead of a carpenter's pencil. Hook the end of the line at one end, hold down and snap to make the line. Works for drywall, too.

Yardstick Handle

Attaching a handle to the flat side of a yardstick makes the measuring device easier to move about and assures better hand control. A lightweight metal drawer pull, screwed in place midway along the yardstick, provides an excellent and inexpensive handle.

Cutting Veneer

If you've tried to cut or trim veneered pieces like a flush panel door, you know that splintering can be a problem. A solution is to use a sharp utility knife and straightedge to mark the trim line. Make sure to mark both sides, and cut in deeply. You can complete the cut using either a saw or plane without making a mess of things.

Thin-Sheet Cutting

Also use a utility knife to scribe your cutting line on the back side of thin sheets of material like plywood or paneling to get a cleaner cut. Use masking tape on the good side, on one side of the cutting line.

Storing The Square. *Nail a 6″ piece of tongue-and-groove flooring to your shop wall, groove-side up. Then, to hang your square, just drop its short bar into the groove of the flooring piece. It's secure, looks neat, and keeps the square visible, easy to retrieve and replace.*

Spark Protectors

Grinders and metal cut-off saws in the shop can throw off sparks, small red-hot particles of metal. Some can end up in electrical outlets, or may also pass through electrical motor vents and cause serious shorts or motor failure. Appropriate shields of sheetmetal can be easily cut and bent to form a base for attaching to your benchtop. Round corners to avoid injuries.

Mixing Glue

Before removing the cap from a partially used tube of glue that hasn't been used for awhile, squeeze the contents from top to bottom several times. This remixes the ingredients, which may have separated. Do the same with other compounds left in tubes for long periods.

Gluing Dowels

A good fit is when you can push the dowel into the hole with your fingers, but don't make the hole so large that the dowel wobbles. Don't put glue only in bottom of hole and hope it will squeeze up. Apply glue to both the dowel and the sides of the hole.

Glue Removal Tools

A couple of very sharp paint scrapers and a sharp, ½″ wide wood chisel are good tools to remove excess glue after it is slightly dry. Press the sharp scraper square to the surface and in a couple of swipes you can get rid of any glue squeeze-out. Use the chisel to scrape excess glue from inside corners or next to moldings. Make sure scrapers are sharp. Touch them up with a fine file or sharpen on a 1″ belt grinder. You can use the shank of a screwdriver to burnish the edge and roll it over to get more of a hook on it.

Finishing Projects

Make up a finishing support for small projects by simply driving small box nails through a piece of ¼″ plywood or other scrap wood. Turn it over to support the project

To rejuvenate sanding belts, try using the sole of a crepe rubber shoe. Place your hand inside the shoe and apply the sole to the moving belt.

so you can paint or finish all sides at one time.

Paint On Glass

Forget the masking tape when painting next to glass. Allow a small strip of paint to go onto the glass, then when done just use a razor blade-type scraper to remove the paint from the glass surface.

Paint Tray Saver

To save time in cleaning up paint trays, either line the tray with aluminum foil before starting, or simply slip a small plastic trash bag over it. When done, turn the bag inside out and toss, along with worn-out roller covers.

Removing Old Paint

Use a heat gun to remove old paint instead of paint remover. It goes much faster and is less expensive and messy. Heat until the paint bubbles up, then remove the softened old paint with a sharp paint scraper. Since the wood stays dry, you can sand it immediately.

Neater Brushes

To keep the metal ferrule on a paint brush clean, cover it with masking tape before starting a job. The tape keeps the metal part clean, and you can dispose of it easily when you are through using the brush.

Hydraulic Jack Care

Use only hydraulic jack oil in your jacks. Don't add brake fluid. Even though it's a hydraulic jack and your car has hydraulic brakes, brake fluid contains alcohol which can eat the cup leathers used in hydraulic jacks. If you add brake fluid, you will mess up the internal working parts. Also don't add hydraulic oil when the jack is jacked up; when you let it down it may become damaged.

Power Paint Mixing

Use a power drill to mechanize paint mixing. To eliminate splattering, use a paper plate. Punch a hole in the center and push the end of your stirring attachment through the hole before chucking into your drill. Then hold the paper plate down over the open can while stirring to prevent splattering.

Paint Level Indicator

Instead of putting a smear of paint across the outside of a can to mark the level of paint inside, which can be messy and obliterate the label, use a rubber band. Put it around the can and roll it down to the level of the paint. Just by glancing at the rubber band, which is visible all the way around, you can see how full it is.

Half-Turn Trick

When painting large areas, give the paint can a half turn periodically throughout the job. Dipping the brush into the can alternately on one side of the can, and then the other, automatically keeps the contents stirred at the surface and prevents formation of a drying film. Also occasionally sweep the tip of the brush back and forth through the paint, especially with fast-drying latex.

Two-Brush Painting

To avoid hold-ups, use two brushes when applying latex. This lets you keep one brush under a wash of water to remove accumulated, drying paint. When the brush is clean, wrap in cloth or absorbent paper to remove excess moisture. Switch to a clean brush when the one in use has filled with paint and needs a good rinse.

Painting Over Screws

One problem with painting over screws is that the dried paint seals the screwheads to the wood and causes chipping when you try to remove them. To avoid this, back each screw out a couple of turns before the paint dries and then re-seat after painting.

Paint Color Test

It is often hard to tell what paint will look like until it is dry. To test, spread some onto a white desk blotter or a similar absorbent material. You won't have to wait until the paint dries to see what it will look like. The liquid part of the paint absorbs quite fast while the pigments remain suspended on the surface to give you a preview.

No-Strain Paint

If you find dried lumps in a can of paint, you don't have to strain the paint into another can to get rid of them. Instead, cut a circle from a piece of wire screen slightly smaller than the can's inside circumference. Put the circle of screen on the surface of the paint. With a little help, it will sink to the bottom of the can, taking the lumps with it.

Lump-free paint stays above the screen.

Spring Clip Hanger

A large, strong spring-type paper clip clamped to the bristles of a cleaned paint brush can serve double duty. It helps maintain a chisel edge on the brush, and provides an eye to suspend the brush from a nail in your workshop.

Drip-Free Paint

The next time you break open a can of paint, try this trick to keep paint from dripping down the side. Use a regular screwdriver to punch four holes in the rim of the can (in the groove where the lid fits). You will find that paint drains back into the can, and the lid seals the holes when set back on the can.

Paint Ring Preventer

To avoid leaving a ring of color where you set a paint can during a job, keep a paper plate under the can. Use doubled-over masking tape on the can bottom and press the can to the paper plate. The plate, sticking to the can, provides you with a handy over-sized coaster.

Roller Touch-Ups

Touching up a small spot on a wall is a hassle after you have finished painting and cleaning up. To avoid messing up a paint tray, transfer paint from the can to the roller with a small square of sponge. Spread what you need onto the roller, then finish the job.

Slick Brush Holder

Use a thumbtack on wooden handled brushes to help in cleaning. Put the brush in a can partly filled with solvent, press the tack halfway into the handle, and set the head of the tack over the lip of the can. You can move the tack up or down the handle to adjust the depth of the bristles in the solution.

Brush Straightening

If a good paint brush has bent bristles, try straightening them instead of throwing the brush away. Jam the brush in a container of thinner, wedging the handle so the bristles are bent in the direction opposite the original bend. The bristles should straighten after about 48 hours.

Drilling Light. If you have to use a power drill in a recess where light doesn't quite reach, try this. Tape a pocket or pencil flashlight to the top of the drill. Then turn it on and its light will shine down across the bit to illuminate the spot you need to drill.

Finishing Secret

You can buy polyurethane in flat, semi-gloss, or gloss. But the secret to using it is thinning. If you apply thin coats it is easy to rub down to get a beautiful soft luster or a mirror gloss. For a lacquer look without spray equipment, apply gloss polyurethane thinned as follows: 3 parts polyurethane to 2 parts mineral spirits.

Sawdust Help

When refinishing furniture, keep a supply of clean, fine-grained sawdust handy. As you scrape away loosened varnish, sprinkle a bit of it over the entire cleared area. The sawdust absorbs the residue of the varnish remover and clings to the surface until scraped into a bag for disposal.

Emergency Brushes

If you run out of throw-away brushes, or if you don't want to waste one putting oil on a small project, try this: Roll up some paper toweling tightly, fold it over, put a couple of rubber bands around one end, and you have a cheap throw-away brush. It won't last long, but

Clean up tools used to apply tile cement or mastic by putting them in the freezer. You'll find the material easier to chip off.

for a small project it will spread the finishing oil evenly and keep your hands clean.

Finish Test

Apply nail polish remover on cotton ball and apply on a glossy part in an inconspicuous place. If the ball sticks, it's varnish, lacquer, or shellac, and you need a refinisher. If it doesn't stick, you need a paint remover.

Saving Brushes

If you plan to put several coats of oil stain on a project and don't want to clean the brush or use a new one each day, try this: Dip the brush in the oil, then place it in a small plastic bag and put a rubber binder around the top. The brush will stay soft for several days, and you take half the work out of your finishing job.

Finishing Tip

When finishing a project, stand it up vertically when applying the stain or oil. This way, when the stain is drying, any seepage will collect where it is easier to see and remove. You can mask hardware before staining, but it may be easier to remove it for finishing. Keep notes so you can get the hardware back on quickly and efficiently.

Inside Finishing

Don't forget to finish the inside of your project to help prevent stress due to uneven moisture exchange. You don't have to sand as much inside, but it is important to put the same number of coats of oil, stain, or wax on the inside as you put on the outside.

Wet Sponge Trick

When soldering two joints that are close together, simply apply a wet sponge to the first joint soldered. This will prevent heat from the second joint from loosening the first joint.

Undoing Hide Glue

Hide glue was the glue of choice in years past for fine furniture and is still a good glue. It is water soluble, so if a part breaks, just wrap wet rags around the joint until it loosens up so you can remove the part to replace it.

Soft-Touch Punch

You can make your own brass-tipped punch to use when driving out a soft pin, or when you want to make sure that a part isn't damaged. Make several in a few different sizes by simply brazing a heavy layer of brass onto the ends of some scrap steel rods. Dressed up with a file, they become serviceable tools which will last for years.

Rusted Nut Solution

If you are faced with a rusted nut on a bolt and no penetrating oil, try ordinary household vinegar. One or two applications should loosen the nut.

Smoothing Glass

To smoothen the edge of a glass pane, fold a piece of sandpaper into the groove of a length of tongue-and-groove flooring. Then insert an edge of the glass into the groove and run the sanding block along it.

Won't Start Solution

If you car or pickup won't start after a rain or during humid conditions, you can try two things: First spray WD-40 over the distributor cap and along each of the spark plug wires. If that doesn't help, remove the plug wires at the distributor and spray inside. If you don't have any WD-40, dig out the hair dryer from the bathroom. Pull the major wires from the distributor, one by one, and train the dryer on the ends.

Plug Wire Mix-Up

If you need to replace spark plugs, try this to avoid getting wires mixed up: Use clip-type clothespins, numbered, on each of the wires before you remove them.

Scouring Copper

To scour copper tubing for sweat soldering, try a small device available at auto parts stores called a battery post cleaner. It comes in two parts for cleaning the outside of the battery post and the inside of the cable connection. You can use it the same way on copper tubing, and it's easy to carry around in your toolbox.

Removing Trim

To save trim or molding for reuse, use two small flat prybars. Slide the thin end of one behind the molding, then insert the second bar and use both alternately to inch the trim off. If there are thin finishing nails protruding from the back, use a Channelock-type pliers to pull them out; the rounded edge over the upper jaw acts as a perfect fulcrum.

Small Part Catcher

Smooth shop or dish towels are handy when making repairs. Clean off a section of your workbench and spread out a towel. As you take something apart, the towel will keep small parts from rolling onto the floor. Square shop rags also can be used, but may not cover a big enough area on your bench.

Cotter Pin Saver. Sometimes the fit is so snug when trying to drive a cotter pin you know that forcing it will probably flatten the eye of the pin. To keep this from happening, insert a nail through the eye of the pin before driving it into the hole.

Soldering Helper

Keep a mound of modeling clay handy when soldering. You can use it to hold small pieces of work at odd angles to each other. Push the ends of the items into the clay and position them to meet each other. The clay will hold the pieces securely and eliminate the possibility that metal contact (like a vise) will conduct heat away from the work.

Emergency Levels

In a pinch, a glass measuring cup with calibrated lines on two sides can be used as a level. Fill with water to one of the markings and put on the surface to be leveled. The waterline will touch equal calibrations on both sides once the surface is level. If you don't have a measuring cup, you can scribe lines on any glass container. Use a felt-tipped marker to make points opposite each other, at equal distance from the bottom.

Reading V-Belts

Identifying the numbers on worn-out V-belts is often difficult, especially on those belts that run over belt tighteners. Tip: Rub the area over the number with a piece of chalk, then wipe. The numbers on the belt may show up enough to read them.

Precision Oiling

To slow the flow of oil from an oil can, put a straight pin in the spout and crimp the spout to hold the pin in place. Push the pin all the way into the crimped spout until it rests against the spout opening. This closes off the spout so only the smallest drop of oil can squeeze out, and it allows you to apply controlled amounts to small tools or motors.

Unsticking Saws

If your saw has accumulated a sticky resin build-up which makes it bind, clean off the gunk with an oven cleaner such as Easy Off. This also works for items such as power saw blades and router bits. Take proper precautions, clean off right away, then coat metal with light oil.

Replacing Window Glass

You can use a small propane torch to soften putty on windows so it can easily be removed. Use a spreader attachment if possible, otherwise play the torch gently over the putty, watching not to damage paint or wood.

Checking Contacts

If you have appliances that abruptly quit, first unplug and check electrical connections, especially clip-type. Pulling the electrical connections or jiggling them will often solve the problem. Another way is to spray electrical contact cleaner (it also can be used on switches). Fixing such simple problems instead of calling a repairman can save you big money.

Musty Odor Fix

To mask musky odors common to old furniture, put a pound of red cedar shavings in the toe of a worn-out nylon. Tie, cut off the excess and attach along the back of a drawer, on the back, or underneath the piece.

Recycling Saw Blades

Save any bandsaw blades that break before becoming dull to make your own scrollsaw blades. Break or snip the long blade into lengths to fit. If necessary, grind off the teeth on each end of the blade so it will fit in the saw chuck.

Drill-Bit Scriber

You can make an excellent scriber for scratching patterns onto sheet-metal from a worn-out or broken high-speed drill bit. Grind it to a sharp point. Before grinding the end down to a point, drive the shank of the bit into a hole drilled to size in the end of a rounded wooden block. The block will serve as a handle for the scriber.

Sharpening Tools

The single-bevel blade in wood planes, chisels, and jointers are often mis-sharpened. Most such new blades need to be tapered back more from the edge. The taper should be about 20 to 25° instead of about 30°. The real secret is to never touch the back side to a hone. Grind a burr only on one side, then remove the burr by gently working the blade flat on a fine abrasive.

Shrink-Tube Splicing

For professional-looking splicing without electrical tape, use heat shrinkable tubing. Slip the tube over a splice, apply heat with a heat gun and it will shrink down for perfect coverage. You can get the tubes in multiple sizes, as well as shrinkable wire caps for use in place of screw-on wire nuts. They are perfect for work on vehicles, trailers, underground and pool wiring, outdoor lighting, and sprinkler systems.

Free Funnels

A used plastic detergent, bleach or oil container can make a good substitute funnel, sometimes better than those you buy. Rinse out the bottle and pencil out the shape you want the funnel to be. Then use a sharp utility knife to cut off the bottom. A bonus with bleach bottles is that your free funnel will have a built-in handle.

Carpet Protectors

Keep one or more pieces of old carpeting in the shop to help protect your finish work. Spread the carpeting over your workbench, or drape it over a sawhorse; it also provides a solid surface to work on. You can also affix a carpet section to one end of your workbench if you do a considerable amount of fine woodworking.

One-Hand Oiling

To help with oiling jobs on hard-to-reach motors with flip-top oiler tubes, try this: Solder a small washer about ¼″ back from the end of the spout of a squirt-type oil can. With this you can reach into the motor area with one hand, and use the spout end to flip up the top of the oiler tube. The washer will hold the flip-top so you can stick the spout in the tube.

Beating Tool Rust

To protect something like a drill press column, which never contacts the workpiece, a coat of oil is acceptable. A tablesaw top, where the wood rides on the metal surface, can be protected with a coat of paste wax. For other tools, consider gun blueing. It is a process by which steel is acid etched and then coated with an oxide that, in reality, is controlled rusting. Cold gun blue is available at gun shops for about $3 a bottle.

Spark Plug Tool

If you are changing spark plugs in a vehicle, use a 6″ length of 5/16″ or 3/8″ fuel line hose to start the new plugs back in the head. If the plug gets cross threaded, the hose will slip. For best results, try to keep the hose as straight as possible.

Drill Bit Cleaning

To clean corrosion from a twist drill bit, let the drill help you. While applying oil to the turning bit, drill repeatedly into a block of hardwood secured in your vise. Apply the oil to the bit steadily, at its point of entry into the wood. Friction of the bit against the wood and abrasive wood particles provide a scouring action.

Cigarette Chars

To remove char marks caused by cigarettes on finished furniture, rub with nail polish remover on cotton swabs to dissolve the black residue. If a hollow remains, apply several coats of equal parts of nail polish remover and clear nail polish. Let dry between coats.

Battery Cleaner

Use a paste of 3 parts baking soda and 1 part water to clean corrosion from vehicle battery terminals. The slightly alkaline paste neutralizes the corrosion. Clean up with a wire brush, then wipe the terminals with petroleum jelly.

ROOM DIVIDERS

A Build-It-Yourself Project That Creates Storage And Sets Off Areas With Style

You can build this 7′-foot-high divider storage unit yourself, and reap several benefits at the same time. With its enclosed cupboards and see-through shelves, it's a great storage-maker. And, because of the unit's two-sided design, it can be used to define and separate areas of your home, wherever you place it.

For example, you can use it to separate dining from living areas, while taking advantage of the ample storage it offers for china, glassware, and linens. Or, you could use it to create an entry where none now exists. Its storage and the display space can be used for books, games, or electronic equipment. And the unit was designed to divide space without visually reducing the size of the room or cutting off needed light.

According to the designers at Western Wood Products Association, you also could add lights to the unit's recessed top. They will reflect against the ceiling to produce a soft, ambient light.

Built of solid western woods, this project requires moderate woodworking skills, but nothing beyond the ability of experienced weekend carpenters. The drawings on the following pages show some of the basic dimensions and details so you can decide if you would like to build it. If so, complete step-by-step plans are available (see address below).

This divider provides storage that stands out beautifully, and it's movable as well. Except for the door trim, all lumber used in this project is cut from standard sizes.

Cupboard doors on the lower storage area open from one side only, making it easier to build. However, the front and back of the unit look identical, so it can be used freestanding, as a divider, or against a wall. Fixed frames are used as a design feature on the open shelves in the upper storage area.

To simplify construction and installation, the cabinet is built in three sections: base, upper section, and top. If you ever want to move, you just take it apart and carry it with you—an advantage over built-in units.

The unit can be finished in deep wood tones or contemporary pastels to fit into your home's decor. The designers suggest that you precondition the lumber before starting construction by storing it indoors for a couple of weeks. This allows it to adjust before cutting so you get nice tight-fitting joints. Note: When preconditioning lumber, use wood spacers across the stack to separate each layer to provide good air circulation.

Tools needed for the project include a hammer, nail set, precision power saw (table or radial-arm saw), drill, screwdriver, tape measure, framing square, dado blade or router, bar clamps, chisel, and plane. A belt or finish sander is also helpful.

Note: The complete plans for the room divider include detailed drawings and step-by-step directions. Plans are available for 75¢ postpaid. Write to the Western Wood Products Association, Yeon Building, 522 SW Fifth Ave., Portland OR 97204-2122. Ask for Plan No. 57.

TECH NOTES: BUILDING THE DIVIDER

Building this room divider is quite straightforward; here are some of the highlights:

The construction starts by assembling a base frame of 2x4s, then adding end frames and a top frame, and fastening with glue and screws. Add 1½x2″ nailers around the bottom and top of the frame.

Next, cut seven 1x4 boards to 69¾″ in length for the bottom shelf and install. Then 1x4 boards are installed on the ends, and six 1x4s are glued and clamped to make a center partition for the bottom unit.

Uprights of 1½x2″ pieces from 2x3s or 2x4s are cut to assemble uprights on both sides which fit onto the base unit. A frame is built of 2x2s for the upper shelf and 1x4s are attached to the frame.

Next, the center partition above the upper shelf is built of 2x2s and also is covered with 1x4s. Ledgers of 1x1 stock are used to hold the top shelves, also made of 1x4s.

The top is made using a 2x8 frame. Then the frames for the lower doors and panels are built using half-lap joints, covered with wood.

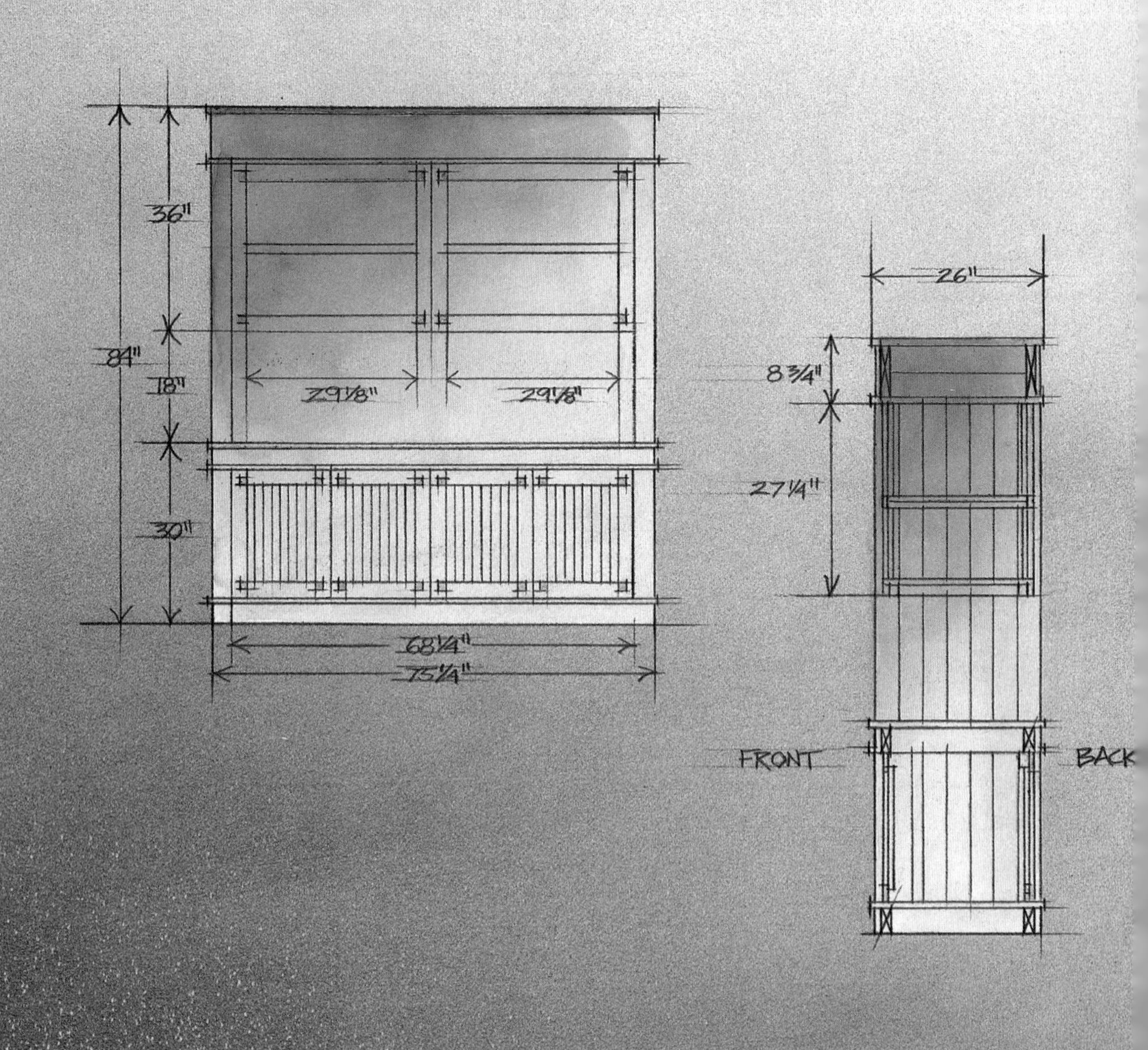

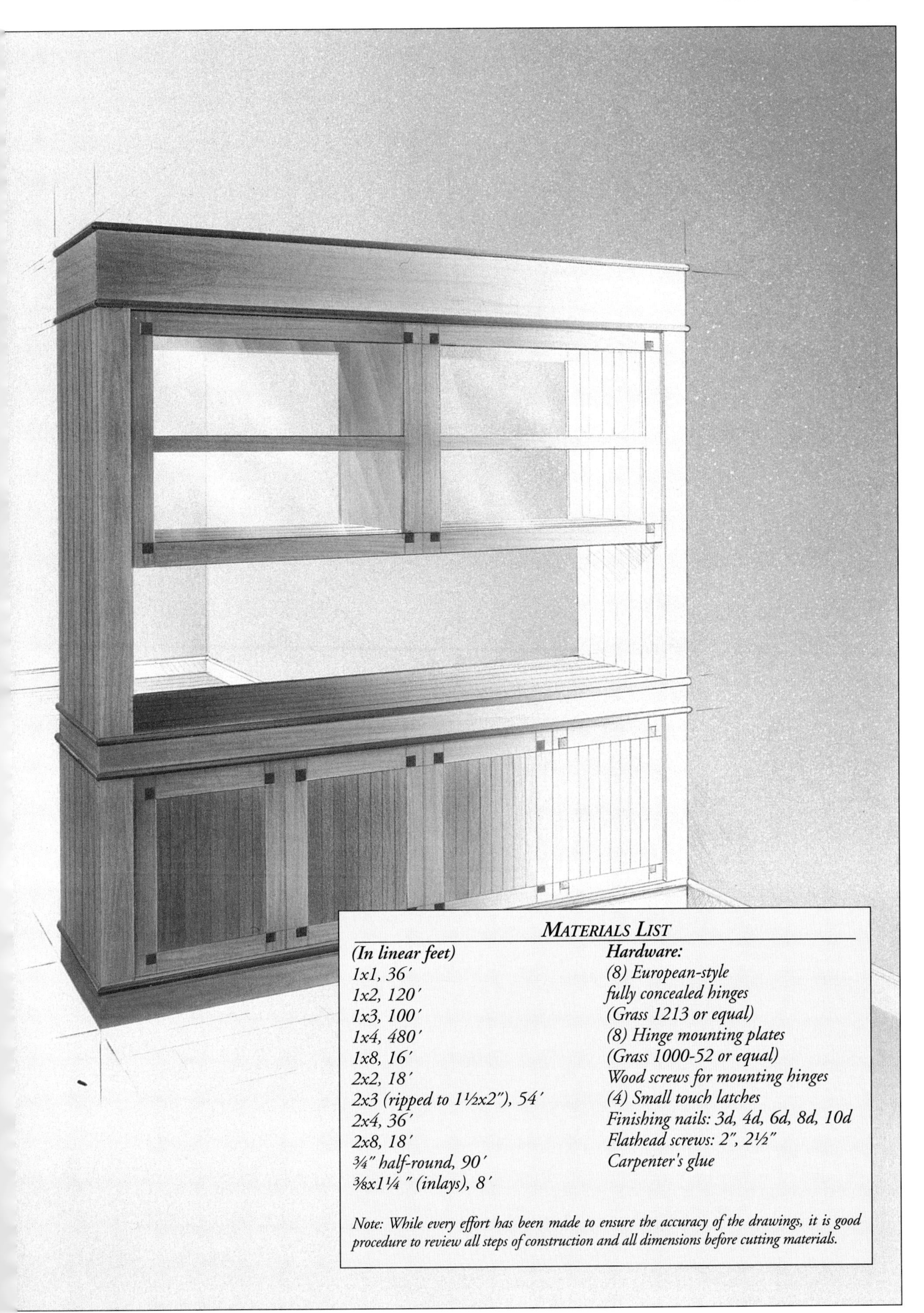

Materials List

(In linear feet)
1x1, 36′
1x2, 120′
1x3, 100′
1x4, 480′
1x8, 16′
2x2, 18′
2x3 (ripped to 1½x2″), 54′
2x4, 36′
2x8, 18′
¾″ half-round, 90′
⅜x1¼ ″ (inlays), 8′

Hardware:
(8) European-style fully concealed hinges (Grass 1213 or equal)
(8) Hinge mounting plates (Grass 1000-52 or equal)
Wood screws for mounting hinges
(4) Small touch latches
Finishing nails: 3d, 4d, 6d, 8d, 10d
Flathead screws: 2″, 2½″
Carpenter's glue

Note: While every effort has been made to ensure the accuracy of the drawings, it is good procedure to review all steps of construction and all dimensions before cutting materials.

Pouring Cement

How To Make Concrete Part Of Your Do-It-Yourself Project Arsenal

Just one generation ago, knowing how to use cement was as much a part of life as pounding nails.

Back in the 1920s, when a farmer needed to build a barn, the first order of business often was to track down the one engine-powered cement mixer that was passed from farm-to-farm on an "as needed" basis. (Who actually owned it had faded from the collective memory long before.) That one mixer poured all the new cement in the township.

Back then, cement was just a part of getting something built. Today, however, do-it-yourselfers often think cement work is out of their realm of possibilities. But that's changing, say Robert Scharff and John Corinchuck, co-authors of a book published by Meredith Press called *How To Build And Repair Concrete, Brickwork, And Stone.*

Larger continuous pours are best done by professional crews with the muscle to unload trucks fast. For slab-work, like the driveway here, adequate sub-base preparation, forms, and reinforcement are critical to success.

"There is no reason to back away from these types of projects," advises Scharff. "While there is much to learn, the basics are relatively simple and definitely can be mastered by the average do-it-yourselfer."

One of the first things Scharff will tell you is that the word *cement* is often technically misused. Most of us say *cement* when we mean *concrete.*

"They are not the same," he says. "Portland cement is only one ingredient in a concrete mix. Others are aggregates like sand, gravel, and crushed stone, plus water. The aggregates give strength and volume to the mix. Cement is the 'glue' that holds the mix together, while the water triggers the chemical reaction in the cement known as hydration."

Estimating Concrete

As Scharff points out in the easy-to-read guidebook, estimating the concrete needed for a project is not difficult. Just multiply the thickness (height) of the project by its width and length, and then divide this number by 12 to get the cubic feet.

Or, divide this number by 27 to find the number of cubic yards. One yard of concrete is equal in

Wire mesh is used most often for slab-work reinforcement, photo above. When possible, whole pieces are used; if combined, they are overlapped 6". To avoid paying for extra driver time, both forms and crew must be ready for delivery.

volume to one cube measuring 3'x3'x3', or 27 smaller cubes 1'x1'x1', or nine thinner slabs measuring 3'x3'x4".

Always be sure you will have enough concrete to completely fill the forms within a reasonable amount of time. Concrete must set up and age as a single mass. Some larger pours can be broken down into distinct sections, but consider each section a single mass. To be safe, calculate your needs accurately, and then add up to 10% for possible spills, uneven subgrades, or trial batches.

There are three basic ways to get concrete for projects: 1) buy it from a ready-mix company that will deliver by truck to your site, 2) buy aggregates and cement to mix your own concrete on-site, or 3) buy packaged premixes that only require adding water. Which you choose will likely depend on the amount of concrete you need.

Screeding, photo above, is done with a length of 2x lumber using the top of the forms as a guide. The surface is then floated to get a final finish. Guiding a wheelbarrow full of cement takes muscle; some crews use motorized versions.

Ready-Mix Concrete. Ready-mix is the most convenient and economical for larger jobs, such as the driveway shown in the photos. Doing business with a local ready-mix company makes their expertise available to you at no extra cost. They know the local codes pertaining to concrete mixes that can be used for different projects. They can also blend in admixtures to produce air-entrained concrete, fast- or slow-setting mixes, or colored concrete.

Unfortunately, many ready-mix companies will only deliver a minimum of one cubic yard. However, there may be companies in your area that supply to homeowners. These will generally accept orders for less than a yard, and often offer metered delivery, which eliminates the need for estimating.

Some companies offer self-hauling service. You rent a small mixing trailer that is filled with mix at the plant, and hook it to your vehicle with a universal hitch. The trailers normally hold up to one cubic yard, which is mixed during the ride back to your job site. Plain hopper trailers have no mixing capability and aggregate can settle during transport.

Unloading into forms or wheelbarrows is easy with the trailer's dumping mechanism. Saturdays are prime time for rentals, so reserve the work date well in advance. Since you will be charged by the hour, or even half-hour, it is a good idea to assign one crew member the duties of picking up, washing out, and returning the trailer, while the other workers finish the concrete.

Check out several suppliers, comparing minimum order amount, cost per cubic yard (or foot), cost for delivery, time the driver may stay on site at no additional cost, and cost for additional driver time (if needed). Don't be afraid to go with a company that appears to service mainly contractors if it offers more advantages.

Packaged Premixes. Premixes are convenient for small jobs or where handling separate ingredients is difficult. Premixes contain cement and aggregates in the same bag. You simply add water to produce a mix with a plastic-like consistency. The aggregate in premixed concrete is normally only ½″ in diameter, which makes mixing, placing, and finishing easier.

Premixed bags are sized by weight; the typical 60-lb. bag will produce about one-half cubic foot of concrete. Always set some premix aside so you will have material to add to the mix if you make the first batch too soupy. Note: Keep in mind that premixes are rarely air-entrained because hand mixing is not rigorous enough to generate the tiny air bubbles within the concrete.

Premixes can be used when several cubic feet of concrete are needed, such as when setting posts, casting molded projects, or constructing small service walls, entrance landings, mounting slabs, small footings, short curbs, or stoop steps. You can batch up premix faster by using a power mixer.

Larger premix jobs are possible if you break down the work into smaller sections. A patio with a permanent grid of treated lumber is a good example. Grid sections can be filled one at a time. To make sure each section cures to the same shade, keep the water used per bag constant and use the same curing technique on all sections.

Premix manufacturers use cement as their main bonding agent, but aggregates and additives vary to meet specific needs. For example:

- Concrete mix, also called gravel mix, contains cement, sand, and gravel. It is used for all general concrete work.
- Sand mix (fine topping) is a mix of cement and fine sand designed for jobs where concrete is less than 2″ thick. Sand mix cures to a stronger finish than ordinary premix concretes because of its higher cement content. It can also be used for filling cracks, resurfacing, stuccoing, and laying flagstone, and paving brick.
- Fast-setting premix is ideal for setting posts and poles and for slab work 2″ or thicker. The initial set can be in as little as 15 minutes, with walk-on time in less than an hour.
- Surface-bonding mixes are specialty mixes containing additional bonding agents or fiber-reinforced materials. Typical jobs include top bonding to damaged walls and slabs, bonding together dry stacked masonry block, or paraging over rigid insulation board.

Mixing From Scratch

Scratch mixing is common for small to medium-sized projects requiring between one-half and two yards of concrete. Working at a steady pace, two people using a power mixer should be able to mix, place, and finish between one and two yards of concrete per day.

Scratch mixing is less expensive than using premixes. Premixes usually have a maximum aggregate size of ½″, but scratch mixing lets you select larger sizes. You can also alter the mix proportions for the most economical mix possible.

When ordering aggregates, always add at least 10% to the estimate to allow for waste and error. It takes work to move the aggregate and cement, so carefully plan the drop point. If your property is sloped, it is better to unload above the job site rather than below it.

There are two basic ways to mix proportions: by weight and by volume. Working by volume is more common. You can measure by the shovelful, but using containers is recommended. A "part" can be any volume you select as long as you remain consistent. It's useful to remember that each 94-lb. bag of cement contains one cubic foot of material or about 7½ gallons.

The bottom chart at right shows the strongest practical mixes using various aggregate sizes. These proportions are used for concrete exposed to outside weather, de-icing agents, and the like. These mixes can be used for concrete used in walks, driveways, patios, swimming pool decks, or floors.

By increasing aggregate content, less expensive but slightly weaker mixes are possible. For example, the 1:2¾:4 mix shown in the top chart produces moderately strong concrete useful for most foundations, walls, and structures not directly exposed to the weather. A 1:3:5 mix can be used for heavy, massive foundations, thick retaining walls, and masonry backing.

Adding the right amount of water is the most difficult part of mixing. Sand usually contains moisture, which must be accounted for as part of the mixing water. Check the water content of the sand by squeezing it with your hand. Damp sand falls apart when squeezed and released. Wet sand forms a ball but leaves no moisture on your palm. Very wet sand forms a ball and leaves moisture.

A word on water-cement ratios: One gallon of water weighs about 8⅓ lbs., and one cubic foot of water weighs almost 62 lbs. Combining one 94-lb. bag of cement with 6 gallons of water (50 lbs.) results in a water-cement ratio of 0.53. This is the highest ratio recommended for home use.

When using a power mixer, begin by loading all of the coarse aggregate and half of the mixing water. If a liquid air-entraining agent is being used, add it as part of this mixing water. Start the mixer and add the sand, cement, and remaining water.

Once all ingredients are loaded, continue mixing for at least three minutes. When properly blended, the concrete will have a uniform color. Streaking indicates dry patches in the mix.

Put the concrete in the forms as soon as possible after mixing. If the concrete shows signs of stiffening in the drum, remix it for about two minutes to restore its workability. If remixing does not result in a plastic mix, discard the concrete. Never add water to concrete that has stiffened to the point where remixing does not restore workability.

ALTERNATE MIXES TO MAKE ONE CUBIC YARD

1:2¼:3 Concrete	
Cement	6 bags
Sand (wet)	14 cubic feet (0.51 cubic yards)
Coarse aggregate	18 cubic feet (0.66 cubic yards)
Water	36 gallons
1:2¾:4 Concrete	
Cement	5 bags
Sand (wet)	14 cubic feet (0.51 cubic yards)
Coarse aggregate	20 cubic feet (0.74 cubic yards)
Water	30 gallons
1:3:5 Concrete	
Cement	4.5 bags
Sand (wet)	13 cubic feet (0.48 cubic yards)
Coarse aggregate	22 cubic feet (0.8 cubic yards)
Water	27 gallons

Note: "How To Build And Repair Concrete, Brickwork, And Stone" is an all-inclusive project guidebook for working with the materials of the mason's craft. Containing 700 illustrations, it shows how to plan, execute, and complete hundreds of projects around the home. Priced at $34.95, it's available where how-to books are sold. If you can't find a copy, write Meredith Books, 1716 Locust, Des Moines, IA 50309-3400.

MIXING BY VOLUME FOR SMALL JOBS

Maximum-Size Coarse Aggregate (in.)	Air-Entrained Concrete				Non-Air-Entrained Concrete			
	Cement	Wet, Fine Aggregate	Wet, Coarse Aggregate	Water	Cement	Wet, Fine Aggregate	Wet, Coarse Aggregate	Water
⅜	1	2¼	1½	½	1	2½	1½	½
½	1	2¼	2	½	1	2½	2	½
¾	1	2¼	2½	½	1	2½	2½	½
1	1	2¼	2¾	½	1	2½	2¾	½
1½	1	2¼	3	½	1	2½	3	½

Tech Notes: Mixing By Hand

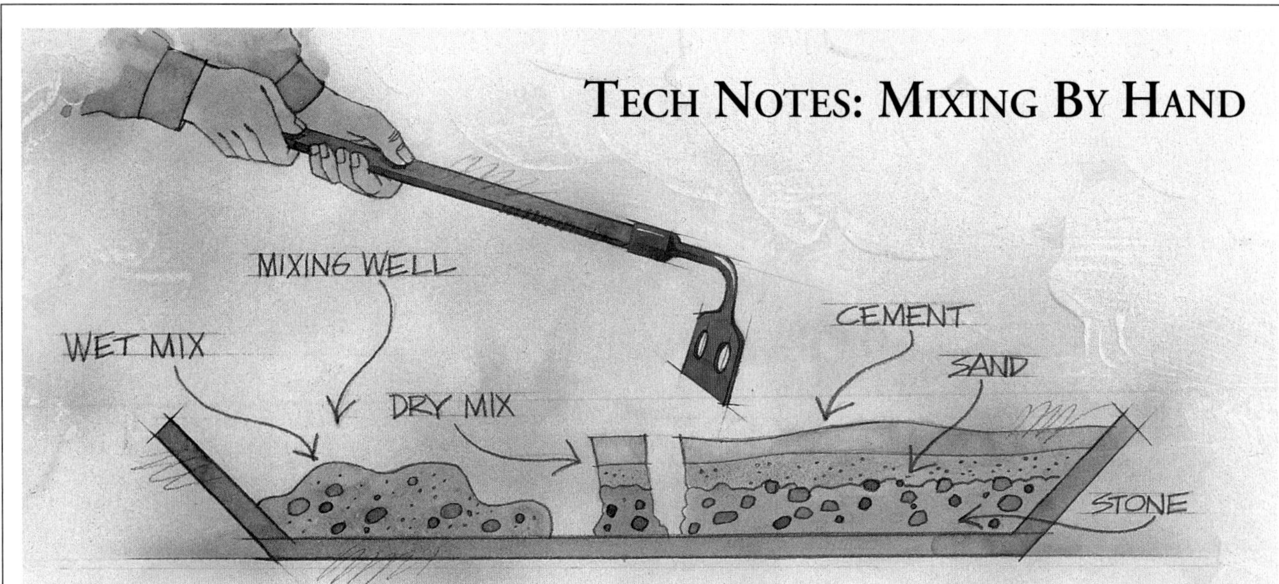

For small jobs requiring less than a few cubic feet of concrete, it is sometimes more convenient and less expensive to mix by hand. Hand mixing is not vigorous enough to make air-entrained concrete, even if you use air-entraining cement or an air-entraining agent. Hand mixing, therefore, should not be used for concrete exposed to freezing-thawing conditions or de-icers.

Mortar Box. Place the mortar box on a level surface and wet down its inside surface. Spread out all the coarse aggregate in an even layer in the bottom of the box. Leave about one-fourth of the box clear to act as a "mixing well." Spread sand on top of the coarse aggregate and follow with the cement. You should now have a three-layer sandwich of stone, sand, and cement in the proportions called for by your mix formula.

Pour a portion of the mix water into the well area of the box. Using a hoe, slice down through the sandwich and pull a small cross section of dry materials into the water. Turn it over several times to blend thoroughly and then cut off another small section. Continue working in this manner until the mix in the well area of the box reaches the proper consistency.

You can then remove and place this concrete or add more water and continue to work forward through the entire sandwich of dry materials. You should only be mixing a very small amount of the total material at a given time. When you finish, the mixing well will be at the opposite end of the box from where you started.

Wheelbarrow. You can't use the mortar box technique in a wheelbarrow; there just isn't enough space. Instead, spread the sand on the bottom of the wheelbarrow, followed by layers of coarse aggregate and cement. Add water in increments, and mix with a hoe or shovel. Hold the hoe short to help control it, and don't lift a shovel any higher than needed to clear it when you turn it sideways. Limit amounts to one to two cubic feet at a time or mixing will be cramped and difficult.

Flat Surfaces. This technique is similar to using a mortar box except that the materials are positioned in a ring on a hard, smooth surface such as a concrete floor or driveway or a heavy sheet of plywood. The center of the ring is the mixing well.

Layer the ring with coarse aggregate on the bottom, followed by sand and cement layers. Add water to the center of the ring and pull ingredients into the mixing area with a hoe. As the mix reaches the proper consistency, remove it for immediate placement.

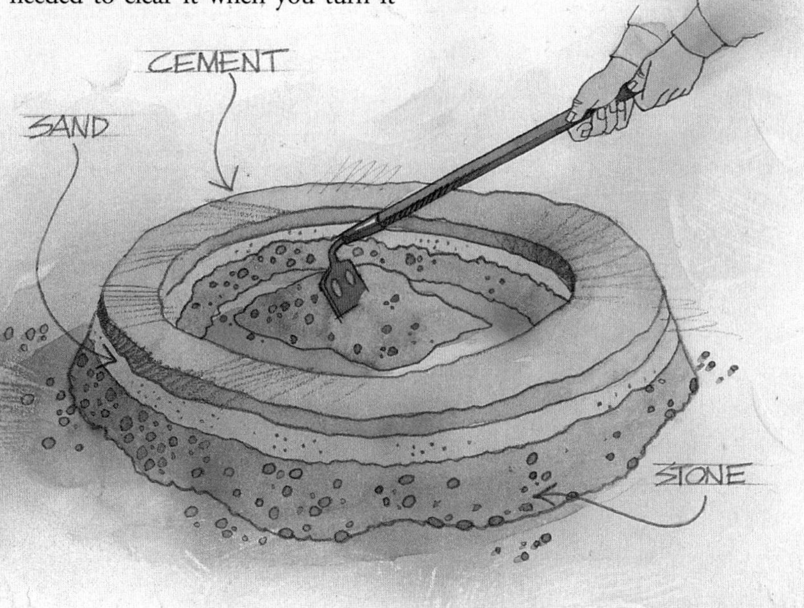

Nails And Nailing

Basic Advice On The Most Common Type Of Wood Fastener

Like so many things, using nails falls in the "nothing is ever simple" category. Although many hammers and nails are multipurpose, each type has its advantages and disadvantages, depending on the use intended. Knowing a few basic facts about both hammers and nails can eliminate much of the confusion.

For rough carpentry work, most professionals will use a 22-oz. framing hammer. These hammers often are exactly 16″ from the end of the handle to the top of the head, and can be used to mark off 16″ centers. Rookie carpenters often will lay their hammer down and measure out the centers with their tape, not realizing that they could use the hammer itself.

For finish and trim work, professionals will generally use a 16-oz. hammer. For both hammer sizes, the preference leans toward the straight claw type over the curved claw type because straight claws don't require reaching as far when pulling nails.

Good claw hammers can cost $20 or more. Look for high carbon steel, ground and polished, with the rim tempered to reduce chipping.

To do any serious hammering, get a leather nail pouch. Many professional carpenters prefer a belt with side pouches on the job because the pouches stay out of the way when they are kneeling down to nail, or when they are climbing ladders.

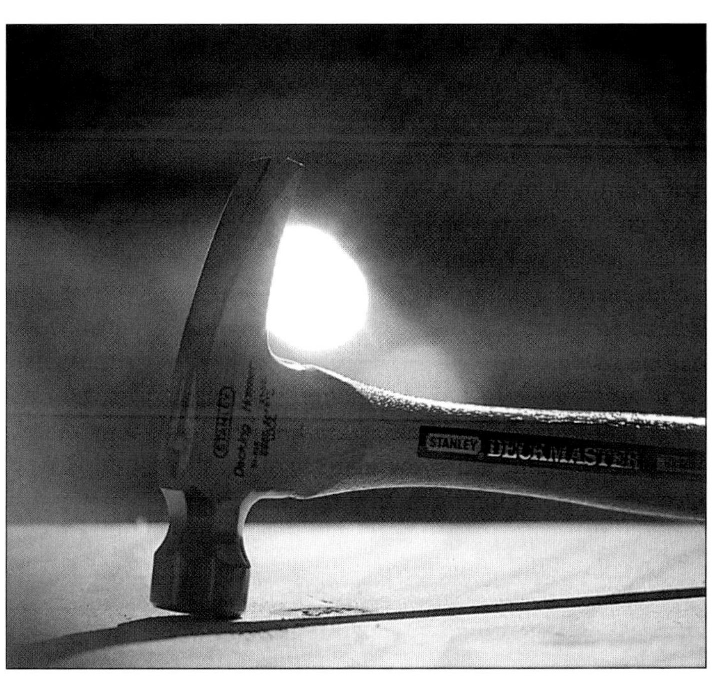

A professional carpenter's hammers get rough treatment; pros generally will buy a 22-oz. hammer for framing and a 16-oz. hammer for finish work

Hammering Techniques

If you watch a professional carpenter closely, you will see that he positions the nail to match the arc of the hammer. In other words, he will angle the nail toward himself slightly so that when the hammer strikes it hits the nail squarely on the head.

In rough framing, nails are usually driven at an angle toward the center of the board to increase holding power. Beginners often tend to bend nails because they push the hammer instead of swinging it. Holding the hammer at the end of the handle allows you to swing the hammer like the pendulum of a clock. Keeping your eye on the nail, and not on the hammer, also helps.

Another key step to avoid bending nails is to keep the hammer face clean. Run a piece of fine sandpaper or emery cloth over the face of the hammer occasionally, especially if you are working around glue or adhesives, or pounding cement-coated nails. In these situations the hammer's face can tend to get slippery or dirty. Regular cleaning of the face helps avoid bent nails and black marks on the wood.

A couple of hammers will serve the average do-it-yourselfer quite well for most jobs. But there is one notable exception; hardened masonry nails should never by driven with a carpenter's hammer. For striking any hardened steel object, like masonry nails, cold chisels, star drills, or other steel tools, use a machinist's, engineer's, or hand-drilling hammer or hand sledge.

Carpenter's hammers don't have the right temper of steel for striking hard steel, and they can chip or break if used incorrectly, sometimes with disastrous results.

According to the Consumer Safety Commission, about 30,000 people are injured each year using hammers. Most of these receive eye injuries, and the most common cause is using the wrong hammer for the job. A simple precaution for masonry nails is to cut a piece from a plastic drinking straw and fit it over the nail to reduce the danger of it snapping. The straw is mashed and comes off as the nail is hammered home. Even with this technique, be sure to wear safety goggles.

Choosing Nails

The holding power of a nail depends on how big a nail you use, the type of nail you use, where you position that nail, and what kind of wood you are nailing into. Nail suppliers have many charts on what nail to use where. But in rough carpentry only a few nails are used for a majority of the work:

- 16d cement-coated sinkers for rough framing.
- 8d cement-coated sinkers for flooring and roof sheathing.
- 16d galvanized casing nails for hanging windows and doors.
- 4d, 6d, or 8d finish nails for interior trim work.

When selecting nails for length, one thing to keep in mind is the thickness of the lumber. Generally, nails are driven first through the thinner board into the thicker board. The nail should penetrate two-thirds of the way into the second board. (See page 171 for more tips on nail length.) When nails must penetrate beyond the second board, you can increase their strength by clinching.

Use two hammers, with one hammer held against the head of the driven nail. Use the other to bend over the point of the nail with the grain. It is possible to get a good clinch using only one hammer if you approach it correctly. First, hit the nail at the side of the point with the edge of the hammer face. This will bend the nail without backing it out. Continue to bend the nail over by hitting it under the point to complete the clinch.

When framing up walls of a home, some professional carpenters like to drive three or four nails into the studs, toenailed from both sides at about 30°.

How many nails you use depends on what you are nailing together. Professional carpenters often will use two nails at the ends of 2x4s, three nails for 2x6s and 2x8s, and four nails for 2x10s and 2x12s. Generally, they will position the nails 1″ to 1½″ in from the edges of the board. Some carpenters like to nail as far as possible from the ends of boards; they will move back on the board and angle the nail into the second board. The angled nail will have more holding power than one nailed straight into the end grain. Carpenters use different methods of toenailing. One key to success is to use 8d nails, two on each side, instead of bigger spikes. If nailing a stud onto a plate, for example, first position the stud next to a pre-marked line, then move it back ⅛″or ¼″ and tap a nail straight in to hold the stud as it is nailed from the opposite side. Drive two nails in on one side, then come around and drive in the opposite two. Then pull out the holding nail. The idea is to have the nails come through the center of the stud into the plate.

Another toenailing trick is to use spacer blocks. After getting one stud in place, cut a spacer of 2x4, even 2x2, to go between the studs. If the studs are 16″ on center, the spacer block should be 14½″ long. Simply lay one end against the stud that is already nailed and use it to hold the next stud to be nailed in.

In other nailing, the basic idea is to position the nail so that the load will fall across the nail, rather than with the length of the nail. You want the strain to be crosswise to the nail. This takes advantage of the nail's shear strength. You can pull a nail out easily, but it is tough to shear it off.

Another basic rule of thumb is to try to position nails so any weight will push the nail deeper.

Reducing Splitting

One problem that plagues carpenters is board splitting. The farther from the end of the board that you nail, the less likely that the board will split. If the boards you are nailing still are splitting, one trick is to blunt the end of the nail before driving it. A blunt nail will tear, rather than spread, the wood fibers.

Some carpenters, if they have a hammer with a wooden handle, may use the old carpenter's trick of boring a ¼″ hole an inch deep into the butt of the handle, and filling it with beeswax. Then, when nailing through very tough wood, a nail can first be stuck into the beeswax to lubricate it and make it easier to drive home.

There are other ways to reduce splitting. For example, if you are nailing close to the edge of a board and you know it will split, you can nail the board first, then cut it to length after the nails are in. You can also pre-drill holes for the nail. One way is to cut the head off a nail, chuck it in your drill and use that nail to make a hole. Another slick device, especially for interior trim, is called a "nail spinner" that fits in a power drill. You insert the nail and drill it into position. The nail will go to within ¼″ or so of its desired position, then you can drive it home with a hammer and a nailset.

Keep in mind that nailsets, used to drive nails below the surface of the wood, come in different sizes. Usually three sizes will be all that you will need. Try to avoid using a nailset that is too big; you can end up making the nail hole larger than it needs to be. A nailset, with its concave head, can also be used to drive nails back out of boards.

Fastening Helpers

Mastic adhesives, clips, and brackets can be used to help nails with their fastening job. Metal clips for joists and posts can save time on projects such as decks, and can increase the strength of the joints significantly over nails alone. Mastic works great to increase the holding power of furring strips on masonry walls. It also can help prevent squeaks when installing ½″ CDX plywood over joists for subflooring. Some framing carpenters putting up interior walls on a slab use mastic under the bottom plate, as well as masonry nails.

In some situations nailing patterns can be important. These include nailing in windows and doors, and nailing finish flooring, roof sheathing, and drywall. Generally nails should not be driven through window jambs. When installing sheathing, try to follow the instructions of the manufacturer. Plywood sheets, for example, will call for a different nailing pattern than waferboard.

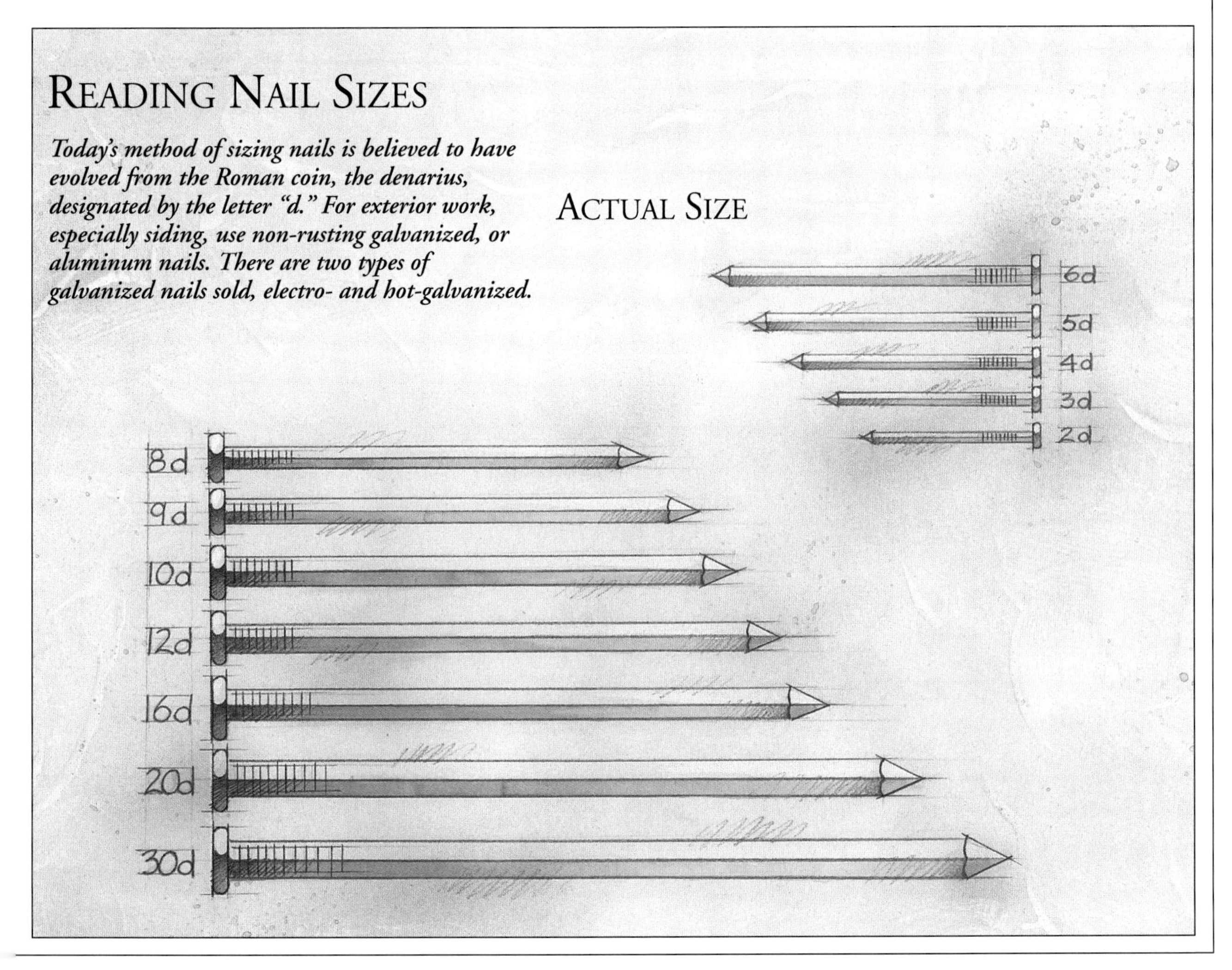

Tech Notes: Selecting The Right Nail

According to Northwestern Steel and Wire Co., manufacturers of Sterling-brand nails, two elements to consider when selecting nails are the shape of the nail and the finish on it. Every nail has three parts—head, shank and point—and these are put together in different combinations to make a wide variety of nail types. Finishes are easier to remember; there are only three or so types commonly used.

The Head. Most nails used in general-purpose carpentry will have one of three types of heads: flat, countersunk (in different degrees), and brad. Flat heads, which are flat on both the upper and lower surfaces, are found on the most widely used nails. Examples are common, box, and roofing nails.

Critical nail parts are the head, shank, and point. The most widely used nails have flat heads, as found on common, box, or roofing nails.

Common nails are just that—the most commonly used for general-purpose nailing. Box nails are similar, except they have a thinner shank than common nails of the same length. Roofing or shingle nails also have self-explanatory names, as do most of the special-purpose nails.

Countersunk heads are slightly countersunk, making it easier to drive the nail head flush with the surface of the wood. An example of countersunk heads is found in the casing nail, which has a deep cone-shaped head, intended to be driven flush with the surface. Casing nails are used to install window and door casings, where a sturdy nail with an inconspicuous head is needed. They are thicker—length for length—than their close cousins, the finishing nail.

Nail Gauges and Sizes

Gauge

1 2 3 4 5 6 7 8 9 10 11 12 13 14 15 16 17 18

Sizes of Wire

Steel Wire Gauge No.	Inches (Decimally)	Millimeters (Decimally)
1	.2830	7.188
2	.2625	6.668
3	.2437	6.190
4	.2253	5.723
5	.2070	5.258
6	.1920	4.877
7	.1770	4.496
8	.1620	4.115
9	.1483	3.767
10	.1350	3.429
11	.1205	3.061
12	.1055	2.680
13	.0915	2.324
14	.0800	2.032
15	.0720	1.829
16	.0625	1.588
17	.0540	1.372
18	.0475	1.207

Brad heads are found on finishing nails. These are made to be driven below the surface of the wood and covered up in woodwork and furniture. Finishing nails sometimes have "cupped" heads, with a small indentation in the center. That's so you can drive them below the surface of the wood with a nailset, and avoid marring the wood with the hammer.

A couple more types of nail heads are worth knowing about. One is the "dish head drywall" type, with a concave head that makes it easier to nail drywall securely. Another type is the double-headed or duplex nail, used in jobs where you expect to pull the nail again, such as in temporary braces, scaffolding, or concrete forms.

The Shank. Nail shanks are either smooth or threaded. Common, box, finishing, and casing nails are usually smooth, although sometimes you can find threaded versions of these. (Note that "Sm" on a carton means smooth, not small.)

Threaded shanks come in many different types. Ring-shanked (RS) and annular threaded (AT) are very similar. Other types are twisted, barbed, fluted, and screw-shanked. Some roofing nails and most drywall nails are ring-shanked, but another highly effective drywall nail is barbed. Flooring nails and hardboard siding nails are often screw-shanked. Roof rafter and truss nails may be either ring-shanked or screw-shanked. Masonry nails may be fluted or smooth.

Threading increases the holding power of the nail, since the rough surface interlaces with the wood fibers. Threaded nails generally have less tendency to split wood, since these shanks tend to tear or break the wood fibers rather than shoving them apart like a wedge.

Screw-shank nails combine the holding power of a screw with the driving power of a nail. They screw themselves through the wood as they are driven to provide very great holding power. Another type of shank is square, found most commonly in "cut" masonry nails. These nails are cut from hardened steel rather than round stock.

You also may encounter a shank type called "stiff-stock." These are nails made from heat-treated steel to make them harder. The next hardness level is "oil quenched."

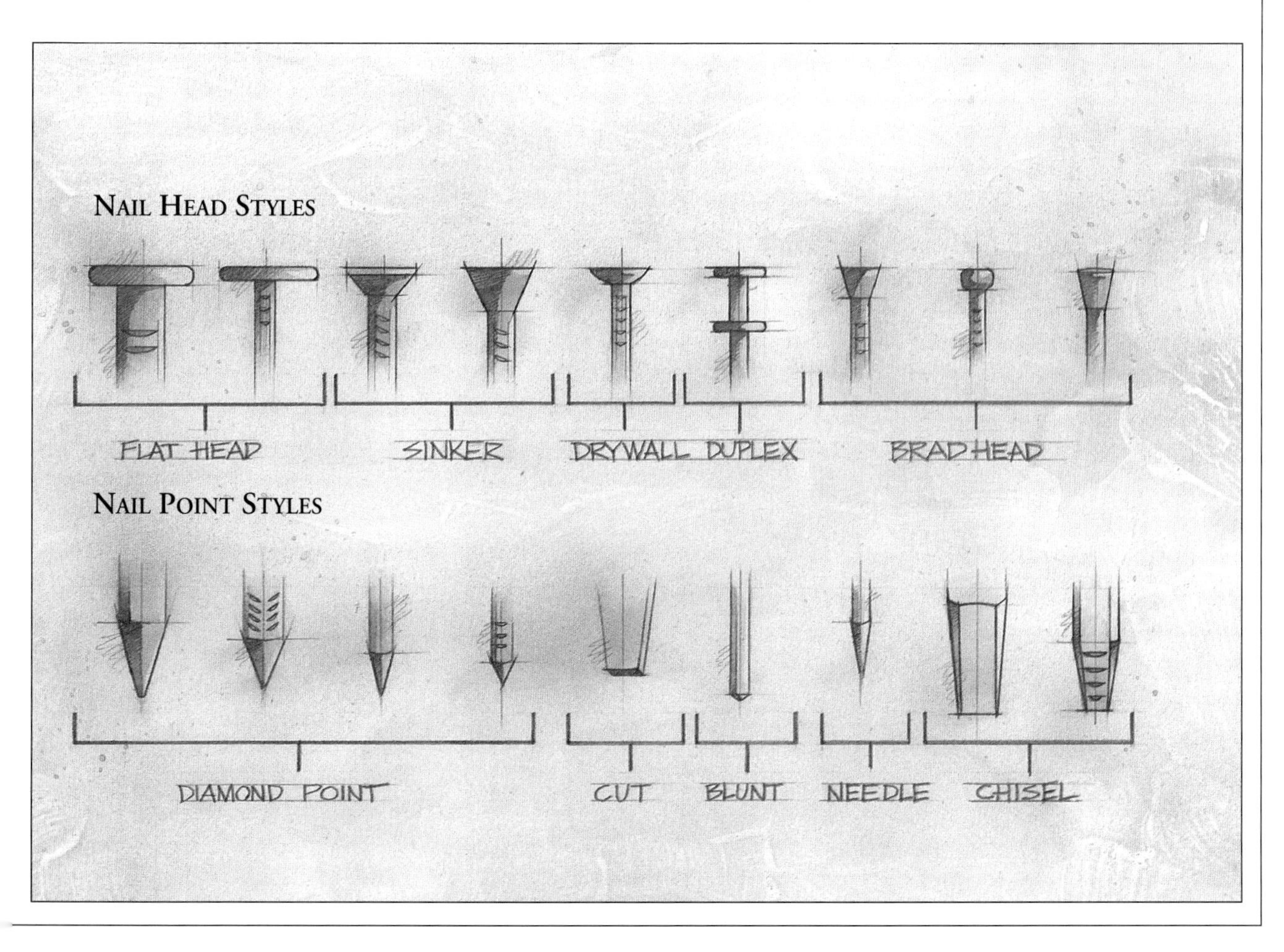

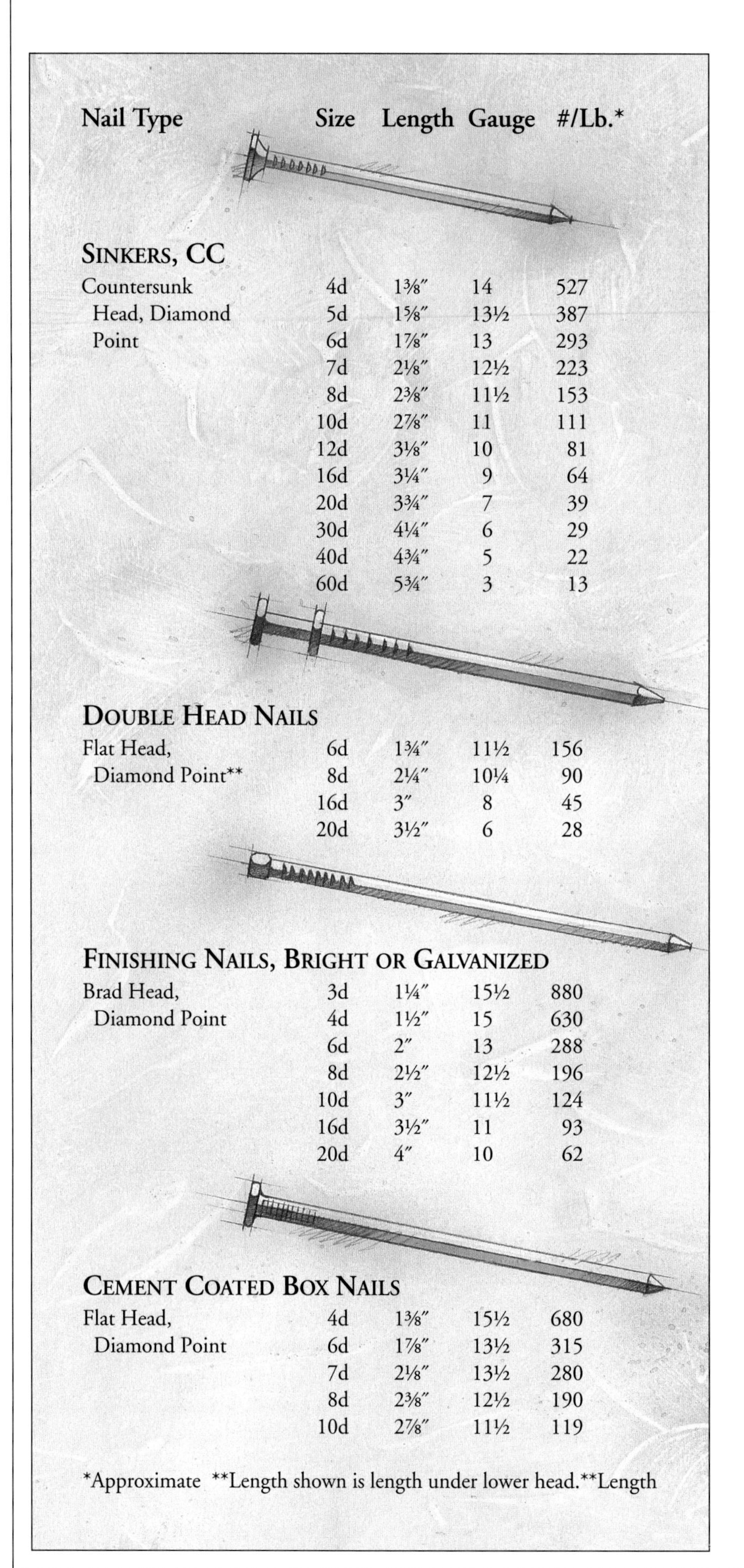

Nail Type	Size	Length	Gauge	#/Lb.*
SINKERS, CC				
Countersunk Head, Diamond Point	4d	1⅜″	14	527
	5d	1⅝″	13½	387
	6d	1⅞″	13	293
	7d	2⅛″	12½	223
	8d	2⅜″	11½	153
	10d	2⅞″	11	111
	12d	3⅛″	10	81
	16d	3¼″	9	64
	20d	3¾″	7	39
	30d	4¼″	6	29
	40d	4¾″	5	22
	60d	5¾″	3	13
DOUBLE HEAD NAILS				
Flat Head, Diamond Point**	6d	1¾″	11½	156
	8d	2¼″	10¼	90
	16d	3″	8	45
	20d	3½″	6	28
FINISHING NAILS, BRIGHT OR GALVANIZED				
Brad Head, Diamond Point	3d	1¼″	15½	880
	4d	1½″	15	630
	6d	2″	13	288
	8d	2½″	12½	196
	10d	3″	11½	124
	16d	3½″	11	93
	20d	4″	10	62
CEMENT COATED BOX NAILS				
Flat Head, Diamond Point	4d	1⅜″	15½	680
	6d	1⅞″	13½	315
	7d	2⅛″	13½	280
	8d	2⅜″	12½	190
	10d	2⅞″	11½	119

*Approximate **Length shown is length under lower head.**Length

The Point. Oddly enough, the more blunt the nail point, the less likely it is to split the wood. Sharp, thin points spread the fibers, while blunt points tear and break them, placing less strain on the wood. Of course, blunt points are harder to start and drive. Here are five nail points you are most likely to encounter.

Diamond-point is the most common, representing an all-purpose compromise between the blunt and needle points. Blunt points are often found on hardwood flooring nails. This type of wood splits easily if sharp nails are used, and blunt points help reduce splitting.

Chisel points are found on heavy-gauge spikes to facilitate driving them into thick timbers.

Needle points are often found on nails used on insulated building board and fiberboard. The needle point makes the nail easy to start and drive into materials where splitting isn't a problem. Cut points are found on cut masonry nails, as mentioned earlier.

The Finish. Besides the shape of the nail, it pays to know about nail finishes. Usual finishes are "bright," "galvanized," and "cement coated" (often abbreviated as CC). Bright nails have bare, clean metal, with no finish added. Galvanized (galv) nails are coated with a zinc alloy to resist rust, making these especially suitable for outdoor use. "Electro-galvanized" nails have a thin, smooth, shiny coating.

Cement coated (CC) nails are treated with a special resin which melts from the heat of friction as it is driven, then sets like glue when it cools, giving the nail greater holding power. Just remember that cement coated nails have nothing to do with Portland cement; they are not concrete nails. Rather, the cement involved is an adhesive.

Other Nails. A couple of other general purpose nail types are "wire brads" and "wire nails." These are small nails, usually 1½″ or less in length, with accordingly thin shanks, usually 18 gauge or smaller. The wire nails have flat heads; wire brads have brad heads. Such nails are usually smooth shanked and bright, except for painted, threaded nails used for paneling.

Most special-purpose nails have fairly descriptive names, such as drywall, roofing, shingle, flooring, siding, underlayment, concrete, and masonry nails. Some of these are sized in penny sizes, others in length and wire gauge. Still others designate the head size on the package, too. The cryptic code, **1¼x11x7/16 galv rfg**, designates a galvanized roofing nail 1¼″ long, with an 11-gauge shank, and a 7/16″ diameter head.

Nail Sizes. Many nails are sized in the ancient "penny" system. The origin of this isn't certain, but it is widely believed to have started in England, where nails sold for so many pennies per 100 nails. The smaller nails cost less per 100, the larger nails more. Hence they came to be known by their price. While they cost a lot more today, the old system stuck for designating sizes.

You can use this bit of history to help you remember that the larger the penny number, the larger the nail. Shank and head sizes also go up in proportion to the length. The "penny" is represented by the symbol "d," which probably comes from the Roman *denarius* coin, the "penny" at the time the nail sizing system evolved. Therefore, a nail marked "16d" on the carton is read as 16-penny and it is 3½″ long.

Nail Length. There aren't many hard and fast rules on how long nails should be for specific jobs. Usually, for general framing and

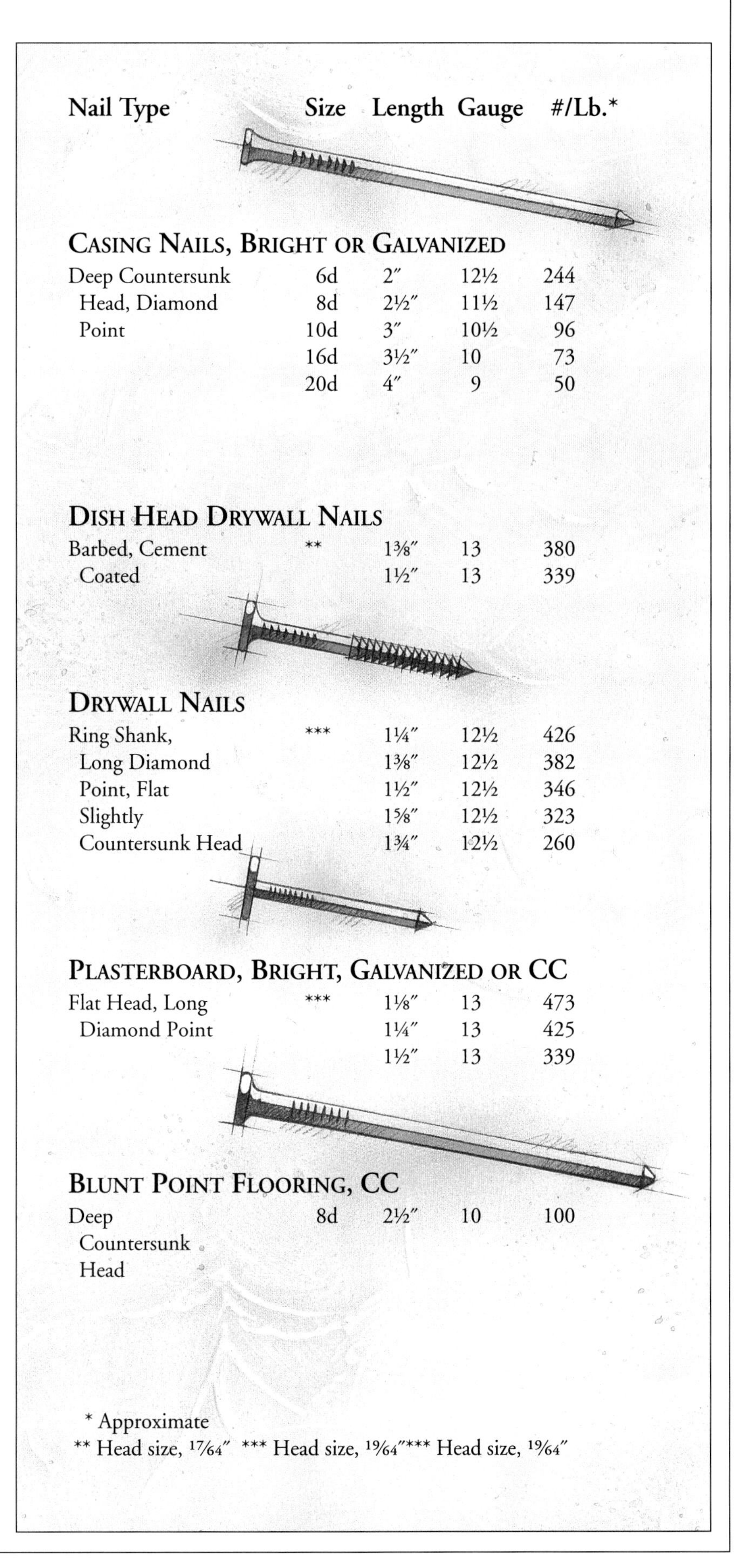

Nail Type	Size	Length	Gauge	#/Lb.*
CASING NAILS, BRIGHT OR GALVANIZED				
Deep Countersunk	6d	2″	12½	244
Head, Diamond	8d	2½″	11½	147
Point	10d	3″	10½	96
	16d	3½″	10	73
	20d	4″	9	50
DISH HEAD DRYWALL NAILS				
Barbed, Cement	**	1⅜″	13	380
Coated		1½″	13	339
DRYWALL NAILS				
Ring Shank,	***	1¼″	12½	426
Long Diamond		1⅜″	12½	382
Point, Flat		1½″	12½	346
Slightly		1⅝″	12½	323
Countersunk Head		1¾″	12½	260
PLASTERBOARD, BRIGHT, GALVANIZED OR CC				
Flat Head, Long	***	1⅛″	13	473
Diamond Point		1¼″	13	425
		1½″	13	339
BLUNT POINT FLOORING, CC				
Deep Countersunk Head	8d	2½″	10	100

* Approximate
** Head size, 17/64″ *** Head size, 19/64″*** Head size, 19/64″

construction, 16d and 10d common or CC sinkers are most useful, with 8d often used for toenailing to avoid splitting.

Box nails are often a good choice on general work with 1″ and 2″ (nominal) lumber, because they have a thinner shank and have less of a tendency to split the wood. CC sinkers have a relatively slim shank and good holding power.

One rule of thumb on nail length is that the nail should penetrate about two-thirds of the way into the second piece of wood being joined. For example, if you're nailing two 2x4s together to make a 4x4 corner column, the nail should be at least 2½″ long (8d), but probably most carpenters would use a 3″ (10d) for this job. A 16d (3½″) would go all the way through, leaving a short point that would be hard to clinch over. On the other hand, a 16d, driven at an angle so that it wouldn't protrude, would provide extra strength. If you are end nailing—for example, driving a nail through a top plate into the end of a vertical stud—you would probably use a couple of 16d. To toenail a stud in place, use 10d or 8d, going to the smaller size if splitting is a problem.

Note: A good source for more information on nails is Northwestern Steel and Wire Co., manufacturers of Sterling-brand nails. Write them at 121 Wallace St., Sterling, IL 61081, or call 815/625-2500.

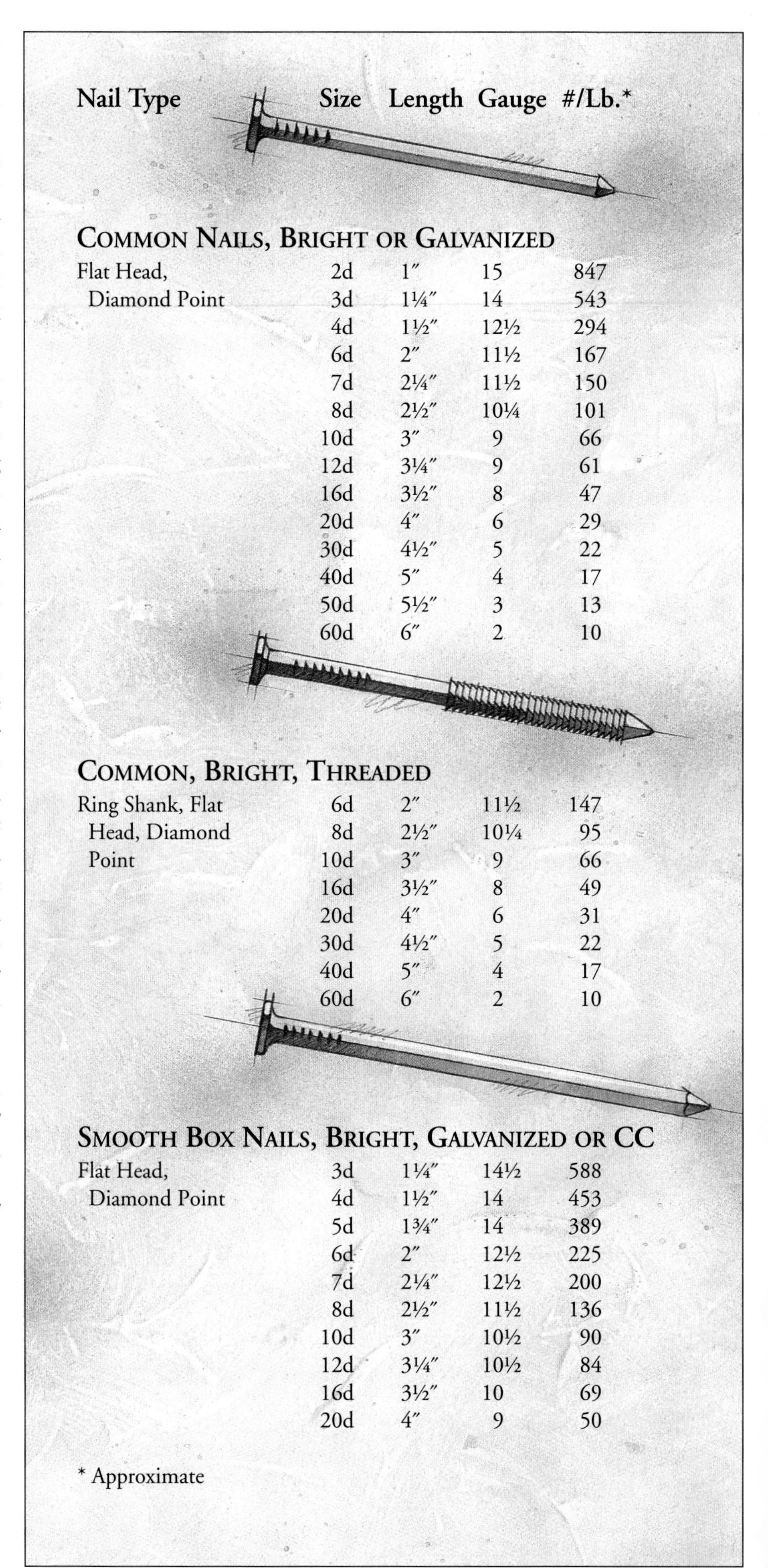

Nail Type	Size	Length	Gauge	#/Lb.*
COMMON NAILS, BRIGHT OR GALVANIZED				
Flat Head,	2d	1″	15	847
Diamond Point	3d	1¼″	14	543
	4d	1½″	12½	294
	6d	2″	11½	167
	7d	2¼″	11½	150
	8d	2½″	10¼	101
	10d	3″	9	66
	12d	3¼″	9	61
	16d	3½″	8	47
	20d	4″	6	29
	30d	4½″	5	22
	40d	5″	4	17
	50d	5½″	3	13
	60d	6″	2	10
COMMON, BRIGHT, THREADED				
Ring Shank, Flat	6d	2″	11½	147
Head, Diamond	8d	2½″	10¼	95
Point	10d	3″	9	66
	16d	3½″	8	49
	20d	4″	6	31
	30d	4½″	5	22
	40d	5″	4	17
	60d	6″	2	10
SMOOTH BOX NAILS, BRIGHT, GALVANIZED OR CC				
Flat Head,	3d	1¼″	14½	588
Diamond Point	4d	1½″	14	453
	5d	1¾″	14	389
	6d	2″	12½	225
	7d	2¼″	12½	200
	8d	2½″	11½	136
	10d	3″	10½	90
	12d	3¼″	10½	84
	16d	3½″	10	69
	20d	4″	9	50

* Approximate

PROJECT PACKHORSE

It's A Portable Toolbox, Workbench, And Equipment Organizer All Combined Into One

As most do-it-yourselfers soon begin to realize, a constant project challenge is to keep tools, equipment, and materials accessible and organized. An additional challenge is to keep project gear portable because the bulk of home projects are done "on-site" and not at a workbench.

This handy project companion has been designed by Mark McClanahan of Clio, Michigan. It provides a home for the gear that needs to be transported to the project at hand. It can help you speed up your projects, improve your efficiency, and reduce the frustration of not being able to find what you need.

You can keep it in your garage and simply wheel it to where it's needed; it will go a long way in helping you reduce your run-around time and let you concentrate on doing the best project work possible.

Only a sheet and a half of plywood is needed for this do-it-yourselfer's packhorse. It's designed to hold tools and equipment of all sizes and types; plus it has a work surface that folds down. In the down position, tools and parts are within easy reach. When the work is done, the entire unit (including a top cabinet) retracts into a manageable, wheeled rectangle so you can easily stow it away until your next project.

The plans for this project come from the American Plywood Association. It's a straightforward design that is easy to cut and assemble. The association recommends using ½″ APA-trademarked Medium Density Overlay (MDO) panels, overlaid both sides, if available, or APA-trademarked A-B or A-C plywood. For a unique appearance, you could also consider using APA-trademarked reconstituted wood panels.

Other materials you will need include a 1″x23″ wood dowel, a pair of 1″ wide by 6″- or 8″-diameter wheels with axle, four nuts and six washers (drill the axle holes in the plywood sides according to the wheel size). You will also need a pair of 1¹⁄₁₆x18″ continuous hinges for attaching the tabletop; four 1x1½″ butt hinges for attaching the toolbox doors; two barrel bolt latches for securing the toolbox; two magnetic catches for the toolbox doors; and perforated hardboard, measuring 24x21⅞″, plus the necessary miscellaneous hanger hardware.

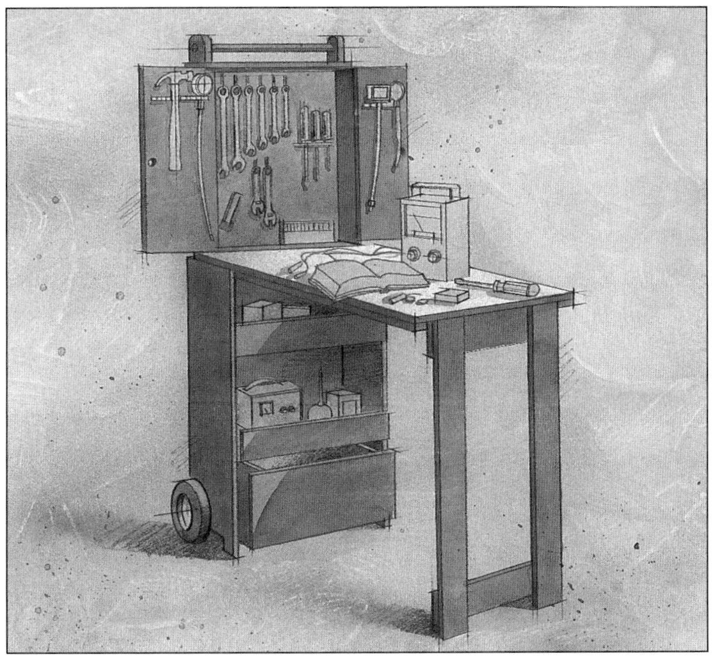

Made of ½″ plywood, this unit stores and organizes tools and equipment for a wide variety of projects. With its bench surface pulled down, equipment is instantly within easy reach.

Also acquire, as needed, wood screws, finishing nails, white or urea resin glue, wood dough or synthetic filler, fine sandpaper, and finishing materials.

When you cut out parts from the plans, be sure to follow all safety precautions. Also, make sure each part is cut to the exact dimensions shown so that matching parts are the same size. The completed unit can be protected with your choice of finish.

Note: To get more information on the many other plywood project plans offered by the association, send $2 for a copy of their Handy Plan Catalog. Write American Plywood Association, P.O. Box 11700, Tacoma WA 98411-0700.

Tech Notes: Building A Project Packhorse

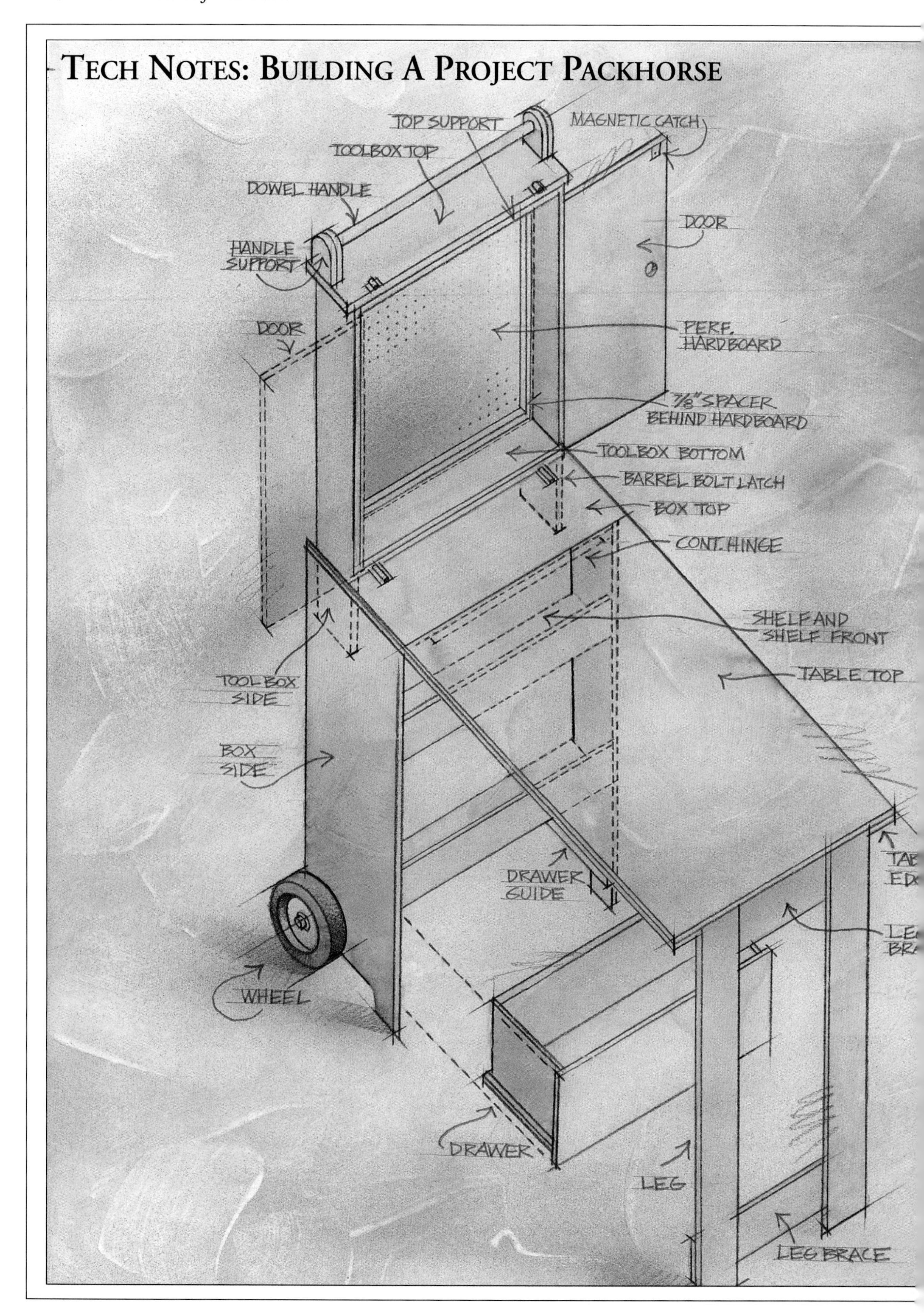

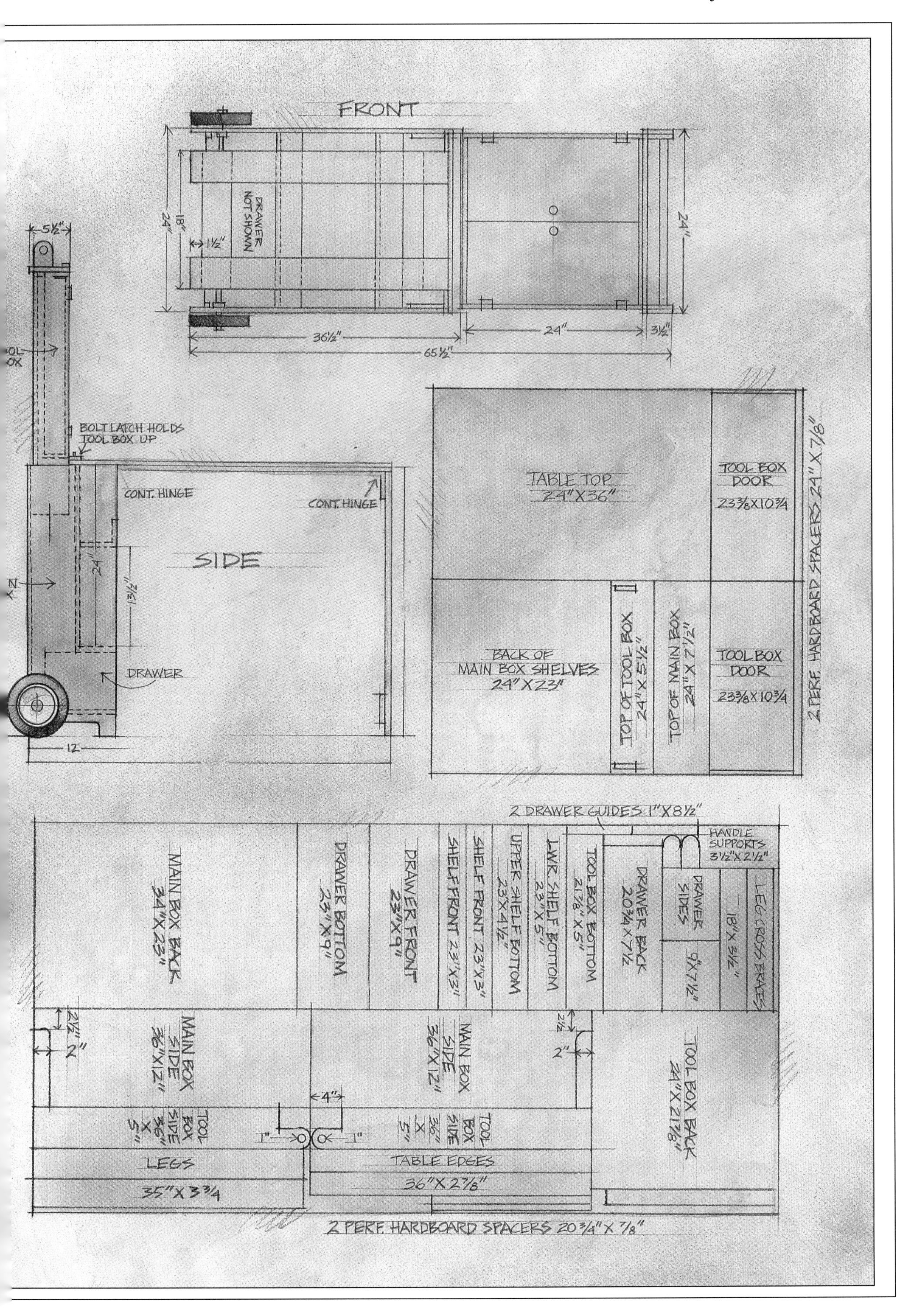
FRONT
DRAWER NOT SHOWN
24"
18"
1½"
36½"
24"
3½"
65½"
24"
5½"
BOLT LATCH HOLDS TOOL BOX UP
CONT. HINGE
CONT. HINGE
SIDE
24"
13½"
DRAWER
12
TABLE TOP
24"X36"
TOOL BOX DOOR
23⅜X10¾
BACK OF MAIN BOX SHELVES
24"X23"
TOP OF TOOL BOX
24"X5½"
TOP OF MAIN BOX
24"X7½"
TOOL BOX DOOR
23⅜X10¾
2 PERF. HARDBOARD SPACERS 24"X⅞"
2 DRAWER GUIDES 1"X8½"
HANDLE SUPPORTS
3½"X2½"
MAIN BOX BACK
34"X23"
DRAWER BOTTOM
23"X9"
DRAWER FRONT
23"X9"
SHELF FRONT 23"X3"
SHELF FRONT 23"X3"
UPPER SHELF BOTTOM
23"X4½"
LWR. SHELF BOTTOM
23"X5"
TOOL BOX BOTTOM
21⅞"X5"
DRAWER BACK
20¾X7½
DRAWER SIDES
9"X7½"
18"X3½"
LEG CROSS BRACES
2½"
2"
MAIN BOX SIDE
36"X12"
MAIN BOX SIDE
36"X12"
2½
2"
TOOL BOX BACK
24"X21⅞"
4"
TOOL BOX SIDE
36"
X
5"
TOOL BOX SIDE
36"
X
5"
1"
1"
LEGS
35"X3¾
TABLE EDGES
36"X2⅞"
2 PERF. HARDBOARD SPACERS 20¾"X⅞"

WORKING METAL

Even For A Hard-Core Woodworker,
Knowing How To Work Metal Can Pay Off

Even if most of your do-it-yourself projects involve working with wood, you may want to consider equipping your home workshop with welding capabilities. The equipment can not only be used for occasional repair jobs, but to help in maintaining or building other workshop tools.

Don't be scared off by the cost. Buying an oxygen/acetylene welding outfit with tanks can admittedly be a major investment for home use. But there are ways to get started on a limited budget. You can buy small tanks or rent the larger conventional-sized tanks instead of buying them. Once you get welding equipment, you can save money by using it to make your own two-wheeled tank cart. Another way to trim the initial purchase price and cut the maintenance costs of gas welding is to use propane instead of acetylene, along with oxygen.

According to professional metalworker Vince Koebensky, the propane will allow you to cut up to 1"-thick steel without problems. A variety of propane tank sizes are readily available at much cheaper prices than acetylene tanks. A 100-lb. propane tank will accommodate about 15 large tanks of oxygen tanks before having to be refilled. Normally acetylene will be used up at about the same rate as oxygen.

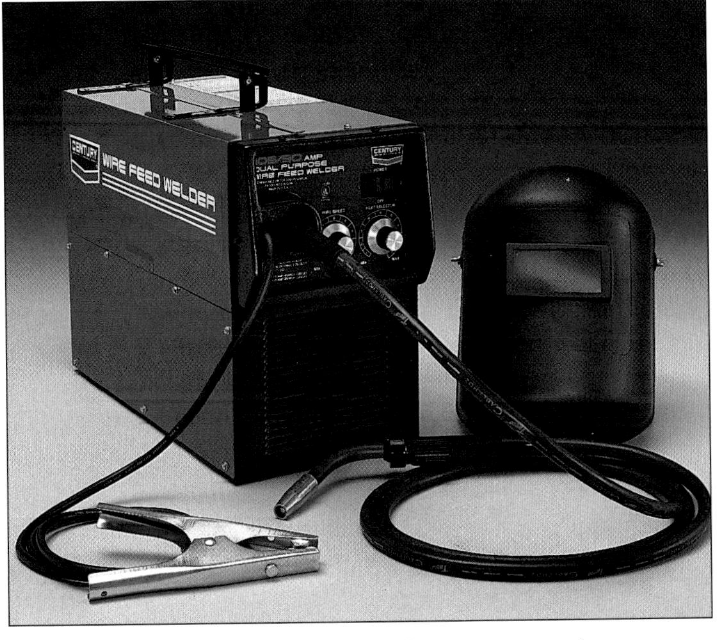

Whether you opt for gas or electric welding equipment, there are ways to start on a limited budget and work up. Many advanced do-it-yourselfers are eyeing wire-feed welders like this Century model.

One of the metalworker's best friends, besides welding equipment, is the right-angle grinder, opposite page, which can be fitted with a wide range of discs to either cut or smooth.

When switching to propane, the only additional investment, besides the propane tank, is for propane cutting tips. Get a few different sizes; they cost about $10 each.

Propane burns slightly cooler than acetylene, and in the worst case with propane you will need to pre-heat slightly longer on thicker material, and move a little slower while cutting. But, besides the cost saving of using propane, propane won't leave unburned residue like acetylene can.

Also, if you run out of propane on a weekend, you can get the propane tank refilled at almost any service station. An acetylene tank must go back to the company where it was purchased or leased to be refilled; companies usually won't take acetylene tanks other than their own for refilling or exchange.

To get started with an arc welder, many shop owners first buy a small AC welder, or what is called a "buzz box." However, this type of welder limits what you can do because only a few welding rods work well with it. A better investment is the AC/DC welder, which works well with all welding rods and in all welding positions. Because it is about twice the price of an AC welder, your budget may determine which unit you buy. However, an AC/DC welder will do a nicer job and is easier to use.

Regardless of the equipment you use for welding or cutting, Vince recommends certain precautions. First, make sure you have a "clear zone" free of flammable material where welding takes place. Metal

TECH NOTES: MAKING WELDING REPAIRS

Once you get set up with welding equipment and personal gear, you won't be limited to only working with wood. The most often performed job with any welding equipment is repair work. Here are tips on key procedures from Vince Koebensky, who works metal for a living in his own shop called "Hot Iron" near Buffalo, Minnesota.

• Any repair areas first must be cleaned with a grinding wheel and/or a wire wheel. Because layers of paint and/or grease often exist on the work, also clean a spot for the ground-cable clamp when using an arc welder. Good grounding is essential. Beware of trying to "burn out" debris. Instead of burning it out, you actually will burn it in. Debris will mix with the molten metal and result in a poorer weld, usually with pinholes throughout.

• When a break requires a simple butt weld, always bevel both sides of the break to allow a good root pass, followed by a cover pass or passes, depending on the metal thickness (see illustrations). Groove out cracks using a rotary grinder; an ultra-thin, 3″-dia. flat abrasive wheel works well. To weld any crack without grooving it is fruitless and will only be cosmetic in nature. The same applies to butt welds. Without beveling the ends, you will get only marginal penetration and end up redoing the job.

• Success with cast repairs depends on the type of cast iron. Making repairs on machinable cast (which usually has threaded holes or machined flat surfaces) is easier than making repairs to cast iron of the type that is used in exhaust manifolds. NIROD, a nickel rod, works well for cast repairs and is worth its extra cost. When working on cast repairs, always prewarm the piece slowly (from 300° to 400° F.) after cleaning and beveling to relieve the internal stress. Prewarming reduces the shock to the cast when an arc of instant hot heat is struck. Skipping the prewarming will result in additional fractures in and around the welded area.

• Annealing should also be used for cast iron and any tool steel or other metals with carbon content. It is done by wrapping the repaired work in an asbestos-like blanket immediately after welding to allow the repair to return to room temperature very slowly, usually over a 4- to 6-hour period. This slow cooling helps reduce the internal stress of the metal to prevent any new cracks and help the repair survive the external stress that originally broke it.

• Many parts needing repair may have a piece missing, especially cast iron. If the metal is a good grade, such as machinable cast, a missing piece can be made of mild malleable steel and "married" to the cast using a nickel rod. After the repair is made, don't grind the finished weld to clean it up unless absolutely necessary. If fit-up requires a flush weld, it is critical to have beveled or grooved the work to have allowed 100% penetration.

Grinding a finished weld beyond what is required for fitting will only weaken a repaired area unnecessarily. If your weld requires grinding, find out what you are doing wrong. Under the proper conditions, by using the right rod (or wire), proper heat range setting, and proper preparation, you should not have to do a thing to a completed weld.

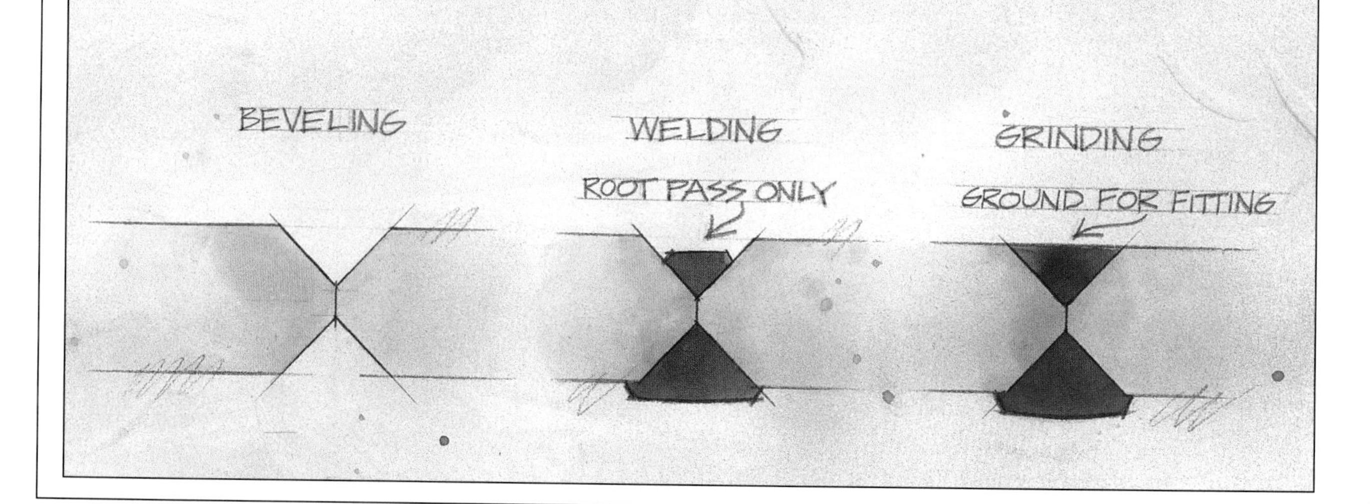

interior walls and concrete floors are best in welding areas. A fire extinguisher is a must.

Also, don't overlook exposure protection. When welding, wear a heavy-duty, long-sleeved, dark-colored work shirt. It is best to wear 100% cotton or denim shirts because hot sparks "roll off" this material better than shirts made of cotton/polyester blends, which can burn through very quickly. Wear a shirt that fits tight around the cuffs and collar because you can get a burn on your neck similar to sunburn if you don't cover up.

Heavy denim cotton jeans are excellent welding attire. Duckcloth bib overalls offer the advantages of heavier cloth and also allow more air movement. Never stick pant legs inside of your shoes or boots, or wear pants too short to cover your footwear. If you get a hot piece of slag or spatter down inside your footwear, you will never get it out quick enough to avoid getting burned.

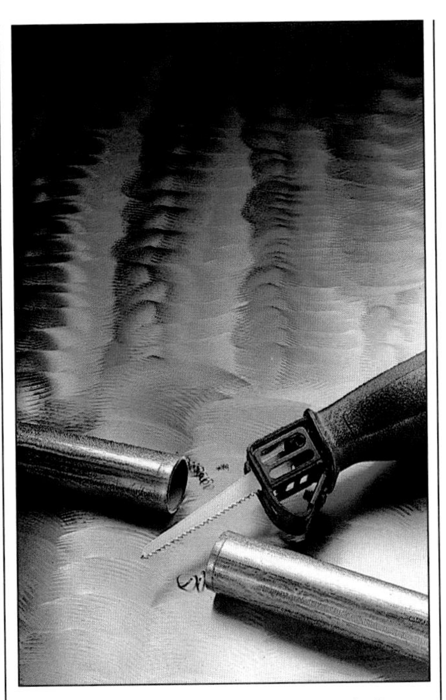

Working metal usually requires heftier tools than those for woodworking, such as the Sears reciprocating saw shown above, as well as adequate safety gear.

A good arc welding helmet is a lightweight unit which adjusts so a nod of the head brings the shield down into place. (New versions are available with glass that instantly darkens.) If the helmet you buy doesn't have additional protection at the bottom front, secure a 4″ strip of leather across the bottom to provide extra protection from arc flashes in the neck and throat area.

For arc welding, many welders use only a #10 green lens. However, some professionals use two dark lenses together, a #10 gold-covered lens plus a #2 to #5 green lens to darken the flash even fur-

Identifying Metals

To get the best welding job, you need to know exactly what type of metal you are welding. Here is a simple test. Hold the material lightly but steadily against a grinding wheel that is clean and free of foreign material. Study the pattern and compare it with the following descriptions. A handy way to identify metal is to keep a box of labeled pieces next to the bench grinder and compare the unknown metal to the known sample.

Machinery steel (or low-carbon steel) produces long, white spark streams with a few forked spurts or bursts.

Medium- and high-carbon tool steel gives a shorter stream of sparks with many fine repeating spurts.

Gray cast iron has a pattern similar to carbon steel, but the stream is much shorter and red in color.

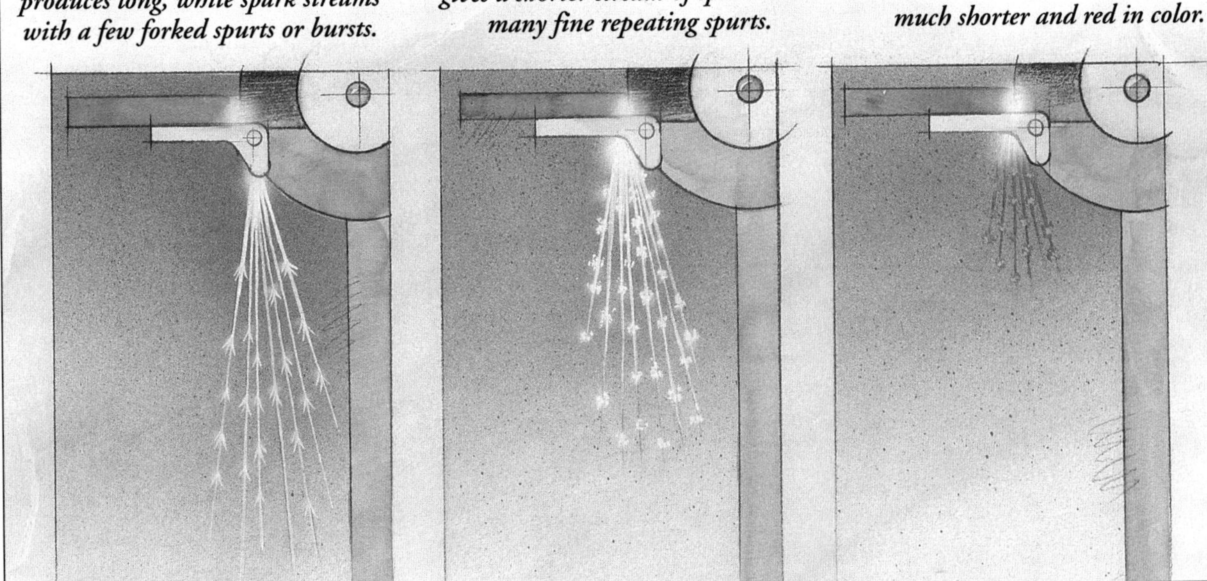

ther. The gold lens provides better filtering of ultra-violet rays. When cutting with an acetylene torch, many pros wear #5 green-shaded safety glasses for eye protection. With the shaded glasses, it is easier to see what you are cutting, and the glasses also offer protection when the torch pops back with something hot in the direction of your eyes.

In any shop where others are welding, keep your back to the flash because your eyes can be burned even when you are not looking directly at it. You can also burn your eyes with a flash picked up by your peripheral vision. The only immediate indication of burning is a momentary inability to see. But later in the day, your eyes may feel like somebody threw sand in them. It is an experience to be avoided.

A Shop-Built Hydraulic Press

Many shop owners needing a special tool or piece of equipment will use welding gear to build it themselves. Doing so not only saves cash, but provides an abundance of satisfaction. This powerful hydraulic press, handy for working metal, is an example of a tool you can easily make. And it will serve its purpose well over the years.

Smaller hydraulic presses are very simple to build. The specific size will depend on how many tons of pressure you want, or on which hydraulic jack you use. A small hydraulic press works well for bending metal and for straightening flat, round, square, angle, or channel iron. Good steady pressure applied to a piece straightens it much better than beating on it. Certain jobs for the hydraulic press require hanging the jack upside down so that the ram of the hydraulic jack pushes downward. An example of this is when pressing off bearings. It is much easier to see what is happening when the jack is reversed.

Most newer hydraulic jacks will work in any position (horizontal, sideways, upside down), and that fact is usually stated on the side of the jack. Check for this when buying a jack for a hydraulic press. If nothing is stated on the jack about working in all or any positions, then assume it will only work vertically (right side up).

Keep in mind that the unit shown is not an adjustable (pinned) press as are larger commercial presses, but rather a small, powerful, mobile press that works well for tough, smaller jobs. To build this press, acquire a 10-ton hydraulic jack. Use four pieces of steel: two 4x¼" channels 28" long, and two 8x½" H-beams, one 13½" long and the other 17" long. Weld the 4" channels to serve as vertical supports between both H-beams. Note that the press is built using the shorter H-beam on the bottom, with the flat surface down. Both beams are in the horizontal position, but the top H-beam is turned to be 90° offset from the bottom beam, with its face in the vertical position.

Angle-iron brackets are mounted on the shorter H-beam to secure the hydraulic jack, especially when the unit is turned over. Cut a 2½"-dia. hole in the center of the other H-beam to accommodate items with a shaft. This allows the shaft to stick through while the item is being worked on. As you begin using the hydraulic press, you will find that several different shop-made spacers and jigs will be helpful, depending on the thickness of material being worked.

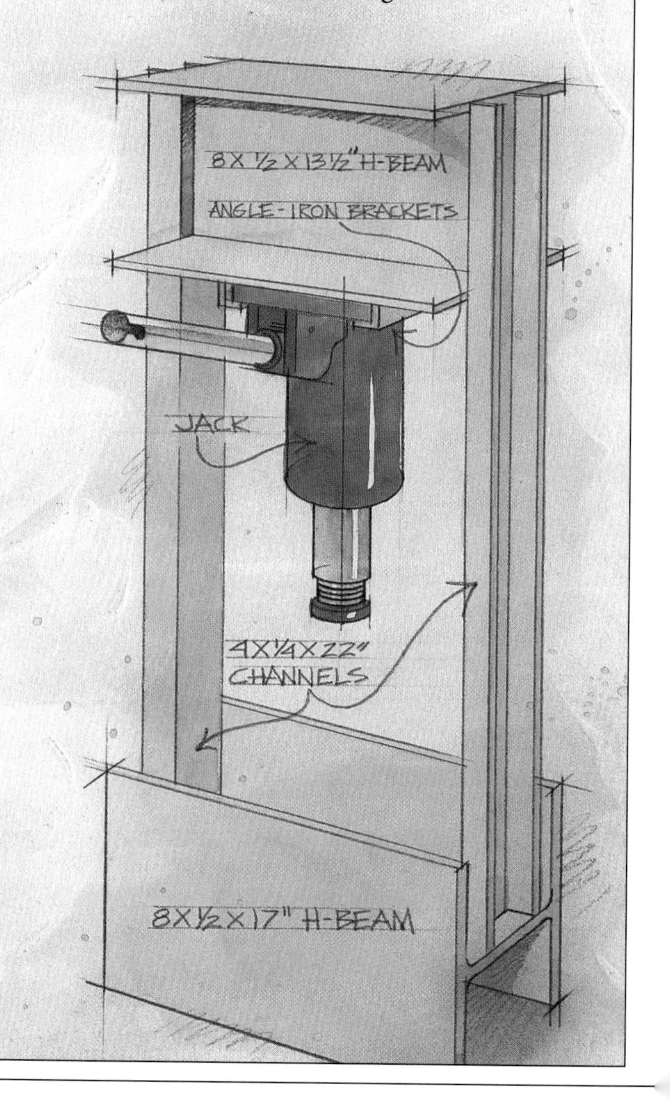

Tech Notes: Working Sheetmetal

Each type of material used in the home workshop requires a different touch. Steel, cast iron, and aluminum all are metals, yet each will machine differently.

Thickness of materials is another variable; thin metals like sheetmetal require special approaches. When filing metal bar stock, for example, each stroke of the file removes material from a large surface area. And the thicker the material, the greater the pressure you may safely apply.

With sheetmetal, however, the part must be well supported, the tool pressure applied must be lighter, and the number of teeth on the file must be reduced.

Drilling sheetmetal also is different than drilling thicker materials, explains aeronautical engineer Jacob Schulzinger. Drill-bit manufacturers recognize this by offering sheetmetal-length bits that are significantly shorter than the standard length. They are ground with a 135° "included" angle instead of the 118° angle that is used for thicker materials.

When drilling thin material, make sure that the part is firmly supported to prevent bending, and securely clamped to prevent spinning when the drill breaks through. A pilot hole is recommended when working with large bits to reduce the drill-point pressure and to compensate for the lack of drill point surface speed.

When drilling sheetmetal, it is best to start with a center-punched mark to keep the bit from skipping, with a pilot hole of about ⅛″ diameter. Enlarge the hole gradually until you reach the desired size. If you decide to skip the pilot hole and the gradual increase in drill-bit size, you will likely produce an out-of-round hole, with ragged edges on both sides.

Here is a good rule of thumb to get maximum strength when placing holes in sheetmetal parts: the closest a hole should be placed to the edge of the part is 1½ to 2 diameters. Holes placed closer than this, to either the edge of the part, another hole, or the nearest bend, can crack.

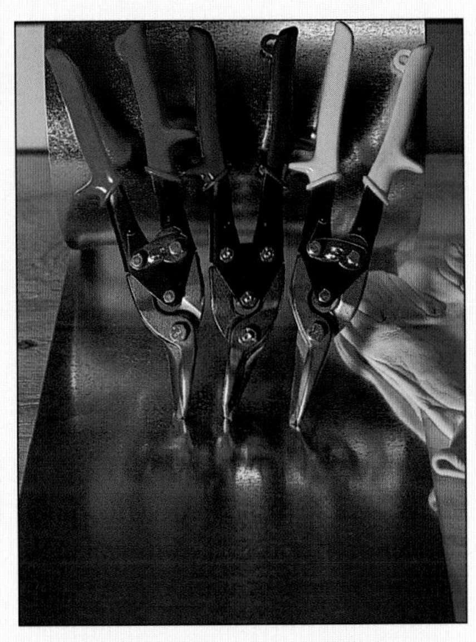

Aviation snips make straight cuts, but specific versions are designed to also make wide curves (yellow), tight curves right (green), and tight curves left (red).

Another good rule is that a fastener needn't be any closer than 4 to 6 diameters from the next one. Therefore, if you are using a ⅛″-dia. Pop rivet, the nearest another rivet should be placed is ½″ to ¾″. By using this rule, you will reduce the chances of damaging the part, as well as make optimum use of your fasteners.

Sheetmetal parts should be handled with care because of the sharp edges produced when the material is worked. Those few extra moments spent deburring are always worthwhile. While special deburring tools are available, the average do-it-yourselfer doesn't really need them and can get by with just a countersink for deburring and a file to dress the edges.

Use layout fluid or a wide felt-tipped marker to darken the material's surface, and then a metal scribe or bench knife to mark layout lines cleanly so they can be seen easily. For circles, a pair of dividers with one leg sharpened to a chisel point does a good job. When all of the work has been done on the part, the layout fluid can be removed with solvent.

When selecting a hacksaw blade for sheetmetal, at least three teeth should touch the metal at all times to give a smooth cut. If the material is too thin for even your finest blade, try sandwiching the sheetmetal between two pieces of thin plywood.

When plywood isn't available or practical, cut out the shape with a pair of tin snips. If you are cutting out a large opening, try making a starting hole with a sharp chisel instead of drilling one. The starter hole will be ragged, but it will be faster than drilling. There are a wide variety of snips available for sheetmetal use, including straight-blade cutters, right- and left-hand cutters, and hand-operated nibblers. Select the type that best suits the nature of the work you are doing.

Bending sheetmetal isn't much of a problem if you remember that the radius of the bend should be no less than 1½ times the thickness of the material. If, for instance, you are trying to bend a 1⁄16″-thick piece of metal, then the smallest bend radius used should be 3⁄32″. If the metal cracks when it is bent, try increasing the bend radius to 2 times the material thickness.

A steady, even pressure is needed for good bending, and making simple bends isn't difficult. Clamp the part securely in a vise or to a bench over a formed block, then use a piece of scrap wood or metal to apply even pressure to bend the free end of the part. Formed radius blocks can be made by routing the edge of a piece of hardwood to the desired shape.

Sheetmetal should not be bent by pounding or by heating; reserve those operations for thicker pieces. Good tools for straightening and working sheetmetal include the body and the tinsmith's hammers. A ballpeen hammer is not recommended for this application. Always back up the metal to be worked, and take your time when trying to straighten a part or generate a bent shape.

Both the hammer and the back-up block should have polished surfaces to prevent transmitting surface irregularities to the part. A good source for back-up blocks is an auto parts store that sells body tools.

Even if you are just an occasional sheetmetal worker, you can find a good supply of material at reasonable prices at your nearest metal-building manufacturing plant. These manufacturers use 22- to 29-gauge steel in both galvanized and prepainted form, and always have coil ends and roll-form ends that are in the scrap bin. A little time spent on the phone with the salesmen at these plants can save you money.

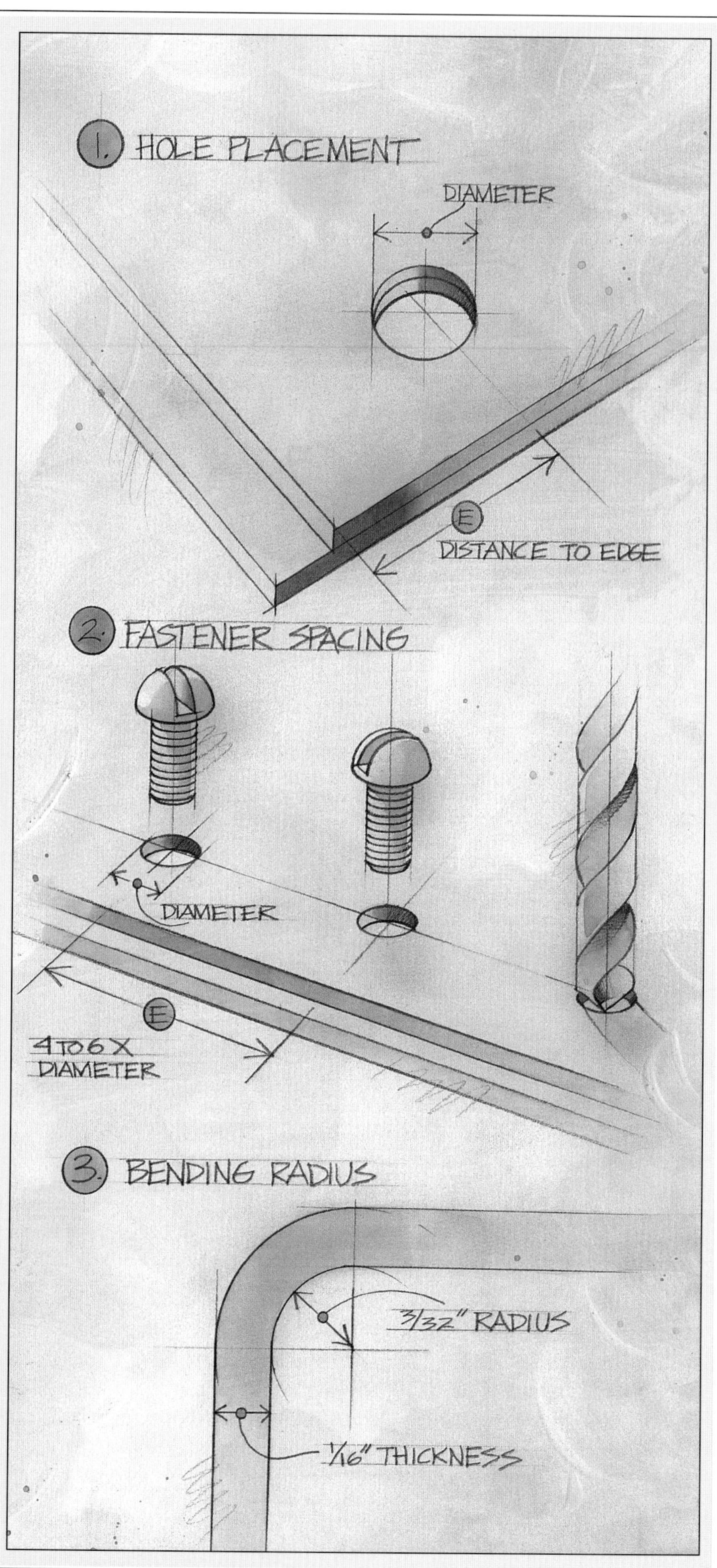

On The Level

The Tool That Helps Keep You In Line With The World

Back in the old days, pioneers who couldn't afford a level would use a pan of water. When the surface of the water was the same distance from the rim all the way around the pan, the board it was sitting on was level.

One thing as true today as it was then is that keeping things square and level in the beginning stages of building will pay off many times over before the project is done. And, there is hardly a do-it-yourselfer who can't afford a good, all-purpose 2′ level today.

Levels under $10 are adequate enough for the occasional project around the home. Beyond that, the choice of levels can be almost overwhelming. If you have the money to spend and the need for them, you can buy traditional levels 18″, 24″, 28″, 30″, 48″, 72″, even 78″ long. You will find torpedo levels, line levels, combination squares with leveling vials, even stick-on vials to make your own leveling tools. You can buy leveling devices that capitalize on laser beam technology. Then there's the transit—a more expensive, precision leveling tool.

It used to be that levels were only available in wooden frames with vials held in place with plaster. You now can buy levels with frames made of cast-aluminum, magnesium, and even high-impact structural foam, with vials that are easily replaced and/or adjustable. You can buy magnetic levels to use with steel framing. You can find levels with vials that light up at a press of the button for working in dark areas, and levels that give you a digital readout, much like a calculator.

The common 24″ level, in the carpenter trade, is primarily a tool for rough work. The 18″ level is used mainly by plumbers, steamfitters, and pipe fitters; it fits nicely into a 19″ toolbox. The 28″ level was originally popular with finish carpenters back in the early 1900s. Window casings were 30″ wide, and this level would cover maximum surface and still fit into the casing. The 42″ level was originally sold mainly to tile setters because older bathrooms were usually tiled and were just a little more than 42″ wide.

The 48″ level is the classic mason's length. At one time, concrete blocks were 15″ long, so this level would span three blocks at once. The 72″ level is the original level for the 6′x8″ door jamb.

One principle to remember when using levels is that the bubble should be centered exactly with the vial. Do-it-yourselfers often believe that the reading is level if the bubble is touching one line or the other; this will be close, but not precise. Another thing to remember is that levels can get out of whack, especially if they have been dropped, nicked, or tossed around. It is a good idea to occasionally check the accuracy of your levels, then either adjust the vial or replace it if need be.

The three levels most commonly used on the job by a finish carpenter include the 24″, 48″, and 78″. The 78″ level is reserved for work on large-scale projects.

Level Accuracy

Stores that sell expensive levels to tradesmen often have a special jig to test the accuracy of a level before it is taken home. If you are paying $50 for a level, you want it to be accurate. One thing to keep in mind when using a level is that its accuracy is directly related to the amount of surface it covers. For example, the vial in a combination square is useful, but the level is measuring a surface of only about 4″. The longer the surface covered, the more accuracy the level will have. Professionals will use a 6′ level when they need super precision, or, for example, when they are working on projects that will span 20′ or so.

Sometimes you need extra length for accuracy; other times you need the length just to reach the spot you want to mark. But there are ways to extend the reach of a level in rough carpentry. For example, you can set a 2′ level on top of a carpenter's square or straightedge to get level marks for a header. You can even use a 2x4 that is 4′ long or so, but eyeball it to see that it is straight and true before using it.

The illustrations on the opposite page show how to check a level for accuracy. Here is the basic procedure: With the level on its working edge, lay it on a flat surface and check the position of the bubble. Then turn the level 180° (swap end for end), and check the bubble again. It should be in the same position. That is the first test.

The second test is to do the same thing, but this time turn the level over on its opposite working edge (swap top for bottom). Again the bubble should stay in the same position.

You can also check for plumb by holding the level against a flat surface perpendicular to the floor. Check the bubble in the plumb vial, then turn the level over so the opposite working edge is against the wall. The bubble should be in the same position.

When using a line level, try to keep the string as tight as possible, and adjust for any depression in the line.

Using Levels

The line level is handy for leveling over long distances. The key to using a line level is to keep the line (or string) as tight as possible and to keep the level centered on the string. Most professionals use nylon line instead of cotton. Try to keep the line as tight as possible, then give it an extra pull to get it extra-taut. Even so, over 20′, the line level will still depress the line slightly, and you will need to adjust for this slight depression.

Clear plastic hose can be used to extend a level line over distances (see Using Water Levels). Hold one end vertically next to the mark you want to transfer and fill with liquid until it is level with the mark. The level of the liquid at the other end will be exactly the same height. This works well for leveling posts, for example, or for getting a level line around a room to help you put in a floor or ceiling. However, keep in mind that sun shining on one end of the hose can change the level of the liquid.

Levels can also be used to help find pitch or slope; in fact, some torpedo levels have markings to indicate ⅛ or ¼ pitch. These make it simple to position plumbing pipes that need to drain. But you can also use a level on top of a 2x4 to determine slope. For example, let's say you want a brick patio to slope ¼″ per foot. With your level on top of an 8′ 2x4, you should have a 2″ drop at one end when the bubble reads level.

Likewise, you can use the same technique to estimate how far walls are out of plumb. Let's say you hold your level with one end on the floor along a wall and center the plumb vial. You see that there's a ¼″ gap between the level and the wall. If you are using a 2′ level and the wall is 8′ high, you will know the top of the wall is 1″ out of whack if the stud is straight. And don't forget that the plumb bob is also a leveling device; it gives you a perfectly vertical line.

Caring for Levels

Levels deserve good care, not so much because of their cost, but because you want them to be accurate. If your level gets a nick in it, take time to smooth it out. Professional carpenters in snow country will often make it a habit to take levels into the house at night during the winter to avoid freeze-and-thaw cycles that could affect their accuracy.

Take care when transporting your levels, too. One good way to transport levels is to use the cardboard core of carpet rolls. Saw off a proper length, then cut out wooden ends with your sabersaw. If you should drop your level, it has a better chance for survival if it is inside one of these protectors.

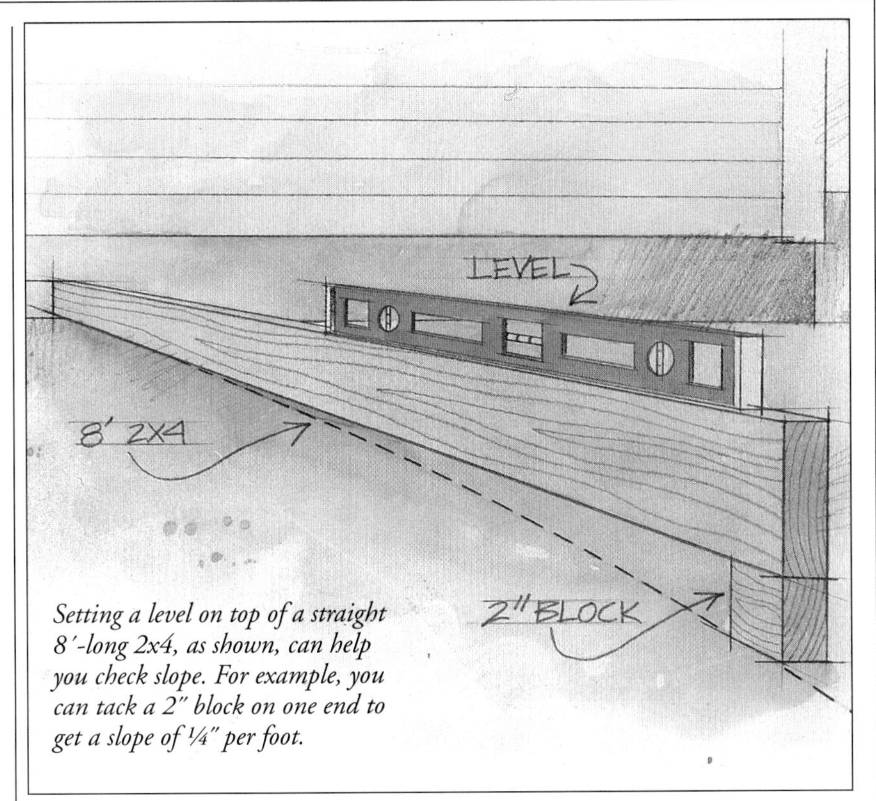

Setting a level on top of a straight 8′-long 2x4, as shown, can help you check slope. For example, you can tack a 2″ block on one end to get a slope of ¼″ per foot.

Using Water Levels

Sometimes you need to check the level of objects that are at a distance from each other, or figure out how to establish a slope. A way to do these jobs is to use a water level.

One version of a water level is simply a clear plastic tube and a plastic jug. To make one, first measure the diameter of the tube, then cut a hole of the same size in the jug lid. Fill the jug with water, screw on the lid, and push one end of the tube far enough into the hole so that it extends well below the surface of the water.

Then, suck on the other end of the tube to create a siphon effect so the water will flow into the tube. When water starts to flow out the free end, lift the end of the tube a little higher than the top of the jug.

Checking a Level

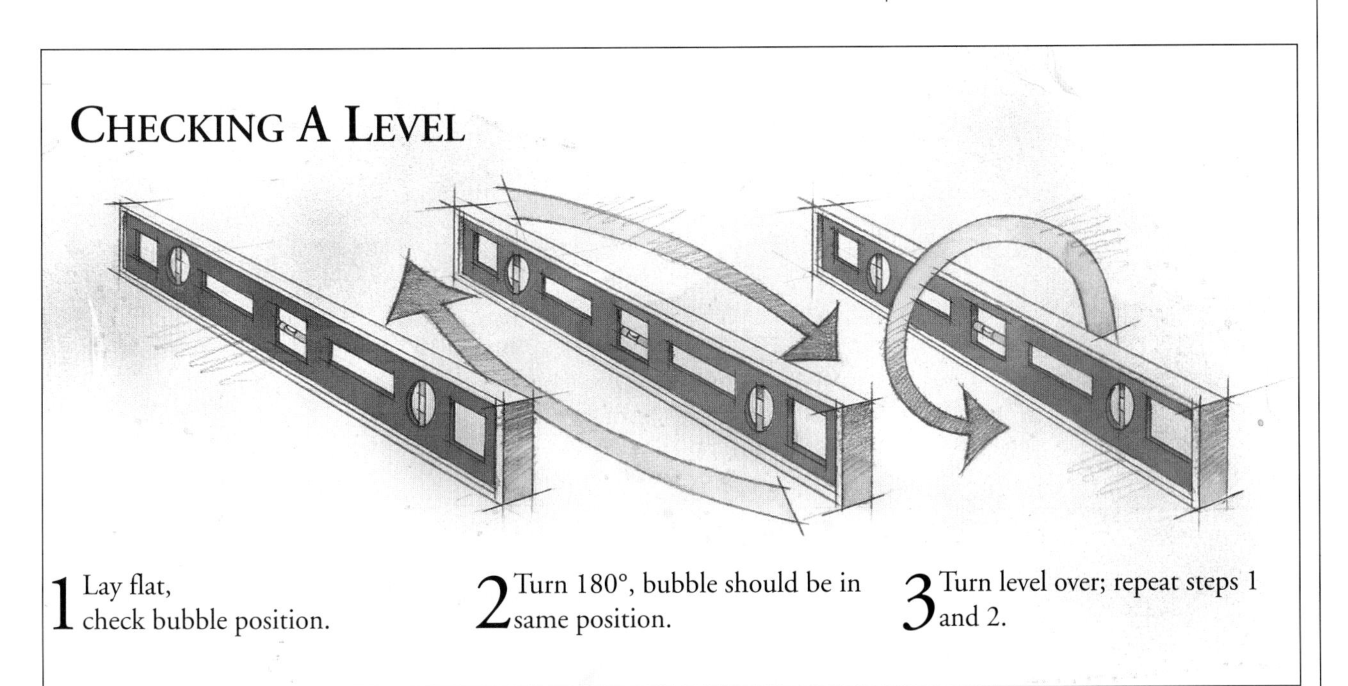

1 Lay flat, check bubble position.

2 Turn 180°, bubble should be in same position.

3 Turn level over; repeat steps 1 and 2.

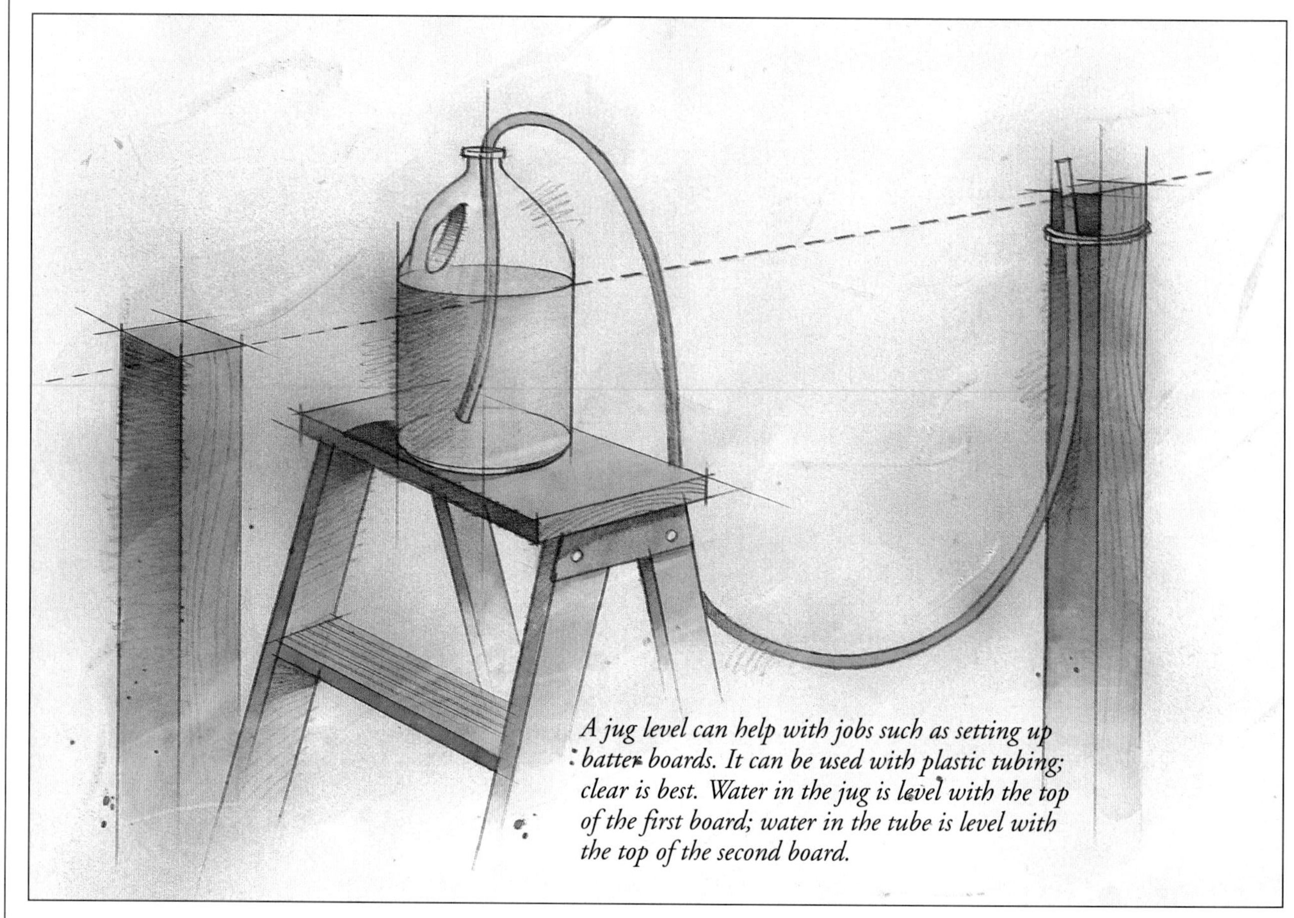

A jug level can help with jobs such as setting up batter boards. It can be used with plastic tubing; clear is best. Water in the jug is level with the top of the first board; water in the tube is level with the top of the second board.

The water in the tube's free end will stabilize at the same level as the water in the jug. If you put the jug next to an object and hold the end of the tube next to another object, you'll be able to tell if the two objects are level with each other.

In building projects, a water level can help you make sure the ledger boards are level and that the batter boards are level with each other. Batter boards are used to help set up building lines. They are set about 4′ or more away from the corner layout stakes, with 2x4s used for stakes and 1x6s for ledgers. Put the jug on a milk crate or some lumber so the water in the jug is slightly lower then the top of the first set of batter boards. Next, tie the end of the tube to the second set of batter boards.

After sucking on the tube and the siphoning action stops, pour more water into the jug. The water will rise in both the jug and the tube because water always seeks its own level. Keep pouring water into the jug until the surface of the water in the jug is even with the top of the first set of batter boards. At this point, you'll have three things level with each other: the top of the first set of boards, the surface of the water in the jug, and the surface of the water in the tube.

Now compare the surface of the water in the tube with the top of the second set of batter boards. If they are level with each other, then you know that the second set of boards is level with the first set.

There are several tricks in using a water level. First, sight along the bottom of the cup-shaped surface inside the tube for your readings. You can also put food coloring or some other dye in the water to make it easier to see. Don't get any air bubbles in the tube; they can cause inaccurate readings. (If bubbles get in, remove them by letting all the water drain out of the tube, then start over.) Also be sure to use a clear tube so you can inspect for bubbles. The best is ¼″ vinyl tubing from a plumbing supply store. Don't get kinks in it or the readings may be off. When using the device outside, be sure it is either completely in the sun or completely shaded to avoid inaccurate readings due to solar gain on part of the tubing being used.

If you don't want to invest in clear plastic tubing, an alternative is to add about 18″ of clear plastic tubing to each end of a garden hose using hose couplings. If, for example, you want to use the device to establish a slope on your lawn, tape one plastic end to a 4′ stake pounded in the ground. Then tape the other plastic end to a portable 4′ stake with a yardstick attached. First put the two tubes side by side and mark the water level on the yardstick. By standing the portable stake at various places in the yard and checking the reading, you can figure out how much dirt you will need to move to get the slope you want.

Using Laser Levels

More recently companies have begun to blend the technologies of electronics and optics to produce low-cost leveling devices that shoot visible laser beams. They replace strings and water levels for interior and exterior level and plumb work.

The basic idea of an eye-visible laser beam used as a measuring devise is not new; rotating laser systems that create a circular plane of light have been used to level road beds, lay out fields, and install ceiling tile. But the low price of these new devices is now making this space-age technology feasible for the home do-it-yourselfer.

One company, Laser Tools Co., Inc. of Little Rock, Arkansas, packages laser beam leveling devices in a price range from $139 to $599, all using a built-in, eye-visible laser beam to extend the level reference for measuring, aligning, leveling, or pointing.

The laser levels are attracting the attention of professional builders because they allow one person to do a job that otherwise would require two.

The lowest price version, called the L25 Laser Handy Line, projects a beam of light from the end of the level, extending a safe, eye-visible laser dot that can be seen on almost any surface up to 50′ away. It allows fast, precision leveling of construction site layouts, a complete floor from wall to wall, a concrete slab and forms, or a ceiling line.

How does it work? The level is measured using the vial that is built in and factory-set. The laser is activated by turning the battery cap switch. A laser beam shoots out to where you want a level mark. To help mark the laser dot, a built-in target is also transmitted which indicates the exact center of the laser dot. The center is marked, then ½″ is subtracted to compensate for the height of the beam over the bottom of the level. The device, with a case of aircraft aluminum, weighs less than 12 ounces. Three size-N alkaline batteries provide over eight hours of use.

The laser level, as well as others sold by the company, can be used with builder or camera tripods and is especially useful and accurate in laying out, leveling, or sloping interior and exterior pipework, wiring, ductwork, and plumbing. Some other uses include installing acoustic tile, positioning studs, aligning trusses, laying brick and block, laying out decks, building fences, setting cabinets, squaring timber, plumbing rafters, aligning door headers and doors, leveling siding, installing appliances, measuring drainage slopes, positioning wallboard, aligning gutters, leveling platforms, setting batter boards, laying out stairs, and determining roof pitches.

The company also sells accessories for its laser levels, including cases, tripods, special clamps and brackets, and a "beam bender" that creates two laser beams 90° apart for use in layouts. For a complete listing of the levels, prices, and more information, you can write Laser Tools Co., Inc., 12221 Arch Street Pike, Little Rock, Arkansas 72206, or call or fax (501) 888-8831.

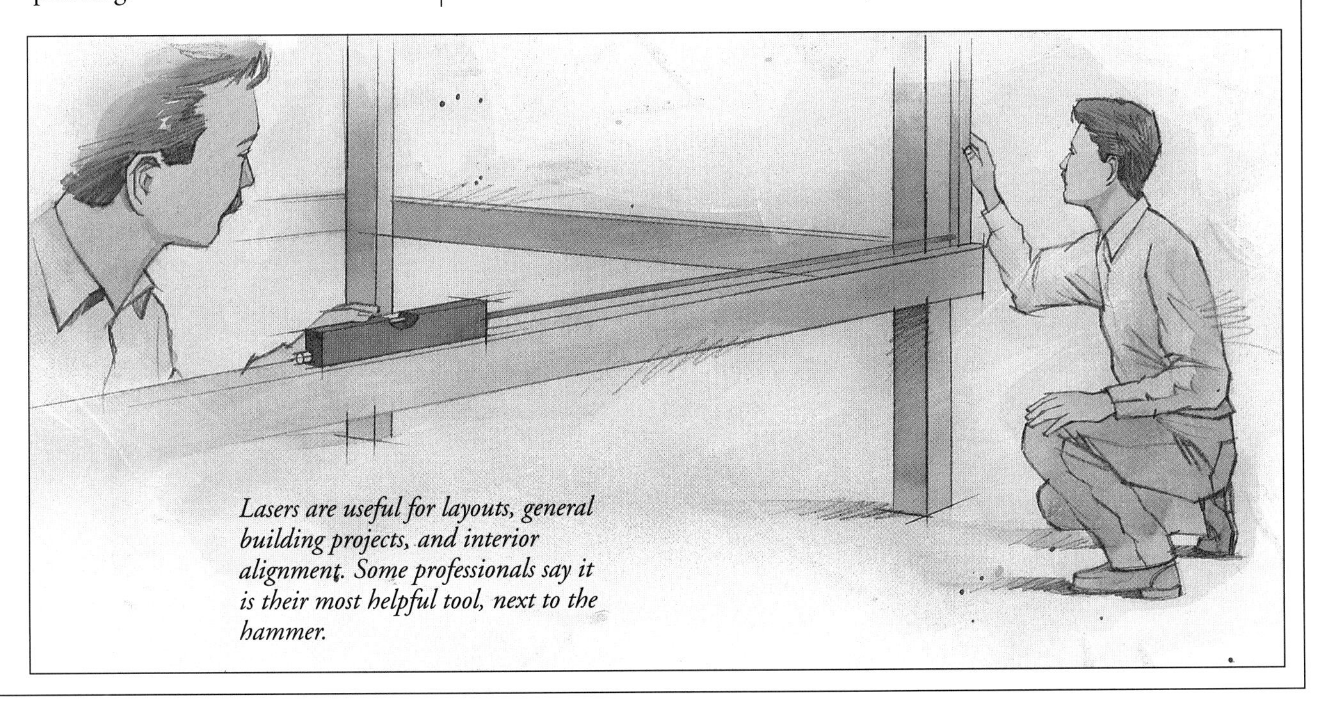

Lasers are useful for layouts, general building projects, and interior alignment. Some professionals say it is their most helpful tool, next to the hammer.

Hard-To-Reach Places

An Easier Way To Sand, Polish, And Deburr The Cracks And Crannies

No matter how basic or simple finishing techniques seem to be, often there is more to them than meets the eye. By trial and error, most shop professionals eventually develop their own favorite procedures to get the job done.

For example, even the most expert of do-it-yourselfers have to admit that there are just some places where regular sheet sandpaper doesn't work well. Specifically, it's the cracks and crevices that are a pain. If you find yourself turning out projects with hard-to-access surfaces, consider a convenient solution to the problem: abrasive cords and tapes.

The sketches show some of the various ways flexible cords and tapes can be used in the home workshop. Both the round cords and flat tapes can be used on common project materials like wood, metal, or plastic. For woodworking, abrasive cords and tapes are especially useful in finishing new wood spindles, or for removing old, hardened paint and varnish from grooved areas of chair legs, spreaders, spindles, and table legs.

Where the cords and tape really come to the rescue is in deburring, grinding and polishing hard-to-reach areas which are inaccessible to most standard tools. For example, they are ideal for cleaning up narrow slots and grooves, small holes, and curved surfaces.

One manufacturer of both round abrasive cords and flat abrasive tapes is the E. C. Mitchell Co. in Massachusetts, which has been in business for 75 years. Their cords and tapes were initially used in the metal industry and are still known

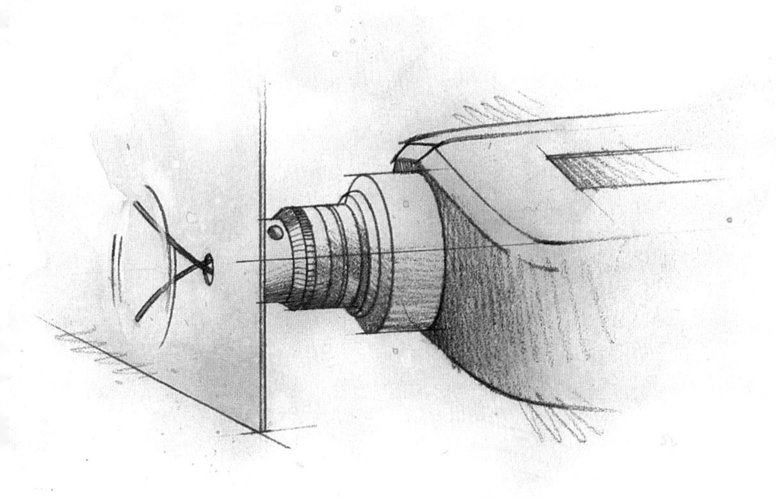

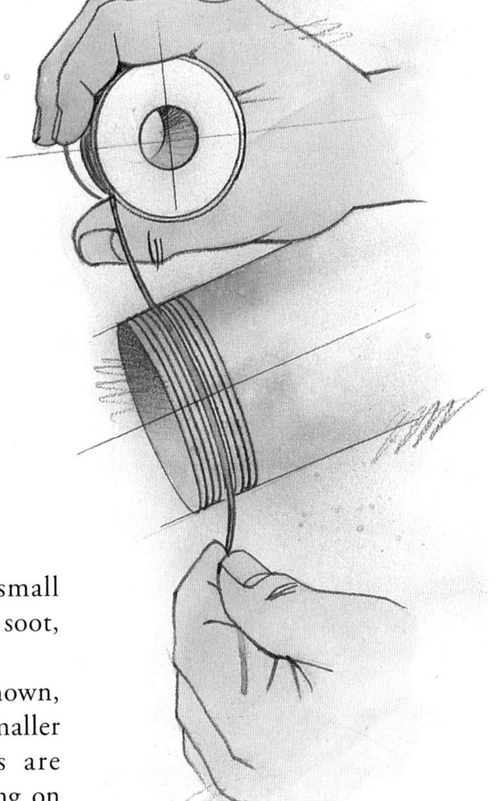

as "the machinist's friend."

Impregnated with either aluminum oxide, silicon carbide or crocus (for ultra-fine polishing), the cords are available in .015″ down to .012″ diameters. That's about as thin as a line drawn by a lead pencil. The tapes come in widths from 1⁄16″ to 1⁄4″. Both the cords and tapes come on 50′ spools.

The cords and tapes are used primarily by hand, simply holding them taut with only a light pressure during use. The larger diameter cords, from .093″ to .150″, can be used with speed chucks or other power tools. To polish the inside of a hole, for example, you can make a loop long enough to fit into the hole, push the loop into the chuck of a power drill, then feed the two loose ends into the hole. To smooth it, just turn on the power.

The tapes, with abrasives on both sides, are an excellent substitute for emery cloth strips; they won't tear or fray and can be cut to any length. The cords also can be used to deburr and remove rust, paint, and sludge from pipe threads and other contoured surfaces. The smallest, ultra-fine cords can be used to clear blockages in small tubing or nozzles caused by soot, rust, or corrosion.

Besides the applications shown, the company reports that smaller diameter cords and tapes are excellent helpers when working on printed circuit boards. They can be used to prepare a surface before soldering, and also for removing solder flash afterwards. The tapes can easily reach around components or leads and through holes.

Prices for aluminum oxide cords and tapes range from about $12 on up to $26 for a 50′ roll. Silicon carbide cords and tapes cost about double that of aluminum oxide. (Prices are for orders of less than six spools.) The aluminum oxide cords come in a grain range from 120 on up to 200, while the tapes range from 150 to 180.

Note: The E. C. Mitchell Co. will send you free literature along with 2″-long samples of 13 types of cords and tapes. Write the company at 80-90 Boston St., P.O. Box 607, Middleton, MA 01949-0907, or call 617/774-1191.

INDEX

CREDITS

This book was produced by NORTH COAST PRODUCTIONS, with assistance from the following. All text, photos, and illustrations, except as noted, are by NORTH COAST PRODUCTIONS, 650 Mount Curve Boulevard, St. Paul, MN 55116.

DIY ENHANCEMENTS (Section I, pages 6 and 7): BUNGALOW UPDATE (page 8): text, photo and illustration source, Western Wood Products Association. WOOD HEAT (page 13): text and illustration sources, Fiber Fuel Institute and Waterford Irish Stoves; photos pages 12 through 16 as identified, Waterford Irish Stoves and Pyro Industries. NORTHERN EXPOSURE (page 21): text and illustration sources, photos, FinnLeo. MASTERING MOLDING (page 27): text and illustration source, photo, Georgia-Pacific. PARADISE OUTDOORS (page 31): text source and photos, California Redwood Association: pages 30 and 31, photos Michael Landis; page 32, photos Earnest Braun, design Richard Schwartz; page 33, design John Paletta; page 34 and top 35, photos Dan Sellers, design Jamie Turrentine; photo bottom page 35, Andrew McKinney. DIMENSIONAL DRYWALL (page 36): text sources, United States Gypsum Co.; Gypsum Association, and Association of the Wall & Ceiling Industries; illustration source and photos, United States Gypsum Co. BACKYARD BEAUTY (page 45): text and illustration source and photos, American Plywood Association.

DIY IMPROVEMENTS (Section II, pages 50 and 51): REAL GRANITE (page 52): text source and photos pages 52 and 53, Cold Spring Granite Co.; photos page 54, Mitch Kezar. CONCRETE PAVERS (page 56): text sources, Pave Tech, Inc., Borgert Products, Interlocking Concrete Paver Institute; illustration source, Pave Tech, Inc.; photos, Symrah Licensing, Inc. HOME PLUMBING (page 61): text sources, Milford Roubik, Richard Day, and Genova, Inc.; illustration source, HomeStyles Plan Service. TRUSS RAFTERS (page 69): text source, Truss Plate Institute. CARPENTER LORE (page 73): text sources, contributors to Trade Secrets; ROOF RESCUES (page 81): text and illustration sources, photos, Georgia-Pacific Corp.; ATTIC VENTILATION (page 88): text and illustration sources, Cobra Ventilation Co. PAINTING SHORTCUTS (page 90): text source, John A. Gordon. PROJECT HELPERS (page 94): text sources and photos, Performax Products, Irwin Co., Autodesk, Polaroid Corp., Ornamental Mouldings, Hirsh Co.

DIY INVESTMENTS (Section III, pages 96 and 97; background photo, Sears, Roebuck & Co. and Affinity Marketing): OLD HOUSES (page 98): text, Constance Schrader; photos, Susan B. Storch. HOMESTEAD HERITAGE (page 102): text sources, Nancy Roberts and Minnesota Historical Society. AN OLD-HOUSE INSPECTION CHECKLIST (page 105): text, editors of Old-House Journal. CINDERELLA SAWS (page 110): text and photo sources, Makita USA and Sears, Roebuck & Co. SHOP KIDS (page 114): text sources, contributors to Home Shop News. WASTE DISPOSERS (page 117): text source, Emerson Electric. WONDER TOOL (page 121): text source, Patrick Spielman; photo, Sears, Roebuck & Co. and Affinity Marketing. SHOP SPACES (page 124): text source, Russ Barnard; illustrations, Barbara Bowen; photo page 124, Sears, Roebuck & Company and Affinity Marketing; photo page 125, Mark Duginske and Gregory Foye. MULCHING MOWERS (page 128): text source, illustrations page 130, The Toro Co. WORKBENCHES (page 131): text, illustration source, and photos, Stanley Tools.

DIY ACHIEVEMENTS (Section IV, pages 142 and 143): DO-IT-YOURSELF HINTS (page 144): contributors to Home Shop News; photo, Stanley Tools. ROOM DIVIDER (page 155): text source, photos, illustration page 156, and source for other illustrations, Western Wood Products Association. POURING CEMENT (page 159) text source, Robert Scharff. NAILS AND NAILING (page 165): text and illustration source, Northwestern Steel and Wire Co. PROJECT PACKHORSE (page 173): text and illustration source, American Plywood Association; design, Mark McClanahan. WORKING METAL (page 176): text and illustration sources, Vince Koebensky and Jacob Schulzinger; photo page 176, Sears, Roebuck & Co. and Affinity Marketing. ON THE LEVEL (page 183): text sources, Brian Ringham and Laser Tools Co. HARD-TO-REACH PLACES (page 188): text and illustration source, E. C. Mitchell Co.

ADDRESSES

American Plywood Association, P.O. Box 11700, Tacoma, WA 98411; Association Of The Wall & Ceiling Industries, 307 E. Annandale Rd., Falls Church, VA 22042; Autodesk, 11911 North Creek Parkway S., Bothwell, WA 98011; Borgert Products, Inc., 8646 Ridgewood Rd., St. Joseph, MN 56374; California Redwood Association, 405 Enfrente Dr., Ste. 200, Novato, CA 94949; Cobra Ventilation Co., Inc., Subsidiary of GAF Building Materials Corp., 1361 Alps Rd., Wayne, NJ 07470; Cold Spring Granite Co., 202 So. Third Ave., Cold Spring, MN 56230; E. C. Mitchell Co., Inc. 88-90 Boston St., Middleton, MA 01949; FinnLeo, 575 East Cokato St., Cokato, MN 55321; Georgia-Pacific Corp., 133 Peachtree St. NE (30303), P.O. Box 1763, Norcross, GA 30091; Gypsum Association, 810 First St. NE, #510, Washington, DC 20002; Hirsh Co., 8051 Central Park Ave., Skokie, IL 60076; HomeStyles Plan Service, 275 Market St., Ste. 521, Minneapolis, MN 55405; Interlocking Concrete Paver Institute, 1323 Shepard Dr., Ste. D, Sterling, VA 20164; Irwin Co., P.O. Box 829, Wilmington, OH 45177; Laser Tools Co. 12221 Arch Street Pike, Little Rock, AR 72206; Makita USA, 14930 Northam St., La Mirada, CA 90638; Northwestern Steel and Wire Company, 121 Wallace St., Sterling, IL 61081; Old-House Journal, Two Main St., Gloucester, MA 01930; Ornamental Mouldings, 1907 Nuggett Rd., P.O. Box 4257, High Point, NC 27263; Performax Products, 12211 Woodlake Dr., Burnsville, MN 55337; Polaroid Corp., Cambridge, MA 02139; Pave Tech, Inc., P.O. Box 31126, Bloom-ington, MN 55431; Sears Merchandise Group (Craftsman Power Tools), D3 181A, 3333 Beverly Rd., Hoffman Estates, IL 60179; Stanley Tools, Box 1800, Dept. WBB, New Britain, CT 06050; Truss Plate Institute, 583 D'Onofrio Dr., Ste. 200, Madison, WI 53719; Toro Co., 4640 W. 77th St., Ste. 179, Minneapolis, MN 55435; Western Wood Products Association, Yeon Building, 522 SW Fifth Ave., Portland, OR 97204; Wood Truss Council Of America, 5937 Meadowood Dr., Ste. 14, Madison, WI 53711; Waterford Irish Stoves, 16 Airpark Rd., Ste. 3, West Lebanon, NH 03784; Wood Moulding and Millwork Producers, 1730 SW Skyline Blvd., Ste. 128, Portland, OR 97225.